译苑新谭 / New Perspectives in Translation Studies

New Perspectives in Translation Studies (《译苑新谭》) is a scholarly peer-reviewed international academic journal co-hosted by Translators Association of Sichuan and Chicago Academic Press. The journal is published semi-annually, focusing on theories, ideas, and methods in translation studies. It provides a high profile, leading edge forum for academics, professionals, educators, practitioners and students in the field to contribute and disseminate innovative ideas on translation studies. *New Perspectives in Translation Studies* invites original, previously unpublished research and survey papers written in English or Chinese on theoretical or practical aspects of translation studies. These areas include, but are not limited to, the following topics:

- ♦ Translation theories
- ♦ Literature translation
- ♦ Translation teaching
- ♦ Translation techniques
- ♦ Machine translation
- ♦ Literary translation
- ♦ Scientific translation
- ♦ Empirical studies
- ♦ Personnel training
- ♦ Translation industry

The current and past issues are made available on-line at: http://chicagoacademicpress.com/.

荣誉主编：连真然
主　　编：魏清光

Honorary Editor-in-Chief: Lian Zhenran
Editor-in-Chief: Wei Qingguang

编 委

Nicole Bergstrom	Mark Bender	桂清扬	
旦增杰布	黄昌佑	黄一凡	江久文
江丽蓉	李跃平	李在辉	连　益
连真然	梁真惠	廖国强	廖　红
刘永志	落桑旺秋	龙仕文	宋　达
唐晓云	童代丽	王维民	吴永强
张道振	张　玲	章上游	朱宪超

Editorial Committee Members

Nicole Bergstrom	Mark Bender	Gui Qingyang	Tenzin Gyalpo
Huang Changyou	Huang Yifan	Jiang Jiuwen	Jiang Lirong
Li Yueping	Li Zaihui	Lian Yi	Lian Zhenran
Liang Zhenhui	Liao Guoqiang	Liao Hong	Liu Yongzhi
Lobsang Wongchuk	Long Shiwen	Song Da	Tang Xiaoyun
Tong Daili	Wang Weimin	Wu Yongqiang	Zhang DaoZhen
Zhang Ling	Zhang Shangyou	Zhu Xianchao	

学术顾问

董晓波	辜正坤	李克兴	李志民
林巍	邵璐	孙迎春	王大伟
王东风	王建开	文军	赵友斌

Academic Counselors

Dong Xiaobo	Gu Zengkun	Li Kexing	Li Zhimin
Lin Wei	Shao Lu	Sun Yingchun	Wang Dawei
Wang Dongfeng	Wang Jiankai	Wen Jun	Zhao Youbin

法律顾问：魏志刚　李玉红

Legal Counselors: Wei Zhigang Li Yuhong

出版日期：2023 年 10 月 15 日
本期总号：第 8 期
本年期号：2023 年第 2 期
创刊日期：2020 年 4 月 20 日
国际刊号：2691-6649

Date of Publication: October 15, 2023
Total: 8
Issue: No. 2, 2023
Date of Inception: April 20, 2020
ISSN: 2691-6649

编辑部信息
地址：5923 N Artisan Ave Chicago IL 60659
　　　成都市武侯大道顺江段 77 号 1 栋 5 楼
投稿邮箱：fyxh028@163.com
网址：http://chicagoacademicpress.com/

Contact Information
Address: 5923 N Artisan Ave, Chicago, IL 60659
　　　　 5th-floor office, Ste 1, 77 Shunjiang Section,
　　　　 Wuhou Avenue, Chengdu
Email: fyxh028@163.com
Website: http://chicagoacademicpress.com/

目 录
CONTENTS

The Translation and Reception of Taizhou School in English-speaking Countries from the Perspective of Bourdieu's Sociological Theory: A Case Study of Li Zhi's Works .... ZHANG Junchao（1）

Translation and Research of Taizhou School Thoughts in the Western World since the 20th Century .... CAI Lili（12）

The Enlightenment of C-E translation of Li Zhi's Thought on Chinese Classics Culture "Going Global": A Case Study of *Fenshu* and *Xu Fenshu* .... ZHANG Weiyi（22）

C-E Translation in Ancient Books of Propagating Value of Emperor Yan Di Culture .... CUI Qingling WAN Jialin（34）

人工智能技术在翻译项目中的应用研究 .... 崔启亮（41）

AIGC 时代的翻译研究：挑战与路径 .... 王华树 李 丹（52）

ChatGPT 辅助翻译的潜力与局限——以《后维多利亚时代人》的翻译为例 .... 侯广旭（60）

国内外五种机器翻译平台对比——以特斯拉公司简介中文译文为例 .... 毛佳敏 张继光（69）

评价理论视角下 ChatGPT 与人工汉英翻译对比研究——以《主席新年贺词》为例 .... 林泽钦（78）

中医西传第三方译者研究——以文树德《黄帝内经·素问》英译本为例 .... 俞森林 雷佳豪（89）

郑振铎对清末民初翻译家的批评及启示 .... 管新福（99）

加强中国法律典籍外译 促进中西文明互鉴——董晓波教授访谈 .... 骆怡然 董晓波（107）

翻译大众化与大众翻译话语——德布雷媒介学视阈下的考察 .... 肖维青 王 景（118）

党的"十九大"以来《习近平谈治国理政》翻译研究综述 .... 戴若愚 王玥月（128）

2021 年中国翻译研究年度综述 .... 皮伟男 赖春梅 蓝红军（141）

传承优秀文化 规范景区英译 讲好中国故事——泉州著名世界遗产点九日山景区信息英译问题及解决方案 .... 陈 彬 李跃平（156）

《三国演义》三个英文全译本中典故的英译策略研究 .... 冉明志（169）

国家形象自塑视阈下外交话语隐喻英译策略探析——以 2020 年外交部例行记者会发言为例 .... 肖志清 李静霞（178）

从翻译美学角度比较许渊冲和翁显良的汉诗英译策略 .... 张紫涵（186）

"跨语际性"视阈下国产动画英译研究——以《大理寺日志》为例 .... 雷 静 李明明（194）

翻译目的论视角下《列女传》日译本对比研究 .... 杨梅竹 敬卓越（202）

基于语料库的立法文本模糊语英译策略研究 .... 黄宇柱（212）

《搜神记》日本馆藏刊本调查及译介与研究论析 .... 刘 毅 陈芳（225）

"一带一路"推动下中国应用翻译研究的新领域——《工程技术翻译学导论》介评 .... 梁富录（234）

《人生》民俗文化形象俄译重构研究 .... 周一钦（240）

接受美学视角下《中国疫苗百年纪实》日译策略研究 .... 卢俊宇 王晓梅（248）

CONTENTS
目 录

布迪厄社会学视阈下泰州学派在英语国家的翻译与接受——以李贽作品为例......................张竣超（1）
20世纪以来泰州学派思想在西方世界的译介与研究..蔡丽丽（12）
李贽思想英译对中国典籍文化"走出去"的启示——以《焚书》和《续焚书》英译本为例
....张薇依（22）
古籍英译：炎帝文化的传播价值..崔庆玲 万家麟（34）
A Study on the Application of Artificial Intelligence Technologies in Translation Projects..... CUI Qiliang（41）
Translation Studies in the AIGC Era: Challenges and Pathways............................WANG Huashu LI Dan（52）
The Potentials and Limitations of ChatGPT Assisted Translation: A Case Study of the Translation of
 After the Victorians..HOU Guangxu（60）
Comparison of Five Domestic and Foreign Machine Translation Platforms: Taking the Chinese Profile of
 Tesla Company as an Example..MAO Jiamin ZHANG Jiguang（69）
A Comparative Study Between ChatGPT and Human C-E Translation Based on the Appraisal Theory:
 A Case Study of the *"New Year Address by President Xi"*..LIN Zeqin（78）
On the Third-Party Translator in the Western Transmission of Traditional Chinese Medicine:
 With Unschuld's English Translation of *Huang Di Nei Jing Su Wen* as a Case of the Study
 ....YU Senlin LEI Jiahao（89）
Zheng Zhenduo's Criticism and Enlightenment to the Translators in Late Qing Dynasty and Early Republic
 of China...GUAN Xinfu（99）
Strengthen Foreign Translation of Chinese Legal Classics to Promote Mutual Learning between Chinese
 and Western Civilizations: An Interview with Professor Dong Xiaobo......LUO Yiran DONG Xiaobo（107）
Mediological Review of How the Discourse of Mass Translation Forms and Develops
 ....XIAO Weiqing WANG Jing（118）
Literature Review on Translation Studies of *Xi Jinping: The Governance of China*
 ....DAI Ruoyu WANG Yueyue（128）
An Annual Literature Review of Translation Studies in China in 2021
 ....Pi Weinan LAI Chunmei LAN Hongjun（141）
Inheriting Excellent Traditional Chinese Culture, Normalizing Scenic Area English Translation, Telling
 Chinese Stories Well: Problems of English Translation of Information in Jiuri Mountain Scenic Area,
 a Famous World Heritage Site in Quanzhou and Their Solutions........................CHEN Bin LI Yueping（156）
A Comparative Study of Strategies for Translating Allusions in the Three Complete English Versions of
 San Guo Yan Yi.. RAN Mingzhi（169）
The Translation Strategies of Metaphors in Diplomatic Discourse from the Perspective of National
 Image Self-shaping: A Case Study of Foreign Ministry Spokesperson's Remarks on Regular Press
 Conferences (2020) ....XIAO Zhiqing LI Jingxia（178）
A Comparative Study of the C-E Poetry Translation Strategies of Xu Yuanchong and Weng Xianliang
 in the Light of Translation Aesthetics.. ZHANG Zihan（186）
Translation Study of Chinese Animation from the Perspective of Translingualism: A Case Study of
 White Cat Legend... LEI Jing LI Mingming（194）
Contrastive Study of the Japanese Versions of *The biographies of Chinese Women* Based on Skopos Theory
 .... YANG Meizhu JING Zhuoyue（202）
A Corpus-based Study on Fuzzy Language Translation in Legislative Texts.................... HUANG Yuzhu（212）
Investigation, Translation, Introduction and Research of *Sou Shen Ji* in Japanese Library Collections
 ....LIU Yi CHEN Fang（225）
An Emerging Area of Pragmatic Translation Studies in China Driven by the Belt and Road Initiative:
 Comments on *An Introduction to Translatology of Industrial Engineering Interpretation & Translation*
 ....LIANG Fulu（234）
Reconstruction of Folk-culture Images in the Chinese-Russian Translation of *Life*................ZHOU Yiqin（240）
A Study on the Strategy of Japanese Translation of *A Century Record of Vaccine in China* from the
 Perspective of Aesthetic of Reception...LU Junyu WANG Xiaomei（248）

传承江南文脉，对话世界文明：泰州学派译介研究专栏

主持人：董晓波（南京师范大学外国语学院 博士生导师）

"派以地名，地以派闻"，作为明清思想史上重要的学术流派之一，泰州学派继承和发扬了王阳明的哲学思想，使得儒学更加为大众百姓所接受。其创始人王艮提出的"百姓日用即道"的民本思想，彰显了中华优秀传统文化的核心价值。发源于江苏泰州，泰州学派的思想不但传遍神州大地，更穿越空间的距离，在国际汉学研究中产生了巨大的影响，加深了西方学者对于儒学和中国哲学思想的理解。

南京师范大学泰州学院外国语学院泰州学派译介科研团队在院长黄文的带领下，立足泰州大地，深入挖掘泰州地域文化精粹，向世界宣传传播泰州学派的思想精华与价值内涵，有效地推动了中华优秀地域传统文化的创造性转化、创新性发展，为建设中华民族现代文明做出了贡献。本专栏是科研团队三位青年教师张竣超、蔡丽丽、张薇依的最新研究成果。通过对泰州学派及其代表人物在英语国家的译介与接受的深入研究，进一步厘清了泰州学派对外传播路径，建构了新时期中国地域文化在构建中国对外话语体系和中国叙事体系中的重要价值，打造了中国地域文化人文外宣新名片。

Taizhou School Studies 1

The Translation and Reception of Taizhou School in English-speaking Countries from the Perspective of Bourdieu's Sociological Theory: A Case Study of Li Zhi's Works

⊙ ZHANG Junchao (Nanjing Normal University Taizhou College, Taizhou)

Abstract: As one of the most important and revolutionary schools of thought in the middle and late Ming

Dynasty, Taizhou School (*Xuepai*) inherited and developed the philosophical ideas embedded in Yangmingism, making Confucianism more accessible to the people from all walks of life. Started from Taizhou in Jiangsu, the thought eventually spread across the nation and was studied by both historians and philosophers over centuries. Nevertheless, most research of Taizhou School is still limited to its concept as well as the value to modern society. Few studies have focused on the translation and reception of this vital school in English speaking countries despite the influence of it in international sinology academia. Therefore, by applying Bourdieu's sociological theory, this essay takes Li Zhi, one of the most important figures in Taizhou School, as a case study to understand the translation and reception of Taizhou School in English-speaking countries. It is found that the translation of Li Zhi's works has witnessed four phases and are influenced by three different "fields".

Key words: Taizhou School; Li Zhi; translation; Bourdieu; sociology

布迪厄社会学视阈下泰州学派在英语国家的翻译与接受——以李贽作品为例

张竣超（南京师范大学泰州学院，泰州）

[摘 要] 作为明代中晚期最重要的学术流派之一，泰州学派继承和发扬了王阳明的哲学思想，使得儒学更加为大众百姓所接受。发源于江苏泰州，泰州学派的思想最终传遍全国各地。几个世纪以来，许多史学家和哲学家都对其进行了深入的研究。然而，尽管泰州学派在国际汉学研究中具有巨大影响力，大多数对泰州学派的研究还仍限于其概念内涵和它对当代社会的意义，很少有研究真正关注泰州学派在英语国家的翻译和接受现状。因此，本文基于布迪厄的社会学理论，对泰州学派代表人物李贽的作品进行个案研究。研究发现，李贽作品的翻译主要经历了四个阶段，并受三种不同场域的影响。

[关键词] 泰州学派；李贽；翻译；布迪厄；社会学

1. Introduction

The introduction to Confucianism in western society can be traced back to the 16th century when Michael Ruggieri (also known as Luo Mingjian 罗明坚), the very first priest visiting mainland China, translated the Confucianism classics *Four Books* (*Sishu* 四书) in Latin (Zhang Xiping, 2001). Together with other prominent Jesuits like Matteo Ricci (Li Madou 利玛窦), Ruggieri not only published some translated texts of Confucianism but carefully studied the essence of Confucius's thoughts, making the study of China into a comprehensive discipline now known as sinology. Thanks to those sinologists, the impact of Confucianism was no longer limited to East Asian countries but spread to a wider world.

Nevertheless, in this first round of translation, emphasis was put primally on Confucius himself (Mei Qianli, 2008). Other well-known branches of Confucianism like ChengZhu Neo-Confucianism (程朱理学) or Yangmingism (阳明心学) had not been fully covered yet. In fact, Jesuits at that time intentionally avoided mentioning Zhu Xi (朱熹)'s theory although *Four Books* were mostly codified by Zhu Xi (Mei Qianli, 2008: 136-137). Ricci and his student Prospero Intorcett (Yin Duoze 殷铎泽) all regraded Pre-Qin Confucianism (i.e., Confucius-Mencius doctrines) as the orthodox and belittled Neo-Confucianism. They believed that the theories of Neo-Confucianism like "*Li*" (理) and "*Gewu zhizhi*" (格物致知) embodied the tendency of atheism which was obviously contradictory to their Catholic belief (Cummins, 1993; Janik, 2020:33-37). Under such circumstances, as a Confucianism school which claimed all things were complete in the body (Wang Gen, 2001) and emphasized body-based (*Shen Ben* 身本) philosophy,

Taizhou School would not have the opportunities to be translated or simply introduced to western society by those Jesuits. It was not until the Republican era (1911-1949) that Taizhou School amid the development of New Confucianism[①]began to appear in various academic books and journals. In this primitive introduction, Li Zhi (李贽; also known as Li Zhuowu 李卓吾), one of the radical representatives of the Taizhou School, was identified and often discussed in sinology due to his rebellion against Confucianism traditions. In the subsequent studies on Taizhou School, western sinologists even compared Li Zhi to the "Enlightenment thinkers" who ran counter to the traditional Catholic beliefs (Hou Wailu, 1987/2005). Li Zhi received extra attention because of his rebellious social identity. Thus, it is not enough to study the translation of his works merely from a linguistic aspect. A more comprehensive socio-cultural approach must be carried out to understand the multifarious "power" behind the translation. By applying Bourdieu's sociological theory, this essay aims to analyze how various social "fields" influence translation as well as the reception of Li Zhi's works in European countries. Four major phases are identified with each of them controlled by one or several fields.

2. Taizhou School and Li Zhi

2.1 The formation and spread of Taizhou School

Before elaborating on the translation of Taizhou School, it is necessary to first provide an overview of this school. A basic understanding of how the school was formed and why it prevailed in the middle and late Ming Dynasty can contextualize further studies on its spread to the western society.

It should be first noticed that while Taizhou School is often classified as a branch of Neo-Confucianism and Yangmingism, the central tenet of this school is somewhat contradictory to either theory as it believed that "sagehood should belong to everyone, regardless of social status" (Cheng, 2009: 46). Initiated by a lower-class salt merchant Wang Gen who discontinued his studies in school at the age of eleven (Wang Gen, 2001), the well-educated intellectuals (also known as *Shi Da Fu* 士大夫) were no longer in the central position in Taizhou School. According to the school, all men have the ability to "know without deliberating and to know how without learning how" (Bary, 1999: 862). There is no difference between the ordinary "I" and the sage. Moreover, like other Confucianism theories which actively engaged in politics, Wang Gen also proposed a bold political agenda that local officials should be elected by the people instead of being chosen through traditional meritocratic examinations known as *Ke Jü* (科举). This agenda was often seen as the "rudimentary" form of "representative democracy" (Lidén, 2018). Considering the sociopolitical system in Ming Dynasty, such beliefs were not only innovative but rebellious. The rebellion became one of the salient features of Taizhou School when being formed. As indicated in Huang Zongxi (黄宗羲)'s seminal work *Ming Ru Xue An* (明儒学案 *The Records of Ming Scholars*) where Taizhou School was first thoroughly introduced and analysed (Wu Zhen, 2009), followers of Taizhou School were "no longer within the boundaries Confucian moral philosophy" and had already "turned Heaven and Earth upside down" (Huang Zongxi, 2008). In this situation, the formation of the school is more like an activism movement and the disciples of Wang Gen as well as other followers of Taizhou School were no longer Confucians but brave activists.

Akin to the formation of the Taizhou School, the dissemination of it was also distinct from the previous Confucianism school. Through various public meetings and gatherings (*Jianghui* 讲会), practitioners of Taizhou School discussed the "practical ethical questions" as well as concerning social issues rather than the theoretical significance of the Confucianism classics. In addition, Taizhou School leaders seldom impose strict restrictions on people's personal life, nor did they fast or go on any diet (Lidén, 2018: 16). Unlike ChengZhu Neo-Confucianism and Yangmingism which emphasized the significance of "regulating the self or *Xiushen* (修身)" (Chen Lai, 2008: 276), Taizhou School advocated "self-preservation" and there would be no other things more important than "securing the self" (Wang Gen, 2001: 29-30). The Taizhou School movement came to the climax in the late Ming Dynasty whilst gradually declining amid the collapse of the Ming Dynasty (Wu Zhen, 2009). After the foundation of the Republic of China in 1911, due to its strong anti-traditional features, Taizhou School was rediscovered by many Chinese scholars who were eager to reform society. Like the followers of the Taizhou School, Chinese scholars in the Republican era not only studied Confucianism but were committed to changing the social and political systems through their own endeavors (Liang Shuming, 2020).

2.2 Li Zhi: an anti-traditional Confucian

Despite the debates over Li Zhi's identity and his connections with Taizhou School, most historians still regard him as a representative figure of the Taizhou School (Wu Zhen, 2009: 30-35). Therefore, studies on the translation of his works can undoubtedly reveal the translation of Taizhou School in English-speaking countries.

Like Wang Gen developed his mentor Wang Yangming's theory, Li Zhi was more progressive and aggressive in criticizing Confucius-Mencius doctrines (Bary, 1999: 865). In Ray Huang's famous book: *1587, A Year of No Significance: The Ming Dynasty in Decline*, Li Zhi was introduced as an anti-traditionalist to western society. Born in a Hui family[②] that possessed strong Muslim traditions, Confucius-Mencius doctrines seemed to be trivial to Li Zhi from the very beginning. At the age of twelve, Li Zhi (2000: 78) had already dared to point out Confucius's inadequacy. After struggling in bureaucracy for thirty years and witnessing the death of his two daughters, Li Zhi started to contemplate the true meaning of life as well as individuals' relationship with society (Xu Sumin, 2006:86). He identified the hypocrisy of the traditional moral standard and despised Confucianism classics. From his point of view, the *Analects* (*Lun Yu* 论语) and *Mencius* which were often used as the textbooks for Imperial Examination (*Ke Jü*) prevented individuals from knowing the genuine feelings and desires of their own (Lee, 2012). When Li resigned as a prefect of Yao'an (姚安) County in Yun'nan in 1580, his behaviors seemed to become more "lunatic" and "iconoclastic" as he allowed females to attend the class and took the tonsure like a monk (Xu Sumin, 2006: 107-112). In 1590, Li Zhi's most influential book: *A Book to Burn* (*Fenshu* 焚书) eventually came out and three years later (1593), *A Book to Hidden* (*Cangshu* 藏书) was also published, which immediately gained popularity over the intellectuals. The two books contained most of Li Zhi's essays, letters and commentaries and the subjects covered were various and "kaleidoscopic" including "aesthetics, politics, historiography, ethics, and the relationship between the sexes" (Lee & Haun, 2016: 29).

3. Influence of Field on the Translation and Reception of Li Zhi's Works

Previous research on the English translation of Li Zhi's works was often descriptive with a vague timeline. In Wu Wennan's study (2019), the entire spread process was simply divided into two stages: 1930-1980s and 1980s-2018. Considering the great social changes in China over the centuries, such a taxonomy seems to be rather general and arbitrary. Moreover, while Wu provided an overview of how Li Zhi's works were introduced to western society, he did not probe into the underlying reasons behind such a spread. Under such circumstances, Bourdieu's sociological theory of field is applied to fill this research gap in the current study.

Centered on Bourdieu's theory, the "field" was defined as "a network, or a configuration of objective relations between positions" (Bourdieu & Wacquant, 1992: 97). Such a concept was coined to analyze the social activity in a particular "social space in which interactions, transactions and events occurred" (Thomson, 2008: 67). It should be noted that the "social space" in Bourdieu's theory is not static but changeable and thus, the structure of field was also dynamic (Hanna, 2016: 21). Individuals or institutions compete with each other for their own purposes, trying to dominate the field. A social phenomenon is nothing but an outcome of a struggle between different powers. As indicated by Bourdieu (1993: 27), newcomers always try to "break through the entry barrier and the dominant agent who will try to defend the monopoly and keep out the competition". Obviously, both newcomers and "old power" were social creatures and were shaped by their own "social experience". In Bourdieu's theory, such an experience was called "habitus" which served as a vital "property" of all agents. It comprised "a structured and structuring structure" (Bourdieu, 1994: 170). To be more specific, the habitus was a systematically ordered structure which was structured by individuals' "past and present experience" and was structuring or "shaping one's present and future practice". For instance, translators' habitus that helps them to decide which text should be translated and what strategies should be employed were "structured" by their personal experience like cultural backgrounds or professional translation training experience (Liu Xiaofeng & Ma Huijuan, 2016: 58). After being structured, the habitus then controlled translators' practice, subtly influencing the field where translators lived in.

In terms of the translation and reception of Li Zhi's works, they were controlled mainly by the Confucianism study field, Ming study field and the Chinese classics (*Dianji* 典籍) translation field. The three fields were interrelated, hindering or advancing the spread of Li Zhi's works in western society. When studies on Confucianism or Ming dynasty thrived in the international sinology, Li Zhi would by all means be noticed and when a large number of resources were invested in the translation of Chinese classics, Li Zhi's works would be covered as well due to his importance in Chinese philosophy history. In the following discussions, such interrelations are concluded into four phases (See Figure 1).

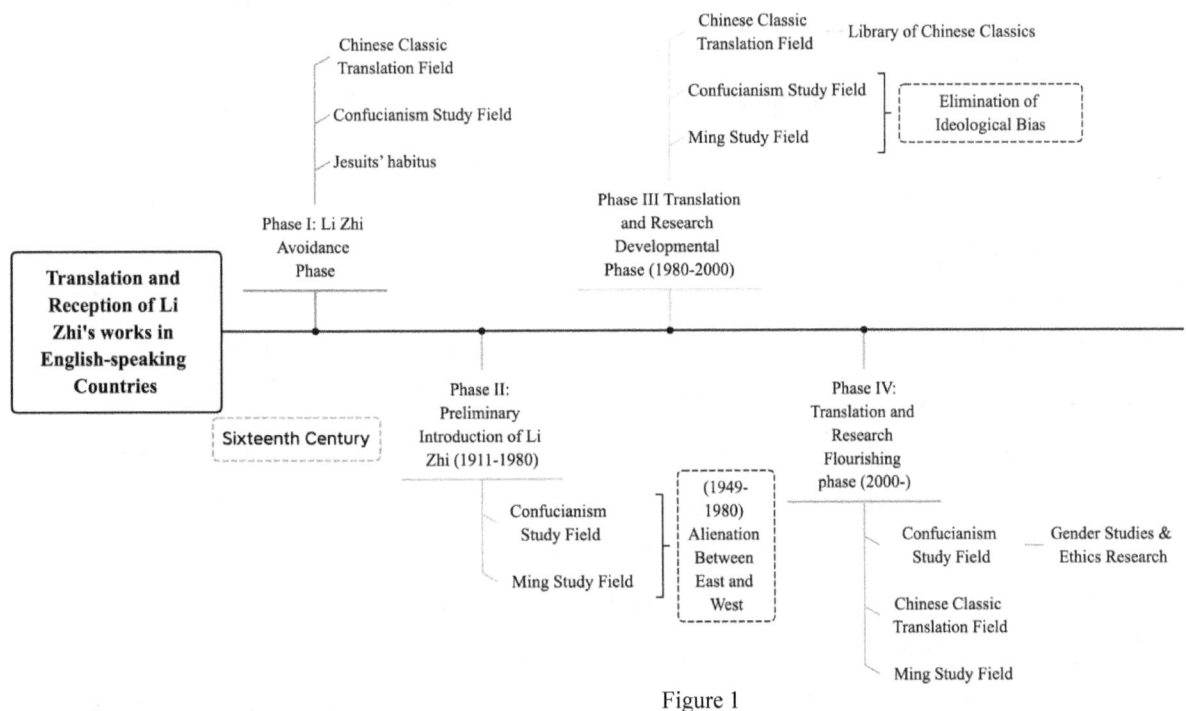

Figure 1

3.1 Phase I: Li Zhi avoidance phase

Although it was vital to understand the motivation of the initial introduction, it was still meaningful to figure out why Taizhou School and Li Zhi had not received much attention in the western acidemias until the late 1930s. As a matter of fact, when Matteo Ricci first arrived in Nanjing, the southern capital of the Ming Dynasty in 1599, he made acquaintance with many Confucians including Li Zhi (Chen Dubin, 2020). In his biography, *De Christiana expeditione apud Sinas* (*China in the Sixteenth Century: The Journals of Matthew Ricci,* 利玛窦中国札记), Matteo Ricci (1953: 334) described Li Zhi as an "apostate from the literati" and a "distinguished scientist with many followers." After the first encounter, the two scholars met again in Ji'ning, Shandong Province in 1600. They were both exhilarated by this reunion and had a thorough discussion on religion and philosophy. Matteo Ricci even intended to preach Catholicism to Li Zhi(ibid). Nevertheless, despite the friendship between Li Zhi and Matteo Ricci, none of Li Zhi's works or Taizhou School classics was translated at that moment. The brief mentions of Li Zhi in Matteo Ricci's journal were all the westerners knew (Wu, 2019: 76). The reasons for such avoidance or "neglect" were as follows.

First of all, Jesuits' habitus had already decided that they were less likely to introduce Neo-Confucianism classics to European countries. As mentioned earlier, Neo-Confucianism scholars all possessed a tendency towards atheism. They believed that reality did exist and can be understood through individuals' own endeavors (Craig, 1998: 552) which obviously could not be accepted by the Catholic Jesuits.

In addition to the subjective reason arising from the Jesuits' habitus, the Confucianism study field and Chinese classics translation field resulted in such an avoidance more objectively. While the western world had been aware of the greatness of the Chinese empire for a long time due to the Skill Road and Marco Polo's story, the interactions between the two cultures were always "sporadic and indirect" before the expansion of Europe from the 16th century (Stavrianos, 1990: 347). There existed almost no translation of Chinese classics until the arrival of the Jesuits. Therefore, the priority for the Jesuits was to present an overview of Chinese cultures and society. There was no need to illustrate the complex schools of Confucianism before understanding the basic concepts of Confucianism. Moreover, the Confucianism study field in the middle and late Ming Dynasty also influence the Jesuits' choices of translation. Despite some disagreements, the central position of Confucius had not been challenged or questioned (Wu Zhen, 2009: 426-427). Even for Taizhou School which possessed the strongest rebellious features against traditional Confucianism, it still emphasized the spirit of Confucius-Mencius doctrines (ibid: 433). Meanwhile, the Confucianism study field had been under official's strict supervision and regulations during that period. In 1579, the Grand Secretary (*Shoufu* 首辅) Zhang Juzheng (张居正) issued an edict to ban private academies (Lidén, 2018: 18). Many Taizhou School followers like Yan Jun (颜均) and He Xinyin (何心隐) were arrested and prosecuted by the officials (Wu Zhen, 2009). Thus, considering the western readers' knowledge of China and the official's edict, Jesuits chose not to translate other schools of Confucianism.

3.2 Phase II: preliminary introduction to Li Zhi in western society (1911-1980)

When Dr. Sun Yat-sen led the democratic revolution and founded the Republic of China in 1911, one important political slogan was "Expel the Tartars, Restore China" (驱除鞑虏, 恢复中华). The Tartars obviously referred to the

Manchu who defeated the ethnic Han-ruled Ming Dynasty. Such a slogan was in line with many ethnic Han intellectuals' dissatisfaction with the Manchu's ruling. They mourned the collapse of the Ming Dynasty and began to conduct comprehensive studies on the rise and decline of the Ming. In this situation, a new field: the "Ming study" field was gradually formed and together with the previous Confucianism study field, the Chinese classics translation field influenced the following translation activity of Li Zhi's works.

As the Republican scholars looked back the history of the Ming Dynasty, the modernity and the iconoclastic features that emerged in the late Ming dynasty immediately attracted their attention. They came to realize that they were not the first group of people that dissented from the traditional Confucianism moral standards. During the New Culture Movement (1915-1923), an increasing number of studies on the Taizhou School were carried out and after three centuries, Li Zhi eventually regained his influence in the Confucianism study field. He was pushed into the frontline against traditional Confucianism, becoming a hero in many Republican scholars' eyes. Historian Wu Yu (吴虞) admired Li Zhi's courage and resonated with his ideas. His publication (Wu Yu, 2013): *The Supplementary Biography of Li Zhuowu in Ming Dynasty* in 1916 not only illustrated Li Zhi's thoughts but more importantly, called on the public to reform Confucianism based on Li Zhi's theory. Under such influence, K.C. Hisao (also known as Xiao Gongquan 萧公权) published an English article *Li Chih: An Iconoclast of the Sixteenth Century* in 1938, which served as the first comprehensive introduction to Li Zhi in English-speaking countries. The English translation of some excerpts from Li Zhi's *A Book to Burn* and *A Book to Hidden* was also included in this essay. Receiving his PhD in politics at Cornell University, Hisao was familiar with the western research paradigm as well as the academic discourse. Therefore, his essay was more accessible to western sinologists, inspiring international sinology to conduct more research on Li Zhi. Overall, the collapse of the Qing Dynasty advanced the studies of the Ming Dynasty during the Republican era (1911-1949). More Ming intellectuals and Confucians were identified under the influence of the Ming study field and Li Zhi stood out as an effective "tool" to reform Confucianism. The English translation of Li Zhi's works was merely the outcome of the struggle that happened in the Ming study field and Confucianism study field.

The establishment of the People's Republic of China (the PRC) in 1949 marked a new era in which Marxism first served as the main ideology in the country and became the "guiding thought" in academia. Many researchers started to use Marxism to investigate those long-standing issues in Chinese history. For instance, from the theory of "Historical Materialism" Hou Wailu et la., (1960) indicated that Li Zhi epitomized the anti-feudalism fighter in the Ming Dynasty. Unfortunately, due to the impact of the cold war, the entire western society followed the foreign policy of the United States, adopting a hostile attitude towards New China. The fresh research findings made by Chinese scholars were strange to western sinologists. In international sinology, research on Li Zhi or Taizhou School was often conducted as a supplementary study of the Ming Dynasty. From Eng-chew Chen's (1973) dissertation *Li Chih as a Critic: A Chapter of the Ming Intellectual History* to Ray Huang's monograph, the translation of Li Zhi's works was often "secondary" and served as the offshoot of the Ming study field (Wu, 2019: 75). Under such circumstances, although some of Li Zhi's articles were translated in English between 1911-1980, the full-scale of translation did not start until 1980.

3.3 Phase III: translation and research developmental phase (1980-2000)

Due to the "Reform and Opening-up Policy" at the end of 1978 in mainland China, western sinologists could eventually have opportunities to conduct their studies in China and exchange ideas with Chinese scholars. Such exchanges greatly changed the Ming study field and Confucianism study field. The ideological bias was gradually eliminated in the two fields. Researchers in this phase focused on every aspect of Li Zhi ranging from his philosophical and political ideas to his aesthetic theory. Many of Li Zhi's articles and thoughts were therefore introduced to English-speaking countries. For instance, Hong Kong scholar Chan Hok-lam (陈学霖) visited mainland China in 1980 and identified some important publications on Li Zhi which were unknown to him (Wu, 2019). Collaborated with mainland scholars, new findings were reported in his subsequent studies (Chan, 1980).

At the same time, the Chinese classics translation field also had a significant impact on the translation of Li Zhi's works. In 1994, China's National Press and Publication Administration initiated an ambitious project: the "Library of Chinese Classics" (大中华文库), which aimed at introducing Chinese classics to western society (Lü Jianlan, 2021:170). With the endeavors made by translators from all over the world, a total of 110 Chinese classics were translated into English. Although Li Zhi's works were not included in the project, the thriving translation industry undoubtedly expand the influence of Chinese classics. Thus, Phase III was more like a transition stage which made preparations for the comprehensive translation in the new millennium

3.4 Phase IV: translation and research flourishing phase (2000-)

As a large number of resources were invested in Chinese classics translation field, Chinese culture was greatly promoted in the western world. Many research institutions and foundations were established to advertise and research the uniqueness of Chinese culture. For example, the "James P. Geiss and Margaret Y. Hsu Foundation (the Geiss Foundation)" was established in 2001 and was dedicated to supporting Ming studies. Such a foundation benefited the all-around research on Li Zhi in the new millennium.

In addition to the financial support from the Ming study field, one vital factor that motivated the English translation of Li Zhi was the popularity of feminism. In 1995, the Fourth World Conference on Women was held in Beijing and a bold blueprint for women's rights known as *The Beijing Platform for Action* was made. The "action" aimed at empowering women and removing all "obstacles to women's active participation" (United Nations, 1996: 7). With such an agenda, the feminism movement came to a new climax and emerged as one of the most important social trends in the new millennium. This new trend penetrated every aspect of life, and the Confucianism study field could not be an exception either. An increasing number of scholars, especially females, started to doubt Confucian's opinions on women because for a long history Confucianism had been seen as "women oppressive" (Li, 2000: 2). In order to solve this issue, Chenyang Li, a professor of philosophy at Nanyang Technological University edited a book: *The Sage and the Second Sex: Confucianism, Ethics, and Gender* to discuss the relationship between feminism and Confucianism. This important book made great contributions to the reform of Confucianism. It provided strong arguments and evidence to show that Confucianism was capable of coming to terms with modern feminism (Cahill, 2001). In the sixth chapter, Li Zhi was depicted as a Confucian feminist by Pauline Lee. Later in her doctoral dissertation (2002), "*Li Zhi (1527-1602): a Confucian Feminist of Late-Ming China*", Lee further elucidated the feminism ideas embedded in Li Zhi's works. From Lee's perspective, Confucianism possessed a tradition of feminism in Chinese history with a particular focus on "self-cultivation" and Li Zhi was one of the proactive feminists that advocated gender equality (Lee, 2002: 4). Through Lee's research, Li Zhi intertwined with the gender studies and ethics research and an increasing number of scholars outside the Confucianism study field started to conduct studies relevant to Li Zhi. Handler-Spitz, a professor at the University of Chicago adopted a comparative method to analyze Li Zhi's most important book: *A Book to Burn*. In her dissertation (Handler-Spitz, 2009), some of Li Zhi's writings from *A Book to Burn* were translated into English and were compared with the French writer Montaigne's essays. In the following years, the interdisciplinary studies on Li Zhi continued to develop and ultimately in 2016 sponsored by the Geiss Foundation, the first comprehensive English translation of Li Zhi's works was published. Edited and translated by Handler-Spitz, Li Zhi's two important books: *A Book to Burn* and *A Book to Hidden* (Li, 2016) were presented to the western audience in a considerably detailed way. Not only did three translators translate Li Zhi's letters, poems and essays, they considerately offered many useful annotations which help western readers to better understand Li Zhi's thoughts. Overall, it can be seen that the comprehensive translation fulfilled in 2016 was driven by the thriving interdisciplinary research trend in Confucianism study as well as the capital from the Ming study field.

4. Conclusion

Despite the significance of Li Zhi in Confucianism and Chinese history, scant attention has been paid to the translation and reception of his works in English-speaking countries (Lee, 2002: 4). It seems rather surprising that few researchers are curious about how Li Zhi is introduced to the western academia. Many of them somehow take it for granted that due to the great impact of Confucianism, the introduction to the other branches of Confucianism would occur spontaneously. Nonetheless, as discussed in the essay, the introduction to Taizhou School and Li Zhi was much later than that of Pre-Qin Confucianism schools and the social backgrounds for such an introduction were also different. By using Bourdieu's sociological theory, the translation of Li Zhi's works is analyzed from a border social aspect. It is found that the introduction to as well as the translation of Li Zhi's works are strongly connected with the Confucianism study field, the Ming study field and the Chinese classics translation field. Every time Confucianism faces challenges, Li Zhi would be revisited by the reformists. Those reformists as the newcomers compete with the traditional thoughts and by introducing and translating Li Zhi's works to a wider readership, they used Li Zhi as a weapon to attack the old power. Additionally, as a vital figure in the late Ming Dynasty, the rapid development of the Ming study field in international sinology also benefits the translation of Li Zhi's works. Ultimately, the increasing capital investment in the Chinese classics translation field financially supported the introduction to Li Zhi's works in English-speaking countries.

Notes

① Distinctions should be made between Neo-Confucianism and New Confucianism. The former was initiated in the Song Dynasty by Zhu Xi (朱熹), Cheng Yi and Cheng Hao and thus, the school was often called *ChengZhu Lixue* (程朱理学). On the other hand, the latter refers to a political thought emerging in the May Fourth Movement which aimed at reforming Confucianism to be more adapted to modern society.

② Li Zhi's ethnic identity remains to be disputable with some arguing him to be Han. Nonetheless, there was no denying that Li Zhi's family had strong connections with Arabic culture (Xu Sumin, 2006: 73:75).

References

[1] Bary, W.T. Self and Society in the Ming [G]// Bary, W.T & Bloom, I (eds.) *Sources of Chinese Tradition, Vol 1.* New York: Columbia University Press, 1999: 841-871.

[2] Bourdieu, P. & L. Wacquant. *An Invitation to Reflexive Sociology* [M]. Cambridge: Polity, 1992.

[3] Bourdieu, P. *In Other Words: Essays Towards a Reflexive Sociology* [M]. M. Adamson (trans,). Cambridge: Polity, 1994.

[4] Bourdieu, P. *Sociology in Question* [M]. London: SAGE Publications, 1993.

[5] Cahill, S. "Book Reviews: *The Sage and the Second Sex: Confucianism, Ethics, and Gender*" [J]. *The Journal of Asian Studies*, 2001: 60(4).

[6] Chan, Hok-lam. "Li Chih (1527-1602): Additional Research Notes" [J]. *Chinese Studies in History*, 1980, 13(3): 81-84.

[7] Chen, Dubin (陈笃彬). "The Different Type of Collision between Chinese and Western Civilizations in the Late Ming Dynasty—When Li Zhi Meeting Matteo Ricci" (晚明中西文化的别样碰撞——当李贽遇上利玛窦) [J]. *Journal of Quanzhou Normal University* (泉州师范学院学报), 2020, 38(03): 59-64.

[8] Chen, Eng-chew. *Li Chih as a Critic: A Chapter of the Ming Intellectual History* [D]. Seattle: University of Washington, 1973.

[9] Chen, Lai (陈来). *Songming Lixue* (宋明理学[M]) Shanghai: East China Normal University Press (华东师范大学出版社), 2008.

[10] Cheng, Y. "The Taizhou School (Taizhou Xuepai) and the Popularization of Liangzhi (Innate Knowledge)" [J]. *Ming Studies*, 2009, 60: 45-65, DOI: 10.1179/175975909X12589849512374.

[11] Craig, E. *Routledge Encyclopedia of Philosophy* [M]. London: Taylor & Francis, 1998.

[12] Cummins, J. S. *A Question of Rites: Friar Domingo Navarrete and the Jesuits in China* [M]. London: Scolar Press, 1993.

[13] Handler-Spitz, R. *Diversity, Deception, and Discernment in the Late Sixteenth Century: A Comparative Study of Li Zhi's 'Book to Burn' and Montaigne's 'Essays'* [D]. Illinois: The University of Chicago, 2009.

[14] Hanna, S. *Bourdieu in Translation Studies: The Socio-cultural Dynamics of Shakespeare Translation in Egypt* [M]. New York & London: Routledge, 2016.

[15] Hou, Wailu (侯外庐) et la. *Zhongguo Sixiang Tongshi vol 4* (中国思想通史第四卷[M]). Beijing: People's Publishing House (人民出版社), 1960.

[16] Hou, Wailu (侯外庐). *History of Neo-Confucianism in Song and Ming Dynasties* (宋明理学史[M]). Beijing: People's Publishing House (人民出版社), 1987/2005.

[17] Hsiao, K. C. "Li Chih: An Iconoclast of the Sixteenth Century." *T'ien Hsia Monthly*, 1938, 6 (4): 317- 341.

[18] Huang, R. *1587, A Year of No Significance: The Ming Dynasty in Decline* [M]. New Haven: Yale University Press, 1976.

[19] Huang, Zongxi (黄宗羲). *Ming Ru Xue An* (明儒学案[M]). Beijing: Zhonghua Book Company (中华书局), 2008.

[20] Janik, M. Early Modern European Atheism with Chinese Characteristics: First Jesuit Descriptions of Neo-Confucianism and Their Spinozist Reception [G]//Wróbel, S & Skonieczny, K(eds.) *Atheism Revisited*. Cham: Palgrave Macmillan, 2020: 33-44.

[21] Lee, P. *Li Zhi (1527-1602): A Confucian Feminist of Late-Ming China* [D]. Stanford: Stanford University, 2002.

[22] Lee, P. *Li Zhi, Confucianism and the virtue of desire* [M]. Albany: State University of New York Press, 2012.

[23] Li, C. Introduction: Can Confucianism Come to Terms with Feminism? [G]// Li, C (ed). *The Sage and the Second Sex: Confucianism, Ethics, and Gender.* Chicago: Open Court, 2000: 1-21.

[24] Li, Z. *A Book to Burn and A Book to Keep (Hidden)* [M]. Rivi Handler-Spitz, Pauline C. Lee, and Haun Saussy (eds&trans). New York: Columbia University, 2016.

[25] Li, Zhi (李贽). *Collections of Li Zhi* (李贽文集[M]). Beijing: Social Science Academic Press (社会科学文献出版社), 2000.

[26] Liang, Shuming (梁漱溟). *The Cultures of East and West and Their Philosophies* (东西文化及其哲学[M]). Shanghai: Shanghai People's Publishing Press (上海人民出版社), 2020.

[27] Lidén, J. *The Taizhou Movement* [D]. Stockholm: Stockholm University, 2018.

[28] Liu, Xiaofeng, Ma, Huijuan (刘晓峰，马会娟). "Key Terms in Sociological Translation Studies and their Explanations" (社会翻译学主要关键词及其关系诠释) [J]. *Shanghai Journal of Translators* (上海翻译), 2016(05): 55-61.

[29] Lü, Jianlan (吕剑兰). "The Spread of Chinese-English Edition of Library of Chinese Classics in the United States"(《大中华文库》汉英对照版在美国的传播) [J]. *Chinese Culture Research* (中国文化研究), 2021(4):170-180.

[30] Mei, Qianli (梅谦立). "Early Translation in Western Languages of Confucian Classics" (《孔夫子》: 最初西文翻译的儒家经典) [J]. *Journal of Sun Yatsen University Social Science Edition* (中山大学学报社会科学版), 2008, 48(2): 131-142. DOI:10.3969/j.issn.1000-9639.2008.02.015.

[31] Ricci, M. *China in the Sixteenth Century: The Journals of Matthew Ricci* [M]. New York: Random House, 1953.

[32] Stavrianos, L.S. *A Global History: From Prehistory to the Present* [M]. New Jersey: Prentice Hall, 1990.

[33] Thomson, P. Field [G]// Grenfell, M (ed.) *Pierre Bourdieu: Key Concepts.* Stocksfield: Acumen, 2008: 67-81.

[34] United Nations. *Report of the Fourth World Conference on Women* [R]. New York: United Nations, 1996.

[35] Wang, Gen (王艮). *Full Collections of Wang Xinzhai* (王心斋全集[M]). Nanjing: Jiangsu Education Publishing House (江苏教育出版社), 2001.

[36] Wu, W. "Li Zhi in English-Language Scholarship" [J]. *The Journal of East West Thought*, 2019, 9(4): 75-88.

[37] Wu, Yu (吴虞). *Collections of Wu Yu* (吴虞集[M]). Beijing: Zhonghua Book Company (中华书局), 2013.

[38] Wu, Zhen (吴震). *Taizhou Xuepai Yanjiu* (泰州学派研究[M]). Beijing: China Renmin University Press (中国人民大学出版社), 2009

[39] Xu, Sumin (许苏民). *Commentaries on Li Zhi* (李贽评传[M]). Nanjing: Nanjing University Press (南京大学出版社), 2006.

[40] Zhang, Xiping (张西平). "Michel Ruggieri, the Founder of Sinology in the West"(西方汉学的奠基人罗明坚) [J]. *Historical Research* (历史研究), 2001(03): 101-115.

Bio

ZHANG Junchao is lecturer of Nanjing Normal University Taizhou College. Academic interest: translation and sociology, intercultural communication. E-mail: junchao.zhang@nnutc.edu.cn.

Taizhou School Studies 2

Translation and Research of Taizhou School Thoughts in the Western World since the 20th Century

⊙ CAI Lili (Nanjing Normal University Taizhou College, Taizhou)

Abstract: The translation and research of classical literary works play a very important role in the exchange and mutual learning of Chinese and foreign cultures. Taizhou School is a typical enlightenment school in Chinese history. The founder of the school, Wang Gen, carried forward the thought of Wang Shouren and led the trend of ideological liberation in the late Ming Dynasty. The domestic research on the translation of Taizhou School thoughts is still in its infancy. This study will systematically search and sort out the translation and research overview of Taizhou School thoughts in the western world since the 20th century. On the one hand, it will investigate the overall appearance of the western academic circle on the translation of Taizhou School thoughts, on the other hand, it will point out the deficiency in the research and dissemination of Taizhou School thoughts in the western world, explore the effective ways of overseas dissemination of its philosophy, political, education and literary theories, and further promote the outbound translation and dissemination of Chinese classics.

Key words: Taizhou School; thoughts; western world; translation

20 世纪以来泰州学派思想在西方世界的译介与研究

蔡丽丽（南京师范大学泰州学院，泰州）

[摘 要] 经典文学作品的译介和研究在中外文化的交流互鉴中起着非常重要的作用。泰州学派是中国历史上一个典型的思想启蒙学派，学派创始人王艮发扬了王守仁的心学思想，引领了明朝后期的思想解放潮流。国内对于泰州学派思想的译介研究尚处于起步阶段。本研究将系统检索并梳理 20 世纪以来泰州学派思想在西方世界的译介与研究概况。一方面考察西方学术界对泰州学派思想译介的整体貌相，另一方面指出泰州学派思想在西方世界的研究与传播问题，探索其哲学思想、政治思想、教育思想和文学理论海外传播的有效途径，进一步推动中国典籍外译和传播。

[关键词] 泰州学派；思想；西方世界；译介

1. Introduction

In the Ming and Qing Dynasties, missionary groups represented by Matteo Ricci brought Western scientific and technological knowledge to China, and at the same time, they turned eyes to the spiritual culture of Chinese civilization. They sent ancient Chinese wisdom to the West through the translation of Chinese classics such as *the*

Four Books and *the Five Classics*, which directly or indirectly influenced the development of western philosophy, politics and other fields. In the 20th century, neo-Confucianism emerged in China, and some representative figures came to the United States one after another, pushing the Chinese culture with Confucianism as the core to spread more deeply and widely in the United States. Since the May Fourth Movement, faced with the impact of modern Western civilization under scientism, a group of people have emerged in China to reinterpret and carry forward traditional culture. They tried to rebuild the value system of Confucian culture and sought the modernization of Chinese society and culture by taking Confucian spirit as the body and Western culture as the use. Their ideology is called as modern Neo-Confucianism. There are two teams for the dissemination and development of neo-Confucianism in the United States. The first team is the Chinese-American scholars, such as Du Weiming, Yu Yingshi, Liu Shuxian, Cheng Zhongying, etc. The second team is the western scholars, who take Confucianism as a pure academic study and expand the influence of neo-Confucianism in the United States by publishing works and teaching. Among them, the representative figures are William Theodore de Bary, Roger T. Ames and Benjamin I. Schwartz, etc. Theodore de Bary's research on Chinese traditional philosophy greatly promoted the translation and dissemination of Taizhou School in the western world. After entering the 21st century, the initiative of "going out" of Chinese culture has been clearly put forward, and the share of cultural export has been greatly increased. Outbound translation of Chinese culture, which is different from the traditional translation field, has gradually come into the foreground. Huang Youyi pointed out that the current new trend is "from the past 'translation world' to continue the 'translation world', while paying more attention to 'translation of China'" (Huang Youyi, 2018). Therefore, in the international situation where national soft power and discourse power are increasingly being paid attention to, how to tell China's story well, and improve China's international discourse power and maintaining China's national image have become major concerns of the translation and dissemination research of Chinese classics.

Taizhou School is an academic school with unique charm and controversy in the history of Chinese thought. It is the first enlightenment school in the late feudal society of China, as well as the first true enlightenment school in Chinese history (Hou Wailu, 1980). For a long time, our research on the dissemination and influence of the Taizhou School thoughts has been more focused on East Asia than on the West, which is obviously not conducive to the urgent needs of current cultural development. At present, there have been a lot of research achievements in the academic circle on the research of Yangming Studies and Li Zhi's thought in the West, but the research on the translation and introduction of Taizhou School thoughts is still in its infancy. This study will systematically search and sort out the general situation of the translation and research of the Taizhou School thought in the western world since the 20th century. Due to the lack of translated works of the Taizhou School, the translations selected in this paper are fragments of the Taizhou School thought translated by foreign scholars. On the one hand, this paper examines the overall appearance of the American academic circle in the translation of Taizhou School thoughts, on the other hand, it will point out the translation of Taizhou School thoughts in the western world, and explore effective ways to spread its philosophy, political, education and literary theories abroad, hoping to attract more scholars' attention to the translation and dissemination of Taizhou School in the English world.

2. The Academic Thoughts of the Taizhou School

In the history of Chinese thought, the Yangming School is regarded as a peak. It had a great impact on the

Neo-Confucianism of the Song and Ming Dynasties and had a great ideological liberation effect on the feudal society of China since the Ming Dynasty. The Taizhou School led by Wang Gen, as a civilian Confucianism with the theme of the study of common People's Daily life, is even more unique in the Yangming School. Some scholars say that the Taizhou School initiated by Wang Gen belongs to the left wing of Wang's studies. Therefore, as the founder of leftist Wang Studies, Wang Gen played a very important role in promoting the influence of Yangming School thoughts on Ming studies both at home and abroad. After the middle of Ming Dynasty, when the dominant position of feudal natural economy was increasingly shaken and the germination of capitalism began to emerge, it dared to break through the barriers of feudal autocratic system, negated traditional values, emphasized human natural instinct and life value, and put forward "Learning for daily use by the common people" and "The Huainan Investigation of Things"(*Huainangewulun*), which were contrary to Confucian orthodoxy and different from Wang Shouren's "heresy". Reflecting the ideological awakening of the common people, it had the heroic spirit of "turning over heaven and earth" and "fighting the dragon and snake with bare hands against the feudal ruling class". It had the fearless rebellious spirit of breaking the famous religion by "the power of non-famous religion" (Bai Shouyi, 1999). This is the essence of the Taizhou School of Wang Gen, the fundamental difference between it and Yangming School, and also the most martial spirit of it. It is an accurate interpretation of the influence of Wang Gen and Taizhou School in the international and domestic ideology at that time and later generations.

In terms of regional influence, the academic ideas of the Taizhou School are not limited to the Taizhou area, but take Taizhou as the central pole of ideological communication, and take the Yangtze River Basin as the main place of diffusion. Spread to more than ten provinces in China, it had been disseminated abroad to Japan, South Korea, Korea and other western countries. In terms of its influence on the ideological field, the Taizhou School's influence on the politics, economy, literature, science, culture, education and other aspects of the late Ming Dynasty society is all-round, brilliant and praised by the world. It is said in *The General History of Chinese Culture* that, "Taizhou School is a school of thought derived from Wang Shouren's mind science, which had a great social influence in the middle and late Ming Dynasty. The most remarkable characteristic of this school is that it has a strong color of populism and maniacal character, and pays attention to the pursuit of self-worth. Therefore, this school became very popular in the late Ming Dynasty." (Chen Wutong, 2004:223)

The contribution of Taizhou School in the field of philosophy is most famous for Wang Gen's "The Huainan Investigation of Things". It emphasizes taking one's own as the "right" to "model" the world, so as to correct oneself and others, to realize self-cultivation and self-preservation. This thought of "cultivating oneself" and "securing the world" is a great deepening and expansion of the Confucian thought of inner sanctification and outer king. Moreover, Wang Gen, starting from the perspective that "body" is the "root" of the universe, put forward the ecological philosophy that "body" is integrated with the universe, and that "nature is the root", actually advocating a kind of "everyone first" concept. On the basis of Wang Gen's philosophical thought, Wang Bi put forward the idea that "spontaneous is called Tao", which changed the elusive Taoism of "heavenly principle" of the moralists into the Taoism of realizing the "harmony" from human to nature and society. By means of a theoretical analysis from the point of view of phenomenology of the body, Hong Yu and Huang Deyuan tried to explain the views of Taizhou School on the body so as to apprehend the essence of Confucian thought, which is a philosophy that seeks to "establish oneself" and "cultivate oneself" rather than a "philosophy of consciousness" (2010). In his thesis *The Life Philosophy of Taizhou School*, Xu Chunlin believed that the life philosophy of Taizhou School is the science of settling down for the common people (2010).

In the political field, the contributions of Taizhou School are highlighted in advocating the idea of "the common People's Daily life is the way" and the idea of caring for the people, diligence and honesty. Starting from the human nature theory to meet the daily needs of the people, the Taizhou School required the rulers to cultivate benevolence and virtue, emphasize kindness and education, conform to the people's wishes, and oppose their tyrannical and greedy behaviors. It requires the rulers to govern the world with filial piety, put virtue before literature and art, and maintain and satisfy the wishes of the common people as the fundamental requirement. It requires the rulers to respect the wishes and concerns of the common people and govern the world by the world. (Lu Peimin, 2015:143)

The contribution of the Taizhou School to the economic leadership is reflected in the fact that, from the perspective of respecting oneself and establishing itself, it emphasizes the essence of economizing on necessities and advocates the development of social production so as to safeguard and satisfy the rights and interests of farmers, workers and merchants. Among the school's souls, Wang Gen was "prosperous in his family" because of his good business practices. Yan Jun was persecuted for his thought of "controlling desires rather than benevolence". He Xinyin dissipated all his family wealth because of his ideal society of "gathering harmony hall". Li Zhi was regarded as a "heretic" for his advocacy of various economic doctrines such as "every man has his own interests" and the rationality of commodity market competition (Cai Guiru, 2018:231-232).

For their contributions in the field of science, Wang Gen began to put forward the practical view that "whatever is done is learned and what is done is the way", and later developed and formed those represented by Xu Guangqi, Li Zhizao and Wang Zheng, who paid attention to absorbing advanced western scientific knowledge and technology in the field of practical studies, combined with traditional Chinese science and technology, and made great achievements in astronomy, mathematics, biology and agronomy. It set off the enlightenment trend of thought of science in the late Ming Dynasty.

In the field of education, the most important feature of Taizhou School education is the civilianization, which has been unanimously affirmed by the historians. The Tai Zhou school thoughts on education was begun by Wang Gen and developed by the likes of Yan Jun, Wang Bi, Luo Rufang, He Xinyin, Li Eli, Jiao Hong and Zhou Rudeng. Each generation of the school outdid the former. Their theory of "searching the solitude far in the mountains, bringing wisdom to the market place" helped to establish universal education for society. They established the notion of an ideal society with their motto "everyone can be a 'gentleman'". They advocated notions of spiritual and physical well-being, completing oneself and completing others and returning to the original mind in pursuing an educational policy beneficial to happiness in life. They employed easy to learn songs and poetry as well as Confucian and Buddhist classics in this pursuit. Ideally, students would use these methods in happy interaction with teachers and other classmates. This would increase their desire to learn and they would progress quickly. The Taizhou School, with their emphasis on social life and their multi-faceted teaching material and activities, has a modern face. The results they achieved could be used for consideration in today's academic world. (Wen-shu Huang, 1998)

In the field of culture, Taizhou School advocates the satisfaction of "nature", Li Zhi's "The Childlike Mind-and heart" (*Tongxinshuo*) holds high the banner of Renaissance in the late Ming Dynasty, the public security school "express the spirit of nature" and form the characteristics of "express the heart directly, without holding a suit" of literature theory, Tang Xianzu boldly sings the true temperament of people and in the literary circle and opera circles of the late Ming Dynasty, etc.

Since the reform and opening up, the Chinese academic circle has published some research results and emerged some excellent works. Lin Ziqiu focuses on the family history, life, works, philosophical thoughts, ethical thoughts, social and political thoughts, economic thoughts and educational thoughts of the founder of the Taizhou School, Wang Dong and Wang Bi, and their academic thoughts and achievements represented by Yan Jun, He Xinyin, Li Zhi, Jiao Hong, Tang Xianzu and Yuan Hongdao. It points out that the Taizhou School, which followed Wang Studies, has the characteristics of popularization of preaching objects, simplification of Confucian theories, popularization of Confucian classics, naturalization of mind, mystification of preaching activities and moralization of social ideals, etc. (2000). In *General Theory of Taizhou School*, it discussed the academic origin, representative figures, academic achievements and influence of Taizhou School from three aspects: the relationship between Hu Yuan and Taizhou School, the establishment of Wang Gen and Taizhou School, and the study of other representative figures of Taizhou School. The authors point out that the emergence of Taizhou School was the logical necessity of the evolution of Neo-Confucianism in Song and Ming Dynasties, and its general development trend was from the theory to the theory of heart. It is a very strange and important academic school of thought in the recent history of Chinese thought, which influenced the Ming and Qing Dynasties and even the May Fourth Movement. (2005) Wu Zhen's *Study of the Taizhou School* starts from the redefinition of the "Taizhou Study Case" by Huang Zongxi, focuses on the thoughts and behaviors of the representatives of the Taizhou School, such as Wang Gen, Wang Fu, Wang Dong, Yan Jun, He Xinyin, Luo Rufang, etc., and probes into the whole ideological picture of the Taizhou School. He believes that the ideological characteristics of the Taizhou School have strong social orientation, political orientation and religious orientation. Most of its ideological positions are based on the theory of "ready-made conscience" of Yangming's mind studies, and also have the idea of "returning to Confucius and Mencius" (2009). Huang Yuanjia focuses on the academic inheritance and transformation process of the Taizhou School, and systematically presents the academic development of the school Huang Yuanjia. (2012) In addition, Qian Mu (1895-1990), Xiong Shili (1885-1968) and Zhang Junmai (Carsun Chang 1886-1969) have all made important comments on the Taizhou School in their works. Most of these excellent works conducted longitudinal studies on the origin and development of the Taizhou School as a whole, and have not conducted horizontal comparative studies with other regional schools or scholars, nor have scholars conducted systematic studies on the translation and introduction of its thoughts abroad.

3. An Overview of the Translation of Taizhou School Thoughts in the Western World

In China, a new interest in the Taizhou movement started when the May Fourth Movement became a real force in the 1920s and 1930s. Scholars later labelled as "Neo-Confucians" were inspired by Western philosophy, Buddhism and Neo-Confucianism from the Song and the Ming dynasties.

In the west, the study of Taizhou School thoughts mainly focuses on the translation and dissemination of Li Zhi's thoughts. According to Bai Xiufang's discussion in the article *Li Zhi Studies Abroad*, as one of the representatives of leftist Wang Studies, Li Zhi's thoughts have also exerted great ideological influence in Southeast Asian countries, especially Singapore, as well as in the United States and Europe (1996). Xiao Gongquan, a professor at the University of Washington in Seattle, wrote his thesis *Li Zhi: A Thinker Who Attacked the Feudal Tradition in the 16th Century*, in which he fully affirmed Li Zhi's anti-feudal tradition, which served as an introduction to Li Zhi's thought for Western scholars (1938).

Many other scholars have conducted in-depth research and dissemination of Li Zhi's thought. Huang Ray is a Chinese-American historian and expert on Chinese Ming history. He is known for his advocacy of a "grand view of history". In 1930, Huang Ray, Professor of history at Paltz College of State University of New York, wrote the famous *1587, a Year of No Significance: The Ming Dynasty in Decline*, which has been translated into German, French, Japanese and other languages, has had a certain influence in the field of the study of the world's history of thought, so that more countries and people in the world know the Ming Dynasty society in history. In the seventh chapter of this work, Professor Huang devoted nearly 30,000 words of ink to writing the chapter "*Li Zhi — A Philosopher in Conflict with Himself*", which gives a detailed introduction of Li Zhi's family and its influence on him, and demonstrates Li Zhi's thoughts from various angles through the analysis of Li Zhi's single-minded character and his ideological disputes with Geng Zhi. Pointing out that Li Zhi is a contradictory thinker... In his article, Mr. Huang Renyu further analyzed that, "Li's teachings were half materialist and half idealistic, which was not uncommon among Confucists at that time... His thought was influenced by Wang Yangming, Wang Ji, Wang Gen, etc. In terms of academic schools, he has always been regarded as belonging to the Taizhou School." (2006)

The important promoter of the spread of the Taizhou School in the United States is the American scholar William Theodore De Bary. In 1960, he published a book, *Sources of Chinese Tradition*, in which he gives a brief overview of Taizhou School, titled *The Taizhou School as a Popular Movement*. The article fully affirmed the Taizhou School's philosophical thoughts, historical thoughts and educational theories, "In the Taizhou School itself personal relationships crossed traditional class lines, intellectual associations crossed political lines, and educational work crossed religious lines." (1960) While the penetration of the movement to the lower levels of society is significant, as contrasted to the type of individuality cultivated almost entirely within the upper class of the Song period, its broad extension to all levels of society and to many areas of life is of more fundamental importance than its class character. Its spreading of Confucianism to the common people should not be underestimated. For its primary engagement in popular education, and what might be called its proselytizing evangelism, the Taizhou school Confucianism for the first time became heavily involved in the sphere traditionally occupied by popular religion. In addition, he translated important fragments from *Mingru xuean*, *Wang Xinzhai yiji* and *Fenshu*, and explained the important thoughts of Taizhou School in depth.

(1) The Huainan Investigation of Things

Before visiting Wang Yangming, Wang Gen had described his own teaching as "the investigation of things," but he recognized that his interpretation of it was similar to Yangming's "innate knowing." The similarity lies in the fact that "investigation of things" means for both essentially the "rectification of affairs." In other words, the starting point of all self-cultivation as formulated in the Great Learning should be an understanding of things, matters, actions, and events, so that these conform to one's own sense of right and wrong, shame and deference, etc., and thus become "rectified". In particular Wang Gen stressed the self as the active center of things. In his view self and society were one continuum, with the self as the trunk or base and society as the branch or superstructure (not unlike Xu Heng's version of the Elementary Learning).

（2）Clear Wisdom and Self-preservation

Wang Gen's brief essay titled "Clear Wisdom and Self-preservation" ("*Mingzhebaoshenlun*"), from which the following passage is drawn, is expressed in a simple style and somewhat repetitious argumentation, which reflects both his own homespun character and his desire to communicate to the simplest people. Clear wisdom is innate knowing. To clarify wisdom and preserve the self is innate knowing and innate ability. When Wang Gen speaks of "my body being cooked alive or the flesh being sliced off my own thighs" and "throwing away my life", he is alluding not only to violence done to one by others but to extravagant gestures of self-sacrifice and protests against a highly idealized view of the self that called for heroic self-denial and an almost religious dedication to one's ruler or parents, so contrary to the natural human instinct for self-preservation.

（3）The Enjoyment of Learning

This ode expresses the natural spontaneity and creative power of the Way manifesting itself through the individual, but a Way that also serves the needs of human beings. Wang Gen's activism is alive with the spontaneous joy of the Dao and finds that joy in learning. Wang Gen was not the first Chinese thinker to find joy in life. This is a common theme among his predecessors, from Confucius and Zhuangzi down through the Song masters to Wang Yangming. But he may be the first to express such rapturous joy in learning of a kind that is available to all and not just the secret delight of the scholar. Wang Gen's joy arises from the fact that learning is so simple and easy. It does not require any erudition or intellectual exertion; it is the operation of ordinary intelligence in everyday life, which should be effortless. Joy is spontaneous when one does not rely on one's own strength, but let nature, innate knowing, the Way be manifested freely through the self.

（4）The Childlike Mind-and heart

Basic assumptions for Li Zhi are, first, the cardinal Neo-Confucian doctrine of the essential goodness of the human mind and second, Wang Yangming's view that the manifesting of this inherent virtue comes through the direct, uninhibited expression of "good [innate, intuitive] knowing." Li contrasted this natural innocence and spontaneity to the glib professions of sagely morality all around him. These seemed to him the hypocritical mouthings of "scholars" whose learning and "virtue" were quite conventional, secondhand, and pretentious — uninformed by the searching self-scrutiny ("self-watchfulness") so emphasized in the Great Learning and the Mean. Once people's minds have been given over to received opinions and moral principles, what they have to say is all about these things, and not what would naturally come from their childlike minds. No matter how clever the words, what have they to do with oneself? What else can there be but phony men speaking phony words, doing phony things, writing phony writings? Once the men become phonies, everything becomes phony. Thereafter, if one speaks phony talk to the phonies, the phonies are pleased; if one does phony things as the phonies do, the phonies are pleased; and if one discourses with the phonies through phony writings，the phonies are pleased. Everything is phony, and everyone is pleased. (De Bary,1997)

4. An Overview of the Research on Taizhou School in the Western World since the 20th Century

Ji Wenfu, a radical scholar who lived from 1895 to 1963, used the phrase "left-wing of the Wang Yangming School" for the first time in his book *Zuopai Wangxue* (1934). Wang Ji and Wang Gen are identified as the prominent members of the "left wing" in this essay, which develops a political language. This description places a lot of emphasis on their political radicalism, but it leaves out the whole picture, which includes their spirituality and perspective on human beings, Dao, and how people interact to one another and the universe. The fact that Ji Wenfu never clarifies what "leftist" and "rightist" mean is problematic.

Following Ji Wenfu, a number of academics with a left-leaning perspective, such as Hou Wailu, have taken an interest in Wang Gen and the Taizhou movement. Wu Yu (1872-1949), who published Li Zhi's biography, also uncovered the Taizhou practitioner who was influenced by Wang Gen and was acquainted with numerous of the May Fourth Movement's participants. Li's writings underwent revisions in the 1950s and 1960s, and many who criticized Confucianism during "the Cultural Revolution" cited Li's critique of the philosophy. Another question is whether or not they correctly comprehended him. These writings provided a strong framework for the study of Taizhou School ideas in the West.

William Theodore de Bary's seminal article "Individualism and Humanitarianism in Late Ming Thought" helped advance Western research on the Taizhou movement and inspired some of his students at Columbia University and other American universities to write PhD theses on various Taizhou practitioners. He Xinyin was the subject of a monograph written by Ronald G. Dimberg in 1974, Jiao Hong (1547-1629) was the subject of one by Edward T. Ch'ien in 1986, and Wang Gen was the subject of a PhD thesis by Lee Sheng-kuang in 1990. Thesis on *Li Zhi, Philosophe Maudit (1527–1602)* by Jean-François Billeter was published in 1979, while Wang Gen was the subject of a monograph by Monika Übelhör in 1986. Up until Yu-yin Cheng's 1996 thesis, which analyzes the socioeconomic context of the Taizhou practitioners and details their organizations, not much more was done after this. Her title *Sagehood and the Common Man*; *T'ai-chou Confucianism in Late Ming Society* has the same title with Lee Sheng-kuang's thesis *Commoner and Sagehood*; *Wang Ken and the T'ai-chou School in Late Ming Society*. Both Cheng and Lee have an interest in the socioeconomic circumstances of Taizhou practitioners, but Cheng is more ambitious and covers He Xinyin and Luo Rufang in addition to Wang Gen, whereas Lee Sheng-kuang solely pays attention to Wang Gen. Since Cheng's thesis was written before the publication of *Yan Jun Ji* in 1996, she didn't pay much attention to Yan Jun. Among these books, Billeter is still studied by academics who are fascinated by the remarkable life and views of Li Zhi. Jiao Hong-related work by Edward T. Ch'ien prompted Yü-ying Shih to write a lengthy (42 page) criticism of his book. In it, Shih criticized Ch'ien for exploiting French structuralism and German phenomenology to make "tortuously labored" arguments and charged that he was using Jiao Hong "to play his own 'game'". Ch'ien's provocations forced Yü to revisit Jiao Hong's universe and provided him the chance to criticize what he saw as errors in phenomenology and structuralism. However, Ch'ien's argument that Jiao Hong blended Confucian, Daoist, and Buddhist concepts and that this combination could be credited to the entire Neo-Confucian movement is what Yü is attacking, not only his use of Western phenomenology and structuralism None of the other PhD theses on Wang Gen and the Taizhou School have come to a similar discussion. However, there is no related research on Yan Jun in the west.

5. Conclusion

To sum up, we can see that there are mainly the following problems in the studies of translation and communication of Taizhou School in the West. First, there is a lack of historical systematic and comprehensive studies, and no researchers have paid comprehensive attention to this topic so far. Second, limited by language, culture, sinology and research methods, the translated works are blank, the range of topics is narrow, the research level is single, and the list of phenomena is too many. Third, the research views and methods are outdated, there is no solid theoretical foundation, so it is unable to obtain valuable results. It can be seen that in the context of globalization, the academic circle fails to pay timely attention to and respond comprehensively to the trip of Taizhou School thoughts to the Western world. In the urgent need of the broad intellectual circle to promote Chinese culture and foreign studies classics, the current research vision, research intensity and research level in this field are far from keeping up with the requirements of the times.

References

[1] Bai, Shouyi (白寿彝). *A General History of China* (中国通史[M]). Shanghai: Shanghai People's Publishing House(上海：上海人民出版社), 1999.

[2] Bai, Xiufang (白秀芳). "Li Zhi Study Abroad" (李贽研究在国外)[J]. Journal of Capital Normal University (Social Science Edition) [首都师范大学学报(社会科学版)], 1996(1)82-87.

[3] Billeter, Jean-Francois. *Li Zhi, Philosophe Maudit (1527-1602*[M]*)*, Genève: Droz, 1979.

[4] Cai, Guiru (蔡桂如). *Study on Wang Gen of Taizhou School* (泰州学派王艮研究[M]). Nanjing: Nanjing Publishing House(南京：南京出版社), 2018.

[5] Cai, Wenjin & Yang, Chengsheng (蔡文锦，杨呈胜). *General Study of Taizhou School* (泰州学派通论[M]). Nanjing: Jiangsu People's Publishing House(南京：江苏人民出版社), 2005.

[6] Ch'ien, Edward T. *Chiao Hung and the Reconstructuring of Neo-Confucianism in the Late Ming*[M]. New York: Columbia University Press, 1986.

[7] Chen, Wutong(陈梧桐). *General History of Chinese Culture (Ming Dynasty Volume)*[中国文化通史（明代卷）[M]]. Beijing: Beijing Normal University Press(北京：北京师范大学出版社), 2004.

[8] Cheng, Yu-yin. *Sagehood and the Common Man: Tai-chou Confucianism in Late Ming Society. Ph.D. Dissertation*[D]. California Davis University, 1996.

[9] De Bary, Wm Theodore. Individualism and Humanitarianism. *Self and Society in Ming Thought*[M], New York and London: Columbia University Press, 1970 (145–248).

[10] De Bary, Wm Theodore. *Sources of Chinese Tradition, Vol. 1*[M]. Columbia: Columbia University Press, 1997.

[11] Dimberg, Donald G. *The Sage and Society: The Life and Thought of Ho Hsin-yin. Monographs of the Society for Asian and Comparative Philosophy, No. 1*. the University Press of Hawaii, 1987.

[12] Hong Yu, Huang Deyuan. "All Things Are Already Complete in My Body": An Explanation of the Views of the Taizhou School on the Human Body[J]. *Frontiers of Philosophy in China*, 2010, 005(003):396-413.

[13] Hou, Wailu (侯外庐). *History of Neo-Confucianism in Song and Ming dynasties* (宋明理学史[M]). Beijing: Beijing People's

Publishing House (北京：北京人民出版社), 1987.

[14] Hou, Wailu (侯外庐). *Outline of Chinese ideological history* (中国思想史纲[M]). Beijing: China Youth Publishing House(北京：中国青年出版社), 1980.

[15] HSIAO,K.C. "Li Chih:An Iconoclast of the Sixteenth Century"[J]. *T'ien Hsia Monthly*,1938, 6(4):317-341.

[16] Huang Wen-shu. "The Tai Zhou School's Educational Philosophy"[J]. *Philosophy and Culture*, 1998, 25(11):1018-1033.

[17] Huang, Renyu (黄仁宇). *1587, a Year of No Significance* (万历十五年[M]). Beijing: Zhonghua Book Company(北京：中华书局), 2006.

[18] Huang, Youyi (黄友义). "From translating the world to translating China" (从翻译世界到翻译中国)[N]. *Guangming Daily*(光明日报), 09-12-2018.

[19] Huang, Yuanjia (黄元嘉). *On the Inheritance and Transformation of Taizhou School: from Wang Gen to Geng Tiantai* (论泰州学派的传承与转化：从王艮到耿天台)[D]. National Chi-Nan University(国立暨南国际大学), 2012.

[20] Ji Wenfu (嵇文甫). *Thoughts and History of Late Ming Dynasty* (晚明思想史论[M]). Beijing: Orient Press (北京：东方出版社), 1996.

[21] Johanna Lidén. *The Taizhou Movement Being Mindful in Sixteenth Century China*[D]. Stockholm: Stockholm University, 2018.

[22] Lee, Sheng-kuang. *Commoner and Sagehood: Wang Ken and the T'aichou School*[D]. Univiversity of Arizona, 1990.

[23] Lin, Ziqiu, Ma, Boliang&Hu, Weiding (林子秋, 马伯良, 胡维定). *Wang Gen and Taizhou School* (王艮与泰州学派[M]). Chengdu: Sichuan Dictionary Publishing House(成都：四川辞书出版社), 2000.

[24] Lu, Peimin (卢佩民). *The Culture of Taizhou School* (泰州学派文化[M]). Nanjing: Nanjing University Press(南京：南京大学出版社), 2015.

[25] Übelhör, Monika. *Wang Gen [1483-1541] und seine Lehre: eine kritische Position im spätem Konfuzianismus*[M]. Berlin: Reimer, 1986.

[26] Wu, Zhen (吴震). *Study on Taizhou School* (泰州学派研究[M]). Beijing: China Renmin University Press（北京：中国人民大学出版社）, 2009.

[27] Xu, Chunlin (徐春林). *The harmony of life —— A study on life philosophy of Taizhou School* (生命的圆融——泰州学派生命哲学研究[M]). Beijing: Guangming Daily Press(北京：光明日报出版社). 2010

[28] Yü, Ying-Shih. The intellectual world of Chiao Hung revisited (Book review of Edward Ch'ien, Chiao Hung the Reconstruction of Neo-Confucianism in the Late Ming) *Ming Studies,* 1988(24-66).

Bio

CAI Lili is lecturer of Nanjing Normal University Taizhou College. Academic interest: translation and cross-culture studies. E-mail: 20201014@nnutc.edu.cn.

Taizhou School Studies 3

The Enlightenment of C-E translation of Li Zhi's Thought on Chinese Classics Culture "Going Global": A Case Study of *Fenshu* and *Xu Fenshu*

⊙ ZHANG Weiyi (Nanjing Normal University Taizhou College, Taizhou)

Abstract: The culture of Chinese classics is extensive, profound and has a long history, which is an important part of cultural soft power. With the proposal the national strategy of Chinese culture "Going Global", improving the quality of translation of cultural books, which are important cultural carriers, is a issue worth thinking deeply. Li Zhi, as an outstanding enlightenment thinker, litterateur and historian in the Ming Dynasty, as well as one of the representative figures of the left-wing Taizhou School of the post-Yangming school, occupies an important position in the history of Chinese thought. He made remarkable achievements in philosophy, history and literature, and wrote many books. His philosophical thoughts, historical thoughts and literary theories are all treasure-houses for reference and exploration in the era of globalization. The study of Li Zhi in the West began in the 1930s, and his translations are still of inspiration and reference significance to the Chinese translation of Chinese classics today. By summarizing the translations of different versions of *Fenshu* and *Xu Fenshu*, this paper explores their inspirations for the translation of classics in the new era, thus improving the translation quality of Chinese classics, telling Chinese stories well and promoting Chinese culture to "go global".

Key words: Chinese Classics Culture; strategy of culture "Going Global"; Li Zhi; translation; *Fenshu* and *Xu Fenshu*

李贽思想英译对中国典籍文化"走出去"的启示
——以《焚书》和《续焚书》英译本为例

张薇依（南京师范大学泰州学院，泰州）

[摘 要] 中国典籍文化博大精深、源远流长，是文化软实力的重要组成部分。我国提出文化"走出去"战略，文化典籍作为一种重要的文化载体，提高其翻译质量是一个值得深思的问题。李贽作为明代杰出的启蒙思想家、文学家、史学家，阳明后学左翼泰州学派代表人物之一，在中国思想史上占有重要的地位。他在哲学、史学、文学诸多方面都卓有建树，著作很多。其哲学思想、史学思想和文学理论对全球化时代的人类社会而言，都是可资借鉴和发掘的思想宝库。西方对李贽的研究始于20世纪30年代，其译著对我们今天典籍汉译仍具有启发和借鉴意义。通过对不同版本《焚书》和《续焚书》译著进行概括梳理，探索其对新时代下典籍作品

翻译的启示，进而提高中国典籍翻译质量，对外讲好中国故事，推动中国文化"走出去"。

[关键词] 中国典籍文化；文化"走出去"战略；李贽；翻译；《焚书》和《续焚书》

1. Introduction

The culture of Chinese classics has a profound and close relationship with the Chinese culture. It is a special spiritual wealth accumulated by the Chinese nation in the long history of development, and also the most vibrant part of the long history of culture. The r*eport to the 20th National Congress of the Communist Party of China* points out that efforts should be put in "extending the reach and appeal of Chinese civilization" through enhancement of international communications capabilities and struggle to strengthen China's voice in international in order to "deepen exchanges and mutual learning with other civilizations and better present Chinese culture to the world"(Xi Jinping, 2022:19). The culture of excellent classics can only become a kind of soft power if it is widely disseminated in the international society and widely recognized by the people of the target country, and even assimilate the other country (Li Zhi, 2010:105-107). Only by letting the world know about Chinese classics and culture can we spread Chinese culture, better tell Chinese stories and promote cultural exchanges between China and other countries. The export of Chinese culture started earlier, but its spreading speed and influence are not satisfactory. Therefore, it is necessary to explore the potential power of classical culture, take it as an important source of soft power of contemporary Chinese culture, and spread it widely in the international community, which can deepen the understanding of Chinese culture in the world and exert the influence of Chinese classical culture.

The translation and international dissemination of Chinese classics is the cardinal way for the world to understand Chinese culture (Wu Tao, 2018:99). Written in ancient Chinese which is difficult to understand, Chinese classics contain extensive and profound traditional culture with unique and distinct national connotation, which generally need text translation to effectively spread. The foreign translation of Chinese classics began 400 years ago with the Chinese cultural transmission movement led by missionaries and sinologists (Wei Siyu, 2023). At present, the translation of classics has become a major camp of Chinese academics and a torrent that helps Chinese culture "go global". With more and more frequent cultural exchanges between China and foreign countries, people all over the world have stronger desire to understand Chinese culture. The widespread use of Chinese language and the establishment of Confucius Institutes all over the world have proved the desire of people all over the world to understand China. However, English is the most popular and widely used language in the world today. To better spread the classical culture containing the essence of the Chinese nation in the world, it is inevitable to rely on the English translation of classical books as an important means (Bi Ran, 2014:277). Against this backdrop, the significance of English translation of classics is obvious, which is of great practical significance to carry forward national culture, promote the integration of Chinese and Western cultures, and maintain the inherent cultural identity of China.

2. Li Zhi and *Fenshu* and *Xu Fenshu*

2.1 Li Zhi and Taizhou School

Li Zhi (李贽), known by his style name Zhuowu (卓吾), was an outstanding philosopher, historian and writer of the late Ming Dynasty and one of the representative figures of the left-wing Taizhou School (泰州学派) of post-Yangming studies (阳明后学). Li, from a commercial family in coastal Fujian, passed the provincial examinations but never went on to the next level, the *jinshi* (进士). As a consequence, he held only minor official posts over the course of his career. In 1585, at the age of fifty-nine, he retired to a Buddhist temple and devoted himself to reading, studying and writing which proved as the most important period of his life. In his later years, Li began to give lectures, revealing a lot about the pseudo-Daoism (伪道学) at that time, and deeply criticizing the feudal ethics (Luo Laiwei, 2014:18). It was his articulation and publication of unconventional ideas led to his death in 1602 in a prison near Beijing. Li produced voluminous works in genres ranging from essays, letters, commentaries to poetry, historiography, and philosophy, those was banned and destroyed repeatedly in the Ming and Qing dynasties although, Li still had a considerable number of works about 87, including *Fenshu* (焚书), *Xu Fenshu* (续焚书), *Cangshu* (藏书), *Xu Cangshu* (续藏书) and so on. Throughout his life, he was a pioneer of his era, with a clear rational goal and a clear destination in life, as he practised anti-false doctrine, advocated the freedom and equality of men and women, reassessed historical figures, and proposed the "the childlike mind" (*Tongxinshuo* 童心说) view of literature and art.

  Taizhou School was one of the most distinctive and diverse schools of thought following the orthodox schools of the Yangming school (阳明学派) in Zhezhong (浙中) and Jiangyou (江右), and was a product of the merging of Confucianism, Taoism and Buddhism under the academic conditions of the time. As a unique and controversial academic school in the history of Chinese thought, the Taizhou School, from the point of view of the history of academic thought, had a tendency to use tradition to move towards anti-tradition and to transition from orthodoxy to heresy. This tendency is inextricably linked to the origins and experiences of the Taizhou scholars, which have led to differences in their personal talents and ideological opinions (Yang Guorong, 2020:47). Nevertheless, their ideological characteristics and the scope of their preaching tended to suit the consciousness and needs of the grassroots, such as the woodcutter, the peasant, and even the illiterate, and were therefore widely accepted and welcomed, with far-reaching effects. In all fairness, the Taizhou School did open up new paths of thought, and while it may have been crude and impure in its cultivation of the mind, it was able to practise its beliefs with a sense of commitment and style (Zhang Kewei, 2012, 31:50). The Taizhou School was undoubtedly the forerunner of the Enlightenment trend in academic thought from the mid-Ming Dynasty onwards, both in terms of the relationship between teachers and the lineage of learning, and in terms of its ideological tendencies that differed from orthodox Confucianism. In the twentieth century, scholars such as Ji Wenfu (嵇文甫) and Hou Wailu (侯外庐), as well as the American scholar William Theodore de Bary and the Japanese scholar Shimada Shinji (岛田虔次), held the Taizhou School in high esteem (Zhou Qun, 2021:16).

  Taizhou School, with its systematic theories and complete writings, belongs to its founder Wang Gen (王艮), his second son Wang Bi (王襞) and his younger brother Wang Dong (王栋), who collectively known as the "Three Geniuses of Taizhou Huainan (泰州淮南三王)". The later scholars were Yan Jun (颜钧), He Xinyin (何心隐), Luo Rufang (罗汝芳), Geng Dingxiang (耿定向), Li Zhi, Guan Zhidao (管志道), Jiao Hong (焦竑), Tao Wangling (陶望龄), Yinling (寅龄) brothers and others. Li Zhi studied under Wang Bi, son of Wang Gen, and inherited the ideological tradition of the Taizhou School of Wang Gen and He Xinyin, and developed it further, thus establishing the ideological system of anti-Daoism. However, there are doubts in academic circles as to whether Li Zhi should belong to the

Taizhou School, but from his own writings and his life experiences, Li Zhi is greatly associated with the Taizhou School (Wu Zhen, 2009:19). He took over the wildman's mind and the sceptical and critical spirit of Yangming and the Taizhou School, lightened the morality and ethics in teleology, highlighted the natural dimension of human nature, raised the independence, freedom and equality of the subject, especially the individual, and showed a strong enlightenment spirit and value (Tan Bing, 2000:54).

2.2 Li Zhi's Thought and *Fenshu* and *Xu Fenshu*

Li Zhi's thought is based on Confucianism, and he also adopted Taoism, Zen and Western thought, forming a unique ideological system (Huang Teng, 2019:2). The main ideas are all reflected in his writings, such as *Fenshu* and *Xu Fenshu*, which include various aspects of philosophy, history, politics and aesthetics, with philosophical ideas serving as the basis for other theories (Yang Ting, 2014:16). His main philosophical thoughts can be summarized from the following aspects.

Firstly, Li proposed "the childlike mind" theory. It has five main connotations: natural purity, mindfulness, self-centredness, and truthfulness. One cannot be said to have a "childlike mind" without one of these. The main purpose of the doctrine of the "childlike mind" was to advocate a return to the heart of the child, a return to the self, and to rectify the unorthodox and hypocritical culture of the time. He advocated that words and deeds should be done out of one's true nature and opposed the trend of hypocrisy. His outstanding contribution to the old sense of regulating the principle of individuality at the time was also manifested in a bold rejection of the authority of Confucius.

Secondly, on the premise of learning from saints such as Yao (尧), Shun (舜) and Confucius, he broke the barriers of false Taoism and false Confucianism, and did not take the right and wrong of Confucianism as right and wrong. Li Zhi put forward a view beyond the mainstream, dedicated to breaking the world's "idolatrous" spirit of Confucius, vigorously attacking Neo-Confucianism (程朱理学), exposing the hypocritical face of Daoists, and criticising Daoism (Guan Shuyang, 2018:97).

Thirdly, Li Zhi adhered to the proper lineage of "cultivating one's own body and self (修身正己)" and held tightly to the platform of "the people's daily use as the way (百姓日用为道)". From Wang Xinzhai (王心斋)'s thought of it, Li developed it into a new theory of "focus on the people". Outside the Taizhou School, no one attached importance to the value and status of everyday life, such as dressing and eating, but Li Zhi argued that daily life should be the object of exploration, transforming it from a monastic tool to an ontological status, which was a transcendence of Confucianism (Luo Laiwei, 2014:19).

Fourthly, Li Zhi acknowledged self-interest versus meritocracy, celebrating individuality and sharing one's strengths (Wei Yixia, 2013:139-144). Li (2000) proposed that "selfishness is the heart of man (私者，人之心也)". He openly declared that selfishness is the nature of human beings and affirmed that human beings have selfishness, and that human selfishness was one with the human heart, and that without selfishness there was no heart. He also put forward the idea of respecting virtue, and the so-called "virtue (德性)" actually means "to act in accordance with one's nature (率性而为)", that is, to act in accordance with one's natural nature and needs (Yu Yunhan, Tongxi, 2003:81).

Li Zhi's main works are *Fenshu* and *Xu Fenshu*. The former likely first published in 1590, and the latter first published posthumously in 1618. In it, Li Zhi showed his contempt for ethical and aesthetic conventions through eccentric views. "Brazenly provocative, his writings challenged authorities of all kinds and championed individual judgement and personal desires" (Li, 2016).

3. The Enlightenment of C-E translation of *Fenshu* and *Xu Fenshu* on Chinese Classics Culture "Going Global"

3.1 *Fenshu* and *Xu Fenshu* in English-language scholarship

Given that Westerners at the time did not have much knowledge of Li Zhi's ideas, the first Westerners to know about Li Zhi would have been Matthew Ricci (Wu Wennan, 2019: 89). In his book *The Journals of Matthew Ricci*, Ricci (2010) recorded the encounters with Li Zhi and collisions of their ideas. After the 1930s, many scholars devoted themselves to the study of Li Zhi's thought, and only then did it begin to spread in the West, with many research findings appearing (Zhang Xianzhong, 2009:145). With the development of cultural exchanges between China and the West, the translation and dissemination of Li's thought in the United States has developed in both breadth and depth through the joint efforts of Chinese and American scholars, and since the 1980s, the study, translation and spread of Li Zhi's thought in the United States has undergone a developmental shift from ideological studies of politics, history and culture to aesthetic studies of literature and art (Li Chao; 2004).

Before 1980, translation was largely secondary to or an offshoot of the more principal goal of producing scholarly studies of Li Zhi. In his article, *Li Chih: An Iconoclast of the Sixteenth Century*, K.C. Hsiao translated parts of Li Zhi's *Li Shih Fen Shu, Chu Tan Chi, Tsang Shu, Hsu Tsang Shu*, and *Li Wen Ling Chi* (Hsiao, 1938). But since 1980, translation work has made a substantial progress. LEE, GONG-WAY (1991:67-82) had the earliest full English translation of Li Zhi's *Tongxinshuo* from *Fenshu* in his article *Interpretations of Li Chih: An Anti-Traditional Thinker of Late Ming China*. Clara Yu translated five of Li Zhi's letters for inclusion in the widely used Ebrey sourcebook, including *Letter to Zhuang Chunfu, To Zeng Jiquan, On Reading the Letter to Ruowu from His Mother*, and *To Liu Xiaochuan* (Ebrey, 1993:257-263). In 1996, Stephen Owen also translated "On the Child-like Heart" (Owen, 1996:808-811). In 1999, Yang Ye published *Vignettes from the Late Ming: A Hsiao-pin Anthology*. After her introduction, she provided five annotated essays, including *Three Fools, In Praise of Liu Hsieh, A Lament for the Passing, Inscription on a Portrait of Confucius at the Iris Buddhist Shrine,* and *Essay: On the Mind of a Child* (Yang, 1999). More extensive translation work has been published in the new millennium. In 2002, in the appendix to her doctoral dissertation, *Li Zhi (1527-1602): A Confucian Feminist of Late-Ming China*, Pauline Lee included annotated translations of some Li Zhi's letters, poems, historical commentaries, and prefaces. Lee (2002, 177) stated that, "The essays have been selected to give the reader an introduction to Li's views on topics central to his works, ranging from the context-sensitive nature of truths, Li's novel concept of the mind, to his disputations with the Neo-Confucian preoccupation with abstract metaphysics." In 2016, Rivi Handler-Spitz, Pauline C. Lee, and Haun Saussy published a translation of a substantial portion of two of Li Zhi's most important works, *A Book to Burn* and *A Book to Keep (Hidden)*, as well as selected historical documents pertaining to his life. This was the fruition of five years of careful translation and editing, and the product is the most comprehensive in its genre up to this point in time. The poems were translated by Timothy Billings and Yan Zina. The translations also include a useful chronology of Li Zhi's life and bibliography. The translations are mainly based on Zhang Jianye's *Li zhi quanji zhu (Annotated Complete Works of Li Zhi)* and they supplemented Zhang's annotation whenever necessary with further research of their own (Li,

2016).

3.2 The enlightenment of C-E translation of Li Zhi's thought on Chinese classics culture "going global"

Chinese classics are the essence of Chinese culture. The "going global" of Chinese culture can effectively demonstrate the cultural heritage of China and enhance China's international status. Professor Wang Hongyin (2009), in his introductory essay on the *C-E translation of Chinese cultural classics*, stated that the translation of Chinese cultural classics into English is an important way for Chinese culture to go global, to achieve reciprocal exchanges between Chinese and Western cultures, and to achieve the integration of world cultures. In addition, the famous translator Wang Rongpei also stated that the goal of English translations of Chinese classics is to look at the world and take root in the local area (Ban Bai: 2018). Therefore, foreign translations of Chinese classics are of great significance to the dissemination and promotion of Chinese culture. The problems and considerations of foreign translations of classics, the kind of translation strategy to be adopted, the quality of translation, the change and innovation of translation consciousness directly affect the implementation of China's culture "going global" strategy and the image of China in the world.

3.2.1 The two carriages of "going global": strategies of domestication and foreignization

The two strategies of domestication and foreignization are commonly used in English translations of classics. In *The Translator's Invisibility*, Lawrence Venuti (1995) presented the concepts as two translation strategies that are both opposed and unified. Domestication means taking the language habits of the target language or the target readers as starting point, adopting the expressions that the target language readers are used to in order to express the meaning of the original, with the aim of localising the source language. Foreignization is where the translator maintains the author's original intentions as far as possible and brings the reader closer to the author. The aim of using the strategy of foreignization is to preserve the cultural differences of the nation, and in this way to show the characteristics of the language style of the foreign nation. For the English translation of Chinese classics, it is important that Chinese culture is fully disseminated, so that the world can understand China's unique cultural background and connotations to the greatest extent possible, and that foreign readers can fully accept the cultural content and ideas conveyed therein, not just as a simple export of culture, therefore the culture is fully understood, accepted and rooted in the ground. In the process of English translation of classics, the two translation strategies, domestication and foreignization, are chosen and selected according to the translation reality. They as two translation strategies are never completely opposed to each other, and both methods should be viewed dynamically, with the more appropriate translation method chosen depending on the actual situation, or the organic combination of the two, so that the translation can achieve the purpose of cultural exchange and dissemination.

The translator's choice between the two strategies depends on the purpose of the translation, i.e. Vermeer's translation purpose theory. This theory puts the purpose of translation in the first place, and the purpose or function of the translation in the target context largely determines the way the translation is presented and its content (Hatim, 2005:74). The main purpose of current English translations of classics is to disseminate Chinese culture; therefore, the translation strategies and translation methods should serve that purpose. In the translation of Chinese classics, it is necessary to take into account both the dissemination of Chinese culture and the acceptance of Western readers, so that domestication and foreignization are organically combined. Otherwise, missing the mark will not lead to good translation results.

For example, Pauline C. Lee and others have translated the book "A BOOK TO BURN AND A BOOK TO KEEP (HIDDEN)", which is a good example of the organic combination of domestication and foreignization. The titles of the selected texts are translated into English and Chinese with Pinyin (拼音). In order to facilitate the reader's understanding of the relationship between the various chapters, the translators added headnotes indicating the year and source of the selection and the connection between the selections. The difficulty in translation is Li Zhi's playfulness and varied style of writing, so the style of translation has been flexible accordingly. The aim of the translation is to be easily understood by readers in the English-speaking world. For this reason, the translation is faithful to the original text, with footnotes explaining the historical and cultural background of the text, and in a few places it is treated in a paraphrased manner, for example, the phrase "童心说", sometimes translated directly in Pinyin as "Tongxinshuo" in order to be faithful to the original text, and sometimes translated in a paraphrased manner for ease of understanding as "On the Childlike Mind". Another example is Yang Ye's (1999) book *Vignettes from the Late Ming: A Hsiao-pin Anthology*, in which the author also selectively translated the "童心说" in Li Zhi's *Fenshu*, and translates it as "On the Mind of a Child". Yang Ye's translation also used a combination of domestication and foreignization, prefacing the translation with a biography of Li Zhi to facilitate understanding of his thought and writing style, and following the translation with notes to provide additional explanations of proper names. This is an effective way to ensure that traditional culture is translated in an authentic manner. Generally speaking, if one focuses on a translation style in which fidelity as value orientation, then most English translators of classics adopt foreignization strategy, i.e. they mostly make direct translation and transliteration. And in addition to translating the original text, they also need to make side quotations, explain allusions and original sources. This kind of translation highlights the narrative and cultural value of the translation (Wang Rongpei, 2009:10), and translators sometimes intersperse the translation with the corresponding ancient Chinese original text, sparing no effort to pursue the method of lineal translation advocated by Goethe, because this seemingly also follow the method of translation aims at trying to strengthen people's understanding of the original work, to bring them closer to it in the process of reading, to complete the cycle of reading in a translation in which difference and familiarity, understanding and non-understanding, approach each other (Robinson, 2006:224).

Clara Yu's (1993) translation of selected texts from Li Zhi's works in *Chinese Civilization: A Sourcebook* appears in the chapter "TWO PHILOSOPHERS", which began with a survey of the relationship between Wang Yangming (王阳明, 1472-1529) and Li Zhi, the most influential Confucian thinkers of the Ming Dynasty after Zhu Xi (朱熹), followed by translations of conversations between Wang Yangming and his disciples and letters between Li Zhi and his followers. Clara Yu's translation of cultural terms such as personal names and place names mostly employed transliteration, with nearly no explanations of the content in the form of complementary translation, and in a few places paraphrases were used. This retains the heterogeneity of the translation, but may cause difficulties for readers to understand and hinder the spread of Chinese culture. Therefore, the difficulty of the target readers in understanding the translation is high compared to that of Pauline C. Lee and Yang Ye's version. However, from another perspective, in the C-E translation of Chinese cultural terms such as "里(*li*)", the use of foreignization strategy, such as the use of Pinyin and the addition of notes, can prevent cultural filtering and cultural loss, which can better enable Chinese culture to be presented in the translated language and allow Chinese culture to successfully go out in its original form. At a time when Chinese culture is being promoted as "going global", this view of translation is of great significance in guiding the practice of translating classics into Chinese and English. Both domestication and foreignization adopt an interpretive approach to translation, the difference being that the domestication strategy uses the target language expression for interpretation, while the foreignization strategy uses the source language expression for interpretation. Considering the respective advantages and disadvantages of the domestication and foreignization strategies, as well as the mission of English translation of classics to spread Chinese culture, the author believes that the English translation of classics should adopt the translation strategy of domestication as a supplement and foreignization as the main one. This will not only meet the expectations of the target language audience, but also effectively disseminate Chinese culture.

3.2.2 Thoughts and reflections on "going global"

The number of participants and publishing activities in the translation of Chinese classics has been increasing year by year against the backdrop of the country's strong advocacy of culture "going global". However, in recent years, the problems and obstacles encountered by Chinese culture going abroad have also come to the fore. The difficulty in translating classical Chinese literature lies in the fact that the translator must not only have strong English writing skills, but also have extensive knowledge of Chinese history and Chinese culture. Who should translate Chinese cultural texts? How well are the translations by domestic or Western translators received in the language of the translator? Does the reader come first or does the original text come first? How to deal with cultural differences? These are the outstanding questions that need to be addressed.

Focus on the cooperation of the principal parts in foreign translations. Most Western scholars have a negative attitude towards the issue of Chinese translators undertaking the translation of classics, for example, the famous British sinologist Graham and the contemporary American sinologist Stephen Owen both hold the view that translators should translate foreign languages into their own mother tongue, not their mother tongue into foreign languages (Song Yang, 2017:160). They believe that Western translators' translations are more fluent, natural and readable than those of Chinese translators. Although the available bibliographical statistics of sinology show that the vast majority of Chinese classics were completed by Westerners independently, or with the help of Chinese collaborators, it cannot be ignored that Western translations misinterpreted and mistranslated Chinese culture in many instances. Just because a translator makes a Chinese classic accessible to a Western audience does not mean that the translator always succumbs to Western reading habits. The main purpose of English translation of classics is to disseminate traditional Chinese culture, promote cultural pluralism and interaction, and ultimately achieve the goal of telling the Chinese story and building a Chinese discourse system. Therefore, in the translation practice of classics, accurately, comprehensively and systematically revealing their historical development, discovering their objective laws and drawing on the achievements of our predecessors will help us to improve the breadth and depth of classics translation, and help us to promote the innovative development of Chinese cultural classics translation in the new historical period on the basis of the equal dialogue between the East and the West. The strategy of translating Chinese classics into foreign languages, be it collaborative translation or "borrowing a boat to go to sea", will ultimately involve close integration between research and translation, with Chinese and foreign translators working together to diversify the translation ecosystem in order to promote the further development of the theory and practice of translating Chinese classics.

Highlight the study of overseas audiences. The target audiences is the focus of translating Chinese classics into foreign languages, and it is also the guiding light for Chinese classics to "go abroad". However, audiences are never passive or static recipients of information. Faced with a certain discourse, audiences may accept or reject it; change or insist on a certain attitude; adopt or not adopt a certain expected behaviour (Chen Xiaowei, 2013). Therefore, research on the target audiences can understand their acceptance and dynamics of the content of the translation, so that they can adjust their translation strategies according to their feedback. According to Bonnie S. McDougall, the potential readers of translated literature can be divided into two main categories: professional readers and general readers. Specifically, readers of Chinese literature in English translation can be divided into three categories: (i) "loyal readers" who are interested in understanding Chinese culture, (ii) professionals in English and Chinese literature and translation studies, i.e. "interested readers", and (iii) "fair readers" who have expectations of the universality of literary values (Qin Jianghua and Liu Junping, 2012). In view of this, when translators translate Chinese classics into foreign languages, they should first clarify the target positioning of the target audience and fully consider the reading needs and acceptability of them. If the target audience is general readers, translators can first publish abridged and rewritten texts that are easy to understand and universal to satisfy their curiosity and interest, or can make appropriate deletions and rewrites of the obscure contents of the original texts to make them more in line with the reading level and acceptability of the target readers and enhance the readability and acceptability of the translations. If the target audience is specialist readers and researchers, the work can be translated in its entirety, or in a series of chronological or genre-specific translations. The translations can be supplemented by quotations and references to meet their research needs on Chinese classics.

Deal well with the differences between Chinese and Western cultures. How can the translation of classics achieve a counter trend of spreading our culture from the weaker cultural circles to the stronger European and American cultural circles and make it acceptable to the latter? When translating classics into English, it is necessary to consider the cultural potential difference and the function of the English translation. In general, when translating, translators are better at translating foreign works into their own mother tongue, and vice versa, they are doing "reverse translation". The domination of C-E translation by local translators in the context of culture "going out" is a kind of reverse translation (Wang Baitao, 2020:318-319). If the Western mind has difficulty in accepting the original expressions, which may easily cause misunderstandings, or if the reader feels that the expressions are awkward, then the flexible adjustments should be adapted. In the process of translation and communication, there is a problem of compromise and adjustment to cultural aspects. Translation is closely related to the cultural context in which the language is spoken and it is not a purely linguistic act. A translation is not just a description of the original text, but also conveys the cultural equivalent of that text in the translated language; it promotes understanding and recognition of the culture of the original language in the target language. The cultural view of translation emphasises the cultural act of communication, translation is the breaking down of various barriers at the linguistic level, with aims to transplant culture and cultural intermingling. The translator should be able to enter the cultural world of the source-language work, but also consider the cultural acceptability of the target language to the readers of the culture into which it is translated. It argues that target readers should try to adapt to cultural differences and achieve intercultural communication. The translator takes this as a basic criterion, stands in the reader's shoes, judges the good and bad of the translation and determines the appropriate way to carry out the translation. Communicate with target readers when conveying cultural information. In C-E translation, one should not pursue the linguistic and textual level of reaching meaning, but rather translate from the perspective of cultural communication and transplantation, actively thinking about how to use the target language to convey the linguistic and cultural characteristics of Chinese itself, thus promoting the spread of Chinese culture in the target language culture.

4. Conclusion

In the process of "going global", Chinese culture must actively integrate into a multicultural and global civilizational context, innovatively interpret the basic values of Chinese culture, achieve the widespread dissemination of outstanding Chinese traditional culture, strengthen cultural confidence, and enhance China's cultural soft power. The essence of Chinese culture going global is to spread Chinese cultural symbols and values to the world in a positive, equal and mutually beneficial, peaceful and friendly, open and inclusive manner, to build cultural awareness and value recognition of China among the people of other countries, to enhance the international influence and international discourse of Chinese culture, and to provide Chinese wisdom for solving world problems and building a community of human destiny. Chinese cultural translation is closely related to national development, international changes and the progress of the times, and it is a long and gradual process. The joint efforts of the state, the writers and the translators are indispensable in order to make audiences hear and see, but also to make them understand and read. In taking the pulse of the times and seizing the opportunity, various communities still need to work hard in various forms to explore, promote, disseminate and promote cultural treasures.

References

[1] Ban, Bai (班柏). "English Translation of Classical Texts and Chinese Culture 'Going Out': an Interview with Professor Wang Rongpei" (典籍英译与中国文化"走出去"——汪榕培教授访谈录) [J]. *Shandong Foreign Language Teaching* (山东外语教学), 2018, 39(06): 3-10.

[2] Bi, Ran (毕冉). "An Analysis of English Translation of Classical Texts and Cultural Soft Power" (典籍英译与文化软实力探析) [J]. *Global Human Geography* (环球人文地理), 2014(18): 277.

[3] Chen, Dubin (陈笃彬). "The Different Type of Collision between Chinese and Western Civilizations in the Late Ming Dynasty—When Li Zhi Meeting Matteo Ricci" (晚明中西文化的别样碰撞——当李贽遇上利玛窦) [J]. *Journal of Quanzhou Normal University* (泉州师范学院学报), 2020, 38(03): 59-64.

[4] Chen, Xiaowei (陈小慰). "Cultural Consciousness and Audience Awareness in Foreign Propaganda Translation" (对外宣传翻译中的文化自觉与受众意识) [J]. *China Translation* (中国翻译), 2013(2).

[5] EBREY, PATRICIA BUCKLEY. *Chinese Civilization: A Sourcebook* [M]. New York: The Free Press, 1993.

[6] Guan, Shuyang (管舒扬). "An Analysis of Li Zhi's Intellectual Achievements" (浅析李贽的思想成就) [J]. *Changjiang Series* (长江丛刊), 2018(32): 97.

[7] Hatim, B. *Teaching and Researching Translation* [M]. Beijing: Foreign Language Teaching and Research Press, 2005.

[8] HSIAO, K.C. Li Chih: An Iconoclast of the Sixteenth Century [J]. *T'ien Hsia Monthly*, 1938, 6(4).

[9] Huang, Teng (黄腾). *A Study of Li Zhi's Enlightenment Thought* (李贽启蒙思想研究) [D]. Zhongnan University for Nationalities (中南民族大学), 2019: 2.

[10] LEE, GONG-WAY. Interpretations of Li Chih: An Anti-Traditional Thinker of Late Ming China [J]. *Chinese Culture*, 1991, 32(1): 67-82.

[11] LEE, P. *Li Zhi (1527-1602): A Confucian Feminist of Late-Ming China* [D]. Stanford: Stanford University, 2002.

[12] Li, Chao (李超). *One Hundred Years of Li Zhi's Research Review* (百年李贽研究回顾) [C]// Quanzhou City Li Zan Thought Symposium (泉州市李贽思想学术研讨会). Proceedings of the Quanzhou Li Zan Thought Symposium (泉州市李贽思想学术研讨会论文集). 2004.

[13] Li, Zhi (李贽). Collections of Li Zhi (李贽文集) [M]. Beijing: Social Science Academic Press (社会科学文献出版社), 2000.

[14] Li, Zhi (李智). "Cultural Soft Power and China's Foreign Communication Strategy" (文化软权力化与中国对外传播战略) [J]. *Journal of Beijing Administrative College* (北京行政学院学报), 2010(03): 105-107.

[15] Li, Z. *A Book to Burn and A Book to Keep (Hidden)* [M]. Rivi Handler-Spitz, Pauline C. Lee, and Haun Saussy (eds&trans). New York: Columbia University, 2016.

[16] Luo, Laiwei (罗来玮). "An Introduction to Li Zhi" (浅谈李贽) [J]. *Theory Research* (学理论), 2014(06): 18-19.

[17] Matteo Ricci, Giannico. *Ricci's Journal of China* [M] Mouth. Translated by He Gaoji, et al. Beijing: China Book Bureau, 2010.

[18] MEYER-FOND, TOBIE. *The Childlike Mind* [Z].

[19] Owen, Stephen. 1996. *An Anthology of Chinese Literature: Beginnings to 1911*. New York: W.W. Norton and Company.

[20] Qin, Jianghua and Liu, Junping (覃江华、刘军平). "The Translation Life and Translation Thought of Bonnie Du - Also on Translators and Readers of Contemporary Chinese Literature in the West" (杜博妮的翻译人生与翻译思想——兼论西方当代中国文学的译者和读者) [J]. *Oriental Translation* (东方翻译), 2012 (2).

[21] Robinson, Douglas. *Western Translation Theory: from Herodotus to Nietzsche* [C]. Beijing: Foreign Language Teaching and Research Press, 2006: 224.

[22] Song, Yang (宋杨). "Research on the Foreign Translation of Chinese Literary Texts in the Context of 'Chinese Culture Going Out'" ("中国文化走出去"背景下的中国文学典籍外译研究) [J]. *Journal of Lanzhou College of Education* (兰州教育学院学报), 2017, 33(12): 158-160.

[23] Tan, Bing (谭兵). "The Spirit of Enlightenment of Li Zhi's *Xinxue*" (试论李贽心学的启蒙精神) [J]. *Journal of Yanshan University (Philosophy and Social Science Edition)* (燕山大学学报(哲学社会科学版)), 2000(04): 54.

[24] Venuti, L. *The Translator's Invisibility: A history of translation* [M]. London: Routledge, 1995.

[25] Wang, Baitao (王白涛). "Chinese Translation of Classics into English in the Context of Chinese Culture 'Going Abroad'" (中国文化"走出去"背景下的典籍汉译英) [J]. *International Public Relations* (国际公关), 2020(11): 318-319.

[26] Wang, Hongyin (王宏印). *English Translation of Chinese Cultural Classics* (中国文化典籍英译) [M]. Beijing: Foreign Language Teaching and Research Press (北京：外语教学与研究出版社), 2009.

[27] Wang, Ning (王宁). *Cultural Translation and Classical Interpretation* (文化翻译与经典阐释) [M]. Beijing: China Book Bureau (北京：中华书局), 2006.

[28] Wang, Rongpei, et al (汪榕培等). *English translation of Chinese classics* (中国典籍英译) [C]. Shanghai: Shanghai Foreign

Language Education Press (上海：上海外语教育出版社), 2009: 10.

[29] Wei, Siyu (卫思谕). "Promoting Chinese classic culture to the world"(推动中华典籍文化更好走向世界) [N]. *China Social Science Journal* (中国社会科学报), 2023, 01-04(001).

[30] Wei, Yixia (魏义霞). "Individuality, Independent Personality, Equality Consciousness and Li Zhi's Enlightenment Thought" (个性、独立人格、平等意识与李贽的启蒙思想) [J]. *Social Science Research* (社会科学研究), 2013, (04): 139-144.

[31] Wu, Tao (吴涛). "The Revelation of Burton Watson's English Translation of Chinese Classics to the 'Going Global' of Chinese Culture" (华兹生的中国典籍英译对中国文化"走出去"的启示) [J]. *Journal of Kunming University of Technology (Social Science Edition)* (昆明理工大学学报(社会科学版)), 2018, 18(02): 99.

[32] Wu, Wennan (吴文南). "The translation and dissemination of Li Zhi's thought in America" (李贽思想在美国的译介与传播) [J]. *Journal of Quanzhou Normal College* (泉州师范学院学报), 2019, 37(03): 89-95.

[33] Wu, Zhen (吴震). *Taizhou Xuepai Yanjiu (Studies in the Taizhou School)* [M]. *Beijing: China Renmin University Press* (中国人民大学出版社), 2009.

[34] Xi, Jinping (习近平), *Report to the 20th National Congress of the Communist Party of China* (中国共产党第二十次全国代表大会报告) [M]. Beijing: People's Publishing House, 2022: 19.

[35] Yang, Guorong (杨国荣). "The Taizhou School in Chinese Thought" (中国思想中的泰州学派) [J]. *Journal of Jianghai Studies* (江海学刊), 2020(01): 47.

[36] Yang, Ting (杨婷). *Heresy, Enlightenment and Return* (异端、启蒙与回归) [D]. Hunan Normal University (湖南师范大学), 2014.

[37] Ye, Yang. *Vignettes from the Late Ming: A Hsiao-pin Anthology* [M]. Washington: University of Washington Press, 1999.

[38] Yu, Yunhan, Tong, Xigang (于云瀚,全晰纲). "From Wang Gen to Li Zhi" (从王艮到李贽) [J]. *Journal of Weifang College* (潍坊学院学报), 2003(03): 81.

[39] Zhang, Kewei (张克伟). "On the Style and Characteristics of the Taizhou School" (论泰州学派之思想风格与特色) [J]. *Journal of Xihua University (Philosophy and Social Science Edition)* (西华大学学报(哲学社会科学版)), 2012, 31(06): 50.

[40] Zhang, Xianzhong (张献忠). *The Essence of Master—Li Zhi* (大家精要·李贽) [M]. Kunming: Yunnan Education Publishing House (昆明：云南教育出版社), 2009:145.

[41] Zhou, Qun (周群). *Studies on the Taizhou School* (泰州学派研究) [M]. Nanjing: Nanjing University Press (南京：南京大学出版社), 2021: 16.

Bio

ZHANG Weiyi is lecturer of Nanjing Normal University Taizhou College. Academic interest: translation and cross-culture studies. E-mail:784012000@qq.com.

人工智能技术在翻译项目中的应用研究

⊙ 崔启亮（对外经济贸易大学，北京）

【摘　要】 人工智能技术推动翻译领域的数字化、网络化和智能化发展。本文从翻译项目流程的视角，对人工智能技术在翻译项目中的应用进行深入分析，探究翻译项目流程的不同过程应用的具体人工智能技术，并以视频字幕翻译和配音项目为例进行案例分析。研究发现在翻译项目流程中，应用最广泛的人工智能技术分别是自然语言处理技术、计算机视觉技术、神经网络技术、专家决策系统技术。翻译项目流程中使用的具体人工智能技术包括图像识别、语音识别、语音合成、机器翻译、机器学习、深度学习等。

【关键词】 人工智能；翻译项目；翻译流程；机器翻译

A Study on the Application of Artificial Intelligence Technologies in Translation Projects

CUI Qiliang (University of International Business and Economics, Beijing)

Abstract: Artificial intelligence (AI) technologies have propelled the digitalization, networking, and intelligence of the translation industry. This paper provides an in-depth analysis of the application of AI technologies in translation projects from the perspective of translation project process. It explores the specific AI technologies applied in different stages of translation project process, taking video subtitle translation and dubbing projects as examples. The study shows that the most widely used AI technologies in translation project process are natural language processing, computer vision, neural networks, and expert decision-making systems. The specific AI technologies applied in translation project process include image recognition, speech recognition, speech synthesis, machine translation, machine learning and deep learning. The findings shed light on the application of AI technologies in translation projects, contributing to the advancement of the industry.

Key words: artificial intelligence; translation project; translation process; machine translation

一、引　言

全球化和数字化时代的翻译内容呈现多样化和专业化特征，客户方和翻译服务提供方需要组建翻译项目团队，制定和实施有效的翻译项目流程，使用多种翻译技术，形成了翻译项目"人员（People）+流程（Process）+技术（Technology）"的"PPT"运行模式。

近年来，翻译技术发展势头迅猛，翻译行业经历着巨大变革，翻译的"技术转向"愈加显著（王华树、刘

本文是中国国家社科基金重点项目"新时期中国翻译教育体系的建设与发展研究"（批准号：22AYY006）的阶段性成果。

世界，2021：87）。根据中国翻译协会（2023）发布的行业调查报告，截至2022年底，国内具有机器翻译与人工智能业务的企业达588家，相较于2021年增长率为113%。90%的受访企业愿意在未来投入更多资金提升企业的机器翻译相关的技术实力。

除了机器翻译技术广泛应用，人工智能技术以其智能化和自动化，成为翻译行业广泛应用的技术。人工智能（Artificial Intelligence，简称AI）是研究如何使计算机模拟和执行人类智能任务的科学和技术领域。2022年美国OpenAI发布的ChatGPT软件，能够即时生成文本、图像和视频等内容，成为全球"现象级"产品，推动人类进入人工智能生成内容（AIGC）时代。

那么，翻译项目实践中应用了哪些AI技术？翻译流程如何与AI技术相结合？翻译流程的各个活动融合了哪些AI技术？本文先介绍AI技术和翻译项目流程的基本内容，然后研究AI技术在翻译项目流程中的应用，最后对视频翻译项目中的AI技术应用进行案例分析，以期探索AI技术对翻译项目的影响，探究翻译项目技术驱动的特征。

二、人工智能技术与翻译项目流程简介

在翻译项目的PPT运行模式中，流程与技术密不可分。为了深入研究AI技术如何与翻译项目流程紧密集成，对AI技术和翻译项目流程进行简介。

（一）人工智能技术简介

人工智能使用计算机解决人类感知、推理、学习、决策、交流问题，人工智能的研究领域包括自然语言处理、自动定理证明、智能数据检索系统、机器学习、模式识别、视觉系统、问题求解、人工智能方法、程序语言、自动程序设计(蔡自兴等，2003：9)。每个研究领域都包括多种AI技术，与翻译有关的AI技术包括自然语言处理、计算机视觉、神经网络等技术。

自然语言处理(Natural Language Processing，NLP)涉及计算机对人类语言的理解和生成。自然语言处理技术包括语义分析、语言模型、机器翻译、文本生成等，它们使计算机能够理解、处理和生成人类语言，实现语音识别、文本分析、智能对话等功能。机器翻译是自然语言处理技术的一个应用分支，20世纪90年代初，由于人工智能领域中深度学习和神经网络的成功，机器翻译引入了这些新技术，于是统计机器翻译发展成神经机器翻译（冯志伟，2018：44）。

计算机视觉包括活动识别、图像识别、机器视觉技术，实现图像识别、目标检测、人脸识别等功能。神经网络是计算机模仿人类大脑神经元结构的技术，分为深度学习（DL）技术和生成性对抗网络（GAN）技术。

（二）翻译项目流程概述

流程是一系列有规律的行动和规范，每个行动和规范是一个操作性的定位描述，贯穿项目的始终，是以持续提高组织业务绩效为目的的系统化方法（崔启亮，2017：101）。中国翻译协会等同采用国际标准化组织（ISO）发布的笔译项目标准"Translation services — Requirements for translation services （ISO 17100:2015）"，于2016年发布翻译行业团体标准："翻译服务：笔译服务要求（T/TAC 1-2016）"，在此标准中，将笔译项目流程分为译前过程和活动（Pre-production Process and Activities）、翻译过程(Production Processes)、交付后过程

(Post-production Processes)三个相互关联的过程。

译前过程包括四项活动：翻译服务提供方回复客户方的翻译询价和可行性分析、报价、签署翻译协议、与项目相关的客户信息处理。其中项目和客户信息处理活动是译前重要的准备工作，内容包括：项目准备、行政管理活动、项目登记、项目分配、项目技术准备、技术资源、译前活动、语言规范、源语言内容分析、术语工作、风格指南。

翻译过程包括六项活动：笔译、自检、双语审校、单语审校（可选）、校对（可选）、最终检验与交付。其中，单语审校和校对不是必需的活动。交付后过程包括两项活动：客户反馈和结项管理。

三、AI 技术在翻译项目流程中的应用

AI 技术是复杂的技术群，由多种不同研究领域和研究范式构成技术网格。在翻译项目流程的各个过程，针对不同的翻译任务，应用不同的 AI 技术，实现提高效率、保证质量、促进交流的目标。下面分别论述翻译项目流程中译前、翻译、交付后三个过程中 AI 技术的应用。

（一）译前过程中的 AI 技术应用

译前过程应用的 AI 技术解决翻译项目准备中的专业知识获取、文件格式转换、术语识别与提取、译员和审校人员匹配等任务。分别应用 AI 中的自然语言处理技术、计算机视觉技术、模式识别技术、机器学习技术、专家决策支持系统技术。

（1）专业知识学习与准备

对于专业领域的翻译任务，译员和审校人员可以借助 ChatGPT 等内容生成工具，快速获得源文件所涉及的专业领域知识。ChatGPT 基于预训练的自然语言处理模型，理解自然语言文本，自动提取关键词和语义信息，并进行相应的处理和推理，提供相应的解决方案和建议。通过知识图谱技术，将源文件中的专业术语、概念、关系等映射到知识图谱中，从而方便译员和审校人员快速获取相关的领域知识。

例 1. ChatGPT 检索专业知识

笔者 2023 年 6 月承接了国际软件测试认证委员会（ISTQB）基础级考试大纲的翻译任务，需要将第三章"静态测试"从英文翻译成中文。作者为了快速学习 ISTQB 测试认证和静态测试方面的知识，对 ChatGPT 进行了如下提问：

> 我 2023 年 6 月承接了国际软件测试认证委员会（ISTQB）基础级考试大纲的翻译任务，需要将第三章"静态测试"从英文翻译成中文。为了快速学习 ISTQB 测试认证和静态测试方面的知识，请简要介绍一下 ISTQB 和静态测试的基本知识。

ChatGPT 快速给出了如下回答：

> ISTQB（International Software Testing Qualifications Board）是一个国际性的软件测试认证组织，其目标是提供全球范围内一致的软件测试认证标准。ISTQB 提供了各个级别的软件测试考试，包括初级、中级和高级。
>
> 静态测试是软件测试过程中的一种方法，它不涉及程序的执行。相反，它是通过检查和审查软件工件来

发现问题和缺陷。静态测试主要包括以下几种形式：

1. 静态代码分析（Static Code Analysis）：静态代码分析是对源代码进行检查，以发现潜在的问题，如语法错误、死代码、代码规范违规等。这种方法不需要执行实际的代码。

……（笔者注：因篇幅所限，此处省略下面的四段文字）

从 ChatGPT 的回答内容来看：针对性高、信息完整、内容准确、格式清晰，对于快速熟悉 ISTQB 认证考试和静态测试知识有很大帮助。当然，ChatGPT 的答复也存在专业术语表达不准确问题，参见例 1 下画线的文字。"初级"应该是"基础级"，"中级"应该是"高级"，"高级"应该是"专家级"。"Review"应该是"评审"，而不是"审查"。

（2）文件格式转换

如果源文件是图片格式的 JPG 文件或者 PDF 文件，无法直接编辑和翻译文件里的文字，需要应用文件格式转换工具（例如，Abbyy FineReader）通过光学字符识别（OCR）技术，将文件转换成 DOCX 或 PPTX 格式。OCR 技术应用计算机视觉和模式识别等 AI 技术，将图像中的文字转换为可编辑的文本，从而实现对图像文件中文字的可编辑和可翻译。

（3）术语识别与提取

对于多人分工翻译和校对的专业内容的翻译项目，为了术语翻译的准确性和一致性，需要在翻译准备过程中进行术语识别和翻译，并导入翻译项目术语库。可以通过自然语言处理和机器学习技术，实现对文本中的术语进行自动识别和标注。例如，可以使用词性标注和命名实体识别技术，识别出文本中的专有名词和术语。可以使用术语库和语料库等数据资源，进行术语的自动识别和分类。为了保证术语识别和翻译的准确率，可以对机器自动识别和翻译的术语进行人工审校，保持术语处理的效率和准确度。

例 2. 自动术语识别与翻译

笔者承接了某国际机器机构的行业报告的翻译，要求将英文翻译成中文，报告中包括许多关于机器翻译技术的术语，这家机构没有提供术语文件，为此，选择"语帆术语宝"在线术语提取工具。这个工具可以在线上传原文文件，设定术语源语言和目标语言，设置术语提取规则，自动提取术语并且自动翻译成目标语言，用户可以全文预览，对提取的术语和翻译文本进行筛选和修改，导出术语文件到本地。语帆术语宝提取术语的界面如图 1 所示。

图 1. "语帆术语宝"术语在线提取与翻译工具

（4）翻译任务分配与人员匹配

对于专业领域的翻译项目，项目经理在分配翻译和审校任务时，可以根据项目的专业领域、源语言和目标语言、翻译质量要求、翻译成本、翻译交稿时间等要求，应用 AI 技术，从人力资源库中匹配合适的译员和审校人员。其中应用到的 AI 技术包括自然语言处理（NLP）、机器学习（ML）、数据挖掘、智能搜索和推荐系统、专家决策支持系统。自然语言处理用于分析和理解源语言和目标语言之间的语义和语法结构，以便更好地匹配合适的译员和审校人员。机器学习通过对历史翻译项目和相关数据的学习，构建模型来预测和匹配最适合的译员和审校人员。数据挖掘通过对人力资源库中的数据进行挖掘和分析，发现译员和审校人员的技能、经验和专业领域，以便更好地匹配项目需求。智能搜索和推荐系统：通过智能搜索和推荐算法，从人力资源库中筛选出最符合项目需求的译员和审校人员。决策支持系统辅助项目经理在分配翻译和审校任务时做出决策，根据不同的要求和约束条件找到最佳的匹配方案。

（二）翻译过程中的 AI 技术应用

翻译过程的主要工作是完成译文的翻译，并且进行译文审校，以提高译文质量。应用 AI 技术中的自然语言处理技术，具体应用机器翻译技术、深度学习技术、强化学习技术、预训练转换技术等。

（1）"机器翻译+译后编辑"翻译模式

AI 技术在翻译过程得到广泛应用，例如，应用机器翻译生成初步的译文，再通过译后编辑人员对机器翻译的译文进行译后编辑，称为"机器翻译+译后编辑"模式，可以提高翻译效率，同时提高译文质量。

机器翻译是 AI 中的自然语言处理技术在翻译领域的应用。当前机器翻译应用最广泛的是神经机器翻译（NMT）技术。NMT 基于神经网络的机器翻译方法，使用深度学习技术建模和学习翻译。NMT 通过将源语言句子映射到目标语言句子的概率分布生成翻译结果。预训练语言模型是机器翻译常用的基础技术，它使用大规模未标注数据进行预训练，可以捕捉语言的统计规律和语义信息，提供更好的翻译质量和泛化能力。另外，机器翻译应用机器学习技术中的强化学习技术，通过定义适当的奖励函数和策略，帮助机器翻译系统自动调整翻译结果，提高翻译质量，实现机器翻译系统的自动优化。

（2）交互式机器翻译模式

交互式机器翻译模式是一种机器翻译的新翻译模式，近年来受到学术界和产业界的关注和应用。王均松等（2023：16-17）认为技术驱动的翻译模式经历了三次转变，分别是从人工翻译到计算机辅助翻译，从计算机辅助翻译到机器翻译译后编辑，从机器翻译译后编辑到交互式机器翻译。

交互式机器翻译(Interactive Machine Translation，简称 IMT)强调在翻译过程中与用户进行实时的交互和反馈。在翻译过程中，系统会根据译员已经翻译的部分文本，自动预测即将翻译的内容，并动态生成后续译文以供参考。译员可以接受系统提供的译文，也可以按照自己的思路进行修改或提出新的译法。系统会将每一次输入作为反馈进行"学习"并实时做出调整和更新，这个交互过程一直持续到翻译任务完成。交互式机器翻译可以解决神经机器翻译中的局限性，如歧义处理、上下文理解和用户满意度等问题。

交互式机器翻译应用多项 AI 技术，包括机器学习、自然语言处理、多模态处理、自然语言理解等。使用机器学习算法来训练模型，以便根据输入的源语言文本生成目标语言的翻译。机器学习可以帮助模型理解语言的语法、语义和上下文。使用自然语言处理技术来分析和理解源语言文本的结构、语法和语义，使用分词、词性标注、语法分析等技术。结合图像、语音和文本等多种输入模态，利用多模态处理技术提高翻译的质量和准确性。使用强化学习优化翻译过程，通过与用户的交互，根据用户的反馈进行学习和改进。

交互式机器翻译的交互技术包括上下文管理、反馈和指导，包括用户的输入、历史对话、之前的翻译结果。通过输入法的译员译文输入、翻译记忆（Translation Memory）、设定的术语库（Termbase）或对话状态跟踪（Dialogue State Tracking）等技术实现，以确保系统能够根据上下文进行准确的翻译和反馈。交互式机器翻译系统可以根据用户对翻译结果的评价、指出错误或提供替代翻译等用户反馈，对机器翻译系统进行调整和优化，以生成更符合用户要求的翻译结果。

例 3. 交互式机器翻译在翻译项目中的应用

交互式机器翻译系统主要有国外开发的 Casmact，Lilt，以及国内腾讯公司自主研发的 TranSmart 平台，甲骨易公司开发的 LanguageX 翻译平台。图 2 是腾讯公司 TranSmart 交互式翻译方式应用实例。

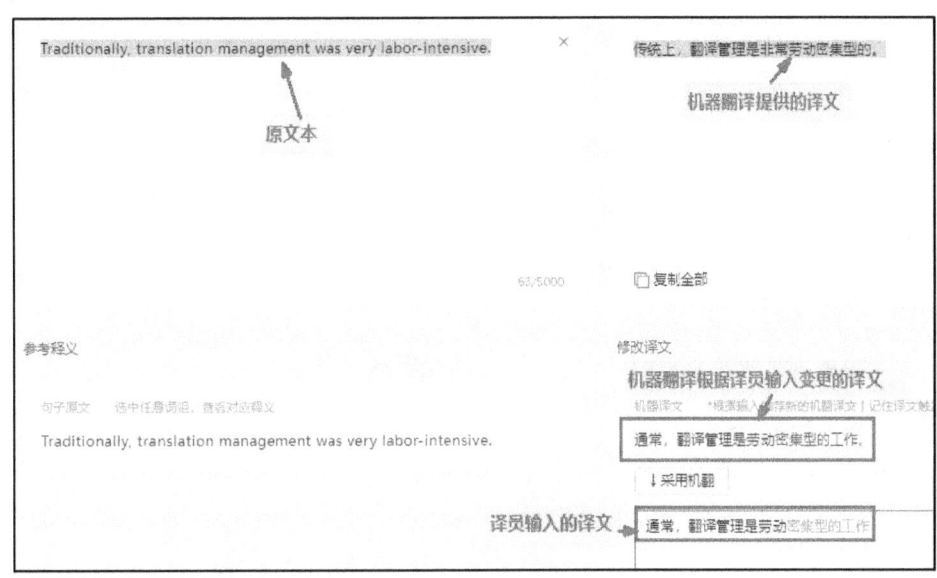

图 2. 腾讯公司 TranSmart 交互式机器翻译方式

在本次交互式机器翻译中，英文原文"Traditionally, translation management was very labor-intensive."显示在左上方，TranSmart 生成的译文显示在右上方，右下方是译员修改译文的区域。如果机器翻译的译文质量高，译员可以点击右侧中间的"复制全部"将机器翻译译文复制到译文区。如果译员对机器翻译的译文不满意，可以输入译文。本例中，机器翻译将"Traditionally"翻译成"传统上"，译员通过输入法改为"通常"，将"translation management"翻译成与机器翻译相同的译文"翻译管理"。译员接着输入了"是劳动"，右下方的"采用机翻"按钮上方显示 TranSmart 根据译员的输入译文，自动改变机器翻译的译文，提供的译文比原文质量更高，译员可以点击"采用机翻"按钮，获得剩下的译文，形成完整的译文。

（3）AI 辅助译文润色和审校

在译文审校方面，AI 技术可以自动检测文本中的语法和拼写错误，并提供纠正建议。AI 技术可以分析文本的语义，检测潜在的歧义或错误。提供关于句子结构、语义关系和逻辑一致性的反馈。根据特定的风格指南或语言规范，检查译文文本是否符合特定的写作规范，并提供改进建议，使文本更加流畅和易读。

在计算机润色和审校翻译译文的工作中，主要应用了 AI 中的自然语言处理、生成语言模型、自然语言理解、机器学习中的强化学习技术。自然语言处理技术包括分词、词性标注、实体识别等，以便更好地理解翻译译文的结构和语义。基于语言模型的生成式模型，可以生成人类类似的文本，使得计算机能够理解和生成润色和审校翻译译文所需的语言表达。自然语言理解技术研究对句子的深层次理解、推理和语义知识的表示与应用，用于问答系统、信息抽取、对话系统等，用于译文修改和润色。强化学习技术使计算机可以根据审校人员的反馈进行学习和改进，提供更准确和自然的润色建议。

关于 AI 技术在译文润色和审校方面的应用，耿芳、胡健（2023：46）对 ChatGPT 进行了研究，认为 ChatGPT 可突破小句层级的限制，从篇章层级入手调整语篇的连贯性，调动词汇、句法等各个语言系统作出译文语域的调整，甚至给出叙述方面的考虑。同时，在与人工交流的过程中，ChatGPT 能够不断调整译文表达，呈现更为恰当的译文，在汉译英译后编辑应用方面具有巨大潜力。下面提供笔者使用 ChatGPT 对译文进行审校和润色的实例。

例 4. ChatGPT 审校和润色译文

使用某机器翻译软件，将国际软件测试认证委员会（ISTQB）基础级考试大纲第三章"静态测试"第一段英文文本翻译成中文文本。然后调用 ChatGPT 进行译文审校和润色，并且总结原来译文存在哪些错误。

笔者对 ChatGPT 进行了如下提问：

> 请校对国际软件测试认证委员会(ISTQB)基础级考试大纲第 3 章第一段的译文。下面第一段是英文原文，第二段是中文译文。
>
> In contrast to dynamic testing, in static testing the software under test does not need to be executed. Code, process specification, system architecture specification or other work products are evaluated through manual examination (e.g., reviews) or with the help of a tool (e.g., static analysis). Test objectives include improving quality, detecting defects and assessing characteristics like readability, completeness, correctness, testability and consistency. Static testing can be applied for both verification and validation.
>
> 与动态测试<u>相反</u>，在静态测试，<u>测试统治下的软件</u>不需要执行。代码、过程规范、系统架构规范或其他工作产品<u>通过人工检查（例如，评审）或借助工具（例如，静态分析）</u>进行评估。测试的目标包括改进质量、检测缺陷和评估可读性、完整性、正确性、易测试性和一致性等特征。验证和确认都可以<u>申请静态测试</u>。

ChatGPT 审校和润色后的译文如下：

> 与动态测试<u>相比</u>，静态测试不需要执行<u>被测试的软件</u>。<u>通过手动检查（例如评审）或使用工具（例如静态分析）</u>，对代码、流程规范、系统架构规范或其他工作产品进行评估。测试的目标包括提高质量、检测缺陷以及评估可读性、完整性、正确性、可测试性和一致性等特征。<u>静态测试可用于验证和确认。</u>

可以看出，ChatGPT 审校和润色后的译文，修改了原译文的两个内容准确性错误，提高了译文表达的规范性（"相反"改为"相比"）。但是，ChatGPT 没有修改术语翻译错误，"specification"应该翻译成"规格说明",不能翻译成"规范",这个术语翻译错误需要审校人员进行修正。

关于原来译文的错误问题,笔者继续提问ChatGPT:

> 原来的译文存在哪些问题?

ChatGPT对原译文错误进行了总结,回复如下:

> 原来的译文相对准确,但存在一些微小的问题:
> "测试统治下的软件"的翻译不够准确,应该翻译为"被测试的软件"或"测试对象的软件"。
> "验证和确认都可以申请静态测试"的翻译不准确,应该翻译为"静态测试可用于验证和确认"。
> 总体而言,译文的意思基本传达了原文的信息,但在部分词汇和短语的翻译上还有改进的空间。

ChatGPT指出了原译文的两个翻译准确性错误,提供了修改后的译文,总结得较为全面,易于理解。

(三)交付后过程中的AI技术应用

翻译项目交付后过程的主要任务包括根据客户的反馈修改译文,对项目进行结项管理。具体包括执行客户满意度调查,完成项目总结报告的写作,与客户总结项目实施情况,与客户进行项目费用结算,进行翻译文件的备份。这些工作可以借助AI技术,提升翻译项目交付后阶段的效率和准确性,同时减轻人工工作负担,使得过程更加智能且高效。

完成这些工作使用的AI技术包括自然语言处理、译文自动修正、情感分析、机器创作等。利用机器翻译修正技术,可以根据客户的反馈和要求,自动修改译文中存在的问题,提高翻译质量和准确性。使用自然语言处理技术,对客户满意度调查进行语义分析,自动识别和提取客户对翻译质量、交付时间等方面的评价和反馈。通过情感分析技术,对客户满意度调查中的文本数据进行分析,自动判断客户反馈的情感倾向,帮助了解客户的满意度和需求。自动化报告生成技术,可以根据项目总结和客户满意度调查的数据,自动生成项目总结报告,包括项目的关键指标、成果总结和改进建议等。通过自动化的费用结算系统,可以根据项目的工作量、时长和费率等信息,自动计算和结算翻译项目的费用,提高结算的准确性和效率。在翻译项目文件的备份方面,可以利用数据备份和存储技术,自动将翻译项目文件进行备份和归档,确保数据的安全性和可靠性。

四、AI技术在视频翻译项目的应用案例

以影视文化翻译为代表的视频翻译成为语言服务市场的"宠儿",根据中国翻译协会(2019, 2020, 2022)发布的中国翻译及语言服务行业发展报告,影视文化翻译连续成为市场需求量前十的语言服务领域。传统的视频翻译依靠译员人工翻译和配音,在字幕文本提取、时间轴调整、目标语言配音方面,耗费了大量的时间和精力,翻译效率很低,成本高昂,后期修改繁琐。

AI 技术在视频字幕翻译和配音方面的应用，改变了传统视频翻译效率。下面以云译公司发布的在线音视频翻译平台 TransWAI 为例，描述 AI 技术在视频翻译中的应用状况。以儿童动画片"小猪佩奇"英文版的中文字幕翻译和配音为翻译项目案例，本案例中的英文视频为 MP4 文件格式，英文视频不带字幕，要求添加中文字幕和中文配音，输出 MP4 格式中文视频文件。

（一）TransWAI 翻译视频字幕

登录 TransWAI 翻译平台，进入"我的工作台"，选择"音视频翻译"，点击"新建"按钮，上传 MP4 视频文件，选择源语言和目标语言，完成项目创建。点击上传的视频图案，进入字幕翻译和审校界面，如图 3 所示。

图 3. TransWAI 的字幕文字提取、翻译与审校界面

由图 3 可以看出，TransWAI 对上传的 MP4 文件完成了字幕英文文本的自动识别，完成了字幕文本的中文翻译，并且对字幕进行了句子切分，添加了每条字幕的开始和结束的时间码。页面右侧可以播放视频，以观看字幕的时间码和文本内容的准确性。视频字幕译者和审校人员可以修改字幕的时间码、字幕的英文和中文文本。完成时间码、英文字幕和中文字幕内容确认和修改后，可以下载字幕文件，导出带有字幕的视频文件。

TransWAI 识别视频的英文字幕文本应用了 AI 语音识别技术、视频识别技术、语音转换为文本（Speech to Text，STT）。TransWAI 生成视频的中文字幕文本使用的是 AI 自然语言处理、深度学习、机器翻译等技术，将识别的英文字幕文本使用机器翻译自动翻译成中文。TransWAI 识别视频字幕的开始和结束时间码使用了自然语言处理技术、视频处理技术、语音识别技术、时间对齐技术。

（二）TransWAI 视频配音

对视频进行中文配音，可以在完成节字幕识别和翻译后，选择"视频配音"，点击"新建"按钮，上传 MP4 视频文件，添加字幕文件，完成项目创建。点击上传的视频图案，进入视频配音界面，如图 4 所示。

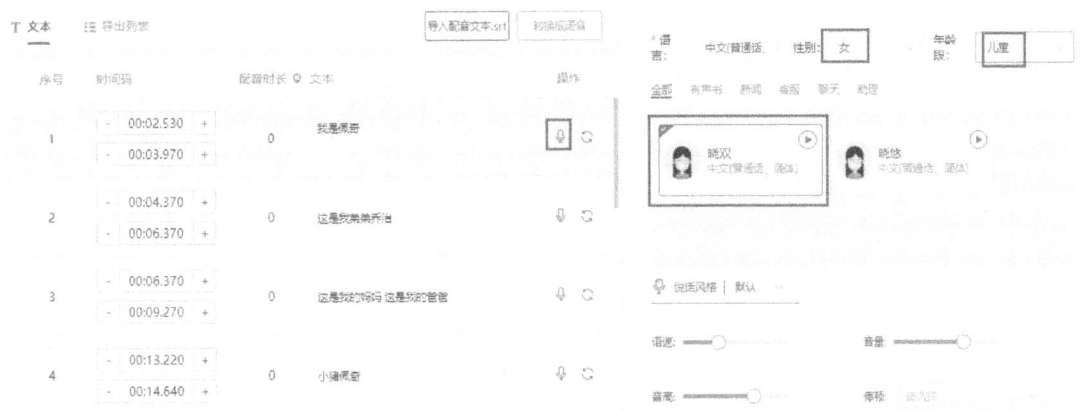

图 4. TransWAI 的视频配音界面

由图 4 可以看出，TransWAI 对上传的视频文件和字幕文件完成了字幕时间码和文本的识别和显示。点击"转换成语音"按钮（话筒形状的符号），页面右侧可以选择配音角色的性别和年龄段，选择合适的配音角色（可以点击配音角色的播放按钮，试听当前角色的发音），右边下方可以设置配音角色的说话风格。可以调整当前字幕的时间码。点击右下方"确定"按钮，完成本条字幕的配音。完成全部字幕的配音后，可以导出配音的视频文件。

TransWAI 视频配音采用的是 AI 中的文本转换为语音（Text to Speech，TTS）技术，TransWAI 将字幕文本自动转换成声音。具体使用的是 AI 的自然语言处理技术、语音合成技术、视频处理技术。

根据以上研究发现，机器翻译是翻译项目中应用最广的 AI 技术。当前主流的神经机器翻译是数据驱动的设计模式，由于某些语言对语料稀疏、语料质量参差不齐，机器翻译的译文还存在质量不稳定问题。由于众多机器翻译系统是以互联网为运行方式，对于需要高度保密的翻译项目，不能使用互联网机器翻译进行翻译。译者需要评估风险，决定是否需要机器翻译以及如何信任机器翻译的译文，并且决定如何进行译后编辑（Bowker, 2023：93；Pięta, Maia & Torres-Simón, 2023：90）。

五、结语

AI 技术快速发展和广泛应用，呈现深度学习、跨界融合、人机协同、群智开放等特征，驱动翻译服务行业的深刻变革，彻底改变传统翻译的工作模式和服务能力。专业的翻译团队在翻译项目实施中将 AI 技术融入流程，形成了"人员+流程+技术"的翻译实施新形式。

在翻译项目流程中，应用最广的 AI 技术分别是自然语言处理技术、计算机视觉技术、神经网络技术、专家决策系统技术。翻译项目流程的各个过程组合使用多种 AI 技术，包括图像识别、语音识别、语音合成、机器翻译、机器学习、深度学习、预训练转换等具体技术，其中机器翻译是使用最广泛的 AI 具体技术。

新一轮 AI 技术正在重塑翻译行业新业态、新模式、新服务，翻译实践者、教育者、研究者需要把握技术带来的发展机遇，迎接技术变革的冲击挑战，主动拥抱技术、学习技术、研究技术、应用技术和发展技术，以驱动和赋能翻译行业跨越式发展。

参考文献

[1] Bowker Lynne. *De-mystifying Translation: Introducing Translation to Non-translators*[M]. London and New York: Routledge, 2023.

[2] Cai, Zixing & Xu, Guangyou (蔡自兴，徐光祐). *Artificial Intelligence: Principles and Applications (Third Editions)*(人工智能及其应用(第三版))[M]. Beijing: Tinghua University Press (北京：清华大学出版社), 2003.

[3] Cui, Qiliang (崔启亮). *Localization Project Management*(本地化项目管理)[M]. Beijing：University of International and Economics Press(北京：对外经济贸易大学出版社), 2017.

[4] Feng, Zhiwei (冯志伟). "The parallel development of machine translation and artificial intelligence" (机器翻译与人工智能的平行发展)[J]. *Waiguoyu (Journal of Foreign Languages)* (外国语(上海外国语大学学报))，2018(6):35-48.

[5] Geng, Fang & Hu, Jian (耿芳，胡健). "New Direction for Post-Editing by Artificial Intelligence Translation: A Case Study of ChatGPT Translation" (人工智能辅助译后编辑新方向——基于ChatGPT的翻译实例研究)[J]. *Foreign Languages in China* (中国外语)，2023(5):41-47.

[6] Pięta Hanna, Rita Bueno Maia & Ester Torres-Simón. *Indirect Translation Explained* [M]. London and New York: Routledge, 2023.

[7] Translators Association of China (中国翻译协会). *2019 Report on Development of Language Service Industry* (中国语言服务行业发展报告2019) [R]. 2019.

[8] Translators Association of China (中国翻译协会). *2020 Report on Development of Language Service Industry* (中国语言服务行业发展报告2020) [R]. 2020.

[9] Translators Association of China (中国翻译协会). *2022 Report on Development of Translation and Language Service Industry* (中国翻译及语言服务行业发展报告2022) [R]. 2022.

[10] Translators Association of China (中国翻译协会). *2023 Report on Development of Translation and Language Service Industry* (中国翻译及语言服务行业发展报告2023)[R]. 2023.

[11] Wang, Huashu & Liu, Shijie (王华树，刘世界). "On Technological Turn of Translation in the Era of Artificial Intelligence" (人工智能时代翻译技术转向研究) [J]. *Foreign Language Education* (外语教学), 2021(5):87-92.

[12] Wang, Junsong, Xiao, Weiqing & Cui, Qiliang (王均松，肖维青，崔启亮). "Technology-driven Translation Modes in the AI Age: Evolution, Causes and Implications" (人工智能时代技术驱动的翻译模式：嬗变、动因及启示) [J]. *Shanghai Journal of Translators* (上海翻译)，2023(4):15-20.

作者简介

崔启亮，对外经济贸易大学教授。研究方向：计算机辅助翻译、本地化翻译、语言服务。电子邮箱：cuiql@sina.com。

AIGC 时代的翻译研究：挑战与路径

⊙ 王华树（北京外国语大学，北京）
⊙ 李　丹（西安外国语大学，西安）

[摘　要] 以 ChatGPT 为代表的新一代技术，对翻译实践产生了深远影响，同时也对翻译理论提出了新的挑战。本文以 AI 生成内容（AI-generated Content, AIGC）技术的发展为背景，探索其对新时代翻译研究带来的挑战，提出未来翻译研究可能的发展路径，包括加强学科交叉融合，拓展研究思路，深化对翻译模式的研究，及扩大翻译伦理研究等多个方面，旨在为 AIGC 时代的翻译研究发展提供新视角和新思考。

[关键词] AIGC；翻译研究；挑战与路径

Translation Studies in the AIGC Era: Challenges and Pathways

WANG Huashu (Beijing Foreign Studies University, Beijing)
LI Dan (Xi'an International Studies University, Xi'an)

Abstract: The advent of new-generation technologies, exemplified by ChatGPT, has profoundly influenced translation practices and posed fresh challenges to translation theories. Set against the backdrop of the development of AI-generated content (AIGC) technology, this paper explores the challenges it brings to translation studies in the new era. It proposes potential future trajectories for translation studies, including strengthening interdisciplinary integration, expanding research approaches, deepening the study of translation models, and broadening the scope of translation ethics research. The aim is to provide new perspectives and insights for the development of translation studies in the AIGC era.

Key words: AIGC; translation studies; challenges and pathways

一、引　言

AIGC（AI-generated content）技术发展迅猛，风靡全球，推动数字人文进入一个全新的发展阶段。AIGC 技术具有强大的内容生成能力，能够进行多模态数据处理、自动特征提取、上下文理解等，同时在数据处理中能够很好地对复杂的语义及其关联关系进行非线性建模，提高数据处理的精度和效果。AIGC 技术不仅提升

本文是 2023 年中央高校基本科研业务费专项资金项目（编号：242500122002）以及 2023 年西安外国语大学研究生科研基金项目（编号：2023SS059）的阶段性成果。

了大规模数字化文本的生成和处理水平，也促进了人类语言的快速生成和深度理解。

在人工智能技术快速发展的时代，翻译研究面临着越来越多的挑战。翻译研究的内容主要涉及数据库建设、翻译文本、翻译史、翻译概念、翻译教育、译者等研究领域（胡开宝、王晓莉，2022）；翻译研究对象侧重翻译文本特征和翻译心理过程，在研究方法上突出量化数据描述与统计，在理论视角方面依赖相关学科理论，在研究模式上重视假设验证（张威、雷璇，2023）；翻译研究呈现量化数据分析程度及数据驱动探索不足、对翻译教学与实践的指导价值不够明确（Ibid）等问题。总体来看，在 AIGC 技术之前，翻译研究的对象局限于传统纸质文本，未能关注自动生成性文本；翻译研究主要关注语言文本的语言学特征，对生成性文本特征考察不足；翻译研究手段主要依赖语料库技术，处理手段较为单一；翻译研究的数据分析和统计不够深入，对研究发现的内在关联和规律阐释有限。

随着算力、算据和算法的突破，AIGC 技术快速发展，迅速席卷全球，进一步推动了翻译研究的技术转向。在技术驱动下，翻译的对象、主体、模式等都发生了技术化转变，翻译的研究对象和内容发生整体性变化（王华树，刘世界，2021），从传统纸质文本转变为声音、图像等数字化的文本类型，以及由众筹翻译、游戏翻译、网站翻译等翻译形式产生的大量原生性数字文本（胡开宝、王晓莉，2022）。在 AIGC 时代，翻译研究呈现显著的变化，如数据的大规模化、研究的自动化和跨学科的融合等，这意味着翻译研究从基于传统个体和小规模文本的研究方式，转向了大规模、复杂且以数字为驱动的研究模式。以往研究者们可能需要花费大量时间进行数据处理，甚至需要学习 Python、R 等编码语言来分析数据，但 AIGC 技术（如 ChatGPT）的出现改变了研究前景（Zhang, Zhang & Li, et al., 2023）。AIGC 技术应用于翻译研究，重塑了翻译研究的流程，改变了翻译研究的方法和手段，对未来翻译研究的开展提出了新的要求，带来了新的挑战。

二、AIGC 时代翻译研究面临的主要挑战

AIGC 技术的发展给翻译研究带来了前所未有的挑战。AIGC 技术催生新的数据类型和研究对象，研究方法和手段亟待更新和完善。传统的理论框架在新的技术环境下显得力不从心，翻译研究对理论创新的需求变得更为迫切。下面将结合 AIGC 技术的特点探讨当前翻译研究面临的四个主要方面的挑战。

（一）研究对象

AIGC 技术催生了很多不同于传统文本的新"文本"，这些文本形式趋向多元化：图片、音视频、动态网页、交互游戏等，呈现多语言、多变量、多模态、非线性、标记化、短语化、去语境化、动态化等特点（王华树，2023：116-117），给翻译研究带来了新的挑战。下面以图片、音视频、动态网页、交互游戏翻译为例分析翻译研究对象的变化特征及带来的挑战：

（1）图片翻译：图片翻译是指将以图片为载体的文字翻译为另一种以图片为载体的语言的翻译活动。如果没有其他模态的内容来协助表达意义，就无法完整地分析文本的意义（Luca, 2020），因此，图片翻译需兼顾图片颜色、场景、情感等非文本元素。随着 AIGC 技术的发展，衍生了许多 AI 图片生成工具（如 Midjourney），借助这些工具能够实现文字自动转换为图片的效果，改变了图片的创作方式。同时对图片翻译研究带来了新的挑战：既要求研究者具备一定的图像解读能力以及对文学和艺术的审美能力，同时又对研究者分析和处理

大量图片翻译数据的能力提出了更高的要求。

（2）音视频翻译：音视频翻译是指借助各种音视频处理技术和软件将音视频作品进行语音识别、字幕翻译等的翻译活动。AIGC 技术衍生出了许多音视频处理技术（如 TransWAI），能够实现对音视频内容的高度智能化翻译处理。音视频翻译研究中，研究对象从传统的词语和句子扩展到了包括声音、画面、镜头语言在内的复合信息，翻译研究的维度更为复杂。Kaindl（2013）指出，"各种模态遵循的形式、功能和感知原则不同。"针对音视频这种多模态文本，翻译研究不仅需要关注文本意义，还需要关注文化、时间、空间等多元素的统筹协调，具有一定的挑战性。

（3）动态网页翻译：动态网页翻译是指对包括网页内容和交互功能在内的整个网站进行翻译和本地化。网站本地化主要针对超文本，对于本地化或任何涉及这些开放和多线性文本形式的研究来说，了解超文本的主要特征至关重要（Jiménez-Crespo，2013：55），因此，动态网页翻译研究更加复杂。AIGC 时代，自动生成的动态网页越来越多，针对动态网页的翻译研究不仅要关注文字本身，还要关注多媒体、动画、链接等超文本互动元素。同时，在动态网页翻译研究中，翻译研究者需要具备一定的网页编程知识和网站本地化经验。

（4）交互游戏翻译：交互游戏翻译是指将电子游戏的文本、图像、声音、动画等内容进行翻译和本地化的过程。Merino（2006）指出，"使用'游戏本地化'来形容翻译并不准确，原因是翻译活动不仅仅指翻译"。AIGC 技术的发展促使更多游戏脚本的自动生成，游戏翻译研究不仅需要处理音频、图像、视频等多模态信息，还需要处理游戏的实时交互、随机生成等动态内容。交互游戏翻译研究中，翻译研究者需兼顾动态文本、游戏情节、审美需求、技术处理等问题。

（二）研究方法

AIGC 时代，大量的生成性文本逐渐成为了翻译的对象，为翻译研究提供了海量的数据，这些数据将成为翻译研究的基本内容。比如，AIGC 技术能够帮助翻译研究者训练翻译模型，生成大量的语料数据用于翻译研究，但同时这种数据驱动的研究方法给翻译研究带来了新的挑战：

（1）翻译数据处理难度加大：AIGC 技术生成的内容包含各种语言和多种模态的文本或非文本内容，翻译研究中需要对这些复杂的数据内容进行归纳分析。如何评估多模态的文本或非文本现象是否得到了准确的解释，如何进行数据可视化分析和解释，以及如何发现数据之下的普遍规律是翻译研究在方法上需要解决的问题。

（2）翻译数据质量难以控制：像 ChatGPT-4 这样的工具能够生成看起来合理的内容，但内容的真实性通常是不可靠的（Cao, Li & Liu, 2023）。AIGC 技术生成的内容来源于网络，语料质量水平参差不齐，其中不乏有文化偏见或误导性信息。针对生成性内容，翻译研究需要对研究内容的质量进行把控，如何确保语料的准确性和可靠性是翻译研究所面临的挑战。

（3）学科交叉研究更加复杂：翻译研究的核心领域不在单模态领域，而是在多模态领域，翻译研究需要进行更多的跨学科工作（Kaindl，2013）。AIGC 技术生成的多模态文本或非文本包含图片、音视频等非文本的媒体数据，这些数据由不同学科知识组成，要求翻译研究通过计算机视觉、语音识别等跨学科研究视角进行，但如何借助跨学科的研究方法科学地分析这些新型的数据具有一定的难度。

（三）研究手段

传统的翻译研究手段，包括文本分析、个案研究、问卷调查和文本对比研究等，尽管在实践中得到广泛的应用，但仍然存在着数据规模有限、分析手段简单、理论指导作用有限以及人为错误较多等问题。面临如今复杂的多模态翻译文本，这些传统手段已经很难满足当前翻译研究的需求，AIGC技术的出现将催生新的研究手段，但同时伴随着新的挑战：

（1）技术应用难度加大：AIGC技术一方面优化和扩展了传统的研究手段和工具，另一方面，要求翻译研究者具备更高的技术应用能力。翻译研究者不仅需要掌握翻译理论，还需要学习和掌握不断出现的新技术和新工具，以适应翻译研究的新趋势。

（2）技术创新难度加大：针对大规模的、多样化的研究对象，翻译研究者不仅需要在现有的技术上融合AIGC技术能力，还需要探索如何创新技术手段推动研究的深入发展，以及如何实现高度自动化和智能化的研究流程。

（四）研究理论

随着生成性人工智能的兴起，传统翻译理论正面临诸多挑战。限于时代局限性，传统的研究视角狭隘，主要关注语言文本分析，未能关注生成内容的多模态特征，对生成内容的随机性和不确定性考量不足。传统的翻译研究理论主要基于语言学、语用学、交际学等语言学理论，理论框架逐渐老化，对新型研究对象和语言模型解释力不足。AIGC技术的发展改变了翻译的方方面面，传统翻译理论的局限性日益凸显，亟待创新翻译研究理论。下面从两个方面加以阐述：

（1）翻译的本质面临挑战：传统的翻译活动中，译者的主体性作用突出，翻译本质上是译者的一种跨文化交际行为。翻译研究主要从语言、文化和社会三个层面来理解译者的翻译实践过程。但随着AIGC技术的发展，多模态文本翻译给翻译研究带来了新的困难，涉及高维结构化数据的生成及其评估（Liang, Zadeh & Morency, 2022）。同时，基于AIGC的大规模翻译模型能够实现文本到图像（Ramesh, Pavlov & Goh, et al., 2021）、文本到视频（Singer, Polyak & Hayes, et al., 2022）、音频到图像（Jamaludin, Chung & Zisserman, 2019）的内容生成，翻译过程和结果都越来越依赖于算法和数据。在这种情况下，翻译的本质可能会被重新定义，翻译研究需要寻找新的翻译理论来解释和指导AIGC时代的翻译实践。

（2）翻译的伦理面临挑战：随着AIGC技术的发展，翻译的伦理问题更加突出。一方面，AIGC技术被广泛应用，翻译的过程和结果越来越不透明，引发翻译的公正性和公平性问题；另一方面，随着翻译数据的大规模化，翻译的隐私和数据安全问题也越来越严重。针对这些问题，翻译研究需要构建新的翻译伦理理论来引导翻译实践的正确伦理行为。

当然，AIGC技术还带来了其它更多方面的挑战，限于篇幅，不再赘述。AIGC时代给翻译研究带来的挑战前所未有，需要研究者紧跟技术时代发展步伐，持续创新，才能推动翻译研究的发展。

三、AIGC 时代翻译研究的发展路径

面对翻译研究的新挑战，我们需要从多方面进行应对，以推动翻译研究在 AIGC 时代的创新发展。以下将就加强学科交叉融合、拓展研究思路、深化翻译模式研究和伦理规范建设等方面进行阐述，这些是 AIGC 时代翻译研究的重要发展路径。

（一）加强学科交叉融合

在利用量化方法收集实证数据来验证理论概念方面，目前的翻译研究虽然已经取得了一定的进展，但在理论层面上仍过于依赖语言学、形象学等相关学科的概念或理论（张威、雷璇，2023）。AIGC 视域下的翻译研究将会呈现更加复杂的多学科属性，翻译研究者需加强跨学科翻译研究：

（1）打破翻译研究的学科界限：在 AIGC 时代，翻译研究者应重新思考语言的本质和翻译的意义，无论是从研究视角还是具体研究手段来看，都要求翻译研究者具有跨学科的研究素养，在不断学习跨学科研究方法的同时，加强与计算机科学、哲学、伦理学等领域的交流。比如，基于丰富的翻译语料资源，研究者可借鉴计算机语言学和语料库语言学的方法分析研究多语言、多模态语料的语言特征；深入学习注意力机制等人工智能领域知识，对人类译员的认知翻译过程进行研究。

（2）借鉴前沿交叉学科研究成果：翻译研究者应主动借鉴前沿交叉学科的研究成果，整合自然语言处理、机器学习、深度学习、对话生成模型等更多 AIGC 技术相关的学科知识，解决 AIGC 时代翻译研究中遇到的新问题。比如，借鉴数字人文的研究成果，翻译研究者可以开展数字化、交互化环境对跨文化传播影响的研究，探寻新的翻译理论；借鉴可视化理论，研究者可以研发翻译过程的可视化分析工具，加强翻译过程研究。

（3）积极关注新兴智能技术应用：AIGC 技术催生了众多的新兴智能技术（如 OpenAI 的 GPT 模型和 DALL-E、Google 的 LaMDA 等），这些新兴技术应用于翻译领域，改变了翻译实践的过程。翻译研究者应积极关注这些技术，主动探索 AI 技术在翻译研究领域中的应用，开拓新的研究路径，拓展新的研究方法和手段。

（4）加强翻译研究跨学科融合交流：AIGC 技术在各个行业领域都得到了创新应用。翻译研究者应积极推动跨学科的融合交流，联合语言学、计算机科学、社会学、心理学等学科的研究者们共同探索 AIGC 时代的翻译问题。此外，翻译研究应关注语言服务的现实需求。由于语言服务具有跨学科、多元化和应用型特征，语言服务需求也呈现多元化和专业化特征（崔启亮、黄萌萌，2022）。翻译研究者应加深与语言服务行业企业人员的交流，掌握语言服务需求变化，将翻译研究的跨学科成果转化为切实的产品和服务。

（二）拓展翻译研究思路

AIGC 技术的发展加速了图片、音视频、动态网页、交互游戏等多模态数据的翻译进程，使得多模态翻译流程更加技术化和自动化，改变了翻译的环境和过程。翻译研究者应紧跟技术发展的节奏，深入思考翻译环境和过程的改变对译员和翻译质量带来的影响，同时以多模态的文本翻译为研究对象，拓展翻译研究的思路：

（1）创新翻译策略研究：针对新生的多模态翻译对象，创新翻译策略研究。例如，在翻译研究中，通过训练人工智能模型并分析不同模态翻译对象之间的关系，研究者可进一步分析、研究各模态之间的转换过程，得出多模态相互转换的规律。

（2）改进翻译评估方式：AIGC 技术的发展促使更多新兴技术在多模态翻译活动中被广泛应用，引发了更多的翻译质量问题。翻译研究者应致力于新技术背景下翻译质量评估方式的研究，基于现有文本评估指标（如 BLEU、TER、ROUGE）加入视觉、听觉等感知因素，为多模态文本的翻译制定更加适用的质量评估指标。

（3）丰富翻译过程研究：AIGC 技术有助于翻译研究中翻译过程数据的收集，如眼动轨迹、进程数据等，推动开展更多针对译员的翻译研究活动，使翻译过程更加透明化、可视化，促进人机协作翻译过程的和谐发展。

（三）深化翻译模式研究

在数字化兴起之前，翻译活动主要依赖于人类译员。随着计算机科技的巨大突破，机器翻译登上舞台并逐渐发展，直到人机协同的翻译模式成为主流。崔启亮（2014）指出："译后编辑是人机交互翻译的重要体现，可为机器翻译的改善提供回馈，代表着未来翻译服务的发展方向。"随着 AIGC 技术的发展，未来的翻译模式将更加依赖于机器，人类译员将主要负责对机器翻译结果进行校验和精细优化。在这种情况下，翻译研究需要以人类译员和人机交互为出发点，深入剖析人机协同的翻译模式：

（1）深化翻译认知过程研究：翻译认知过程研究的核心对象包括翻译过程中的信息处理模式、处理策略以及处理单位（文旭、肖开容，2019）。此外，它还涉及翻译能力及翻译能力获取、翻译专长、译者的认知负担等诸多问题（Albir, Alves & Dimitrova, et al., 2015）。在翻译研究中，AIGC 技术能够帮助处理海量的翻译过程数据，这些数据可用于构建翻译认知仿真模型，揭示译员的认知过程及影响译员认知的相关因素，深化翻译认知过程研究。

（2）深化人机交互模式研究：深入理解和探索人类译员与机器翻译系统之间的协作互动对于提升翻译质量具有关键性意义。为了发挥人机交互的优势，译后编辑是翻译行业中积极采用的翻译实施方式（崔启亮，2014）。翻译研究中，借助 AIGC 技术对大规模的译后编辑译文的过程数据进行观察分析，可以获取构建人机交互编辑模型的精确信息。人机交互编辑模型能够揭示人类译员在机器翻译译后编辑过程中的决策动机和技术行为，深化人机交互翻译的编辑策略研究。

（四）扩大翻译伦理研究

随着 AIGC 技术的快速发展，翻译领域的伦理问题已经超越了基础的翻译规范和数据伦理问题，转向更复杂的技术伦理问题。翻译研究者需要从伦理学的角度出发，关注技术应用及其引发的数据安全等伦理问题，深入研究并提出相应的解决方案：

（1）数据隐私保护：随着大数据技术在翻译中的应用，如何在充分利用数据资源的同时，加强个人数据隐私保护机制，开展翻译数据伦理的系统化研究（王华树、刘世界，2022），是翻译研究的重要领域。面对 AIGC 时代爆发式增长的数据量，尤其是多模态的翻译数据，翻译研究者需关注翻译过程中的数据隐私问题，促进数据的规范使用，同时借助数据加密、识别等技术手段加强隐私安全研究。

（2）知识产权处理：在 AIGC 技术背景下，知识产权问题的复杂性也在加剧。由于网络数据的开放性和共享性（Ibid），很容易产生侵犯知识产权的问题。翻译研究者应关注翻译过程中的数据来源问题，督促翻译人员的行为规范，保护利益相关方的知识产权。

（3）内容质量管控：语言服务提供商和翻译技术企业在不同程度上存在夸大宣传 AI 机器翻译质量的行为（王 Ibid）。鉴于 AIGC 技术赋能的各种翻译技术与工具在翻译中的应用，如何确保翻译内容的质量是翻译研究的重要课题。翻译研究者应关注翻译内容审核流程，同时应针对翻译过程中的内容管控问题展开深入研究，推动翻译质量管控建设。

（4）伦理体系建设：忽视翻译伦理体系的建设将会导致语言服务行业走向畸形发展，甚至会给整个行业生态带来巨大的影响（Ibid）。翻译研究者应关注 AIGC 时代伦理体系的建设，从新技术的开发者、使用者、监管者等多方视角出发，研究制定符合时代发展的翻译伦理规范，同时考虑社会背景、文化影响等多方面因素，确保翻译伦理规范的公正性和科学性。此外，翻译研究应针对技术伦理培训问题展开，促进 AIGC 技术人才培养体系的建设，提高技术伦理共识。

四、结　语

AIGC 技术在推动翻译研究的发展中，无疑提供了前所未有的新机遇，但同时带来了一系列的挑战。在这个新的时期，我们需要对翻译对象进行重新定义和理论阐释，拓展翻译研究视角，深化翻译模式研究，加强翻译伦理研究，并积极寻找翻译研究与其他学科的交叉点。虽然 AIGC 技术能够为翻译研究提供强大的技术和工具，但翻译研究的本质仍然是人文的，我们不能忘记对翻译本质的追问。翻译的研究和实践始终在服务于人文，而不是技术；人文研究学者应善于利用技术赋能，但同时应避免过分依赖技术，努力探寻技术理论创新之路。只有在顺应时代潮流的同时，实现传统与创新的有机结合，翻译研究才能在数字人文的新时代中焕发出新的活力。

参考文献

[1] Aditya Ramesh, Mikhail Pavlov, Gabriel Goh, et al. "Zero-shot text-to-image generation". In *International Conference on Machine Learning (PMLR)*[Z], 2021, 139: 8821-8831.

[2] Amparo Hurtado Albir, Fabio Alves, Birgitta Englund Dimitrova, et al. "A retrospective and prospective view of translation research from an empirical, experimental, and cognitive perspective: The TREC network". In *Translation & Interpreting*, 2015(1): 5-25.

[3] Chaoning Zhang, Chenshuang Zhang, Chenghao Li, et al. "One small step for generative ai, one giant leap for agi: A complete survey on chatgpt in aigc era". In *arXiv preprint arXiv*, 2023.

[4] Cui, Qiliang (崔启亮). "On post-editing of machine translation" (论机器翻译的译后编辑). *In Chinese Translators Journal* (中国翻译), 2014(6): 68-73.

[5] Cui, Qiliang & Mengmeng, Huang (崔启亮，黄萌萌). "Design of language service curriculum based on the analysis of industry requirements" (基于行业需求分析的语言服务核心课程设计). In *Foreign Language Education in China* (外语教育研究前沿), 2022(4): 34-40+92.

[6] Hu, Kaibao & Xiaoli, Wang (胡开宝，王晓莉). "Translation Studies in Digital Humanities: State of the Art, Issues and Future Directions" (数字人文视域下翻译研究：现状、问题与前景). In *Foreign Languages and Their Teaching* (外语与外语教学), 2022(6): 111-121+148-149.

[7] Jamaludin, Amir, Joon Son Chung, and Andrew Zisserman. "You said that?: Synthesising talking faces from audio". In *International Journal of Computer Vision*, 2019, 127: 1767-1779.

[8] Jiménez-Crespo, Miguel A. *Translation and web localization*. London and New York: Routledge, 2013.

[9] Kaindl Klaus. *The Routledge handbook of translation studies*. London and New York: Routledge, 2013.

[10] Liang, Paul Pu, Amir Zadeh, and Louis-Philippe Morency. "Foundations and recent trends in multimodal machine learning: Principles, challenges, and open questions". In *arXiv preprint arXiv*, 2022(1).

[11] Luca, Ion-Sorin. "A multimodal discourse analysis in media". In *Romanian Journal of English Studies*, 2020(1): 74-80.

[12] Merino, Miguel Bernal. "On the translation of video games". In *The Journal of Specialised Translation*, 2006(6): 22-36.

[13] Uriel Singer, Adam Polyak, Thomas Hayes, et al. "Make-a-video: Text-to-video generation without text-video data". In *arXiv preprint arXiv*, 2022.

[14] Wang, Huashu & Shijie, Liu (王华树，刘世界). "On technological turn of translation in the era of artificial intelligence" (人工智能时代翻译技术转向研究). In *Foreign Language Education* (外语教学), 2019(5): 87-92.

[15] Wang, Huashu & Shijie, Liu (王华树，刘世界). "On Translation Data Ethics in the Era of Big Data: Concepts, Problems and Suggestions" (大数据时代翻译数据伦理研究：概念、问题与建议). In *Shanghai Journal of Translators* (上海翻译), 2022(2):12-17.

[16] Wang, Huashu (王华树). *Studies on Translation Technologies* (翻译技术研究). Beijing: Foreign Language Teaching and Research Press (北京：外语教学与研究出版社), 2023.

[17] Wen, Xu & Kairong, Xiao (文旭，肖开容). *Cognitive Translatology* (认知翻译学). Beijing: Peking University Press (北京：北京大学出版社), 2019.

[18] Yihan Cao, Siyu Li, Yixin Liu, et al. "A comprehensive survey of ai-generated content (aigc): A history of generative ai from gan to chatgpt". In *arXiv preprint arXiv*, 2023, 37(4).

[19] Zhang, Wei & Xuan, Lei (张威，雷璇). "A 'turn' towards digital humanities in translation studies: Current situation and reflection" (翻译研究的数字人文"转向"：现状及反思). In *Chinese Translators Journal* (中国翻译), 2023(2): 99-106.

作者简介

王华树，博士，北京外国语大学高级翻译学院副教授。研究方向：翻译技术、外语教育技术、语言服务管理。电子邮箱：wanghuashu@vip.qq.com。

李丹，西安外国语大学高级翻译学院研究生在读。研究方向：翻译与本地化技术。电子邮箱：danaliendeavor@outlook.com。

ChatGPT 辅助翻译的潜力与局限
——以《后维多利亚时代人》的翻译为例

⊙ 侯广旭（南京农业大学外国语学院，南京）

[摘 要] ChatGPT 横空出世已经几个月了，译者们都对这种元宇宙的全新 AI 模型兴趣大发，寄希望于从中挖取更多的助力。但是，对于如何充分利用这种比机器翻译多出了聊天式文本生成功能的 AI 机器人，中国学者尚未能及时拿出层次更深一些的研究成果，多数讨论以预期未来的挑战与机遇为主。笔者在翻译《后维多利亚时代人》的过程中，从理解原文所需的背景信息补充、思维逻辑线索提示等具体角度，而不是从直接用它提供译文角度，咨询与测试了 ChatGPT，发现 ChatGPT 辅助翻译的潜力很大，但也有很多局限。ChatGPT 能为译者提供理解原文所需的有价值的背景信息、语义解读参考、独特的观察推理判断线索等，但是，缺乏对细微差别的辨识能力，难以理解语篇的微妙之处或上下文，从而导致不正确或不适当的反应。译者在使用上要扬长避短，以实现 ChatGPT 辅助翻译的效果最大化。

[关键词] ChatGPT；辅助翻译；《后维多利亚时代人》；潜力；局限

The Potentials and Limitations of ChatGPT Assisted Translation:
A Case Study of the Translation of *After the Victorians*

HOU Guangxu (Nanjing Agricultural University, Nanjing)

Abstract: Several months have passed since the release of ChatGPT, the new AI model emerging in the metaverse. Translators have shown keen interest in harnessing the potential of this AI chatbot, which offers text generation capabilities beyond conventional machine translation. However, Chinese scholars have yet to present substantial research findings on fully utilizing ChatGPT. Most current discussions revolve around future challenges and opportunities. Taking the case of E-C translating *After the Victorians* in which the author consulted and tested ChatGPT, this paper explores the application of ChatGPT in the translation process, specifically focusing on supplementary background information and logical cues for comprehending the original text, rather than obtaining a translated version. The findings reveal that ChatGPT holds significant potential for assisting translators by providing valuable context, semantic interpretation references, and insightful observations, reasoning, and judgment cues necessary for understanding the source text. Nonetheless, its limitations are also evident. Due to its lack of nuanced recognition, ChatGPT occasionally fails to comprehend subtle nuances or contextual nuances in the discourse, resulting in incorrect or inappropriate responses. To maximize the effectiveness of ChatGPT in assisted translation, translators should capitalize on its strengths while navigating its weaknesses.

Key words: ChatGPT; assisted translation; *After the Victorians*; potentials; limitations

一、引 言

ChatGPT 横空出世已经几个月了,比尔•盖茨(Bill Gates)说,"ChatGPT 是他有生以来见到的两个最具革命性的技术进步之一",另一个是 Windows 这样的操作系统。他说,ChatGPT 会改变人们的工作、学习、旅行、交际方式,企业成功将会依赖使用它的技能与技巧(Rampton, 2023)。

"计算机辅助翻译工具广义上涵盖全部帮助翻译人员工作的软件,包括电子词典、搜索引擎以及文字处理软件等。"(黄丹彤, 2022)如今这个大家庭又添了一个"巨无霸"。译者们怎样才能像各行各业一样,也来个"忙趁东风放纸鸢",让翻译工作的效率与质量再"上新台阶"呢?

ChatGPT 对自己翻译能力的判断与腾讯、Intento 和微软的发现相似:"ChatGPT 的翻译可能不如专业翻译工具或专业翻译人员的翻译准确或精确"(Harby, 2023)。笔者也用一些例证进行过测试,总体发现与 ChatGPT 力不从心的自谦是符合的,因此,本文并非探讨 ChatGPT 所提供的英译汉译文的参考价值,而是测试它在帮助译者攻克翻译难点上提供咨询的能力。

笔者在翻译英国通俗史《后维多利亚时代人》(*After the Victorians*)(Wilson, 2005)的过程中,从理解原文所需的背景信息补充、思维逻辑线索提示等角度咨询了 ChatGPT,发现 ChatGPT 辅助翻译的潜力很大,但也有很多局限。

鉴于 ChatGPT 最佳语言训练模型是在英语里进行的(Yang, 2023),笔者与 ChatGPT 的会话均使用英语。为了节省篇幅,具体例证分析主要围绕 ChatGPT 辅助下原文难点的理解与翻译,一般略去整个例证的译文。本文中 ChatGPT 提供的所有咨询结果均来自 OpenAI, ChatGPT (3.5)(OpenAI, 2023),一般不再一一随文标注。

二、ChatGPT 辅助翻译的潜力

对原文的理解是译文读者通过译文感受原作的精华和魅力的前提。根据笔者的使用体验,ChatGPT 对于译者的主要价值在于,当原作的语言与文化背景有一定难度时,它能为译者提供理解原文所需的有价值的背景信息、语义解读参考、推理判断线索等。

除普遍性的优势——省时、可处理分析大文本数据、有些类型的数据提供或答案十分精确(TemPositions, 2023)之外,在为理解原文提供参考方面,同为人工智能的元宇宙,ChatGPT 明显超越了也具有相关匹配"联想能力"的传统搜索引擎,也超越了依赖源文本生成译文文本的机器翻译。ChatGPT 在跟译者的对话中,能够模拟乔姆斯基所说的那种人类语言能力,即能够连续读懂它从来没有读过的话,生成它从来没有读过或写过的文本,能够在一定程度上通过整合信息、分析、推理、联想、归纳、演绎等人类认知训练来应对、回答互联网从来没有问过的问题,提供全新的问题答案,能够承接前题,继续深入探讨后续问题、承认错误、挑战不正确的前提,能帮译者攻克上下文逻辑、一词多义、结构或语义歧义、文化背景缺失等方面的难题,或提供宝贵的提示或线索。尤其是,作为主要建立在英语文本的语言训练模型,它的回答更具有西方文化色彩,因此能补足译者理解源文本时所需要的西方文化视角。它能主动拒绝荒谬、违法、违德等不适当的请求,而且它所分配的应答者,可能是最恰当的聊天机器人,并能在几秒钟之内完成输出,几

乎可以说是秒问秒答。

（一）综合检索，整合输出

ChatGPT虽然达不到作者在场时"八攻八克"的命中率，但它可以同时提供上述多角度的智能辅助，其效率是人工逐条网络检索所不能比的。

例1

原文：The Luftwaffe had destroyed old Coventry—Cuffa's, Godiva's, Shakespeare's—as surely as the RAF would remove the life, the guts of German history.

My question：What does the elliptical phrase "Cuffa's, Godiva's, Shakespeare's" represent?

ChatGPT：The phrase "Cuffa's, Godiva's, Shakespeare's" is used to represent the different aspects of Coventry's heritage that were lost in the bombing. Cuffa's is possibly a reference to the ancient monastery of St. Mary's, which was founded by a Saxon nobleman named Cuffa. Godiva's refers to Lady Godiva, a famous historical figure associated with Coventry, known for her legendary ride through the streets of the city. Shakespeare's refers to the fact that the playwright William Shakespeare was reputedly born in nearby Stratford-upon-Avon, a town close to Coventry, and had connections to the city.

原文中三个所有格式省略结构是英国考文垂市的店铺，还是别的？询问ChatGPT后，它不但补充了省略的中心词"Coventry"，而且详细介绍了这三个词组如何概括了考文垂的历史文化：传说考文垂是如何根据"库法"命名的，"戈蒂娃"怎样与该市有一段美丽的传说，家乡曾与考文垂同属一郡的莎翁也常光顾此地，等等。

（二）知过不讳，重新研判

笔者提醒ChatGPT可能出错时，ChatGPT经常闻过则喜，知过不讳，重启研判过程。

例2

原文：The power of the spoken word was demonstrated in a different way by the Yorkshire novelist J. B. Priestley, whose voice first became familiar to people reading his novel *Let the People Sing*, and who subsequently broadcast talks.

My question：What is the logical subject or doer of "reading his novel"?

ChatGPT：The logical subject or doer of "reading his novel" is the people, as mentioned in the sentence. The sentence states that J. B. Priestley's voice became familiar to people who were reading his novel *Let the People Sing*. Therefore, the readers of his novel are the ones who first became familiar with his voice.

My question：How can the people be familiar with the author's voice by reading his novel?

ChatGPT：I apologize for the mistake in my previous response. Later in the sentence, it's mentioned that J. B. Priestley subsequently broadcast talks, which means that the people who were already familiar with his written work then had the opportunity to hear his actual spoken voice, which would have further reinforced their familiarity with him.

听其说话才能知其口音是个生活常识，怎么"他的声音最初为他的小说《让人民歌唱》的读者所熟悉"呢？ChatGPT先是坚持说他的读者通过阅读熟悉了他的声音。笔者提醒它这有违常识后，ChatGPT主动考虑了第二个定语从句的意义，给出了合乎常识的解读，即熟悉了他的作品及其风格的读者更可能关注他后来的广播谈话节目，因此也就成了最先熟悉他的声音的一批人。这就是所谓事情发展的过程合乎观察者预期判断的事件型逻辑。在笔者追问下，ChatGPT又确认了作家普里斯特利（Priestley）没有在任何电台广播过他的那部小说但介绍过他的小说。为防止误导，笔者特别把后一个定语从句译成了原因从句："他的声音最初为他的小说《让人民歌唱》的读者所熟悉，因为他后来又广播了谈话节目。"

（三）注释背景，显化改写

若找好提问的角度，ChatGPT既能解释句子的文化背景，又能给出该句的语内改写版本。

例3

原文：Hilaire Belloc absurdly believed that any priest who took longer than twenty minutes to say Mass was, or might be, a modernist.

My question：How come any priest who took longer than twenty minutes to say Mass was, or might be, a modernist?

ChatGPT：Hilaire Belloc believed that the traditional Latin Mass should be celebrated in a concise and efficient manner. Modernism emphasized personal interpretation of religious doctrine and Scripture, which Belloc believed was contrary to Catholic tradition. In Belloc's view, a priest who took longer than twenty minutes to say Mass might be a modernist because he might be adding personal interpretations to the traditional Mass. However, it should be noted that the length of a Mass is not a reliable indicator of a priest's theological beliefs.

在译者没太弄懂历史背景的情况下，照字面迻译常是保全的做法，但是把字面背后的意义留给译文读者去"寻味"则可能有违翻译的跨文化交际伦理（滕梅、宋醒，2022）。笔者咨询了ChatGPT，其结果令人惊喜：它既介绍了传统弥撒简短，且使用晦涩难懂的古拉丁语，又指出了现代主义者解释教义常夹带个人观点，又指出了贝洛克（Belloc）以此可信度极有争议的"征候"作为现代主义的标签（悬赏征罪）的荒谬性。经过查阅其他网站支撑资料，笔者决定使用脚注解释历史背景。

（四）拓宽语义，提供选择

例4

原文：It is certainly remarkable that the British adoption of the habit coincided with the period, roughly from the 1890s to the 1950s, of the sand and heat of the Empire, though it's hard to see exactly why the popularity of this observance, hitherto in history of unambiguously religious significance, should be seen as "primarily an imperial phenomenon".

My question：What does "sand and heat" in the above passage refer to?

ChatGPT：The term "sand and heat" refers to the geographical and environmental challenges faced by the British Empire during its expansion and maintenance of control in regions like Africa, the Middle East, and India, which are characterized by sandy deserts and hot climates.

此句中作者暗引了西恩·迈克尔（Sean Michael）的沙漠部族言情小说的书名 *Sand and Heat*（Michael，2003）。其字面既有"黄沙与热浪"的意思，也有"狂躁与发情"的意思。威尔逊巧妙地用这一书名来映射大英帝国的后期，也就是它在两次世界大战期间及前后虽已显倦态但仍在争霸的时期，尤其是阿拉伯的劳伦斯（Lawrence of Arabia）为大英帝国在中东扩展版图的时期。译文是否需要照顾到"激情"之义呢？ChatGPT虽然没有联想到作者对于那部小说名的"暗引"，但它认为，"沙和热"主要指大英帝国在这一时期里在亚非等地争霸时所遇到的自然环境挑战。最后笔者决定将其译成"'沙与热'时期",突出其字面意思。

三、ChatGPT辅助翻译的局限

笔者发现的ChatGPT的不佳表现完全符合一些国际人工智能学术网站对ChatGPT的总体评价:ChatGPT在回答常见问题或提供基本信息方面很有用,但可能无法处理更复杂的任务。"使用ChatGPT的一个重要缺点是它可能缺乏对细微差别的辩识,可能无法理解对话的微妙之处或上下文,从而导致不正确或不适当的反应"(TemPositions,2023)。

人脑对于自然语言及信息语码的解读、加工、创造性的重新编码过程至今仍然是个谜,而智能机器人的工作原理是为人类所知的。ChatGPT无法全面复制人的思维过程,无法全面而灵活地理解与运用人类道德伦理观念。它离不开互联网,只能随着互联网的变大而变大,它依赖"处理""管理""抓取"的大数据集合,具有"高密性""多样性""高速性"及"海量性"特点,但它要在人类不断"调教"训练中学会做出判断,有的判断也可能五岁孩子都能做对,而它做不对。兰姆顿(Rampton)坦言,截至2023年4月,ChatGPT仍然依赖截至2021年的互联网信息,而且这种网络信息既有"真言",又有谣言(Rampton,2023),尤其是在当今人人可以"拿话筒"、发微博的自媒体时代。郑世林等指出,"ChatGPT只能依靠语料库驱动中的概率匹配,在相近数据中得出一个估计值"(郑世林等,2023)。当然,大概率正确的事情是存在的,如投资领域里的基金定投等。但也存在因过多依赖于群体共识而陷入虚假共识的风险。如果入户数据库不更新,智能机器人对同一个问题的回答趋向一致,而人类对于人文社科问题的回答常因人因地因时而有所不同,且更有参考价值。如果是这样,这就成了ChatGPT之于辅助翻译的最大短板。译者所遇到的多数疑难问题大都涉及原文的微妙之处或上下文含义的问题。另外,文科专著不可能都上网,其内容深度与广度都远远大于互联网上"跑"的网文,这些都会使得高度依赖互联网数据的ChatGPT缺少可"参考"的权威数据包括出处(即所谓"互联网无历史")。

(一)联想疏漏,关联错位

ChatGPT擅长按词语的规约意义来解读句子,而不擅长结合句子的上下文来解读句子。如下面例(5)。有时需要提醒,它才注意具体的上下文,如上面的例(2)。

例5

原文:The plot of George Eliot's last great novel, *Daniel Deronda*, published in 1876, had hinged upon the discovery by the central character that he was Jewish, a fact unknown until his mature years. An American critic of our own day remarked that "Deronda had only to look". But not, in 1876, if he had been of Jewish origin, but brought up from birth as if gentile.

My question:"If Deronda had only to look at" what?

ChatGPT:The critic is suggesting that if Deronda had only looked at himself more closely or known more about his own family history, he could have discovered his Jewish identity earlier.

"那位文学评论家"认为百年前的小说《丹尼尔的半生缘》情节有硬伤,原因是"Deronda had only to look",意指"德龙达看看自己的私处(被行了割礼)即可自知自己是犹太人",不会拖到那么晚才发现自己的身世。这也是提出反批评(即在1876年时割礼尚未流行)的威尔逊(Wilson)与"那位文学评论家"的话语语义聚焦。问题是,英文原文字面并没有说"德龙达只消看一看"的是什么。亦即看的对象本可以按常识理解为容貌、肤色等。ChatGPT对笔者提出的原文中"看"的内容的提问的回答"仔细观察自己"和

"了解自己的身世",没有将威尔逊所质疑的"在1876年时,他还不能行那个礼"这个上下文纳入语义解读。而且,"了解自己的身世"的回答还有违养父母一般对抱养的孩子不透露身世的常识。为了正面引导译文读者,笔者对上句进行了显化处理:"德龙达只消看看自己的下面。"

笔者也发现ChatGPT在建立信息关联时有错位或疏漏的情况,如:

例6

原文:And here came the crowned heads of other lands, driving through the rain in their landaus—the big, jolly, laughing queen of Tonga, and opposite her the diminutive sultan of Johore. (Who was that? "Her lunch," replied Noël Coward.)

My question:What does "lunch" imply?

ChatGPT:In this context, Noël Coward was suggesting that the diminutive sultan of Johore was small enough to be the queen of Tonga's lunch. It is meant to be humorous and somewhat irreverent.

ChatGPT只强调喻体"一盒午餐"是用来夸张柔佛苏丹的矮小的,并认为这种玩笑对他有所不尊。我们相信互联网上肯定有东南亚地区的历史传说"食人族"一说,遗憾的是,ChatGPT并没有联想到。

(二) 单向思维,不谙变通

我们不能指望ChatGPT能系统学习一遍伦理学再做出伦理学上道德与功利关系的判断。中国伦理思想中占统治地位的是儒家思想,它主张"重义轻利",甚至走极端到"存天理,灭人欲"一说,而西方的伦理思想则具有功利主义色彩,中国重视动机和手段的合道德性而轻视结果,西方则把结果作为评价的重要标准(汪苗,2016)。如在下面语段的翻译中首先就要考虑到中西方人们伦理判断的差别,才能使读者更好地接受译文。

例7

原文:John Jacob Astor, worth two hundred million dollars: he "would give all he possesses for the place of that woman and child in the lifeboat" ... "The sixteen hundred who went down were typical of mankind..." opined *the Christian Century*. "Manhood triumphed when the Titanic sank."

My question:How come in the face of tragedy, Astor's "would give all he possesses for the place of that woman and child in the lifeboat" request serves as an example of "Manhood triumphed when the Titanic sank"?

ChatGPT:Astor's willingness to sacrifice his own life for the sake of a woman and child demonstrates the noblest aspects of human character and the strength of the human spirit in the face of tragedy.

My question:Please note that Astor wanted to buy the positions in the lifeboat for himself.

ChatGPT:In light of this information, Astor's actions cannot be seen as an example of "manhood triumphing" in the face of tragedy. In fact, his offer to buy his way onto a lifeboat rather than allow a woman and child to get on is selfish. The sentiment expressed by *the Christian Century* is misguided and ignores the selfishness that was also present in the response to the Titanic's sinking.

泰坦尼克海难时,船上规定必须等所有妇孺都上了救生艇后才能让男人上艇。当时富豪阿斯特(Astor)动过那个以钱换命的心思,但是,阿斯特最后不也和679名船员一样赴死海底了吗?从西方的伦理相对论角度,《基督教世纪》的评论"泰坦尼克下去了,人类精神上去了"就是有根据的,因为客观上,这680个人要想活下来是不难办到的。但是,译文如果遵循原作的省略式引用,习惯于道德绝对论的读者就会难以理解，以财换命的阿斯特的例子怎么成了"人类精神上去了"的支撑呢？所以，译文有必要增译"曾动过这个心思""没有造次"这样的词语以排除误导。笔者咨询ChatGPT，结果发现，它先是误认为阿斯特是在用钱给妇女儿童买救生艇上的位置，被笔者否定后，它开始谴责阿斯特的以财求命的不道德行为。

（三）观察失准，悟性不足

在下例里，ChatGPT明显缺乏在人对事物的态度洞察方向上的感悟能力。

例8

原文："The German Emperor is addicted to saying startling things to his own people and others, and our Government may safely be left to clear away any misconception on his part of the facts of this particular case (the Kruger telegram) unless, of course, he really wishes to force at once a quarrel with this country," *the Liberal Manchester Guardian* had written when Willy sent his tactless telegram congratulating Kruger for repulsing the Jameson raid in 1897. But the newspaper editors could have echoed the mood of the band in Portsmouth Harbour on 22 November 1899, when the Kaiser made one of his frequent visits: they played the old melody "Oh, Willie, We Have Missed You".

My question: What changes in the attitude of "newspaper editors" towards Kaiser are reflected in the passage?

ChatGPT: Initially, the editors of *the Liberal Manchester Guardian* expressed their disapproval of the Kaiser's habit of making startling comments and potentially causing conflict with other countries. However, as indicated by the reference to the band playing the melody "Oh, Willie, We Have Missed You" during one of the Kaiser's visits, there seems to be a change in attitude later on. This change could suggest a more light-hearted attitude towards the Kaiser. The editors began to see him in a less serious or influential light.

在"克鲁格电报"这一英德外交危机事件中，《曼切斯特卫报》一开始保持偏中立态度，相信政府应该能够澄清事实，消除德皇的错误认识，因为当时作为皇室彼此通亲的英德两国关系尚处于正常时期。到了第三年，英德贸易战、巴格达铁路等东进政策使得英德关系紧张，媒体也似乎感到了英德终有一战，因此又不去呼应港口热烈迎接德皇的气氛了。笔者就媒体对德态度的变化咨询了ChatGPT，结果令人失望，首先，它没能结合媒体相信政府在化解危机上能有所作为这一点来认识一开始媒体对德的偏中立态度。接着它把媒体后来对德态度说成了轻松、无所谓的态度。很明显，ChatGPT并不懂当时英德关系以及媒体态度前后的微妙变化。

（四）回译效果，乏善可陈

何为回译？A或B国作者用A国语言来写基于B国文化的作品。此时，将作品从A国语言翻译成B国语言时，涉及语际翻译的语码转换和文化特色的回归。A国语作品含有的B国文化中无现成文本内容的回译叫无本回译，当然，偶尔含有的有现成文本的回译叫文本回译（"哪来回哪去"）。笔者测试发现，除了谚语、俗语等高频语料，ChatGPT流于以非回译方法来处理需要文本回译的翻译。在下例中，它明显没有意识到网上已有数个带日文行文特点的中文译文。

例9

原文："Despite the best that has been done by everyone ... the war situation has developed not necessarily to Japan's advantage, while the general trends of the world have all turned against her interest. Moreover, the enemy has begun to employ a new and most cruel bomb, the power of which to do damage is indeed incalculable, taking the toll of many innocent lives. This is the reason why we have ordered the acceptance of the provisions of the *Joint Declaration of the Powers* …"

宣布接受《波茨坦公告》的昭和天皇的《终战诏书》是由日本汉学家模仿古汉语以汉文训读体写成的，网上有多个不具名的汉语版本。此内容只有回译才是上策，因为它能逼近流行于中日之间的具有古汉语特色的日文版本，可给译文增添历史感。当笔者咨询ChatGPT时，无论怎样提示，它给出的都是现代汉语的译文。笔者只好给出一个与各家略有不同的版本："朕之庶众已竭尽全力，但战局并未见起色，世界之大势亦于吾国不利，加之，敌新用残虐炸弹频杀伤无辜，惨害所及，实难逆料。此乃朕令政府接受《列国联合公告》之条款之缘故……"。

四、结 语

笔者在翻译《后维多利亚时代人》过程中，试图"鸟枪换炮"，从偶尔利用机器翻译给自己提供一些免查词典的机会，升级到使用ChatGPT来帮助自己解决翻译中所遇到的"语言图式""内容图式""结构图式"（Carrell & Eisterhold，1983）等方面的问题。笔者发现ChatGPT能拓宽译者的思路，提供更多的理解原文的线索，但也有很多局限。世界上有多少学科，翻译就涉及多少学科。翻译难点攻克必须依赖专门学科的系统专门知识，指望一个"万能"的ChatGPT用其网络"大杂烩"知识支撑来解答本该诉诸专门学科专家的问题，常常是勉为其难的。笔者感到，就攻克文史类英译汉翻译理解难点问题来说，原始的辅助手段的权威顺序尚不能改变：作者在场，咨询英美相关专家或学术性网络论坛，纸媒资料，广义的计算机辅助翻译（ChatGPT、互联网检索等）。

ChatGPT的最大优势是它能在一定可信可靠性的基础上简化改写（paraphrase）英语的句子包括语段，并能给出解释，从而帮助译者攻克难句的理解问题。尽管ChatGPT使用了巨大的文本语料，并进行了多轮训练以增强模型的准确性和泛化能力，译者使用它的时候还是需要巧妙地设计提示问题（prompt），以便使它的辅助翻译功能最大化，同时也为研发者提供使用反馈。

其实，本文研究的最大发现是，没有译者的广开思路在先，ChatGPT就不会发挥得充分。笔者一时记不起那句意思是好工具需要好使用者的英语谚语，于是求助ChatGPT，它不但优质服务，而且还"买一送一"地给出解释（略）："The proverb you are thinking of is likely 'A bad workman blames his tools'."（OpenAI，2023）再深聊几句，ChatGPT又告诉我：19世纪的美国牧师亨利·沃德·比彻（Henry Ward Beecher）曾写道："工具只是人手的延伸，而机器只是一种复杂的工具。"而现代脑科学家又说，"对大脑来说，工具只是工具，而不是手的延伸"。（OpenAI，2023）笔者明白了，确实，"拙匠怨工具"，再好的工具也不是大脑，好工具需要好使用者。

参考文献

[1] Carrell, P. & J. Eisterhold. Schema Theory and ESL Reading Pedagogy[J]. *TESOL Quarterly*. 1983, 4(3)：553-573.

[2] Harby, Abbie. Can I use ChatGPT for translation?[EB/OL]. [2023-5-25]. https://slator.com/resources/can-i-use-chatgpt-for-

translation/

[3] Huang, Dantong(黄丹彤). "Common Computer Aided Translation Tools in China and Abroad"(国内外常见计算机辅助翻译工具一览)[EB/OL]. (2022-02-23)[2023-05-25]. https://mp.weixin.qq.com/s/r4PYj5hktgROE00nFagx4w/

[4] Michael, S. *Sand and Heat*[M]. Torquere Press, 2003.

[5] OpenAI. ChatGPT (3.5)[Large language model]. [2023-05-20].https://chatgptmirror.com/chat?share=ZN306S/

[6] Rampton, John. The Advantages and Disadvantages of ChatGPT[EB/OL]. (2023-04-24)[2023-05-20]. https://www.entrepreneur.com/growth-strategies/the-advantages-and-disadvantages-of-chatgpt/450268/

[7] TemPositions. Examining ChatGPT's Pros and Cons in the Workplace[EB/OL]. (2023-05-11)[2023-05-25]. https://www.tempositions.com/blog/examining-chatgpts-pros-and-cons-in-the-workplace/

[8] Teng, Mei & Song, Xing(滕梅，宋醒). "The Translator's Choice of Responsibility from the Ethical Perspective of the Movie *The Translator*"(从电影《翻译家》看伦理视角下译者的责任选择)[J]. *Journal of Yanshan University (Philosophy and Social Science Edition)*(燕山大学学报(哲社版)). 2022（3）：38-44.

[9] Wang, Miao(汪苗). "The Relativity and Absoluteness of Morality"(道德的相对性与绝对性)[J]. *Business*(商). 2016(22)：151.

[10] Wilson, A. N. *After the Victorians* [M]. London: Arrow Books, 2005.

[11] Yang, Hong. How I Use ChatGPT Responsibly in My Teaching[EB/OL]. (2023-04-12)[2023-05-25]. https://doi.org/10.1038/d41586-023-01026-9/

[12] Zheng, Shilin, Yao, Shouyu & Wang, Chunfeng(郑世林，姚守宇，王春峰). "The Economic and Social Implications of ChatGPT as a New Generation AI Technology" (ChatGPT新一代人工智能技术发展的经济和社会影响)[J]. *Review of Industrial Economics* (产业经济评论). Network Debut (网络首发)（2023-03-12）．

作者简介

侯广旭，硕士研究生文凭（新加坡），南京农业大学外国语学院教授、硕士生导师。研究方向：翻译理论与实践，认知语言学。电子邮箱：1550119709@qq.com。

国内外五种机器翻译平台对比
——以特斯拉公司简介中文译文为例

⊙ 毛佳敏 张继光(江苏师范大学外国语学院,徐州)

[摘 要] 人工智能飞速发展的今天,信息交流与人机交互也在蓬勃发展,大数据、算法等更是日益重要。机器翻译自上世纪产生以来,发展历程经历过波折,但却始终向好。国内外就有关机器翻译的研究与平台应用也在井喷式出现。国外而言,谷歌翻译、微软必应翻译为代表,国内来看,百度翻译、有道翻译占尽主流。此外,最近大火的ChatGPT也占有一席之地。本文将以这些翻译平台为载体,以特斯拉公司英语简介的五种机器翻译译文为考察对象,以期从中发现机器翻译现存的问题与不足,提出相应改进建议,为学者们在机器翻译研究领域提供参考和借鉴。

[关键词] 机器翻译;译文对比;实用类文本;ChatGPT

Comparison of Five Domestic and Foreign Machine Translation Platforms:
Taking the Chinese Profile of Tesla Company as an Example

MAO Jiamin ZHANG Jiguang (Jiangsu Normal University, Xuzhou)

Abstract: Nowadays, the rapid development of artificial intelligence has witnessed booming information exchange and human-computer interaction as well as big data, and algorithms. Since the inception of machine translation in the last century, the development process has experienced ups and downs, but it has always been good. Research and platform applications related to machine translation at home (eg. Baidu and Youdao Translation) and abroad (eg. Google Translate and Microsoft Bing) are also blowing out. In addition, ChatGPT, which recently caught fire, also has a place. This paper will take these translation platforms as the carrier and take the five machine translation translations of Tesla's English introduction as the investigation object, in order to find out existing problems and shortcomings of machine translation, put forward corresponding improvement suggestions, and provide reference for scholars in the field of machine translation.

Key words: machine translation; comparison of translations; practical text; ChatGPT

一、引 言

当今世界是一个高度发展的世界,互联互通的世界,也是高新技术蓬勃发展的世界。国际间信息交流从未像今天这般密切。中国与世界的联系与交流也达到前所未有的状况。信息的大量流动就需要大量的信息交互，语言障碍需要克服，文化差异需要保存，传统习惯需要尊重等。"信息高速"也变成了"信息高铁"。仅靠人工翻译远远满足不了当下各领域需求，人类必须借助技术提高翻译效率，实现更快的信息传递。上世纪 50 年代，自计算机翻译问世以来，人们对机器翻译的研究并不是一直向前进，其间甚至经历过停滞。如今，机器翻译又重新回归大众视野，为世界国家间的信息交换提供便利。

人类对自然语言的认识是没有尽头的，机器翻译的研究也是没有尽头的（冯志伟，1999: 55）。新兴的 ChatGPT 翻译引起了不少轰动。本文就将 ChatGPT 与四种主流翻译平台的特斯拉公司简介中文译本进行对比，分析目前的机器翻译发展现状。

二、机器翻译发展现状

机器翻译 (machine translation) 是自然语言理解 (Natural Language Understanding, NLU) 中最早的一个研究分支，它是利用计算机把一种自然语言转变成另一种自然语言的过程。用以完成这一过程的软件叫做机器翻译系统（黄晨、陈海英，2007: 66）。机器翻译这一概念最早是 Warren Weaver (1955) 在关于《翻译》的备忘录中首次正式提出的，他认为机器翻译是可计算的，可解释为计算机解读密码的过程，自此拉开了机器翻译的研究序幕。然而在 60 年代，由于美国科学院发布的一份报告，认为机器翻译几乎毫无作用，也并未取得可见性成果，随即，机器翻译逐渐被认为无用，进入不受重视时期。机器翻译重回大众视野还是归功于网络的发展。到了 90 年代，世界国家间交流日益密切，信息转换与交互的需求也呈井喷式发展，传统靠人工进行翻译已经满足不了快速的信息交换速度，人们转而把目光投向机器翻译，因此，机器翻译也受到了众多家有需求的公司的追捧。需求带来商机，各公司也在相继开发计算机翻译应用或软件，机器翻译开始得到长足的发展。到了 21 世纪，人工智能成为热捧对象，机器翻译技术不断取得重大突破。随着人工智能、神经网络、深度学习技术不断融入，翻译技术从最初基于规则的机器翻译发展到依托云技术、大数据的神经网络机器翻译，小至手机的翻译 APP，大至翻译行业乃至语言服务领域中的云翻译，翻译技术不断推陈出新，迭代更替（王华树、李智，2020: 87）。目前，国内外几大搜索引擎公司研发的在线翻译系统，比如国外的谷歌翻译、微软必应翻译，国内的百度翻译、搜狗翻译、有道翻译等，是机器翻译的主流。此外，于 2022 年底出现在大众视野的 ChatGPT 也成了风靡全球的翻译引擎。

三、国内外几种机器翻译平台介绍

本文将要进行对比的译文皆来自主流的在线机器翻译软件：谷歌翻译、微软必应翻译、百度翻译、有道翻译和 ChatGPT。选择这几种机器翻译主要有以下原因：一、使用频率最高。单就谷歌翻译来说，2018 年，谷歌翻译提供了 103 种语言之间的互相翻译，每日活跃用户超过 5 亿人，2020 年，谷歌翻译在谷歌应用市场里"热门应用"中排第三名，手机客户端下载量更是超过了 5 亿次，收到评论 713 万条。2023 年，全球最大的中文搜索引擎百度搜索引擎推出的在线翻译语种已经涵盖了 200 种自然语言，每日响应过亿次的翻译需求，手机客户端下载量，以华为应用商店为例，也超过 1 亿次；微软必应翻译的手机移动端下载量甚至超过了两亿次；有道翻译也支持 107 种语言的互相翻译，手机客户端下载量也超过 1 亿次。二、在线语料搜索范围广。百度翻译有云端千万量级词条，并在线提供多种权威字典释义，海量例句、词组用例等。三、对机器翻译实例研究大多选择都是这几种机器翻译平台。以谷歌翻译为例，在知网上搜索"谷歌翻译"，共有相关文献 537 篇；搜索"百度翻译"出现相关文献 163 篇等。

机器翻译方法主要有实例法和统计法两种（马建军，2010: 114)。以实例为基础的机器翻译方法是通过对文本的表层分析和已经获得的经验知识，对文本进行类比，首先是先将原自然语言文本拆分成最小的翻译单位——短语或词汇，然后通过类比，找出合适的译入语短语和词汇，最后再按照译入语的句法结构组成一个完整的长句。而以统计为基础的机器翻译是在海量的语料库和信息库中找到最对应、最合适、匹配最恰当的对应翻译单元。运用统计学原理，找到匹配程度概率最大的翻译单元，得出相应的译入语文本。经过多年的发展和研究，加上机器的"深度学习"，目前，机器翻译也被广泛使用和得到广泛认可。

谷歌翻译于 2006 年 4 月正式推出，主要围绕统计机器翻译。非英语语言转换时必须先翻译成英语，再翻译成相应语种。以英语为中间媒介，实现其他自然语言间的转换。谷歌翻译的翻译过程主要是依靠分析大量的人工翻译文本，比如联合国官方文件和欧洲议会官方文件等。随着人工智能的更新迭代，谷歌翻译已升级为神经网络机器翻译，代替了传统的统计机器翻译提供翻译服务。

微软必应翻译是一种多语言机器翻译系统，由微软公司提供云服务。微软必应翻译集合了跨语种使用者、开发者和应用产品。它通过云服务，为商业文本和语音提供翻译服务。必应翻译首次于 2007 年推出。之前的最初版本是由微软公司于 1999 年到 2000 年间开发的微软搜索系统，该系统以逻辑形式为基础，借助为微软办公软件文本开发的语法纠正系统，发展而来。微软公司现行机器翻译和其他现代机器翻译类似，根据数据驱动而非依靠书面明细规则处理自然语言。

百度翻译于 2011 年首次向公众推出，百度翻译利用深度学习和机器为基础的翻译系统相结合，同时增加了统计学系统提升翻译质量。同时百度翻译还加入了光感识别系统，可以对图片直接进行翻译，使机器翻译的文本类型扩大化，不再仅仅局限于文字和语音。百度翻译使用交叉翻译方法 (Hybrid translation approach)，通过构建系统翻译系统 (statistical machine translation, SMT) 自动抓取互联网上语料库。同时实例法机器翻译也在使用。在翻译具体日期和数字方面，以规则为基础的翻译方法也在译前处理得以使用。

有道翻译隶属于网易有道公司，是中国最大的多语种在线免费机器翻译系统。其特色在于机器翻译是以搜索引擎为基础，释义选取互联网上资源，并根据互联网内容更新而自动更新。有道翻译利用搜索引擎的后台数据和"萃取网页"技术，从海量网页中提取实时更新的词汇短语释义。有道翻译还和几大比较权威的字典出版商，比如朗文、科林斯等合作，为用户提供更为全面且最佳的用户体验。

ChatGPT 是 2022 年底由美国人工智能实验室 Open AI 推出，是一种基于自然语言处理和机器学习的大型语言模型，俗称"聊天机器人"。同时，ChatGPT 也是以深度学习为代表的智能技术长期积累、创新整合的产物（孙伟平，2023: 42)。可以预见，这款软件的面世，对翻译领域产生的冲击是可观的，极大影响了翻译的质量及效率。基于其强大的语料库以及语言处理能力，本文将对该软件产出的译文与其他机器翻译产出的译文进行对比。

四、机器翻译译文质量评价标准

机器翻译系统的目的无非是读入原文，输出译文，系统的优劣及是否可用，关键在于译文的质量，因此译文质量的评估是判断翻译系统成功与否的核心问题（徐剑、梁茂成，1999: 99）。本次采用的语料选自特斯拉官方主页上的公司介绍文本。德国翻译家卡塔琳娜·莱斯 (Katharine Reiss) 提出的文本类型理论将文本类型划分为信息型 (informative)、表情型 (expressive)、操作型 (operative) 三类。基于公司简介文本拥有信息类比较密集，描述较为客观，逻辑性比较强，文体风格不多变的特点，可将该文本归属于信息型文本。对此类文本的翻译策略要求忠实原文、语句通顺。而机器翻译恰好在翻译信息型文本方面有比较优势，故采用实用类信息型文本为载体，分析几种机器翻译平台的译文，进行比较分析。

基于实例的机器翻译的思想最早是由日本机器翻译专家长尾真 (Makoto Nagao) 提出来的（王厚峰，2003: 33）。本次对比，笔者选用了日本机器翻译专家长尾真教授对机器翻译提出的参考标准。长尾真教授就机器翻译问题，提出可懂度和忠实度两个参考标准。两个参考标准分别划分为五个等级，分别标为 1-5。

（1）忠实度等级：

1. 目的语文章忠实地传达出原语文章所传达的意思。
2. 目的语文章忠实体现原语文章意思，少数部分需要修正。
3. 目的语文章基本忠实，但词序不当、词义选择不准确、时态处理不当、短语间关系、名词单复数及状语位置等错误，需要简单的修正。
4. 目的语文章出现漏译、内容丢失等严重现象。
5. 目的语文章完全不能让读者理解。

（2）可懂度等级：

1. 译文语篇清晰，没有歧义和其他令人生疑之处，译文词汇短语、语法规则、文体风格都非常贴切，不用做修改。
2. 译文语篇清晰，但是在词汇短语、语法规则、文体风格上有些许错误，但是不妨碍译入语读者理解。
3. 译文语篇可以基本理解，但是因为词汇短语、语法规则、文体风格有误，对译文的某些细节之处模棱两可。
4. 译文语篇的词汇短语、语法规则、文体风格出现错误多，译入语读者可以猜到原文所传达的基本意思。
5. 译文语篇完全不能够理解，必须经过他人重新翻译。

五、数据分析与讨论

测试文本摘取部分特斯拉公司英语简介，一共4句，单句平均长度均在15个单词以上，属于长句范畴。

在考察译文忠实度的等级时，为了保证忠实度等级标准把握的尺度，笔者选择了10名受过专业翻译训练的英语笔译硕士生，要求她们严格按照长尾真教授所确定的标准、对照原文去评判译文的忠实度等第；而在考察可懂度时我们则选择了10名普通系科本科一年级学生作为译文的等级归属的评判者，让其脱离原文考察译文的可懂度。评判结果均取平均值。这样，在考察过程中，我们就严格地保持了忠实度与可懂度评定的分离，从而更清晰、更独立地考察了机译系统对原文的分析处理能力及译语输出的水平（徐剑、梁茂成，1999：100）。

机器翻译译文举例，每个译文后面括号中的数字表示按照长尾真教授的两个参考标准分别打出的等级分数，前面一个为忠实度等级，后面一个为可懂度等级，最终测试结果见表1：

句一：Tesla believes the faster the world stops relying on fossil fuels and moves towards a zero emission future, the better.

谷歌翻译：特斯拉相信，世界越快不再依赖化石燃料，朝着零排放的未来迈进，那就更好。（4,2）

微软必应翻译：特斯拉认为，世界越快地不再依赖化石燃料，并朝着零排放的未来迈进，情况就越好。（3,2）

百度翻译：特斯拉认为，世界越快停止对化石燃料的依赖，朝着零排放的未来迈进，就越好。（4,2）

有道翻译：特斯拉认为，世界越快停止依赖化石燃料，走向零排放的未来，就越好。（4,2）

ChatGPT：特斯拉相信世界停止依赖化石燃料，转向零排放的未来越快越好。（4,1）

分析：综观这五句译本，在遇到 "the faster.... the better..."这种句式时，虽然各个翻译软件都能意识到比较级，但译本质量欠佳，都存在内容丢失的现象，尽管必应翻译出了"情况"，但内容仍不完整。因此根据忠实度的标准等级，必应翻译划为3等，其他划为4等。在不考虑忠实度的情况下，单从可懂度来看，ChatGPT的译文文字通顺，合乎汉语语法，更易为目的语读者所接受，可划为1等，而其他四种译本，读起来，有内容缺失之感，但不妨碍读者理解，因此只能划为2等。

句二：Today, Tesla builds not only all-electric vehicles but also infinitely scalable clean energy generation and storage products.

谷歌翻译：如今，特斯拉不仅制造全电动汽车，而且制造无限扩展的清洁能源发电和存储产品。（1,2）

微软必应翻译：如今，特斯拉不仅生产全电动汽车，还生产无限可扩展的清洁能源发电和存储产品。（1,2）

百度翻译：如今，特斯拉不仅生产所有电动汽车，而且还生产可无限扩展的清洁能源发电和储存产品。（3,2）

有道翻译：如今，特斯拉不仅生产全电动汽车，还生产可无限扩展的清洁能源生产和存储产品。（3,2）

ChatGPT：今天，特斯拉不仅生产全电动汽车，还生产可无限扩展的清洁能源发电和储能产品。（3,2）

分析：后三句译本分别存在 "all-electric" "generation"的误译，这仅仅是单词的表面意思，不符合语境；以及"today"翻译得不恰当，并不是"今天"这一天。而其他部分译文都能达到部分忠实，因此按照忠实度的标准，百度翻译、有道翻译以及ChatGPT的三句译文只能划为3等；而在可懂度等级上，这三句译文则可以划为2等，因为译文在目标语即汉语的语法和文字上是通顺可懂的。谷歌翻译和必应翻译尽管语义达到忠实，划为1等，但语篇较为生硬，因此可懂性归为2等。

句三：In 2019, Tesla unveiled Model Y, a mid-size SUV, with seating for up to seven, and Cybertruck, which will have better utility than a traditional truck and more performance than a sports car.

谷歌翻译：在2019年，特斯拉推出了Model Y，一款可容纳多达七个座位的中型SUV和Cybertruck，它将比传统卡车具有更好的实用性，并且比跑车具有更高的性能。（4,2）

微软必应翻译：2019年，特斯拉推出了Y型，一款中型SUV，最多可容纳7人，而赛博卡车将比传统卡车具有更好的实用性，性能也比跑车更好。（4,2）

百度翻译：2019年，特斯拉推出了一款中型SUV车型Y，座位最多可容纳7人，而Cybertruck将比传统卡车具有更好的实用性，性能也将超过跑车。（4,2）

有道翻译：2019年，特斯拉推出了中型 SUV Model Y 和赛博卡车 (Cybertruck)，前者最多可容纳七个人，后者的效用将超过传统卡车，性能也将超过跑车。（1,1）

ChatGPT: 2019年，特斯拉推出了Model Y中型SUV，可容纳七人，以及Cybertruck电动皮卡，它将比传统皮卡具有更好的实用性能和跑车级别的性能。（1,2）

分析：综观这五个译本，仅有道翻译是完全符合标准的。ChatGPT单从忠实度来看，可归为1等，而从可懂性标准来看，在语序调整的处理上还欠妥，因此归为2等。其余三个译本，逻辑意义上出现了错误，事实上，特斯拉于2019年是推出了Model Y和Cybertruck这两款产品，所以均存在歧义，并没有准确传达原文的意义。按照忠实度的标准，该三个译文只能划归为4等。从可懂度标准来看，可归为2等。虽然译文在逻辑意义上出现了错误，但在不考虑对原文的忠实与否，只考虑译语是否文从字顺、是否合乎汉语语法时，这一译文是通顺易懂的，在可懂度上是可以接受的。

句四：Launched in 2008, the Roadster unveiled Tesla's cutting-edge battery technology and electric powertrain.

谷歌翻译：敞篷跑车于2008年推出，展示了特斯拉的尖端电池技术和电动动力总成。（3,2）

微软必应翻译：跑车于 2008 年推出，推出了特斯拉的尖端电池技术和电动动力总成。（3,2）

百度翻译：这款跑车于 2008 年推出，推出了特斯拉最先进的电池技术和电动动力系统。（1,2）

有道翻译：这款跑车于 2008 年推出，揭开了特斯拉尖端电池技术和电力传动系统的面纱。（3,2）

ChatGPT: Roadster是特斯拉于2008年推出的，它展示了特斯拉尖端的电池技术和电动动力系统。（1,1）

分析：对于"cutting-edge battery technology"的处理，除百度翻译和ChatGPT译本，都存在问题。cutting-edge意为最先进的、尖端的，通过查找资料，发现并不存在"尖端电池"这种说法，没有"的"会让读者误以为是某个新技术，造成一定的歧义，因此需要修改。从忠实度来看，谷歌、必应以及有道翻译只能划为3等。从可懂度标准来看，前四种译文语篇虽相对清晰，但语感欠佳，还需做修改，因此划为2等。

表1 忠实度与可懂度等级例示

平台 句子	谷歌		必应		百度		有道		ChatGPT	
	忠实度	可懂度	忠实度	可懂度	忠实度	可懂度	忠实度	可懂度	忠实度	可懂度
一	4	2	3	2	4	2	4	2	4	1
二	1	2	1	2	3	2	3	2	3	2
三	4	2	4	2	4	2	1	1	1	2
四	3	2	3	2	1	2	3	2	1	1

六、统计分析

本文按照长尾真教授的标准分析对比了谷歌翻译、必应翻译、百度翻译、有道翻译以及ChatGPT五种机器翻译的译文，统计出以下结果：表格第一列表示对译入语的评判等级，其他数字为在该等级中出现的句子数量（见表2）。

表2 各系统在忠实度及可懂度上各等级的总句子数对照情况

平台 等级	谷歌		必应		百度		有道		ChatGPT	
	忠实度	可懂度	忠实度	可懂度	忠实度	可懂度	忠实度	可懂度	忠实度	可懂度
1级	1	0	1	0	1	0	1	1	2	2
2级	0	4	0	4	0	4	0	3	0	2
3级	1	0	2	0	1	0	2	0	1	0
4级	2	0	1	0	2	0	1	0	1	0
5级	0	0	0	0	0	0	0	0	0	0

为了对表格中的数字进行量化，我们对以上的统计结果进行加权计算：目的语文章等级为1级，则加3分；等级为2级，加2分；等级为3级，加1分；等级为4级，减1分；等级为5级，减2分。由此，可以计算出各机器翻译平台的总体得分情况：

谷歌翻译得分：

(1+0)×3+(0+4)×2+(1+0)×1-(2+0)×1-(0+0)×2=10

微软必应翻译得分：

(1+0)×3+(0+4)×2+(2+0)×1-(1+0)×1-(0+0)×2=12

百度翻译得分：

(1+0)×3+(0+4)×2+(1+0)×1-(2+0)×1-(0+0)×2=10

有道翻译得分：

(1+1)×3+(0+3)×2+(2+0)×1-(1+0)×1-(0+0)×2=10

ChatGPT得分：

(2+2)×3+(0+2)×2+(1+0)×1-(1+0)×1-(0+0)×2=16

以上的数据对比可以看出ChatGPT名列第一，其次是微软必应翻译，继而才是谷歌翻译、百度翻译以及有道翻译，这三者不相上下。

七、结论及思考

通过以上的比较与分析，笔者得出如下结论：

1. ChatGPT将为新晋翻译"网红"。在这次的机器翻译译文比较中，新兴的ChatGPT的翻译水平的确比其他机器翻译平台要高得多。在特斯拉公司简介这种非文学翻译中，ChatGPT能够辨析句式，识别专业术语，其产出译文也相对其他翻译平台更符合中文读者的习惯。但从整体来看，ChatGPT的翻译能力还有很大的发展空间。反观其他几种翻译平台，翻译水平不相上下，没有太大的差距。但通过本次分析，可以猜测，此后国内外学者选择翻译平台时，ChatGPT可能会成为首选。

2. 国内外大多数学者研究机器翻译，多数是以谷歌翻译平台为例，众多研究者认为谷歌翻译依靠的是强大的谷歌搜索引擎平台带来的海量数据库和信息库。然而，张克亮（2007）研究发现机器翻译方法依赖于语料库，而语料库的性质和质量参差不齐。可是从这篇实用类文本机器翻译对比情况来看，翻译质量还是有待提高和加强。

3. 机器翻译员平台分别采用各自独有技术，实现了较好的机器翻译。这得益于背后许多工作人员的艰辛努力与付出。过往几十年，机器翻译的结果却差强人意，尤其是其准确性和可读性往往令人失望（刘启源，2016: 123）。但是，随着谷歌公司在2016年发布神经机器翻译系统，机器翻译在译文准确性和流畅性方面比以前的基于统计的机器翻译译文质量有了大幅度提升，机器翻译在语言服务行业的应用更加广泛（崔启亮，2020: 108）。随着技术的发展，这些翻译平台将会受到鞭策而不断发展，产出更佳的译文，低级的翻译平台终将会被取代，译本忠实度以及可懂性正不断提高。

4. 这也要求译者在选择使用机器翻译的同时，注意甄别。根据不同的文本类型采取不同的翻译策略，是否使用机器翻译，对机器翻译有什么样的预期等等。

5. 机器翻译得出的译文还是有很多的漏洞，比如在词汇的选择上不够灵活，在语言的框架组织上不够亲近译入自然语言等等，也印证了"句子结构稍一复杂，修饰成分和限定成分一多，机器处理就开始力不从心"（罗季美，2014: 118）。这也势必需要人工的译后编辑来进一步对译文进行优化，得出更容易使读者所接受的译文。

6. 科技的进步，带动了翻译模式的创新和发展。随着机器翻译借助神经网络技术的发展使译文精度不断提升，译者的角色主要转向译后编辑（闫欣、陈瑞哲等，2019: 25）。译后编辑的发展始终与机器翻译的发展紧密相随，机器翻译的发展是译后编辑的基础（崔启亮，2014: 69）。人机交互的融合是语言服务行业的发展趋势。译者要以包容和接纳的心态对待机器翻译，因为译者不会被机器翻译取代，但技术会不断孕育新的ChatGPT，这是ChatGPT的时代。

参考文献

[1] Cui, Qiliang (崔启亮). "Post-editing of Machine Translation" (论机器翻译的译后编辑) [J]. *Chinese Translator Journal* (中国翻译), 2014(6): 68-73.

[2] Cui, Qiliang (崔启亮). "A Study on the Translators' Technical Practical Competence in the AI Era" (AI 时代的译者技术应用能力研究) [J]. *Foreign Languages and Cultures* (外国语言与文化), 2020(1): 104-110.

[3] Feng, Zhiwei (冯志伟). "Machine Translation: from Dream to Reality" (机器翻译———从梦想到现实) [J]. *Chinese Translators Journal* (中国翻译), 1999(5): 52-55.

[4] Huang, Chen & Chen, Haiying (黄晨，陈海英). "Application of Machine Translation in China-America Digital Academic Library" (机器翻译在CADAL中的应用) [J]. *Library & Information* (图书与情报), 2007(1): 66-68+85+5.

[5] Liu, Qiyuan (刘启源). "Comparison and Evaluation of Two Machine Translations" (两种机器翻译的对比及测评) [J]. *Course Education Research* (课程教育研究), 2016(10): 123-124.

[6] Luo, Jimei (罗季美). "Analysis of Syntactic Errors in Machine Translation" (机器翻译句法错误分析) [J]. *Journal of Tongji University(Social Science Edition)* (同济大学学报(社会科学版)), 2014(1): 111-118+124.

[7] Ma, Jianjun (马建军). "A Comparative Analysis of the Ambiguity Resolution of Two English-Chinese MT Approaches: RBMT and SMT" (基于规则和统计的机器翻译方法歧义问题比较分析) [J]. *Journal of Dalian University of Technology (Social Sciences)* (大连理工大学学报(社会科学版)), 2010(3): 114-119.

[8] Sun, Weiping (孙伟平). "Work Competition between Human and Machine: Challenges and Solutions: from the World's Most Popular ChatGPT" (人机之间的工作竞争：挑战与出路——从风靡全球的ChatGPT谈起) [J]. *Ideological & Theoretical Education* (思想理论教育), 2023(3): 41-47.

[9] Wang, Houfeng (王厚峰). "Method and Issues of Example: Based on Machine Translation" (基于实例的机器翻译——方法和问题) [J]. *Terminology Standardization and Information Technology* (术语标准化与信息技术), 2003(2): 33-36.

[10] Wang, Huashu & Li, Zhi (王华树，李智). "A Study on Translation Technology in the Age of Artificial Intelligence: Connotation, Classification and Trends" (人工智能时代的翻译技术研究:内涵、分类与趋势) [J]. *Foreign Languages and Cultures* (外国语言与文化), 2020(1): 86-95.

[11] Xu, Jian & Liang, Maocheng (徐剑，梁茂成). "An Evaluation of Some Popular English-Chinese Machine Translation Systems" (对几种英汉机器翻译系统的测评) [J]. *Applied Linguistics* (语言文字应用), 1999(2): 97-102.

[12] Yan, Xin & Chen, Ruizhe & Zhang, Jing (闫欣，陈瑞哲，张井). 翻译技术云平台的发展现状与趋势 [J]. *Chinese Science & Technology Translators Journal* (中国科技翻译), 2019(1): 22-25.

[13] Zhang, Keliang (张克亮). "Sentence Category and Format Transformation of Machine Translation" (面向机器翻译的汉英句类及句式转换) [M]. Henan: Henan University Press (河南：河南大学出版社), 2007.

作者简介

毛佳敏（第一作者），江苏师范大学在读研究生。研究方向：机器翻译、翻译学。电子邮箱：MJMSuccess@163.com。

张继光（通讯作者），博士，江苏师范大学副教授，硕士生导师。研究方向：翻译学、语料库语言学。电子邮箱：jsnuzjg@126.com。

评价理论视角下ChatGPT与人工汉英翻译对比研究
——以《主席新年贺词》为例

⊙ 林泽钦（广东外语外贸大学高级翻译学院，广州）

[摘 要] ChatGPT的发布对翻译行业带来一定的冲击，人们对ChatGPT时代人工翻译前景提出了质疑。本文从评价理论态度系统视角出发，对比ChatGPT与人工英译《主席新年贺词》在再现态度资源及其情感极性方面的差异，旨在考查两者对于原文中相关对象情感态度把握的准确性，从而比较两者在原文理解和译文产出上的差异。本文发现人工翻译对于原文态度以及情感的理解和再现能力优于ChatGPT翻译，具体表现为人工翻译对于情绪的捕捉和再现能力、对于事物的鉴赏能力更佳。这些差异表明，人工译者具备译者主体性，而ChatGPT目前所表现出的"涌现"能力具有局限性。通过上述对比，本文发现了人工翻译的优势和ChatGPT的劣势，并为ChatGPT时代人工译者提出了建议。

[关键词] ChatGPT；人工翻译；评价理论；态度系统；新年贺词

A Comparative Study Between ChatGPT and Human C-E Translation Based on the Appraisal Theory: A Case Study of the "*New Year Address by President Xi*"

LIN Zeqin (Guangdong University of Foreign Studies, Guangzhou)

Abstract: People call into question the prospect of human translation in the ChatGPT age in light of the influence that ChatGPT has had on the translation industry. This study evaluates the differences between ChatGPT and human C-E translation of President Xi's New Year Address in terms of reproducing the attitude resources and their sentiment polarity from the perspective of the attitude system of the appraisal system. It seeks to examine the accuracy of the two in grasping the attitude of the relevant objects in the original text in order to assess the differences between the two in comprehending the original text as well as producing the translated text. It is discovered that human translators perform better than ChatGPT translators in capturing and reproducing the attitudes and emotions in the original text, which is evidenced by the higher skill of human translators in capturing and reproducing emotions and appreciating things. These distinctions show that human translators give play to their subjectivity and that ChatGPT's "emergent" capability currently has its own limitations. The advantages of human translation and the disadvantages of ChatGPT are discovered through the comparison above, and recommendations for human translators in the ChatGPT era are provided as a result.

Key words: ChatGPT; human translation; appraisal theory; attitude system; New Year Address

引 言

2022年11月30日，基于"预训练模型（pre-trained models）"范式的大语言模型（Large Language Model，LLM）ChatGPT正式开展了公众测试，能够执行文本问答、论文写作、语言翻译等较为复杂的任务。与过去的"词典+规则""统计模型""深度学习模型"等范式相比，基于"预训练模型"的方法在语言理解和生成方面取得了重大的历史性突破，引起了广泛的关注。

从GPT-1的1.17亿参数到GPT-4的1.8万亿参数，预训练模型的训练参数呈现指数型增长的趋势。训练参数的增加不仅提升了模型的性能，当参数超过500亿时，还出现了目前无法解释的"涌现（emergence）"现象。现代"涌现"概念的提出者Holland将这一现象描述为"复杂的事物从小而简单的事物发展而来"（Holland，2006：2），即从量变到质变的飞跃。这种"涌现"现象表现为ChatGPT的语言能力越来越接近于人类，并具备上下文学习（in-context learning）能力以及初步的逻辑推理能力（冯志伟，2023）。一时间，人工翻译似乎"黯然失色"。在此背景下，人们不禁发出疑问：当前ChatGPT翻译在原文理解和译文产出上与人工翻译还有何差异？

Martin和White所提出的评价系统（appraisal system）是关于系统功能语言学人际意义的赋值系统，主要关注"作者/说话者在语篇中对所呈现的材料和交际的对象所持有的立场"（Martin & White，2012：1）。评价理论对于揭示语篇中所承载的评价资源具有重要作用（刘世铸，2012；王振华，2004；张先刚，2007），优秀的翻译应该"尽可能地把源语语篇的评价意义转换到目的语语篇中来"（司显柱、庞玉厚，2018：98），因此，考查原文和译文语篇中评价意义是否对等是"翻译质量评估的重要组成部分"（同上）。态度系统是评价系统的核心，"态度（attitude）"包括作者的情感反应、对于行为的判定以及对于事物的鉴赏（Matin & White，2012：35）。以评价理论中的态度系统为基础，比较人机翻译有助于研究两者对原文中相关对象情感态度把握的准确性，从而比较两者在原文理解和译文产出方面的差异。然而，目前学界对此方面的关注还不够充分。

综上所述，本文以评价理论中的态度系统为视角，通过比较ChatGPT翻译与人工翻译在再现态度资源及其情感极性方面的差异，旨在揭示两者在原文理解和译文产出方面的差异，并分析这些差异所反映出的现象，为人工翻译发展提供建议。

一、评价理论及该视角下的翻译研究综述

（一）评价理论

评价理论是对系统功能语言学人际意义的发展，主要研究作者如何通过评价资源表达对语篇中涉及对象的态度和立场。实现评价意义的资源（主要依靠词汇实现）归属三个子系统，即态度系统（attitude）、介入系统（engagement）以及级差系统（graduation）。态度与情感、行为以及事物的评价相关，介入是态度的来源，级差则是对态度介入程度的分级。可见，后两者都是围绕着态度系统这个核心。态度既包括正面（positive），也包括负面（negative），态度系统又可分为"情感（affect）""判定（judgement）"和"鉴赏（appreciation）"三个子系统。"情感"涉及构筑情感反应的资源，该系统包含品质情感（affect as quality）、过程情感（affect as process）和评注情感（affect as common）；"判定"是指根据各种规范性原则对行为进行评判的资源，该系统又可分为社会尊重（social esteem）（包括行为规范、能力、韧性）和社会约束（social sanction）（包括行为真实性、正当性）；"鉴赏"则关注构筑事物价值的资源，该系统又可分为反应（作者评价对象的反应）、构成（评价对象的均衡性和复杂性）以及价值（评价对象的创新性和及时性）（Matin & White，2012：35-56）。

（二）评价理论视角下的翻译研究综述

随着研究的深入发展，评价理论的应用逐渐从语言学领域拓展到翻译学领域，对翻译理论和翻译实践都具有重要的指导意义（司显柱、庞玉厚，2018：98）。目前，在评价理论视角下的翻译研究主要集中在人工翻译领域，其中非文学翻译方面的研究较为突出。商业翻译方面，徐珺（2011）将评价理论应用于商务翻译实践，验证了该方法的有效性和可行性。徐珺（2013）还对比分析了英汉公司简介中态度资源的分布特征及实现方法，揭示了其背后蕴含的文化内涵。新闻翻译方面，鄢佳（2013）分析了奥运新闻标题译文评价意义与原文不一致的情况。政治文献翻译方面，司炳月（2019）从评价理论的级差系统研究外宣文本及其英语译本中级差资源类型、分布特点和对文本其他意义的调节效果。于丽（2021）在评价理论框架下研究政治文献汉英翻译中译者的主体性。将评价理论运用于文学翻译研究的学者较少。夏云（2009）、余继英（2010）从评价理论视角分别以《飘》和《阿Q正传》为例探讨小说人物形象和译文意识形态。周晓梅（2017）对《乔布斯情书》汉译本中隐性评价进行了研究，而林国丽（2017）则关注了比较《狼图腾》与《无风之树》译者所采集的显化与隐化策略及其背后所体现的价值取向。

针对评价理论态度系统视角开展的翻译研究数量不多，从研究对象上看也大体可以分为文学和非文学翻译。非文学翻译方面，钱宏（2007）基于态度系统，对比四则国际品牌香水广告的英汉文本以考察译文的"不忠实"现象及其成因。扶丽华（2010）运用态度系统研究商务语篇态度，发现商务语篇明显具有礼貌、体谅等特点，在体现方式上既有显性也有隐性。李成陈（2017）以态度系统为框架对比60篇中英学术专著他序态度资源的分布特征及实现手段。陈曦蓉（2019）基于华为公司相关语料探讨年报致辞语篇态度的表达方式和翻译策略。侯奕茜（2021）结合概念隐喻以及态度系统，搭建了基于态度的政治隐喻翻译模型。文学翻译方面，陈梅（2013）探讨Levy英译白居易诗歌在态度资源方面的忠实性。鞠玉梅（2016）基于判断系统（态度系统子系统）来研究《论语》修辞功能在译本中的再现。

由此可见，近年来鲜有研究者从评价理论态度系统视角对人机翻译进行对比研究。为弥补研究不足，本文从该理论视角出发对比ChatGPT翻译与人工翻在再现态度资源及其情感极性方面的差异，并分析差异所反映出来的现象，并为人工翻译发展提供建议。本文尝试回答以下问题：（1）ChatGPT翻译和人工翻译在态度资源及其情感极性的再现上存在怎样的差异？（2）这些差异反映了什么现象？

二、研究设计

（一）数据来源

为了从态度系统对比ChatGPT翻译与人工翻译的差异，本文选取2019-2023年共计5年的《主席新年贺词》（下称《新年贺词》）作为原文，选取发表于"中国日报网（China Daily）"上的英译作为人工翻译译文，并选取ChatGPT-3.5根据指令（"请翻译下列文字："+《新年贺词》原文）所生成的译文作为

ChatGPT译文。原文共计14814字，译文共计21245词。主席每年通过新年贺词向世界展示中国在过去一年所取得的成绩，展望美好的未来，为中国乃至世界人民送去新春祝福，贺词中不乏对劳动人民、英雄和士兵的赞扬，对受难者的同情，以及对不法行为的批评，因此《新年贺词》的态度资源较为丰富，具有代表性。

本文使用"微词云"在线设计平台®作为数据收集工具。"微词云"是一款功能强大的在线文字处理工具，提供中英文分词、词性标注、情感分析功能。

（二）研究步骤

由于态度资源的主要实现手段为名词、动词、形容词和副词四类实词，而且作为评价词汇时，这些词通常承载着正面或负面的评价情感。因此，本研究重点关注这四类词中具有正面或负面态度的词汇。

首先，使用微词云对《新年贺词》的原文以及人工和ChatGPT翻译进行分词和词性标注，从中筛选出名词、动词、形容词和副词四类词。

其次，使用微词云分别对筛选出来的中英文词汇进行情感分析，剔除中性态度词汇，保留具有正面或负面态度的词汇，并记录词汇情感极性。

再次，将筛选出来的词汇在原文和两组译文中高亮出来，并根据语境，由两名专业译员剔除不具备评价意义的词汇，并对剩下的词汇进行分类标注。若两名标注人员出现标注不一致的情况，则提交至第三名专业译员进行讨论以达成一致。情感资源标注为"Af"，其子系统包含品质情感（AfQ）、过程情感（AfP）和评注情感（AfC）；判定资源标注为"Ju"，其子系统包含社会尊重（JuE）和社会约束（JuS）；鉴赏资源标注为"Ap"，其子系统包含反应（ApR）、构成（ApC）和评估（ApV）。使用霍斯提(Holsti)公式（信度=2m/(m1+m2)）计算两名标注人员的信度，信度达到可用水平（r=0.85>0.80）。

最后，统计原文、人工翻译和ChatGPT翻译各类态度资源及其正负极性数量和占比，并借助IBM SPSS Statistics 26分别对ChatGPT翻译与原文、人工翻译与原文的数据进行Mann-Withney-Wilcoxon检验（非正态分布），最终制成表格。

三、数据收集结果和差异分析

（一）数据收集结果

经过人工标注和数据整理阶段，我们得到原文、人工翻译和ChatGPT翻译各类态度资源和情感极性分布情况，如下表（见表1和表2）：

表1 各类态度资源分布情况

	总计	Af			Ju			Ap			Z	p
原文	387	26 6.72%			210 54.26%			151 39.02%				
		AfQ	AfP	AfC	JuE	JuS		ApR	ApC	ApV		
		8 5.30%	10 6.62%	8 5.30%	158 75.24%	52 24.76%		83 54.97%	19 12.58%	49 32.45%		
ChatGPT翻译	328	23 7.01%			173 52.74%			132 40.24%				

		AfQ	AfP	AfC	JuE	JuS	ApR	ApC	ApV		
		11	8	4	127	46	76	19	37	-2.028b	0.043<0.05
		8.33%	6.06%	3.03%	73.41%	26.59%	57.58%	14.39%	28.03%		
			28		185		150				
			7.71%		50.96%		41.32%				
人工翻译	363	AfQ	AfP	AfC	JuE	JuS	ApR	ApC	ApV	-0.931b	0.352>0.05
		8	13	7	140	45	85	20	45		
		5.33%	8.67%	4.67%	75.68%	24.32%	56.67%	13.33%	30.00%		

态度资源数量方面，原文情感资源共计387个，ChatGPT翻译共计328个，人工翻译共计363个。从三个子系统的角度来看，原文情感、判定和鉴赏资源数量分别为26（6.72%）、210（54.26%）、151（39.02%）；ChatGPT翻译为23（7.01%）、173（52.74%）、132（40.24%）；人工翻译则为28（7.71%）、185（50.96%）、150（41.32%）。对ChatGPT翻译与原文、人工翻译与原文在三个态度子系统下的子类资源数量进行Mann-Withney-Wilcoxon检验后发现，ChatGPT翻译与原文在态度资源分布方面存在显著差异（p=0.043<0.05），而人工翻译与原文在态度资源分布方面的差异性则不显著（p=0.352>0.05）。

表2 各类态度资源情感极性分布情况

	总		Af		Ju		Ap		Z	p
	正面	负面	正面	负面	正面	负面	正面	负面		
原文	365	22	22	4	202	8	141	10		
	94.32%	5.68%	84.62%	15.38%	96.19%	3.81%	93.38%	6.62%		
ChatGPT翻译	317	11	21	2	167	6	129	3	-2.207b	0.027<0.05
	96.91%	3.09%	94.74%	5.26%	96.53%	3.47%	97.73%	2.27%		
人工翻译	343	20	23	5	175	10	145	5	-0.912b	0.362>0.05
	94.49%	5.51%	82.14%	17.86%	94.59%	5.41%	96.67%	3.33%		

态度资源情感极性方面，原文正面评价词汇共计365个（94.32%），负面评价词汇共计22个（5.68%）；ChatGPT翻译正面评价词汇共计317个（96.91%），负面评价词汇共计11个（3.09%）；人工翻译正面评价词汇共计343个（94.49%），负面评价词汇共计20个（5.51%）。通过对ChatGPT翻译与原文、人工翻译与原文在三个态度子系统下的子类资源情感极性进行Mann-Withney-Wilcoxon检验后发现，ChatGPT翻译与原文在态度资源情感极性分布方面存在显著差异（p=0.027<0.05），而人工翻译与原文态度资源情感极性分布方面的差异性则不显著（p=0.362>0.05）。

（二）态度资源分布差异分析

1. 总体差异分析

态度资源数量方面，ChatGPT翻译比原文少了59个评价资源，而人工翻译比原文少了24个。人工翻译评价资源总数更接近原文，说明人工翻译对于原文态度资源的判断和再现能力优于ChatGPT翻译。

从三个子系统的态度资源数量看，原文同ChatGPT翻译和人工翻译在情感、判定、鉴赏三类态度资源数量上的差值分别为3、37、19和-2、25、1。可以观察到，三者在情感资源数量上差异较小。其中，ChatGPT翻译出现欠额翻译（under-translation）现象，未能再现原文全部情感资源，而人工翻译则出现超额翻译（over-translation）现象。ChatGPT翻译和人工翻译对于原文的判定资源转再现都不足，但ChatGPT翻译与原文差距较大，人工翻译与原文差距较小。鉴赏资源方面，ChatGPT翻译与原文差异较大，而人工翻译与原文几乎没有差异。

从三个子系统的态度资源占比看，原文同ChatGPT翻译和人工翻译在情感、判定、鉴赏三类态度资源占比上的差值分别为-0.29%、1.52%、-1.23%和-1.00%、3.30%、-2.30%。通过绝对值比较两者与原文的占比差距，人工翻译与原文的差异大于ChatGPT翻译。究其原因，主要是人工翻译在尽量再现原文情感和鉴赏资源的情况下，判定资源出现了较多的欠额翻译，所以导致三类资源比例略有失调。ChatGPT翻译虽然在三种资源的占比上更接近人工翻译，但在资源数量的还原度上却明显不及人工翻译。

态度资源情感极性方面，ChatGPT翻译和原文相比，正面评价词汇少了48个，负面评价词汇少了11个，而人工翻译则分别少了22个和2个。从情感极性占比看，ChatGPT翻译与原文差距较大，而人工翻译与原文几乎无差别。由此可见，总体而言，人工翻译情感极性再现能力优于ChatGPT翻译。

2. 情感资源差异分析

情感资源数量方面，ChatGPT翻译未能完全还原原文的质量品质、过程和评注情感资源，出现或多或少的欠额或超额翻译，因此三种情感资源的占比与原文相比有高有低。而人工翻译只有过程翻译的情感资源比原文略高，其他两种情感资源数量和占比几乎与原文没有差异。

情感资源情感极性方面，ChatGPT翻译正面评价词汇的占比比原文高出不少，负面评价词汇占比偏低，而人工翻译两种评价词汇的占比则与原文几乎没有差异。

例1：

原文： "两个一百年"奋斗目标历史交汇，我们开启了全面建设社会主义现代化国家新征程，正**昂首阔步（AfP）**行进在实现中华民族伟大复兴的道路上。

人工翻译： At the historical convergence of the Two Centenary Goals, we have set out on a new journey of building a modern socialist country in all respects and are making **confident (AfP)** strides on the path toward the great rejuvenation of the Chinese nation.

ChatGPT翻译： The historical convergence of the "Two Centenary Goals" marked the beginning of a new journey toward comprehensively building a modern socialist country, and we are marching **proudly (AfP)** and **confidently (AfP)** on the road to achieve the great rejuvenation of the Chinese nation.

"昂首阔步"的意思是"抬起头迈开大步向前"，既能形容精神振奋，也能形容态度傲慢。例子中"昂首阔步"主要体现了人们对于"行进在实现中华民族伟大复兴的道路上"自信的情感。人工翻译将其翻译为"make confident (AfP) strides"较为准确，而ChatGPT使用两个副词"proudly (AfP)"和"confidently (AfP)"修饰"march"会让人误以为是"昂首阔步"的后一个意思，与原文态度资源数量和所体现的态度意义不符。

3. 判定资源差异分析

判定资源数量方面，ChatGPT翻译和人工翻译都没有完全还原原文的社会尊重和社会约束两类判定资源，但人工翻译在社会尊重资源的数量上比ChatGPT翻译更加接近原文，两类判定资源的占比也更加接近原文。

判定资源情感极性方面，ChatGPT翻译正负面评价词汇均少于原文，但两者占比与原文较为接近。人工翻译正面评价词汇数量更加接近原文，但负面评价词汇略多于原文，所以导致正面词汇占比略低于原文，负面评价词汇略高于原文。总体上三者正负面评价词汇的占比差异不大。

例2：

原文：无数**平凡**（JuE）**英雄**（JuE）**拼搏**（JuE）**奋斗**（JuE），汇聚成新时代中国**昂扬奋进**（JuE）的洪流。

人工翻译：The **hard** (JuE) work and **dedication**(JuE) of countless **unsung** (JuE) **heroes** (JuE) have all added to the great momentum of China's **march** (JuE) forward in the new era.

ChatGPT 翻译：Countless **ordinary**(JuE) **heroes** (JuE) have **contributed** (JuE) to the surge of China's **advancement** (JuE) in the new era.

从例子中可以看出，原文具有五个社会尊重资源，人工翻译将原文判定资源很好地在译文中再现出来，而 ChatGPT 却省去了"拼搏""奋斗"等关键词，直接以"ordinary heroes"为主语，翻译不充分。

4. 鉴赏资源差异分析

鉴赏资源数量方面，ChatGPT 翻译反应和评估两类鉴赏资源数量都低于原文，未能完全还原原文的鉴赏资源。与此不同的是，人工翻译在反应、构成和评估三类鉴赏资源的数量上几乎与原文保持一致。

鉴赏资源情感极性方面，ChatGPT 翻译正面和负面的评价词汇都低于原文，尤其负面评价词汇远低于原文。与之相比，人工翻译的正面评价词汇接近原文水平，负面评价词汇稍低于原文。ChatGPT 翻译和人工翻译都出现正面评价词汇占比过高，负面评价词汇占比过低的情况。但从两者与原文在正负面评价词汇数量和占比上的差值来看，人工翻译更加接近原文。

例3：

原文：在此，我要向每一位科学家、每一位工程师、每一位"大国工匠"、每一位建设者和参与者**致敬**（ApV）！

人工翻译：Let me take this opportunity to **salute** (ApV) every scientist, every engineer, and every nation builder who made these achievements possible.

ChatGPT 翻译：All of these accomplishments are a testament to the dedication and hard work of every scientist, engineer, "craftsman of the nation," builder, and contributor!

原文中说话人向科学家、工程师等默默奉献的人们表示"致敬"，人工翻译中将这一表达翻译为"salute"，成功地传达了说话人的意图。然而，ChatGPT 在翻译中省略了这一重要意思，导致原文中鉴赏资源中的评估资源未能得到充分再现，也进而影响了译文中鉴赏资源情感极性的占比。

5. 差异小结

经过上述分析我们可用得出如下小结：1）宏观层面，在态度资源及其情感极性总体分布和占比、态度资源子系统及其情感极性分布和占比上，人工翻译都比 ChatGPT 翻译更加接近原文，这反映出人工翻译对于原文态度以及情感的理解和再现能力优于 ChatGPT 翻译。2）微观层面，人工翻译相比 ChatGPT 翻译对于原文的情感资源和鉴赏资源的还原度更高，更加接近原文，这反映了人工翻译对于情绪的捕捉和再现能力、对于事物的鉴赏能力比 ChatGPT 翻译更胜一筹。

四、差异背后的现象

从上述分析我们得知，人工翻译对于原文态度以及情感的理解和再现能力优于 ChatGPT 翻译，具体表现为人工翻译对于情绪的捕捉和再现能力、对于事物的鉴赏能力更佳。从这些差异中可以发现，人工翻译和 ChatGPT "理解"原文、"产出"译文的底层逻辑不同。人工翻译具备译者主体性，而基于"预训练模型"范式的 ChatGPT 所表现出的"涌现"能力具有局限性。

（一）人工翻译：译者的主体性

哲学家普罗泰戈尔曾说过，"人是万物的尺度"。在人与万物的关系中，人是客观世界的主体，而人作用或感知的对象是客体，这即体现了人的"主体性"。这种主体性很大程度上体现在人能够在认识世界和改造世界的过程中发挥自己的主观能动性。译者身上也具备这种"主体性"，即"作为翻译主体的译者在尊重翻译对象的前提下，为实现翻译目的而在翻译活动中表现出的主观能动性，其基本特征是翻译主体自觉的文化意识、人文品格和文化、审美创造性"（查明建，田雨 2003）。在翻译《新年贺词》时，译者在将原文态度资源转换到译文的过程中需要充分发挥主体性。在情绪捕捉、理解和表达方面，译者在文本中涉及情感色彩的地方，可能会根据个人生活经验和情感体验发挥其主体作用。对于事物的鉴赏方面，译者可能会受到自身的文化背景、价值观念和思维方式的影响，而对原文产生自己的理解和阐释，从而选择对应的翻译策略，并在译文中呈现特定的价值取向。同时，根据目标受众、翻译目的以及个人立场的不同，译者可能会对译文作出相应的调整，以确保译文更加符合读者接受程度、翻译目的和个人立场。

例 4：

原文： 面对全球粮食危机，我国粮食生产实现"十九连丰"，中国人的饭碗端得更**牢（ApV）**了。

人工翻译： Despite a global food crisis, we have secured a bumper harvest for the 19th year in a row, putting us in a **stronger (ApV)** position to ensure the food supply of the Chinese people.

ChatGPT 翻译： In the face of the global food crisis, our grain production achieved a "nineteenth consecutive abundant harvest," making the Chinese people's dinner plates more **secure (JuS)**.

从案例中我们可以看出，"中国人的饭碗端得更牢"事实上是对于"我国粮食生产实现'十九连丰'"的肯定评价。人工译者根据自身文化背景和生活体验将其翻译为"putting us in a stronger position to ensure the food supply of the Chinese people"，符合目标读者文化语境，使读者易于理解说话人的意思。但是 ChatGPT 却将其翻译成"making the Chinese people's dinner plates more secure"，将这句话曲解为"饭碗"的质量安全问题，可见 ChatGPT 并不具备主体性。

总而言之，译者在翻译中所发挥的"主体性"，包含了个人在文化、知识、经验、态度等多方面的价值判断和价值选择，这种主观能动性也正是人与机器最本质的区别。

（二）ChatGPT 翻译："涌现"能力的局限性

ChatGPT 所采用的"预训练模型"范式建立在深度学习基础之上，通过预训练建立"预练语言模型"，然后使用面向特定任务的小规模语言数据集，根据迁移学习的原理进行"微调"，从而形成"下游任务的模型"，以此实现的（冯志伟：2023：3）。

随着训练参数的增长，ChatGPT 展现出了相较其他机器模型而言更加优秀的语言理解和生成能力，即"涌现"能力。虽然这种"涌现"能力目前还不具备科学意义上的可解释性，但就其原理而言，ChatGPT 对于语言的理解和生成能力依旧是机械的、有限的，这主要体现在 ChatGPT 对于语言的"理解"和"生成"只是基于对有限的算法与数据的排列组合。事实上，ChatGPT 仍是一个基于马尔可夫假设的 N 元语法模型（N-gram model），即一个单词出现的概率依赖于前一个单词出现的概率。数据统计只能解决相关性问题，而不能解决逻辑上的因果关系问题。因此，这种经验主义的方法只能机械地"解码"文字信息，而无法像人一样将经验和知识结合起来进行真正意义上的语境化理解和思考。其生成文本的方法也并非"创造性活动（Energeria）"，即"有限手段的无限使用"（Humboldt，1988：49）。

从例4我们也可以看出，ChatGPT翻译态度资源似乎是机械性地"字对字"翻译，而并非根据语境选择更加合乎逻辑的译文，这说明了ChatGPT翻译除了不具备主体性，目前也不能采用人类的思维方式来理解原文的态度资源，并在译文中转换和生成对应的态度资源。由此可见，现阶段ChatGPT的"涌现"能力还存在局限性。

（三）对ChatGPT时代人工译者的建议

尽管ChatGPT的语言能力并非尽善尽美，但类似ChatGPT这样的大语言模型的出现无疑会为传统翻译服务行业带来挑战。ChatGPT具有记忆力强、耐疲劳、反应快等优点，还能根据用户需求及时调整文体风格，这些优势都是人工翻译难以企及的。然而，从ChatGPT与人工翻译在态度系统视角的对比中，我们仍然可以发现在挑战之中蕴含着机遇。一方面，人工译者在翻译中应该自觉发挥译者主体性，根据不同的翻译目的和目标受众，基于自身经验和知识，结合文本的语境，发挥译者的主观能动性，以此体现人工翻译的独特优势。但与此同时，译者也需要注重增强自身的翻译素养，提升个人的洞察力和理解力，扩展认知水平，确保能够正确地发挥译者的主体性，避免误译。另一方面，译者可以将ChatGPT视为一种翻译辅助工具，以达到人工翻译和ChatGPT翻译的优势相互补充。译者可以利用ChatGPT响应速度快和记忆能力强等优势，运用自己的主体性和专业知识进行翻译判断和译后编辑。这种人机耦合的方式可以充分发挥ChatGPT翻译的最大价值，帮助译者更高效地完成翻译任务，提升翻译质量，节省翻译时间。

五、结　语

本文从评价理论态度系统视角出发，对比ChatGPT翻译与人工翻译在再现态度资源及其情感极性方面的差异，发现人工翻译对于原文态度以及情感的理解和再现能力优于ChatGPT翻译，具体表现为人工翻译对于情绪的捕捉和再现能力、对于事物的鉴赏能力更佳。这些差异表明，人工译者具备译者主体性，而基于ChatGPT所表现出的"涌现"能力具有局限性。通过上述对比，本文发现了人工翻译的优势和ChatGPT的劣势，并为ChatGPT时代人工译者提出了建议。

注释

① "微词云"在线设计平台检索入口为www.weiciyun.com。

参考文献

[1] Zha, Mingjian & Tian, Yu (查明建, 田雨). "On the Subjectivity of the Translator" (论译者主体性——从译者文化地位的边缘化谈起)[J]. *Chinese Translators Journal* (中国翻译), 2003(01):21-26.

[2] Chen, Mei & Wen, Jun (陈梅, 文军). "A Research on the English Translations of Bai Juyi's Poems from the Perspective of Attitude

in Appraisal Theory" (评价理论态度系统视阈下的白居易诗歌英译研究)[J]. *Foreign Language Education* (外语教学), 2013, 34(04):99-104.

[3] Chen, Xirong (陈曦蓉). "Translation Strategies Related to Appraisal Theory: An Example from Huawei's Annual Reports" (评价理论态度视域下语篇英译策略——以上市公司年报致辞为例)[J]. *Shanghai Journal of Translators* (上海翻译), 2019 (06):41-45+68.

[4] Feng, Zhiwei & Zhang, Dengke (冯志伟,张灯柯). "GPT and Language Research" (GPT 与语言研究)[J]. *Technology-Enhanced Foreign Language Education* (外语电化教学), 2023 (02):3-11+105.

[5] Fu, Lihua (扶丽华). "The Presentation and Translation of Textual Attitudes of Business Texts" (从评价理论看商务语篇态度的表达及翻译)[J]. *Chinese Science and Technology Translators Journal* (中国科技翻译), 2010,23(01):28-30+23.

[6] Hou, Yiqian (侯奕茜). "Research on Attitude-based Political Metaphor Translation Model: A Case Study of the English Version of Xi Jinping:The Governance of China" (基于态度的政治隐喻翻译模型研究——以《习近平谈治国理政》英译本为例)[J]. *Foreign Languages and Literature* (外国语文), 2021,37(04):122

[7] Humboldt W F V, Heath P L, Aarsleff H .*On language: the diversity of human language-structure and its influence on the mental development of mankind*[M]. Cambridge: Cambridge University Press, 1988.

[8] J.R.Martin, P.R.R.White. *The Language of Evaluation: Appraisal in English* (评估语言:英语评价系统)[M]. Beijing: Foreign Language Teaching and Research Press (北京：外语教研出版社), 2012.

[9] Ju, Yumei (鞠玉梅). "The Rhetorical Function of Judgement Resources in the Discourse Appraisal System of the English Translation of *The Analects of Confucius*" (《论语》英译文语篇评价系统之判断资源的修辞功能)[J]. *Contemporary Rhetoric* (当代修辞学), 2016(05):37-48.

[10] Li, Chengchen & Jiang, Guiying (李成陈,江桂英). "A Contrastive Analysis of 'Attitude' in Forewords of Chinese and English AcademicMonographs Within Appraisal System" (评价理论态度系统视角下中英学术专著他序对比研究)[J]. *Foreign Language Education* (外语教学), 2017,38(05):43-48.

[11] Lin, Guoli (林国丽). "The Implicit Evaluative Functions of Ideational Meaning: Comparison between Jobs' Love Letter and Its Chinese Versions" (概念意义的隐性评价功能——"乔布斯情书"英文及汉译本对比分析)[J]. *Foreign Language Research* (外语学刊), 2015(05):77-81.

[12] Liu, ShiZhu (刘世铸). "A Model of Translation Process Within Appraisal Theory" (评价理论观照下的翻译过程模型)[J]. *Shandong Foreign Language Teaching* (山东外语教学), 2012, 33(4):5.

[13] Qian, Hong (钱宏). "Investigating Unfaithful Translations via the Appraisal Theory: A Case Study on Perfume Ads Translation" (运用评价理论解释"不忠实"的翻译现象——香水广告翻译个案研究)[J]. *Journal of Foreign Languages* (外国语), 2007(06):57-63.

[14] Si, Bingyue & Gao, Song (司炳月,高松). "A Study on the Distribution and Translation of Graduation Resources in Discourses forChina's International Communication" (外宣文本中英级差资源分布与翻译——以 2019 年政府工作报告双语文本为例)[J]. *Shanghai Journal of Translators* (上海翻译), 2019 (05):14-20.

[15] Si, Xianzhu & Pang, Yuhou (司显柱,庞玉厚). "Appraisal Theory, Attitude System and Textual Translation" (评价理论、态度系统与语篇翻译)[J]. *Foreign Languages in China* (中国外语), 2018,15(01):96-102.

[16] Wang, Zhenhua (王振华). "Appraisal Values of Material Processes:Their Contributions to the Image Formation of Characters in

Novels" ("物质过程"的评价价值——以分析小说人物形象为例)[J]. *Journal of Foreign Languages* (外国语), 2004(05):41-47.

[17] Xia, Yun & Li, Defeng (夏云, 李德凤). "Shifts of Appraisal Meaning and Character Depiction Effect in Translation-Comparing Two Versions of *Gone with the Wind*" (评价意义的转换与小说人物形象的翻译效果——以《飘》两个译本为例)[J]. *Foreign Languages and Their Teaching* (外语与外语教学), 2009(07):44-47.

[18] Xu, Jun & Xia, Rong (徐珺, 夏蓉). "A Contrastive Study of English & Chinese Business Discourses from the Perspective of Appraisal Theory" (评价理论视域中的英汉商务语篇对比研究)[J]. *Foreign Language Education* (外语教学), 2013,34(03):16-21.

[19] Xu, Jun (徐珺). "Research on Business Translation in the Perspective of Evaluation Theory" (评价理论视域中的商务翻译研究)[J]. *Journal of PLA University of Foreign Languages* (解放军外国语学院学报), 2011,34(06):88-91+109.

[20] Yan, Jia & Li, Defeng (鄢佳, 李德凤). "Rewriting of Headlines in Sports News: A Perspective of Appraisal Theory" (评价意义在奥运新闻标题编译中的改写)[J]. *Chinese Science & Technology Translators Journal* (中国科技翻译), 2013,26(01):52-55.

[21] Yu, Li (于丽). "Study on Translator's Subjectivity in Political Documents Translation from the Perspective of Appraisal Theory" (评价理论视角下政治文献翻译中译者的主体性研究)[J]. *Foreign Language Research* (外语学刊), 2021(06):67-72.

[22] Yu, Jiying (余继英). "Evaluative Meaning and Ideology of the Translation: With the Example of the English Translation of *The True Story of Ah Q*" (评价意义与译文意识形态——以《阿Q正传》英译为例)[J]. *Foreign Language Learning Theory and Practice* (外语教学理论与实践), 2010 (02):83-90.

[23] John, Holland. *EMERGENCE: From Chaos to Order* (涌现:从混沌到有序)[M]. Shanghai: Shanghai Scientific & Technical Publishers (上海:上海科学技术出版社), 2006.

[24] Zhang, Xiangang (张先刚). "Implications of Appraisal Theory for Text Translation" (评价理论对语篇翻译的启示)[J]. *Foreign Language Education* (外语教学), 2007(06):33-36.

[25] Zhou, Xiaomei (周晓梅). "Explicit Implicit Strategy and Translators' Value Orientation Presentation: A Comparative Study Based on the English Translations of *Wolf Totem* and *Trees Without Wind*" (显化隐化策略与译者的价值取向呈现——基于《狼图腾》与《无风之树》英译本的对比研究)[J]. *Chinese Translators Journal* (中国翻译), 2017,38(04):87-94.

作者简介

林泽钦,硕士,广东外语外贸大学高级翻译学院硕士研究生。研究方向:语料库翻译学、翻译技术、口译研究。邮箱:907729513@qq.com。

中医西传第三方译者研究
——以文树德《黄帝内经·素问》英译本为例

⊙ 俞森林 雷佳豪（西南交通大学外国语学院，成都）

[摘 要] 第三方译者（母语既非源语也非目的语）在中医西传的过程中发挥着不可小觑的作用。本文以文树德《黄帝内经·素问》英译本为例，结合第三方译者文树德的自身素养及翻译目的，分析第三方译者身份对《黄帝内经·素问》英译本及其翻译策略的影响。研究发现，在中医西传过程中，第三方译者所采取的以"中"译"中"、以"古"译"古"及"中西"结合的翻译策略，以及采用的"中西合璧"和"宏观—微观"翻译模式，对于医药典籍的翻译实践有着启迪作用。同时，这种翻译策略的选取和翻译模式的选用在一定程度上推进了中医西传的传播进程。

[关键词] 中医西传；第三方译者；文树德；《黄帝内经·素问》英译本

On the Third-Party Translator in the Western Transmission of Traditional Chinese Medicine: With Unschuld's English Translation of *Huang Di Nei Jing Su Wen* as a Case of the Study

YU Senlin LEI Jiahao (Southwest Jiaotong University, Chengdu)

Abstract: Third-party translators whose native language is neither the source nor the target language play an important role in spreading traditional Chinese medicine to the West. This paper takes Unschuld's English translation of *Huang Di Nei Jing Su Wen* as an example and analyzes the influence of the third-party translator's identity on the English translation of *Su Wen* and its translation strategies in light of his own quality and translation purpose. The results show the translation strategies adopted by third-party translators, such as translating "*Zhong*" into "*Zhong*", translating "*Gu*" into "*Gu*" and Combination of "*Zhong* and *Xi*", as well as the "collaboration of Chinese and Western experts" and "macro to micro" modes of translation, are enlightening for the translation practice of medical texts. At the same time, the selection of these translation strategies and the choice of translation modes have, to a certain extent, advanced the process of spreading traditional Chinese medicine to the West.

Key words: the Western transmission of traditional Chinese medicine; the third-party translator; Paul U. Unschuld; *English Translation of Huang Di Nei Jing Su Wen*

基金项目：中国国家社科基金重大招标项目"世界汉学家口述中文与中华文化国际传播史：图文音像数据库建构"（项目编号：20&ZD330）阶段性成果。

一、引 言

《黄帝内经》是中国最早的医学典籍，被称为"医之始祖"，分《灵枢》《素问》两部分。其中《黄帝内经·素问》具有比较完整之理论体系，内容广博而深奥，为中医理论之渊薮。在中医西传的过程中，译者作为翻译活动的主体，肩负着当今中医药典籍文化"走出去"甚至"走进去"的重大使命。根于译者的母语大致可将其分为三类：源语为母语的译者、目的语为其母语的译者以及母语既非源语也非目的语的译者，即"第三方译者"（石小梅，2016：119）。相比之下，学界对于前两类译者的关注也较多，而非英语世界的"第三方译者"尚未得到研究者足够的关注。因此，本文以第三方译者德国汉学家文树德（Paul Ulrich Unschuld，1943-）《黄帝内经·素问》英译本为例，从译者的自身素养及翻译目的两方面，分析这一身份对其译本及翻译策略的影响，从而探讨第三方译者的译者身份对中医西传的作用与启示。

二、第三方译者文树德及其翻译目的

文树德的母语并非汉语或英语，作为第三方译者的他，在翻译《黄帝内经·素问》（下文简称为《素问》）时，不仅要面对医古文与现代汉语、西医与中医的差异，还要面对中、英、德三种语言上的差异，因此，对于译者的汉英语言功底及中西医医学知识都有较高的要求。

他生于1943年8月19日，毕业于慕尼黑大学药学院，是著名的德国汉学家、医史学家，主要研究领域是中、欧洲医学比较史，尤其擅长医学思想史、伦理史的研究，是西方世界著名的中医历史文献学家、中国医学史研究权威专家。1969年，致力于成为一名中苏关系专家的文树德同夫人来到台北师范大学学习中文，接触到中国医药文献史和中国传统药学后，便对其产生了浓厚的兴趣。他认为如果想要更好地了解现代中医，首先需要了解古代的中医。为此文树德走访过一百多名中医医生和药剂师，并研读日本著名中医和中药学文献研究者 Okanishi Tameto 博士的相关著作，向他的妻子请教中国宋、金、元时期的中国古代药学的相关内容[①]。这些经历都为译者文树德随后翻译《素问》奠定了基础，开启了中国医学史研究之路。随后，他以中医药学相关论题展开研究并获得了德国的汉学博士学位，先后撰写、翻译了多部备受赞誉的中医著作，主要包括：《中华帝国的医学伦理》（*Medical Ethics in Imperial China—A Study in Historical Anthropology*，1975）、《中国医学：医药史》（*Medicine in China: A History of Pharmaceutics*，1984）、《中医思想史》（*Medicine in China: A History of Idea*，1984）等12部英语著作；以及《难经》（*Nan-Ching: The Classic of Difficulties*，1986）、《银海精微》（*Essential subtleties on the silver sea*，1997）等6部译著。2017年8月，文树德因其在中医药领域的卓越成就荣获"中华图书特殊贡献奖"（该奖项是中国出版业面向海外的最高奖项）。2019年11月16日，获得"第六届树兰医学杰出贡献奖"（该奖项被誉为中国医药卫生学界的"诺贝尔医学奖"）。由此可以看出，"第三方译者"文树德有着扎实的中国文化素养和中医知识基础及较强的翻译能力。

文树德（2003）认为"《黄帝内经》是中国思想史的重要来源，是中国古代医学及自然知识的宝贵数据库，其地位堪比《希波克拉底文集》在古代欧洲医学文化中的地位。"但是中医在西方却处于不利的地位，他曾在《今日针灸》（Acupuncture Today）谈及："当时95%以上以西方语言出版的关于中医的著作都反映了西方的期望，而并非历史现实。畅销书的作者通常不懂中文，没有机会了解中医史，而且从来没有或者最多只短期去过中国，并不知道中医的起源和根基在哪里。"①为此，他一直努力扭转中医在西方的不利局面，承担起中医传播者的角色，尽力扭转西方学者对于中医文化的偏见。此外，文树德在《黄帝内经·素问》英译本的前言中写道（2011：9）："译本并非着眼于其生理和病理观点，也并非传递适用于当代临床的治疗建议，而是向读者传递中医思想和语言表达，以及这些思想和语言表达是历史长河中的变化历程。"

除了其主观意愿，文树德同样也受到外部力量的驱使。首先是国外"中医热"现象的兴起，正值基辛格和尼克松与中国和解之际，中国重新敞开大门，中医在某种程度上成为中国吸引外界的一点。一些中医学校也在西方世界办了起来，还涌现出大量关于中医类书籍和译本②。此外，中国的崛起一直以来在世界上是个热门话题，世界各国，尤其西方试图从各个角度破解"中国密码"。因而，正是在这种时代背景下，原本致力于成为中苏关系专家的文树德想要通过解读《黄帝内经》中的"阴阳""五行学说"等内容，即关系科学，来探索中国崛起的原因，在一定程度上实现了他最初的"理想"③。总之受到客观因素的影响，文树德这种探索带有一定程度的"政治色彩"。

三、《黄帝内经·素问》英译本特色

文树德《黄帝内经·素问》英译本是首部严格按照西方语言学标准的全译本，展现了西方学者解读中医的独特视角，被誉为"严肃翻译艺术的典范"②。该译本特色鲜明，主要概括为以下四方面。

翻译历时长。文树德于1988年着手翻译《黄帝内经·素问》，历时28年方才完成。在这期间，文树德对《素问》原文相关文献进行了穷尽式研究，并对其涉及的内容进行了深入的探析，于2003、2008年分别出版《黄帝内经素问——中国古代医学典籍中的自然、知识和意象》（*Huang Di Nei Jing Su Wen: Nature, Knowledge, Imagery in an Ancient Chinese Medical Text*）（下文简称为《03版内经》）和《黄帝内经素问词典》（*A Dictionary of Huang Di Nei Jing Su Wen*）（下文简称为《08版词典》），直到2011年，《黄帝内经·素问》（*Huang Di Nei Jing Su Wen—An Annotated Translation of Huang Di's Inner Classic Basic Questions*）全译本才问世。

内容庞大且系统化。文树德《黄帝内经·素问》的英译历程是先宏观再微观。《03版内经》是文树德《黄帝内经·素问》英译本的总述，前半部分探讨《黄帝内经·素问》的源流、题目内涵、版本流传及注疏等问题；后半部分则全面系统地介绍了《素问》所论及的阴阳五行、脏象、气血、经脉、病因、疾病等内容。Larissa Heinrich（2004：190）评价道："无论是否赞同文树德分析的内容，就内容的全面性和文献的完整性方面，其他著作都无法与之匹敌。"《08版词典》是一部提供索引的工具书，收录了《黄帝内经·素问》英译本中的1866个中医术语，列举了术语所在文句、位置及相应的词组，并提供"极简"的英文翻译（省略注释或解释性文本、参考文献和参考书目等），术语的索引按拼音发音及笔画进行排列，并附有一个按频率降序排列的字符附录。在每个词条末尾后用"◇"标注《素问》中出现的次数，添加章节、页码和行号排列，以便读者在该文本的参考版本中可以找到该词条。Bridie Andrews Minehan（2009：338）认为"《08版词典》是一部开创性的参考书，也是所有中医文献的第一本英文字典。"2011年出版的《黄帝内经·素问》英译本则是在前两部著作基础上的具体阐释。

求真求实的译文。该译本首次采用严格的文献学和史学方法，充分运用脚注，共计5912条，并将脚注中涉及的中、日两国1600年间的600多部《内经》专著以及20世纪中国学者撰写的近3000篇相关研究性文章以索引的方式呈现在译著中，以求最大限度反映《黄帝内经·素问》的原义与风貌。因此，文树德也被李照国称为中医翻译"考据派"（2019：137）。Michael Stanley-Baker（2014：143）评价道："文树德《黄帝内经·素问》系列著作为子孙后代打开了一个丰富的内经研究世界，在未来仍将是不可或缺的经典之作。"

中西合璧的产物。文树德积极寻求与各领域专家合作，主要寻求中国中医科学院医学史与医学文献研究所郑金生教授及田和曼教授（Hermann Tessenow，1945-），分别向他们请教中医领域专业知识和语言学专业知识。这种中西专家合作的方式，使得文树德对于《黄帝内经·素问》的理解更加清楚、翻译更加准确、中医思想精髓传递更加深入，同时也使得《素问》英译本更加符合西方读者的阅读习惯。

四、翻译策略

文树德正是受到了"第三方译者"这一身份的影响，使得他能够客观了解并学习汉、英两种语言，对于汉语源语，他高度认同《素问》汉语原文，认为"只有在了解中医的概念的基础上，才能进行翻译，不可以假设古人是一个超人，能够了解我们现在知识"④。对于英语目的语，他严格按照西方语言学标准，使得译文更加地道。因此，文树德主要采取了以"中"译"中"、以"古"译"古"、"中西"结合三种翻译策略。下面结合具体实例对三种翻译策略加以解读。

（一）以"中"译"中"

文树德（2011）提出："《素问》的翻译要尽可能地接近其源文的原始格式和含义，最大程度再现文本，译者可以基于对文本及其原始文化环境的深入了解，要恰当地解释和添加注释，但要与译文分开。"因此，文树德采取以"中"译"中"的翻译策略，即形式上尽量保持与其所对应的原文文体风格、句式构造上的一致，内容上通过添加脚注的方法，对原文的内容进行文献考证及语言训诂。

例如：

（1）原文：弱而能言，幼而徇齐。

译文：While he was [still] weak³, he could speak.

While he was [still] young⁴, he was quick⁵ of apprehension.

脚注：3 1551/63: "In ancient times, children up to the age of 100 days were called 'weak.'"

4 Tanba: "acording to the Li ji, 曲禮, the age of ten years is called 'youth.'"

5 Wang Bing: "徇 stands for 疾, 'quick.'" 1031/40: "徇 is identical with 循 in the sense of 'complete,' 'comprehensive.' 齊 stands for 疾, 'quick.' Tanba comments: ' the knowledge of the sage was comprehensive and his spirit was quick.'" 2753/62: "徇 stands for 侚, 'quick.'"

该句意为"禀赋有余，发言之早，年虽幼而能顺其正"。译文在形式上参照原文的构句单位，也按照小句来排列，一句一行。同时尽量与原文风格一致，采用排比句式，押头韵。文树德充分运用脚注，分别引用任应秋（1551/63）、丹波元简（Tanba）、王冰、赵益夫（2753/62）及李蔚普（1031）五位学者的论述，对"弱""幼"及"徇齐"进行了详细的阐释，"弱"指婴儿出生后的第一百天，"幼"指孩子十岁，"徇"指快、思维敏捷、理解事物迅速。内容上通过引用大量文献，考察了古汉语之意，补充了古汉字的隐含信息，形式上与原文保持一致，充分运用了以"中"译"中"的翻译策略。

（2）原文：秋三月，此谓容平……；冬三月，此为闭藏。

译文：The three months of autumn,

　　　　they denote taking in and balance.¹⁸

　　　　　　...

　　　　The three months of winter,

　　　　they denote securing and storing.

脚注：18 Wang Bing: "In summer the myriad beings grow and blossoms as well as fruits have reached completion. Their 容狀, 'appearance,' does no longer change and is fixed by autumn." Ma shi: "The *yin qi* has started to rise already and the appearance of all beings is finally determined. Hence, the image of the *qi* [in autumn] is called 'appearance settled.'" 2095: "容 is 收納, 'to take in,' and 平 is 平治, 'in peaceful order.'" Fang Wenhui /110 identifies 容 as 搈 with the meaning of "movement", and 平 as 止, "to stop", 靜," quiet." In this case, the passage should read: "The three months of autumn, this means: any movement ceases." Zhang Yizhi et al.: "Tanba interprets 容 as 盛, 'abundance.' This argument is based on the Shuo wen. The commentary in the Sheng ji jing 聖濟經 states: 'at ease (容) and without hurry; balanced (平) and without bias. That is to say 容平.' This is correct."

译文在形式上参照古文的构句单位，按照小句来排列，同时采用排比句式"the three month of…"；"they denote…"，尽量与原文风格一致。脚注中分别引用王冰（Wang Bing）、马莳（Ma shi）、吴缉庵（2095）、方文辉（Fang Wenhui）及张毅之（Zhang Yizhi）五位学者的论述，王冰注云"万物夏长，华实已成，容状至秋平而定也"（2015：8）。马莳又注曰"七八九月，秋之三月也，阴气已上，万物之容，至此乎定，故气象谓之荣平"（1999：13）。另吴缉庵、方文辉以及张毅之则对"容平""容""平"进行训诂，吴缉庵认为"容"即"收纳""平"即"平治"。方文辉认为"容"即"搈（动，不安）"，"平"即（止），该句意为"秋三月，什么行动都停止"。张毅之则引用著作《素问识》及《圣济经》，考究"容""平"之意。文树德通过引古今学者注疏，在内容上，考究词义，传递了自然环境对人的影响，即"天人合一"思想。在形式上，尽可能地贴近《素问》原文的构句单位，体现了以"中"译"中"的翻译策略。

（二）以"古"译"古"

文树德（2011）认为："翻译《素问》应了解当时作者的知识基础，及其所处的知识环境、政治、经济基础等，从思想、历史的角度来分析源文，努力展现古代作家所要表达的思想、理论和事实。"因此，文树德采取以"古"译"古"的翻译策略，即在处理中医中的隐喻文化时，从原文的时代环境背景出发，力求还原原文所表达的意义。

例如：

（3）原文：二七而天癸至，<u>任脉</u>通，太冲脉盛。

译文：With two times seven,

the heaven gui arrives,

the <u>controlling vessel</u> is passable and.

the great thoroughfare vessel abounds [with *qi*].

"任脉"奇经八脉之一，总任一身之阴经，在女子有妊育胎儿的作用，故主胞胎。张志聪注曰："冲脉、任脉，奇经脉也。二脉并起于少腹之内胞中，徇腹上行，为经血之海，女子主育胞胎。"（2015：3）因此，在中医文献中被广泛译为"conception vessel"。美国著名中医执业医师倪茂山（Ni Maoshing）也采取类似的译法，译为"the ren/conception channels"（1995：136）。而文树德则认为应该将"督""任"置于当时所处的历史背景，这两个术语是汉代医学家选自国家行政领域的术语。"督"相对"任"而言，是更高的官员。"督"是领导职位，例如主管或将军。相反，"任"有"肩负""肩负重任""担任官职"的意思。"任"可以是任何下级官员，负责控制或执行某些普通任务。因此，他将"督脉"译为"supervisor vessel"，"任脉"译为"controlling vessel"。文树德正是从历史的角度分析原文作者所处的环境、当时所具备的知识基础等，对于古代政治背景做铺垫性的描述，做到了以"古"译"古"。

（4）原文：肝者，<u>将军之官，谋虑出焉</u>。

译文：The liver is the official functioning as general.

Planning and deliberation originate in it.[6]

脚注：6 Wang Bing: "It is brave and able to pass decisions; hence [the text] states 'general.' It secretly develops that which has not sprouted yet; hence 'planning and deliberation originate in it.'" Hucker 694 (p. 140): "General: throughout history the most common term for the commander of a substantial body of troops." 961/25: "The term 將軍 dates from the Warring States Period. In the Shi zi 尸子 [a work compiled during the Warring States Period] it is said: 'an army of 100 000 without a 將軍 will behave disorderly.'" 226/66: "*The Lü shi chun qiu*, Zhi yi 執一, states:軍必有將."

"将军"武官名，比拟肝脏之性犹如军中之将军，刚强急躁，好动而不好静。肝在志为怒，其性喜条达而恶抑郁。马莳注云："肝主木，木主发生，故为将军之官，而谋虑所出，犹运筹于帷幄之中也。"（1999：76）"肝"属于"五脏"之一，而"五脏六腑"是中医的重要理论，对其阐释尤为必要。但是，由于藏象术语的隐喻关系复杂，并与中华传统文化紧密结合，特别是对于缺少中华传统文化背景的西方读者来说，甚至对于不了解中医的中文读者而言，理解其背后的医理都十分困难。文树德在脚注中引王冰注疏"勇而能断，故曰将军。潜发未萌，故谋虑出焉"阐释句意。又引用 Hucker、学者李今庸（961）和迟华基（226）的观点，解释"将军"一词的含义，强调了"将军"对于军队的重要作用。文树德正是从传统概念出发，运用以"古"译"古"的翻译策略，由浅入深地阐明了"将军"与"肝"的隐喻关系，帮助读者理解中医医理的同时，又传递了中医文化。

（三）"中西"结合

文树德（2011：13）认为："《素问》翻译不仅是语言转换，更是医学文化和医学思想的传递。他严格按照西方语言学标准，但并非用现代生物医学术语代替中国古代技术术语，要考究语源与语境，具体情况具体分析，以尽可能接近原始中文术语所传达的意义。"因此，在处理中医疾病术语方面，文树德采取以"中西"结合的翻译策略，即在术语规范及内容传递方面，做到"中西"结合。

例如：

（5）原文：胸中不便，嗌塞而咳。（至真要大论篇第七十四）

译文：[Patients] feel uncomfortable in the chest.

The throat is obstructed and they cough.[151]

脚注：151 Wang Bing: "These are the five mao and the five you years." Wu Kun: "Yang brilliance [qi] is a metal transformation. When it dominates, then coolness and cold develop in the center. When metal dominates, then wood is harmed. Hence the upper and the lower flanks on the left have pain. Because of coolness in the center, the stool is semiliquid. The virtue of metal is to draw together. Hence the throat is blocked. Hardness is a metal transformation. Hence breakdown and elevation illnesses appear. Hairy creatures are associated with wood. Hence they perish when they encounter metal. The chest center is the location of the lung, [i.e., of] metal. In case of severe dryness, the lung contracts and cannot function any longer. The result is [a feeling of] discomfort, a blocked throat, and cough."

该句意为"胸中即肺部堵塞，咽塞咳嗽"。张景岳云："胸中，肺所居也，燥胜则肺气敛，而失其治节，故有不便而嗌塞为咳也。"（2011：326）文树德在脚注中大量引用明代学者王冰、吴昆的注疏，解释"咳"与"阳明"的关系，即"阳明，金化也，胸中者，肺金所部，燥甚则肺敛而失其治节，故令不便，隘塞而咳也"（1984：355）。阐释了阳明燥金之气，虽与现代西方医学所解释"咳"得致病机理不一致，但是病症相似，因此文树德将其译为"cough"。在形式上采用西方术语便于读者的接受，同时在内容上也较好地传递了中医文化，做到了"中西"结合。类似疾病术语翻译还有：痈（yong-abscesses）、疡（ulcers）、癃（anuria/urine retention）等。

（6）原文：心移寒于肺，肺消。（气厥论篇第三十七）

译文：When the heart moves cold to the lung,

[this results in] fei-xiao.[6]

脚注：6 yang shangshan: "The heart transmits cold to the lung. When the lung receives cold, it develops heat. When the lung burns, this results in thirst. This is called 'the lung dissolves.'" 2241/27: "消 is short for 消瘅, 'wasting dan.' The three terms 肺消, 鬲消, and 消渴 refer to [the condition of] 上消, 'upper wasting,' when [a person] drinks a lot but his thirst does not end." We consider 肺消 to be a term of foreign or non-Han Chinese origin. a literal translation is "wasting lung", corresponding to the Greek term phthisis.

"肺消"，又名上消和隔消。张景岳注曰："心与肺，二阳脏也，心移寒与肺者，君火之衰耳。心火不足则不能温养肺金，肺气不顺则不能行化津液，故饮虽一而溲则倍之。"（2011：286）简而言之，即心火衰弱不能温养肺金，使水液循环失常，不能生化津液，全部流注于膀胱，津液日耗，本元日竭（石冠，1982：523）。文树德首先在内容上引用杨上善及徐荣斋的论述，对"肺消"这一疾病的致病原理进行阐释，并且尝试与古希腊术语相联系，即"肺消"古音读作："phjats sjaw"，与古希腊术语 phtisis 或者 lung phtisis 发音相似。文树德在形式上将"肺消"音译为"fei-xiao"，在内容上追溯到古代西方，做到了"中西"结合，便于读者的理解和接受。

五、 文树德《黄帝内经·素问》英译对中医西传的启示

文树德《黄帝内经·素问》英译在中医西传过程中对翻译实践及文化传播的作用大体可归为以下三个方面：

首先，文树德《黄帝内经·素问》的英译策略对中医西传的翻译实践有重要指导作用。中国的典籍，同西方典籍一样，同属"过去时代的精神创造物"，通过注疏的方式，流传至今，且层层积累起厚重的诠释文献（朱峰，2019：153）。文树德在其翻译的《素问》中，采取了以"中"译"中"、以"古"译"古"，"中西"结合的翻译策略，充分运用脚注，参考古今中外的评注，释典释文、训诂词义，对原文内容充分解读，力争全面还原原文风貌，并尝试追溯到古代西方探寻渊源，使得读者有机会接触不同的解释和观点，自行构建中医形象。

其次，文树德《黄帝内经·素问》英译的合作方式及翻译历程丰富了中医西传的翻译模式。在跨文化翻译过程中，翻译主体是整个翻译活动的灵魂（殷丽，2017：54）。作为译者的文树德，积极与中国中医科学院医学史与医学文献研究所郑金生教授及美国知名学者田和曼寻求合作，分别向他们请教中医领域专业知识和语言学专业知识。这种融合不同民族、语言和文化背景的中西专家合作方式，使得文树德对于中文文本的理解和阐释更透彻，译文更加符合西方语言规范，译本的可读性、忠实性和学科性在很大程度上得以保证，从而更有利于中医文化的传播。此外，文树德《黄帝内经·素问》采取了"宏观-微观"的翻译模式。文树德先详细探究《黄帝内经·素问》的成书背景、内容及主要思想等内容，再对文本中的1866个中医术语进行"极简"翻译，最后才完成整本书的翻译。这种翻译模式，对于外国读者甚至是毫无中医背景的中国读者而言是较为合理的，能够将《黄帝内经·素问》全面且客观地呈现给读者，在很大程度上促进了中医文化的传播。

最后，文树德《黄帝内经·素问》英译推动了中医文化甚至中国文化的传播进程。文树德面对中医在西方的不利局面，承担起中医传播者的角色，逐渐成为西方研究古老中医疗法的著名权威，同时也是最早用系统、权威的方式对待中医的西方学者之一。他的《黄帝内经》系列译著得到了海外学者们的广泛关注，纷纷在各类一流期刊发表书评推广，共计13篇。殷丽（2017：41）认为："海外同行书评的数量多少，不仅仅是译本是否得到海外相关领域认可的反映，更是译本学术价值的直接体现，有利于扩大典籍英译的海外影响力。"此外，他还利用业余时间带领德国政府代表团前往中国，促进两国文化之间的交流，并积极参加中方

举办的医药峰会，共同探讨中医药和传统医药发展。文树德《黄帝内经·素问》英译拓展了中医西传的路径，促进了中医文化的传播。

六、结 语

文树德《黄帝内经·素问》英译本不仅扩大了《黄帝内经》在西方世界的影响，更帮助世界读者充分地领略到中国古代医学和文化的风貌。同时第三方译者文树德采用的翻译策略、模式及合作方式，对于中医典籍的翻译实践有着重要的启示和借鉴意义，尤其随着中医药在全球的影响力不断增强，中医药在治疗新冠肺炎中的作用越来越受到重视的大背景下，我们应肩负时代的使命，学习文树德所采用的"中西合璧"的合作方式，在原文理解与译文阐释方面都要做到精益求精；借鉴文树德以"中"译"中"，以"古"译"古"，"中西"结合的翻译策略及"宏观—微观"的翻译模式，树立文化自信意识，将我们中医中蕴含的"独特理论和技术方法的体系""深邃的哲学智慧"以及"健康养生理念"以恰当的方式传递给西方世界。

注释

① Acupuncture Today, An Interview With Dr. Paul Unschuld BY MATTHEW BAUER ［EB/OL］［2004-07］https://www.acupuncturetoday.com/mpacms/at/article.php?id=28481

② New York Times, An Expert on Chinese Medicine, but No New Age Healer ［EB/OL］［2016-09-23］https://cn.nytimes.com/china/20160928/chinese-medicine-paul-unschuld/dual/

③ 钟明，德国教授用 28 年翻译《黄帝内经》[J].《环球人物》，2016（29）：66-67。

④ 中国日报中文网，文树德：16 年翻译《本草纲目》的理由 ［EB/OL］［2021-05-26］https://cn.chinadaily.com.cn/a/202105/26/WS60adc009a3101e7ce9751ac6.html

参考文献

[1] Baker, Michael Stanley. Reviewed Works: *Huang Di Nei Jing Su Wen: Nature, Knowledge, Imagery in an Ancient Chinese Medical Text* by Paul Unschuld: *A Dictionary of the Huang Di Nei Jing Su Wen* by Hermann Tessenow and Paul U. Unschuld: *Huang Di Nei Jing Su Wen: An Annotated Translation of Huang Di's Inner Classic—Basic Questions* by Paul U. Unschuld, Hermann Tessenow and Zheng Jinsheng [J]. *East Asian Science, Technology, and Medicine*, 2014(1): 138-143.

[2] Heinrich, Larissa. Reviewed Work(s): *Huang Di Nei Jing Su Wen: Nature, Knowledge, Imagery in an Ancient Chinese Medical Text* by Paul U. Unschuld [J]. *Chinese Literature: Essays, Articles, Reviews (CLEAR)*, 2004(1): 187-190.

[3] Li, Zhaoguo (李照国). *Chinese Medicine Translation Studies Tutorial* (中医翻译研究教程 [M]). Shanghai: Shanghai Joint Publishing Company (上海：上海三联书店), 2019.

[4] Minehan, Bridie Andrews. Reviewed Work(s): *A Dictionary of the Huang Di Nei Jing Su Wen* by Hermann Tessenow and Paul U.

Unschuld [J]. *Journal of Chinese Philosophy*, 2010(2), 337-339.

[5] Ma, Shi (马莳). *Huang Di Nei Jing Su Wen Zhu Zheng Fa Wei* (黄帝内经·素问注证发微 [M]). Beijing: Science and Technology Documentation Press (北京：科学技术文献出版社), 1999.

[6] Ni, Maoshing. *The Yellow Emperor's Classic of Medicine: A New Translation of the Neijing Suwen with Commentary* [M]. Boston: Shambala, 1995.

[7] Shi, Xiaomei (石小梅). "Shigeyoshi Obata's *The Works of Li Po: the Chinese Poet*" (小畑薰良英译《李白诗集》的历史价值与当代意义) [J]. *Journal of Xi'an International Studies University* (西安外国语大学学报), 2016(2): 117-121.

[8] Shi, Guanqing & Wu, Mingqin (石冠卿，武明钦). *Huang Di Nei Jing Su Wen (Selected Notes)* (《黄帝内经·素问》选注 [M]). Zhengzhou: Henan Science and Technology Press (郑州：河南科学技术出版社), 1982.

[9] Unschuld, Paul U. & Tessenow, H. *Huang Di Nei Jing Su Wen—An Annotated Translation of Huang Di's Inner Classic—Basic Questions* [M]. California: University of California Press, 2011.

[10] Wang, Bing (王冰). *Chong Guang Bu Zhu Huang Di Nei Jing Su Wen* (重广补注黄帝内经·素问 [M]). Beijing: Ancient Chinese Medicine Press (北京：中医古籍出版社), 2015.

[11] Wu, Kun (吴昆). *Nei Jing Su Wen Wu Zhu* (内经·素问吴注 [M]). Jinan: Shandong Science and Technology Press (济南：山东科学技术出版社), 1984.

[12] Yin, Li (殷丽). "Study on the Overseas Translation Model of the *Huangdi Neijing* and the 'Going Out' of Chinese Medicine Culture" (《黄帝内经》海外译介模式研究与中医药文化"走出去") [J]. *Journal of PLA University of Foreign Languages* (解放军外国语学院学报), 2017(6): 53-61.

[13] Zhang, Zhicong (张志聪). *Huang Di Nei Jing Ji Zhu Su Wen (Volume 1)* (黄帝内经集注上·素问 [M]). Beijing: Ancient Chinese Medicine Press (北京：中医古籍出版社), 2015.

[14] Zhang, Jingyue (张景岳). *Lei Jing* (类经 [M]). Beijing: China Medical Science Press (北京：中国医药科技出版社), 2011.

[15] Zhu, Feng (朱峰). "On the Characteristics and Methods of Thick Translation in Chinese Philosophy Translation: A Case Study of Chin Annping's English Translation of *Confucius' Analects*" (深度翻译中的译者角色与翻译策略——以金安平《论语》英译本为例) [J]. *Chinese Culture Research* (中国文化研究), 2019(4): 149-159.

作者简介

俞森林，哲学博士，西南交通大学教授、中国语言文学译介学方向博士生导师。研究方向：中国典籍英译及海外汉学研究。电子邮箱：yusenlin@swjtu.edu.cn。

雷佳豪，西南交通大学外国语学院在读硕士研究生。研究方向：翻译学。电子邮箱：leileilei@my.swjtu.edu.cn。

郑振铎对清末民初翻译家的批评及启示

⊙ 管新福（贵州师范大学文学院，贵阳）

[摘 要] 郑振铎是我国现代著名的全能型学者，在文学史写作、文学理论、翻译批评、俗文学研究等领域均卓有建树，为我国新文学的发展做出了重大贡献。在翻译研究领域，他对晚清民国时期的很多翻译家都有客观、合理的批评，如严复、林纾、梁启超、伍光建、周氏兄弟等人。在郑振铎的翻译家批评中，他一方面能恪守学术研究的伦理，坚持客观中立的翻译批评观，不走极端；另一方面是有包容的胸怀、不受流派和见解的左右，让事实成为评判孰优孰劣的标准，值得我们今天认真吸收。

[关键词] 郑振铎；清末民初；翻译家；翻译批评；启示

Zheng Zhenduo's Criticism and Enlightenment to the Translators in Late Qing Dynasty and Early Republic of China

GUAN Xinfu (School of Language Arts, Guizhou Normal University, Guiyang)

Abstract: Zheng Zhenduo is a famous all-round scholar in contemporary China, who has made great contributions to the development of "new literature" in China in the fields of literary history, literary theory, translation criticism, and folk literature research. In the field of translation studies, he objectively and reasonably criticized many translators in the late Qing Dynasty and the early Republic of China, such as Yan Fu, Lin Shu, Liang Qichao, Wu Guangjian and the Zhou brothers. On the one hand, Zheng Zhenduo abided by the ethics of academic research, adhered to the objective and neutral view of translation criticism, and did not go to extremes. On the other hand, Zheng Zhenduo had an inclusive mind, independent of different schools and opinions, and let facts become the standard for judging excellence and inferiority, which is worth learning seriously today.

Key words: Zheng Zhenduo; late Qing Dynasty and early Republic of China; translators; translation criticism; inspiration

一、引 言

郑振铎是我国现代著名的文学史家、翻译家、文学理论家，文学研究会的骨干成员，可谓全能型学者。其所涉及的文学、文化活动异常广泛，学贯中西，在文学史写作、翻译批评、文学评论、俗文学研究等层面

2018 中国国家社科基金"近现代报刊翻译理论资料整理与研究"（18BZW112）的部分研究成果。

均卓有建树，为我国新文学的生成和发展做了不少工作。"他长期身居文坛中心、长期领导主持文学社团和文学报刊丛书的工作，他眼光敏锐又有伯乐之才，所以在他一生中发现、帮助、提携、培养的作家及文学研究者、翻译者和编辑者的数量实在不少。这是他对新文学事业重大贡献"（陈福康，2018：25）。而在翻译研究领域，郑振铎对晚清和同时代的很多翻译家都有过相对客观公正的批评，在发生论争时也能保持学术的理性和克制，让事实本身成为评判孰优孰劣的标准，体现出文学史家深思熟虑的中立姿态；同时又能严格恪守学术研究的基本伦理，和研究对象保持客观距离，以科学的态度切进研究对象本身，避免了先入为主之见，其研究结论广受同代文人的认同和后继者的赞誉，值得当下治文学史、翻译史学者的重视汲取。

二、郑振铎对清末民初翻译家的批评

清末民初是中国翻译史上的重要时段之一，涌现出众多名噪一时的翻译家，其中重要代表如严复、林纾、梁启超、包天笑、伍光建、鲁迅、周作人等，合力推动了西学在中国的译介和传播，为中国近现代文学文化的转型奠定了理论和实践基础。作为稍后或同时代见证者的郑振铎，对清末民初很多翻译家的翻译行为和译本都有过较为客观、中肯的批评，表现出一个学者价值判断的严谨性，有的批评已成盖棺之论，不失为当下翻译家研究的有益借镜。

对清末民初翻译家的批评，严复是第一个绕不开的点。作为晚清翻译家的卓越代表，严译八大名著成为近代中国翻译史上的里程碑，是后世翻译研究常提的标志性成果。郑振铎虽然没有专论严复的文章，但在很多涉及翻译研究的论述里都有对严复的评论。比如1935年在《世界文库·编例》一文中，具体评价了严复"信、达、雅"翻译三要素。他说："翻译者往往奉严又陵氏的'信达雅'三字为准则。其实，'信'是第一个信条。能'信'，便没有不能'达'的译文，对原作的忠实程度，便也颇可怀疑。'雅'是不必提及的；严氏的'雅'往往是牺牲'信'以得之的。不过所谓'达'者，解释颇有不同。直译的文章，只要不是'不通'的中文，仍然是'达'。加入将原文割裂删节以迁就译文方面的流行，虽'雅'却不足道矣。所以我们译文是以'信'为第一义，却也努力使其不至于看不懂。"（郑振铎，1935：23）这段论述中，郑氏能辩证看待严复的翻译三原则，既强调重要性又能发现欠合理之处。后来在《鸦片战争后的中国文学》一文中，特别对严复的翻译贡献进行定论："严复以其谨严秀雅的文字，切切实实的从事于《天演论》《名学》《原富》等等重要名著的介绍，其入人最深。"（郑振铎，1937：15）

与严复受到评价大部分是正面和肯定的不同，作为"译才并世数严林"的林纾，学界的评价则明显两极分化，赞誉有之，批评者亦不少。如刘半农和钱玄同的"双簧信"事件、鲁迅的"引车卖浆者流"之喻等，主要集中在林纾不谙外语、翻译中对原文主观增减等给予嘲笑和批评；另外一些稍显温和的新文化运动者，如周作人、胡适等人也对林纾有过批评，甚至措辞严厉。与上述诸人不同的是，郑振铎则更多看到了林纾的优点，持论比较客观公正，既不隐忍林译小说的问题和瑕疵，又能看到林纾翻译的时代意义。特别在1924年林纾去世后，他撰有《林琴南先生》一文进行悼念和评说，持论客观公允，不失为林纾的盖棺定论之文。在郑振铎看来，正是林纾的翻译和创作推动了我国文学现代性的发生，不管同时或稍后的文人们对林纾持何种态度，其"功绩却是我们所永不能忘记的，编述中国近代文学史者对于林先生也决不能不有一段记载"

（郑振铎，1924：35）。郑振铎认为林纾及其翻译小说是值得近代文学的史家们专书的。而对于林纾由之前维新倒向晚年保守这一转型，郑振铎则说："大约与他的环境很有关系，戊戌之前，他时常与当时的新派的友人同在一起，所以思想上不知不觉的受到了他们的渲染，后来清廷亡了，共和以来，人民也不能有自由的幸福，于是他便愤慨无已，渐渐变成顽固的守旧者了，这样的人实不止林先生一个，有好些人都是与他走同样的路的。"（Ibid）可以说，郑振铎这样实事求是、一分为二对翻译家进行批评，是值得翻译研究者借鉴的。

除严、林之外，郑振铎对梁启超的评论也十分精准。他高度认可梁氏在推动中国现代思想、学术转型方面的贡献，在《梁任公先生》一文中将其贡献归纳为六大方面，第二方面就是针对梁氏的翻译贡献所作的评价：

> 正是中国受外患最危机的一个时代，也正是西欧的科学，文艺以排山倒海之势输入中国的时代；一切旧的东西，自日常用品以至社会政治的组织，自圣典以至思想，生活，都渐渐的崩解了，被破坏了，代之而起的是一种崭新的外来的东西。第二方面是介绍西哲学，经济学等等的学说，所介绍有霍布士，斯片挪莎，卢梭，培根，笛卡尔，达尔文，孟德斯鸠，边沁，康德诸人。他的根据当然不是原著，而是日本人的重述，节述或译文。然因了他的文笔的流畅明达，国内大多数人之略略能够知道培根，笛卡尔，孟德斯，鸠卢梭诸人的学说一样的，却不是由于严复几个翻译原作者而是由于再三重译或重述的梁任公先生。这原因有一大半是因为梁氏的文章明白易晓，叙述又简易无难解之处，也有一小半因梁氏的著作流传的范围极广，我常常觉得很可怪：中国懂得欧西文字的人及明白欧西学说的专家们都算不少，然而除了严复马建忠等寥寥可数的几位之外，其他的人每都无声无息的过去了。一点也没有什么表现；反是几位不带懂得西文或者学问的人如林琴南，梁任公他们，倒有许许多多的成绩来。（郑振铎，1929：28-29）

严复、林纾、梁启超是晚清三大著名翻译家，是翻译研究者经常举例的对象，对上述三人的翻译贡献、翻译理论等，郑振铎均有客观到位的批评和定位。

晚清另一翻译家伍光建也是对我国文学翻译事业做出积极贡献之人，在伍光建生前，郑振铎就充分肯定了其翻译贡献："他自己说他的翻译是有目的。他曾经译了些拿破仑传，法国大革命史……可是他时常大胆的删节原作的一部分。这是不对的，他以'君朔'的名字译的大仲马的《侠隐记》等却是很好的。在清末的翻译界总算是一个重要的人，特别是因为他是用白话文译的。"（郑振铎，1936：14）伍光建去世后，他又写了《悼伍光建先生》一文刊出，评价更为全面具体，他说：

> 光建先生的翻译工作，开始于译大仲马的侠隐记。他曾经告诉过我，他的翻译都是有点用意的。他译这部侠隐记，用意并不浅。他译好后，用"君朔"的笔名，交商务印书馆出版。那时，林琴南先生"古文"的译笔正风靡一时，但光建先生却以水浒传般的精悍的白话文来翻译侠隐记。当时似未为人注意，至多不过视作迦因小转，十字军英雄记一类的一部翻译名作而已。到了五四运动以后，胡适之先生发现了这一部书，大为惊异，便向高梦旦先生询问：这书究竟是出于谁的手笔，君朔是何人的笔名？高先生告以即是光建先生。于是他们俩便自此定交，成为相当密切的友人。而光建先生自此便开始以译书为生涯。自林琴南先生绝笔后，他是最努力的一位译者了。即以此一支译笔，维持着他的生活，过惯了艰苦的译介生涯，过惯了清贫的淡薄生活，他不诉苦，他不旁骛，他没有什么嗜好和享用。他安于这样的译人的清苦的生涯。（郑振铎，1943：18-19）

清末民初的文学、文化界，作家和翻译家们意气风发，感情用事的现象不在少数，一些翻译家甚至还受流派之见的左右，相互之间不留情面的笔战时有发生，能给予同代翻译家中肯客观评价是件不容易的事，郑振铎的《悼伍光建先生》一文可谓是对伍光建人品、译品、文品的定论之言。

对于鲁迅的翻译，郑振铎也有过梳理和评价，他将鲁迅比作苏联的高尔基。二者共同的贡献是推动本国文学的世界性进程。"他以同样喜爱的态度，来对待《死魂灵》、百图凯绥、柯勒惠支版画，以及北平笺谱，陈老莲画博古牌；他以同样的热忱来介绍爱罗先珂的童话，阿志巴绥夫的小说……，他对一切好的，美的东西都是喜爱的。它决不有意的排斥某一时代或某一个地方或国度的美好的东西"（郑振铎，1936：296）。他认为鲁迅有"三绝"：辑佚、创作与翻译（郑振铎，1938：405-406）。将鲁迅置于学者、作家和翻译家的位置给予审视，鲁迅的翻译虽然被作家和学者的名头盖过，但作为三绝之一的翻译，也是值得鲁迅研究者所重视的。

翻译家研究历来是翻译研究的重镇，郑振铎对此较有认识，早在1921年他就在《俄国文学史中的翻译家》一文指出："无论在哪一国的文学史上，没有不显出受别国文学的影响的痕迹的。而负这种介绍的责任的，却是翻译家。威克立夫(Wyclif)的《圣经》译本，是'英国散文之父'(father of English prose)；路德(Luther)的《圣经》译文也是德国的一切文学的基础。由此可知翻译家是如何的重要了。……翻译家的功绩的伟大不下于创作家。他是全人类的最高精神与情绪的交通者。……唯有文学是满含这人类的最高的精神与情绪的，由文学的交通，也许可以把人类的误会消除掉了不少。所以在世界没有共同的语言之前，翻译家的使命是非常重大的。"（郑振铎，1921：70）翻译家因此应该受到重视，而郑振铎对晚清民国这些代表性翻译家的评价，为后来翻译家的批评提供了一个较好的样板和思路，既不掩盖他们在具体翻译中的失误和瑕疵，也不刻意去贬低翻译家们应有的成就和贡献，他总是以客观、科学和中立的姿态，从文学史本身出发，本着还原事物面目的严谨性来评价周边的世界和研究对象，这是一种非常值得倡扬的科学研究态度。

三、郑振铎翻译家批评的价值立场及现代启示

当前的翻译研究已经向各个领域纵深推进，翻译批评也受到较为深入的探讨，其也被认为是推动翻译研究的重要手段之一。一般认为，"翻译批评是以翻译艺术的欣赏为基础，对译本或者翻译理论问题作出科学的分析和评价，以便指导翻译实践和翻译艺术的欣赏活动"（郑海凌，2000：19）。当然，翻译批评不但要批评客体——译文，也要批评翻译的主体——译者。李文俊指出："为了使中国的文学翻译水平再提高一个层次，不应回避以高水平的译家、译品为批评的对象。相反，应该有那么一些有心人，除了总结他们的成功经验之外，也应该着重指出尚可改进之处，并且最好能有较深入细致的分析。"（引自杨自俭、刘学云，1994：626）我们认为，翻译批评的出发点应在于规范翻译家的翻译行为，提高翻译质量，推动翻译事业的进步，更好地服务文化之间的交流。在这一点上，郑振铎的翻译批评可谓深思熟虑、身体力行，实乃业界标杆。

从前面郑振铎对晚清民国翻译家的批评来看，有几点值得我们今天的翻译批评汲取。

一是强调翻译家应该立足翻译实践，全面认真思考翻译问题。在20世纪二三十年代，作为二十出头的年轻人，郑振铎就开始关注翻译问题了。他陆续发表了10多篇文章论述翻译问题，广泛涉及诸如"为何翻

译""翻译什么""翻译可能""如何翻译""为谁翻译"等译学研究领域的重大问题，且新见叠出，文笔老道。当然，这些见解是筑基于他的翻译实践之上的。虽然郑振铎的文学活动重心在于文学批评和编辑出版等，但也间接从事翻译活动，他的翻译经历十分丰富。在文学翻译上，一是翻译了当时几乎能见的文体，西方世界的神话、戏剧、诗歌、小说、儿童文学、散文等都有译文刊发；二是翻译范围十分广泛，古希腊、罗马、印度、苏俄、英法等国的文学作品皆有译介。这样丰富的翻译经历，使郑振铎既能成为翻译场上的"运动员"，又能充当"裁判员"的角色。而且，他通过编辑《小说月报》等重要刊物，能接触到当时的优质译者和译稿，故对翻译问题看得较为深入。"郑振铎在二三十年代在翻译方面作过一系列比较系统、完整的论述，有一些重要理论问题甚至是他第一个提出来的，具有启蒙和开拓的意义。在许多基本问题上，鲁迅的见解与他完全一致。他的这些翻译论述，不仅在当时起了很好的作用，而且经过历史的检验，至今仍基本正确"（陈福康，2010：198-199）。作为翻译家，郑振铎有艺术家的气质和秉赋，感情丰富、思想细腻、生性敏感、善解人意，长于形象思维；作为学者，善于分析、洞察世情、细心严谨、坚忍不拔，善于逻辑推理。他身上有着艺术和科学的完美结合，理想和现实的和谐统一，这也能使他能坚持相对客观的评判标准。1936年在《清末翻译小说对新文学的影响》一文中提出："中国的翻译工作是尽了它不小的任务的，不仅是启迪和介绍，并且是改变了中国向来的写作的技巧，使中国的文学，或可以说是学术界，起了很大的变化。"（郑振铎，1936：116）但他也指出清末的翻译小说也存在五点问题：

> 1. 妥协——在翻译的工作中，无论如何要顾及中国的读者的口味和伦理观点，要不相违背的才翻译；2. 利用——清末的翻译每每是利用外国小说著作想来做改革政治的工具；3. 消遣——一般的读者把翻译小说当做茶余饭后的消遣，故翻译者又要迎合读者起见，故无聊之侦探言情小说甚多；4. 无正确的文学常识——从事翻译的多半是当时一些政客及洋行买办，他们根本不懂得什么是文学；5. 不忠实——一般的翻译者似然抱着小说不过是街谈巷语的东西，根本不十分重要，就马马虎虎一点也没有多大关系，故在翻译的时候，名称的错误、事实的不合，却一概置之不理。（Ibid:117）

郑振铎所指出的这些晚清民国时期的翻译小说的缺点，切中要害，看得精准，今天看来也十分让人信服。

二是只认事实不走极端，坚持客观中立的翻译批评立场。批评毕竟具有主观性，因此在翻译研究和翻译家批评中恪守客观中立的批评立场并不容易。在《世界文库发刊缘起》一文中，郑振铎就指出很多批评家眼光狭窄，缺少科学批评视野的问题。他说："许多批评家们每执持着极偏窄的批评见解。是古者便非今，崇拜莎士比亚的便蔑视关汉卿。抱定了所知的数册书，偏以为天下之美，尽在于此。缘所知太窄，所见遂不免于偏窄。"（郑振铎，1935：22）另外在《人的批评》一文中，他提出批评的两条原则："（一）要以'人'的眼光，为一切批评的标准；（二）要以人道的态度，来批评一切的事物。现在的批评者的眼光，都是非常狭隘的；不是为国家，就是为阶级，等等的单面的感情，把自己的心灵蒙瞽着。他们只看见事物的一面，永不能概观他们的全体——不能以人类为批评的本位。"（郑振铎，1920：1）以此为批评路径，在他看来，清末民初的翻译家就算有各种不足，但其筚路蓝缕之功是不容抹煞的，因此，我们对翻译家的批评应对事不对人，只认真理。王佐良认为中国翻译家有三大独特传统：一是有高度的使命感，为了国家民族的需要不辞辛苦地去找重要的书来译；二是不畏艰难，不怕难书、大书、成套书；三是做过各种实验：直译，意译，音译，听人口译而下笔直书等（王佐良，1987：2）。这一代翻译家通过自己的翻译向中国读者介绍了外国的文学文化成果和社会知识，他们对翻译事业执著，不计较名利；专业功底深，外文中文都精通，不少人熟悉几种外语，而且知识面广，有译德；思想与时俱进，思想开放，善于吸收新事物，视野开拓，让中国人看到了色彩斑斓的外部世界，有力地促进了我国现代文学和文化的转型。这和郑振铎的翻译批评观高度一致，也是促使中国翻译繁荣发展的内生动力。郑振铎在上世纪二三十年代就能持客观中立的批评视域，体现出一个批评家应有的价值立场和民族大义观，就在今天也不过时。他阐述翻译观点，如"文学是可译的""外国诗歌也是可译的""翻译如同创造"，对翻译功能的提炼等，都是长期思考翻译问题、归纳翻译现象的结果；当然，作为学者型的翻译批评家，他深知翻译之不易，对翻译家的批评也不能求全责备，都各有自己的优点和不足，但每个翻译家的译介实践都在为中国的翻译事业添砖加瓦，个人的恩怨不应成为对翻译家进行不恰当批评的借口，郑振铎所倡导的客观评价、务实中立的翻译批评俨为学界清流，为后世翻译批评的科学展开树立起了标杆。

三是有兼容并包的胸怀，对翻译家的批评不受流派和个人成见所干扰。一般而言，批评总会涉及批评方法和立场等问题，也会间有流派之见和个人好恶等主观因素，但郑振铎总会以兼容并包的心态来处理批评对象，避免翻译批评失去客观性。其中最为著名的有两个例子。一个例子是对周作人的评价问题。在周氏成为汉奸后，郑振铎深表痛心，十分惋惜，但也没有刻意抹煞周作人对文学史和翻译研究的贡献，他评价说："周作人是五四时代成长起来的。他倡导'人的文学'，译过不少俄国小说，他的对于希腊文学的素养也是近人所罕及的，他的诗和散文，都曾有过很大的影响。……假如我们说，五四以来的中国文学有什么成就，无疑的，我们应该说，鲁迅先生和他是两个颠扑不破的巨石重镇；没有了他们，新文学史上便要黯然失光。"（郑振铎，1946：18）另一例子是青年批评家梁俊青批评郭沫若译《少年维特之烦恼》的失当之处，和郭沫若同为创造社成员的成仿吾大为光火，来信让承担编辑工作的郑振铎给予声援，认为青年梁俊青不应该批评郭沫若的译文，其中甚至有人身攻击的言辞。但郑振铎坚持编辑的中立原则，只将成仿吾的来信发表出来，并作出具体说明："关于译文究竟错不错，且让深通德文的先生们去批评。关于梁君的一方面的话，有梁君自己去答复，我们也不去代他辨说。我们所要声明的，只是编者的责任问题，"最后劝说郭、成二人，对于翻译，难免出错，要能容忍别人的批评之声，"不必以闻逆耳之言即忘了自己前途的'事业'，而悻悻然欲与言者拼命"（成仿吾，1924：3），争做和事佬。其实，在当时有过很多以文学研究会成员为中心的翻译论争，甚至有些带有流派之见和意气用事的成分，人身攻击的争吵时有发生，但郑振铎能摒弃门户之见，坚持真理，发表了很多令人信服的观点，也是值得今天积极肯定的。

郑振铎所坚持的翻译批评观给我们带来不小启发：正确的翻译批评，应坚持实事求是的原则，坚守客观中立的批评立场，重视译文的社会价值和影响力，不应带任何个人偏见，既不因人熟而相互赞扬捧场，也不因观点相左而诋毁谩骂，一切以翻译成就和学术贡献为出发点进行批评，这才是翻译批评的价值和意义之所在，也才能彰显翻译家研究之于翻译史、文学史、文化史及社会发展史的价值及意义。

四、结 语

杨义指出,郑振铎"一生的建树,乃是作家、理论家、学者、社会活动家大眼光、大魄力的综合效应所致,而且他总是和时代的方向一致,在现代历史的每个重要阶段,均对中国文学及文化做出了开拓性和推动性的贡献"(杨义、邵宁宁,2008:16)。在翻译领域也是如此,他对中国翻译理论的建构做出的贡献是实实在在的,不管是翻译对象的选择、翻译理论的申述,都十分具有代表性。"郑振铎在二三十年代在翻译方面做过一系列比较系统、完整的论述。有一些重要理论问题甚至是他第一个提出来的,具有启蒙和开创的意义"(陈福康,2000:230)。可以说,他从理论上和实践上推动了中国现代翻译理论的规范化进程,为后世的翻译研究树立了标杆。他不但身体力行进行域外文学文化的翻译引进,也对外国翻译家和翻译理论进行介绍,体现出文学研究的世界性视野和比较意识;再是对同时代的翻译家及其翻译成就进行较为详细和客观的评价,他一方面能恪守学术研究的伦理,坚持客观中立的翻译批评观,不走极端;二是有包容的胸怀,不受流派和见解的左右,让事实成为评判孰优孰劣的标准,他的这些做法,就在今天也是非常值得认真梳理和借鉴的宝贵经验。

参考文献

[1] Chen, Fukang (陈福康). "Keeper, Pioneer and Builder: On Zheng Zhenduo's Contribution in the History of Literature" (保存者·开拓者·建设者——论郑振铎在文学史上的贡献)[J]. *Literary Review* (文学评论), 2018(6):15-27.

[2] Chen, Fukang (陈福康). *History of Chinese Translation Studies*(中国译学史)[M]. Shanghai: Shanghai People's Publishing House(上海:上海人民出版社),2010.

[3] Chen, Fukang (陈福康). *History of Translation Theory in China*(中国译学理论史稿)[M]. Shanghai: Shanghai Foreign Languages and Education Press(上海:上海外语教育出版社),2000.

[4] Cheng, Fangwu (成仿吾). "Correspondence: Cheng Fangwu and Zheng Zhenduo"(通信:成仿吾与郑振铎)[J]. *Literature Magazine*(文学旬刊), 1924 (125):3.

[5] Wang, Zuoliang (王佐良). "Translation in the New Era: A Speech at a Symposium on Translation" (新时期的翻译观——一次专题翻译讨论会上的发言) [J]. *Journal of the Translators Association of China*(中国翻译),1987(5):2-4.

[6] Yang, Yi & Shao, Ningning (杨义,邵宁宁). "The Outstanding Pioneer of Chinese Renaissance: On Zheng Zhenduo"(献身中国文艺复兴的卓越先驱——郑振铎论)[J]. *Literary Review* (文学评论),2008(3):5-17.

[7] Yang, Zijian & Liu, Xueyun (杨自俭,刘学云编). *New Theory of Translation* (翻译新论)[M]. Wuhan:Hubei Education Press (武汉:湖北教育出版社),1994.

[8] Zheng, Hailing (郑海凌). "On the Basic Theory of Translation Criticism"(谈翻译批评的基本理论问题)[J]. *Journal of the Translators Association of China*(中国翻译),2000(2):19-22.

[8] Zheng, Zhenduo (郑振铎). "World Library·Compiled examples"(世界文库·编例)[J]. *New weekly*(新生周刊), 1935, 2(16):23-24.

[10] Zheng, Zhenduo (郑振铎). "Chinese Literature after the Opium War"（鸦片战争后的中国文学）[J]. *World Library Monthly Bulletin*（世界文库月报）, 1937 (4-5):15.

[11] Zheng, Zhenduo (郑振铎). "Mr. Lin Qin Nan"（林琴南先生）[J]. *Fiction Monthly*（小说月报）, 1924, 15(11):24-35.

[12] Zheng, Zhenduo (郑振铎). "Mr. Liang Rengong"（梁任公先生）[J]. *Fiction Monthly*（小说月报）, 1929, 20(2):10-29.

[13] Zheng, Zhenduo (郑振铎). "The Influence of Translated Novels on New Literature in the Late Qing Dynasty"（清末翻译小说对新文学的影响）[J]. *Contemporary Literature and Art*（今代文艺）, 1936(1):112-118.

[14] Zheng, Zhenduo (郑振铎). "Condolences to Mr. Wu Guangjian"（悼伍光建先生）[J]. *Middle School Students*（中学生）, 1943(67):18-19.

[15] Zheng, Zhenduo (郑振铎). "Mr. Lu Xun Is Not Narrow-minded"（鲁迅先生并不偏狭）[J]. *Backbone of Force*（中流）, 1936,1(5):295-296.

[16] Zheng, Zhenduo (郑振铎). "Summary of Lu Xun's Lost Work: For the Second Anniversary of Lu Xun's Death"（鲁迅的辑佚工作：为鲁迅先生逝世二周年纪念而作）[J]. *Field of Literature and Art*（文艺阵地）, 1938,2(1): 405-406.

[17] Zheng, Zhenduo (郑振铎). "A Translator of Russian Literature"（俄国文学上的翻译家）[J]. *Transform*（改造）, 1921，3（11）:69-78.

[18] Zheng, Zhenduo (郑振铎). "The Origin of the World Library"（世界文库发刊缘起）[J]. *New Weekly*（新生周刊）,1935, 2(16):22-23.

[19] Zheng, Zhenduo (郑振铎). "Criticism from People"（人的批评）[J]. *Republic of China Daily*（民国日报）,1920(1):1.

[20] Zheng, Zhenduo (郑振铎). "Hibernate and Write: Cherish Zhou Zuoren"（蛰居散记：惜周作人）[J]. *Weekly*（周报）, 1946(19):18.

作者简介

管新福，博士，贵州师范大学文学院教授、博士生导师。研究方向：近代中外文学关系、翻译理论与批评。电子邮箱：paper8226@163.com。

加强中国法律典籍外译 促进中西文明互鉴
——董晓波教授访谈

⊙ 骆怡然（金陵科技学院外国语学院，南京）
⊙ 董晓波（南京师范大学外国语学院，南京）

[摘 要] 本文是对国内著名法律翻译研究专家董晓波教授的访谈。法律典籍是域外了解中国法律文化、形成对中国法治形象认识的第一手资料，积极开展法律典籍外译及相关研究对推动中国法律文化走出去、重塑中国的域外法治形象、增强中国法治话语权具有重要意义。在访谈中，董教授阐述了中华优秀传统法文化的内涵，提及了中国法治形象的域外变迁及其深层原因，从历史价值、文明互鉴层面解释了中华法律典籍外译的必要性，并就我国法律典籍译介面临的挑战提出了对策，对新时代背景下我国法律典籍翻译的研究现状给出了可行建议。

[关键词] 中华法律典籍翻译；对外传播；文明互鉴

Strengthen Foreign Translation of Chinese Legal Classics to Promote Mutual Learning between Chinese and Western Civilizations: An Interview with Professor Dong Xiaobo

LUO Yiran (Jinling Institute of Technology, Nanjing)
DONG Xiaobo (Nanjing Normal University, Nanjing)

Abstract: This paper is about an interview with Professor Dong Xiaobo, a famous legal translation expert in China. Legal classics are the first-hand materials for understanding Chinese legal culture outside the region and forming an understanding of the image of Chinese rule of law. It is of great significance to actively carry out foreign translation of Chinese legal classics and related research to promote Chinese legal culture to go global, reshape China's image of rule of law outside the region, and enhance the voice of Chinese rule of law. In the interview, Professor Dong elaborated the connotation of excellent traditional Chinese legal culture, mentioned the extraterritorial changes in the image of Chinese rule of law and its deep causes, explained the necessity of foreign translation of Chinese legal classics from the perspective of historical value and mutual learning of civilizations, and put forward countermeasures on the challenges faced in the translation of Chinese legal classics, and the research

---

中国国家社科基金重点项目"中国特色法治术语翻译与对外法治话语能力建构研究"（20AYY008），2023年度南京师范大学重大培育项目："中华优秀传统法律文化的译介与传播研究"（23ZD07）阶段性成果。

status and feasible suggestions on the translation of Chinese legal classics in the new era.

Key words: translation of Chinese legal classics; international communication; mutual learning among civilizations

引 言

中国文化源远流长，中华文明博大精深。法律是一种有着丰富内涵的文化载体，中华法制文明具有深厚底蕴和独特魅力。党的十八大以来，以习近平同志为核心的党中央将"中华优秀传统文化创造性转化、创新性发展"摆在突出位置，推动中华优秀传统文化与时俱进，焕发新的生机活力。新时代中华民族的复兴离不开传统法律文化的浸润和滋养，先贤创造的无数法律典籍承载着极具民族特色的法律智慧，引领中华民族将中国建设成为和谐、有序、富强的国家。积极开展法律典籍翻译与研究，有助于牢牢把握法律典籍译介的主动权，客观还原中华法律典籍的真实面貌，促进国际社会对中华法律文化的接受和认同，扭转国际社会对中华法系的刻板印象。同时，也有利于积极传播中华法文化的核心价值，推动中华法系与其他法系平等交流，增强中国在国际法治建设中的话语权，为全球法治命运共同体贡献中国智慧。由此，我们邀请了国内著名法律翻译研究专家、中国法治现代化研究院"一带一路"法治发展研究中心副主任董晓波教授，与我们谈谈中华法律典籍译介的相关问题。

一、中华法文化与法律典籍

问：董老师您好，首先恭喜您的三部英文法学系列专著《新时代中国法律翻译及语言规划》(Chinese Legal Translation and Language Planning in the New Era)、《当代中国法律体系研究》(On Contemporary Chinese Legal System)、《中国立法语言规范化研究》(On the Standardization of Chinese Legislative Language)近期在施普林格(Springer)出版发行。您长期在法律翻译教学及研究领域耕耘，10多年来，主持参与江苏省、广东省地方性法规规章的译审工作，与团队累计翻译500多部法规规章，翻译"国家海上丝绸之路"申报世界文化遗产和国家"一带一路"埃塞俄比亚东方园建设相关法律文件。与此同时，主持国家社科基金重点项目"中国特色法治术语翻译与对外法治话语能力建构研究"，完成国家社科基金一般项目"我国法律法规翻译的统一与规范化研究"，在《中国法学(英文版)》发表《习近平法治思想的人民性探究》《涉外法治人才培养探究》《中国法律典籍的翻译研究》《提升我国法治文化软实力的路径研究：以法律法规外译为视角》等系列学术论文，成果斐然。

回顾您的研究历程，近年来您的研究重心似乎渐渐从立法语言规范研究向法律典籍译介与国家形象研究转变，这一研究转向的动因是什么呢？

答：谢谢你的问题。准确来说，两者均属于法律文化研究，可以说是一体两面、相互成就的关系。法律规范、法律制度是制度形态的法律文化，法律思想、法律学说等属于观念形态的法律文化。本质上都为提升国家形象，推动中国法律文化走出国门而服务。它们同等重要，是推进当代中国法治建设的两个抓手。

自从中国加入WTO后，法律法规逐渐透明化，立法语言的失范既降低立法质量，影响法律实施的权威及执法、司法活动，也有损国家形象。因此，立法语言的规范化研究围绕立法技术与法律语言展开，侧重当代立法语言研究，以期提升立法活动和执法、司法活动的质量，助推法治建设。法律典籍译介研究则是追根寻源。中国特色社会主义现代法治文化不仅沿袭着传统法律思想，在立法、司法和法律监督等实践上也都可以在古代法律文化中找到源头。法律典籍是中国传统法律文化及法律思想的载体，关注中国法律典籍译介，旨在真正展示中华法制文明精髓，推动中国优秀传统法律文化走出去，纠正西方汉学家塑造的中国法律刻板印象和偏见。

由于缺乏挖掘和研究，每每提及法律思想史，必称西方的古希腊、古罗马，给人造成中国法律思想言之无物的错觉。中国的法律思想非常丰富，从甲骨金石、秦简汉帛、经史子集，无所不有。据文献著录的不完全统计，以《九章律》为上限，《大清律例》为下限，仅法典就有160种之多。中国的封建法律和注释这些法律的"律学"，比西方中世纪时拥有更完备的体系。历史上，许多关键人物的独到见解还具有相当的超时代性。早在西周初年，政治家周公就有"父子兄弟，罪不相及"的论述；他还主张定罪量刑时，故意累犯应重罚，过失、偶犯可减免，这在一些西方国家中直到资产阶级革命时期才被提出。又如明清之际的启蒙思想家黄宗羲在其代表作《明夷待访录》中，提出"天下为主，君为客"等一系列具有鲜明启蒙性质的民主观念，反对封建帝制，主张民权，要求加强平等，扩大社会对执政者的监督权力等，这些思想已具备近代民主政治思想的特征。可贵的是，这些思想并非借鉴西方文明，而是从中国传统文化中发展而来，比卢梭在《民约论》中提出的主权在民思想要早了近一个世纪。中华法文化博大精深，许多人文化不自信的根源还是在于不甚了解。

问：面对如此丰富的法律思想与文化，我们该如何理解中国优秀传统法律文化的内涵呢？

答：历史地看，法律文化是一个国家或民族长期积累的结果。自古以来，我国形成了世界法制史上独树一帜的中华法系。它以中国古代传统法制与法律文化为根基，有很多优秀的思想和理念值得我们传承。其指导思想是发端于先秦的中华儒家思想，主要内涵体现在五个方面：(1)"天人合一"的哲学观。中华法系提倡"天人合一"，倡导天人相通、以人为本、以德配天，由于天人相通相合，自然形成"天人感应""以德配天"和"德主刑辅""明德慎罚"等法律思想原则。(2)人本主义的伦理观。儒家之"仁爱"思想渗透在中华法系的思想内涵与立法司法实践活动中，表现为礼法结合、注重教化，重视人学、关注现世，宽仁恤刑、重惜民命，轻徭薄赋、政简狱清等方面。在司法上，慎刑慎杀的刑事诉讼基本理念是我国传统法律文化的重要组成部分。(3)追求"无讼"的和谐观。我国传统文化中"和谐"的思想多源于道家老子和庄子的哲学，"天人合一""道法自然""万物与我为一"体现的是天人和谐观。古代法律文化中有厌讼的传统思想。孔子云，"讼，吾犹人也，必也使无讼乎！"《朱子家训》中有言"居家戒争讼，讼则终凶。"自古以来，百姓相安无事，和睦相处，是一种美好的向往。(4)成文法与判例法相结合的立法实践。历史上，《唐律疏议》《宋刑统》《大明律》《大清律例》等一脉相承，是东方世界先进法律文化的代表，对日本、朝鲜、越南诸国都产生了深远影响。西汉以后开始大量适用判例法，西汉有"春秋决事比"，晋有"议事议制"，唐有"法例"，明有《大诰》等。(5)重视法律监督。我国古代王朝大都重视监察与监督，不同程度地建立了自上而下的司法监督体系。秦朝从中央到地方都设有监察官；隋唐五代，御史台是中央行政监察机关，也是中央司法机关之一,负责纠查、弹劾官员、肃正纲纪;明代都察院由御史台发展而来,主掌监察、弹劾及建议。

可见,中华法系显示了中华民族的伟大创造力和中华法制文明的深厚底蕴。传统法文化中"以法治国""以人为本""德法并治"等理念不仅对中国法治现代化建设的理论和实践发展均发挥了不可忽视的作用,还深深地影响和塑造了我们对于"法"的认知和理解,塑造了我们对中华法文化的共同记忆。

二、中国的域外法治形象与法律典籍译介

问:我国的现代法治建设从传统法文化中汲取了丰厚的养分,让世界了解中华优秀传统法律文化也极其必要。推动中国法律文化走出去,法律典籍的外译是重要的一环。有学者指出,中国法律典籍翻译研究在演进过程中形成了三大范式,即语言学范式、文化学范式和历史学范式。您作为文化学范式的领军人物,多次在《人民日报》《光明日报》《中国社会科学报》《中国法学(英文版)》等发表系列研究成果,主要从历史价值、文化交流、文明互鉴的宏观层面考察法律典籍的外译,能否谈谈您如何看待法律典籍译介的必要性呢?

答:第一,法律典籍外译既是传承中国传统法律文化的需要,也是时代的需求。一方面,推进全面依法治国需要汲取传统法律文化精华;另一方面,法律典籍的译介担负着塑造传统法律文化记忆的重要作用,有助于增强民族自尊心,提振民族文化自信。

在封建社会后期,中华法系受制于封建专制主义发展举步维艰,近代以后,国人照搬西方法治模式的尝试也均以失败告终。但我们从革命、建设、改革的实践中探索了一条适合自己的法治道路。历史和现实告诉我们,在我国社会主义法治建设过程中,我们既要借鉴国外法治的有益成果,也需深入研究中华法系,从中提炼出超越时空的法律思维、法律理论以及立法、司法的原则与制度、经验与教训,科学总结中华法系发生、发展的规律性,找到其与当代法治的契合点,使其有机地融入现实的法治建设中。法律典籍的译介肩负着挖掘传统法文化新价值、阐释古代法思想新意义、赋予旧法治实践新生命的历史重任。

重新聚焦法律典籍译介不仅能够带我们重走前人的法治"长征路",更能以古鉴今,为当下中国法治现代化进程中存在的问题和隐忧提供参照,为全面建设社会主义现代化国家、实现中华民族伟大复兴夯实法治基础。

第二,法律典籍外译是树立中华法治新形象的需要。中国法律形象的塑造在历史上并不具备主体性。从13世纪初期到19世纪,中国的域外法律形象经历了巨大的变化,中国从西人向往的"乌托邦"国度跌落神坛,成为"野蛮""落后"的代名词。18世纪末19世纪初,外国人一边倒地将中国描述为社会破落、政府无能、司法黑暗、道德沦丧的异国,中国的法律制度也被用作贬损中国形象的工具。到了近代,西方汉学家和学者占据着翻译和阐释中国古代法律典籍的主动权,相关的译作和研究成果是以西方法文化空间构建的理论和实践经验为指导的,展现给国际社会的中华法文化形象往往是一种"西化"的、存在诸多误解和偏见的形象。至今,西方对中国传统的法律制度仍存有偏见,甚至持批评态度。中国传统法律文化要想得到其他文化的认同、全面展示中国的法治形象和重塑中华法系,对外译介在当代是十分必要的。

第三,法律典籍外译是促进中外文明平等交流互鉴的需要。无论是批判或肯定的角度,中国法律文化作

为西方文化的"他者",成为西方文化眼中的"变色龙",甚至是被意识形态化或者被误读,这些并不能改变中国法律文化的自身价值及其它在世界文化史上的地位。在一定意义上讲,这恰恰说明中国法律典籍的外译使中国法律文化成为塑造西方文化的一个重要的外部因素,中国法律文化具有世界性意义。

中国传统法律文化体现了中国传统文化的主要精神,具有自身独特的价值判断和文化结构。例如,民惟邦本的民本理念,以和为贵的价值追求,明德慎罚的慎刑思想等,都彰显了中华优秀传统法律文化的智慧。为了提升中华传统文化的感召力和说服力,让世界尊重和认同中国的文化价值,我们要将传统法律文化中优秀的部分译介出去,给世界上那些"既希望加快发展又希望保持自身独立性的国家和民族提供新的选择",为解决国际争端、地区冲突提供中国智慧,为促成一个具有机制约束力和道德规范力的全球机制、构建人类命运共同体贡献中国力量。

问:说到中国法律的域外形象,西方文明视域下的中国法治形象并非一成不变。您与学生在《是文化交流,还是文化霸权?》一文中提及,翻译中的文化误读可分为基于特定目的的蓄意性误读和基于认知局限的无意性误读。中国的"他者"形象从13世纪"乌托邦"式的理想国度到18-19世纪"落后"的东方蛮国,其中不免透露出译者对原文本的权力操纵。这样的蓄意误读是否源于更深层次的文化心理或是其他因素呢?您能展开具体说说吗?

答:翻译是跨文化传播活动,但受限于译者主体意识和历史社会语境,中西解读、古今解读之间存在差异是必然的。翻译中的文化误读有合理与不合理之分,合理的误读反而能使文化保持一种动态、平衡的张力,形成一种文化发展的动能;不合理的误读则会加深民族隔阂。蓄意性误读包含了译者的价值判断、意识形态和文化心理等多方面因素。

早期中国的法律形象在西方之所以呈现出完美的乌托邦形象,首先在于中华法系背后代表的文明,在世界上呈现出一定的优越性,中华法制文明在历史上曾走在世界前列。中华法系作为世界五大法系之一,在唐代达到一个高峰,并影响了东南亚国家,在这一地区形成了相近的法律传统。而中国古代经济发展的自给自足也催生了法律文化的独特性、孤立性,使得中华法系不受世界上其他法律文化的影响,中华法系的法律得益于儒家文化的滋养,形成了相对完备的法律体系和法律部门,其发展水平不逊于任何同时代的其他法系。其次,中国美好的法律形象符合欧洲人精神内核的"乌托邦"冲动。"理想国"是埋藏在西方人意识中的"底层代码",乌托邦则寄托着西方人的美好夙愿,两者在地理位置上都出现在遥远的国度。文艺复兴时期的游记文本和乌托邦文本之间存在着共同的叙事方式和特征,无论是地理位置,还是政教制度,中国的出现都符合理想国或乌托邦的特征,从马可·波罗的游记到门多萨的历史,中国的形象都在一步一步逼近西方人对乌托邦的期待,中国实现或是接近了理想国中人类正义与幸福的目标。

到了18、19世纪,西方得益于工业革命进入帝国主义殖民劫掠贸易时代,而中国的专制主义则渗透进政治、文化的方方面面,让中国的法律文化孤立于世界法律文化之林。这种孤立与封闭阻断了中国与世界进行法律文化交流的可能,成为中国社会文化进步的桎梏。此时的西方文明正需要一个他者来对自身进行认同。与中国的天人和一、讲求和谐的文化不同,经济飞速发展的西方要行其对外扩张之实。为了找到合适的理由，掩盖真实意图，中国便成为西方意识形态所否定和排斥的"他者"，成为"以欧洲为世界中心"的他者镜像对比的落后代表。在这一时期，"东方专制主义"的政治想象开始占据主流，从孟德斯鸠到黑格尔，一些重要的欧洲思想家基于本民族法律史的发展脉络，用西方法的概念去理解中国法，把中国描述为远远落后于西欧各国的文明体系。

在西方的现代化历史与现代性的思维结构中，用西方的一套"文明"来衡量世界各国的国际行为及法律权利，把"文明"看作一种相对于"野蛮"的社会进步状态并且通过将"文明"与种族差异、外交政策、国际法、国际秩序等联系起来建构出一套"文明"话语体系。在这样的话语体系之下，中国法律形象是西方现代文化的"他者"镜像，西方的中国法律形象是西方现代历史中生成的有关现代性"他者"的一整套规训知识。当这种认知逐渐标签化，它便具备了全球的散播性，演变成为一种认识论，成为西方人法律理性的话语，而不是事实真理的话语，从而成为将中国从国际法的权益中排除出去的正当性。

问：如此看来，面对西方强势文化这一整套关于"他者"的话语规训，我们要打破西方法治话语体系下的"他者"观念，重塑中国的域外法治形象，是一项紧迫、必要且充满挑战的任务。

答：是的。法律文化总是与社会经济发展相适应的，不同的文化与文明之间并不存在高下之分，不同的法律文化本应平等交流，互相尊重，互相借鉴。全球化进程中，法律的全球化也表现为一种竞争性，以美国为代表的西方法治成熟国家，在法治制度实践能力和法治话语的产出与输出能力上都起到了压倒性的强势作用，形成了全球化时代的法律帝国主义与法治话语的霸权。

文化的交流互鉴是建立在双方具有平等话语权的基础之上的。重视法律经典的重译和研究，跳出西方法文化主导的解释和评价体系，从本土的、现代的视角解读原汁原味的中国传统法治文化，取其精华、去其糟粕，只有牢牢把握解读自身文化的主动权，才能真正增强中国的法治话语权。

三、中国法律典籍外译面临的挑战及对策

问：法律典籍作为传统法文化的载体，是构建我国法治话语体系的重要组成部分。现阶段我国法律典籍的外译已经取得了不错的阶段性成果，但也面临诸多挑战。您认为我国的法律典籍译介所遇到的困难主要体现在哪些方面呢？

答：目前来看，法律典籍译介确实存在不少问题。简单来说，一是译本数量少、种类匮乏。目前已有的中国法律典籍全英译本仅有《洗冤录集》《唐律》《大明律》和《大清律例》。正律元典尚且如此，待译的法学思想、文化著作更是数不胜数。二是典籍译介的主动权掌握在国外汉学家和学者手中，中国学者尚未把握法律典籍对外译介的主导权。三是缺乏专业的法律典籍翻译人才。古代法律典籍翻译涉及语内和语际双重翻译，对准确性要求极高，译者不仅要有丰富的法学和外语知识，还得有较高的古文造诣，难度高、耗时长、出成果难的特点使不少译者望而却步。四是法律典籍的外译本涉及的语种种类很少，多集中于欧美国家，面向"一带一路"沿线国家的译介几近空白。五是国内外学者对法律典籍的译介和学术研究工作重视程度尚且不够，研究成果少。六是中国法律典籍译本的域外传播途径单一，效果并不理想。

问：目前法律典籍译介的现存问题是多方面的，需要各方持久的协同努力。若要改善现有局面，切实推

动法律典籍外译的进程，您认为首要任务是什么呢？

答：做好法律典籍译介的战略规划。要构建我国的法治话语体系，增强我国的国际法治话语权，最终还要落实到翻译实践上。例如，翻译过程中如何处理不同法系中的术语和法律文化，如何保留源语文化的"异质性"，等等。目前学界不乏相关的微观研究，宏观视角相对欠缺也因而更为必要，所以话语规划也是我的另一研究侧重点。

不同于过去少数国外译者出于个人学术旨趣进行的个性化、零散化行动，战略规划既是一种政治行为，也是一种研究活动。就法律典籍译介来说，做好战略规划是提纲挈领的总任务，需由政府主导，制定兼具科学性、系统性、针对性、开放性的统筹规划，然后多方主体才能从文本、译者与策略选择等微观层面开展具体的实践任务。具体来说，战略规划应涉及四个方面的内容。

第一，地位规划。当前，法律典籍翻译不受重视，主要源于学界对中华法系、传统法律文化的价值认识不足，对法律典籍翻译进行地位规划，就是要高度重视法律典籍翻译在讲好中国历史、传播中国法文化方面的重要性。思想上，不仅要重新认识中华法系的价值，也要充分认识法律典籍译介的战略意义；在实践中，应由政府的相关部门牵头组织，在实施国家重大项目时，要将法律典籍翻译项目纳入研究的范畴和视野，给予法律典籍和其他文化典籍同等的地位和政策支持，以吸引更多研究者加入，逐步提升对法律典籍译介的重视程度。

第二，本体规划。法律典籍翻译具有独特性、专业性、文化性。法律术语是构成法律文本的基本要件，中国古代法律术语是集合了古代法律语言文化符号形式与意义二元结合的体系。翻译古代法律术语需要超越时空、文化情境的牵绊，这决定了翻译法律典籍并不能直接套用其他类型文本翻译的话语体系。中国古代法律典籍成果丰富，既有法典、制度及其补充形式，也有思想、学说，还有民族法律智慧的成果结晶，需抓住重点，系统梳理，去粗取精，立足于古代法律典籍翻译的本体，做好内部系统规划，完善对法律典籍翻译的规范、原则、策略、标准、评价及翻译批评等多方面建设，构建一套与之相匹配的、独立的学科话语体系。

第三，教育规划。随着国际合作在典籍翻译领域愈发形成一种共识，这就要求我们必须做好前瞻性、长远性的教育规划，发现和培养潜在的法律典籍翻译实战家、理论家和批评家，为法律典籍翻译储备充足的后备力量，占领中国法律典籍对外译介话语权的制高点。目前法律典籍翻译教育规划并不能自给自足，法律典籍翻译对译者要求极高，其跨学科、跨专业的特质对学科交叉、渗透和转型发展大有裨益，从人才培养目标、知识体系构建、理论与实践结合等诸多方面尝试推进，形成古代法律典籍翻译的教育体系。

第四，传播规划。传播规划的另一面其实也是声望规划，中国法律典籍的声望是在国际传播中建立起来的，传播规划和声望规划是一体两面的关系。译本的传播并不是自动自发的，翻译的完成并不代表传播的完成，总需要依赖于传播手段和技术，借由特定的传播渠道，向受众发送完整的信息。传播规划是一项系统工程，既需要传播主体的主动介入，也要考量传播的受众、内容、媒介、效果等诸多因素。针对不同的传播环境、目标读者的文化需求和层次，制定不同的传播策略，实现媒介方式的精准定位；同时，做好传播效果的反馈、评价，对传播效果进行评估，以调整和确定新的翻译项目、文本选择及传播方式。

问：法律典籍译介的战略规划是一个涉及多方主体的浩大工程，既涉及政府宏观层面的配套政策，也牵涉微观层面具体的文本和译者的选择以及传播策略和方法的采用，各个层次的规划内容和任务也是不尽相同的，您可以具体谈谈各方的明确职责吗？

答：政府、行业、学术届、媒体都是法律典籍译介战略规划的主体。首先，政府在翻译规划中扮演了重要角色。虽然政府主导的翻译活动具有可控的规范体系，但受制于源语文化的内部因素，最终的翻译作品未能达到预期的传播效果，未能发挥有效的文化外交作用。有研究显示，20世纪80年代的"熊猫丛书"中只有10%左右的译本吸引了英美读者的阅读兴趣，而大部分译作基本达不到"文化传播"的目标（耿强，2010）。新时代的典籍译介应该市场话语和政治话语并重，政府在典籍译介中的角色应从原来的"规则制定者"转变为"扶持者""推动者"，在今后的法律典籍外译工作中，政府应加强对法律典籍外译工作的重视，借鉴其他领域典籍外译的做法，借助政府与外界建搭的合作平台，进一步提高法律典籍译介作品在海外的曝光率和接受度，逐步让海外人士从更广泛的角度了解中国的传统法律制度。

其次，行业层面主要涉及出版机构，通过加强国内外的出版机构合作，既负责典籍原作作品的确定、语种的选择、确定合适的译者等核心工作，也负责对目的语国家读者阅读习惯、读者阅读需求以及图书发行出版的模式等充分调研，以利于典籍译本在海外市场的发行和营销。有实力的出版机构可以扶持"一带一路"沿线国家出版机构的发展，或直接在海外建立分支机构，实现出版、发行的本土化运营，更能有效地把握住目标环境的文化心理、文化氛围，及时得到反馈并加以调整。近几年，在海外建立中国文化中心不失为通过学术外交推动文化"走出去"的有效方法。

再次，学术团体和科研机构等是推动中国法律典籍"走出去"的"智囊库"。一直以来，学术界对法律典籍翻译的研究几近空白。有学者对近10年来古代典籍翻译学术研讨会结集出版的论文和学术期刊的500篇论文统计发现，有关古代法律典籍翻译研究的文章仅6篇，且限于唐代和清代法律的两个英译本（熊德米，2018：006）。学术界要对法律典籍的译介发挥出更加重要的作用，就需加强对法律典籍翻译的多层次、多角度、系统性研究，既可以从宏观层面的政策出发，也可以从微观层面的翻译技术、翻译人才培养出发，还可以从传播学、法制史的角度进行跨学科、协同性的研究，为法律典籍"走出去"提供理论支撑。

最后，媒体是文化传播的载体，扮演着传播的"先锋"角色。从结构组成上，应同时囊括国内媒体与国外媒体，通过国内外媒体合作搭起文化传播和交流的桥梁；从传播的方式和载体上，既包括专业的学术期刊，也包括大众媒体、大众影音，为法律典籍"走出去"铺就多元化、多层次的传播渠道。近几年来，中国开始运用媒体传播学术思想，以现代化技术手段为支持、创新传播方式，借助影视影响力带动法律典籍的接受，这也是一个创新思路。

四、新时代中国法律典籍翻译研究的现状及展望

问：法律典籍的译介承担着塑造传统法律文化记忆、彰显法律文化自信等使命。如何推动优秀法律典籍"走出去"，是时代的考题，是译者的责任，也是学者的担当。您认为我国的法律典籍翻译研究目前存在哪些问题呢？

答：我国法律典籍翻译研究已走过萌芽期和起步期，现阶段的成果主要聚焦在译者研究、翻译策略与技巧研究、译介与传播研究、翻译对比与批评研究这几个主题，研究成果不断增加、视角逐渐多元、内容也逐渐深入。当然，也存在一些问题。

首先，研究成果较少。这主要是由于业已译出的、可供研究的法律典籍译本较少，主要集中在四部已在海外出版全译本中华法系代表作，分别是《大清律例》《洗冤集录》《唐律疏议》和《大明律》，它们均诞生于我国法律典籍外译的初期，且多由外国译者完成。尽管我国已启动并推进了多个向世界推出外文版文化典籍的重大出版工程，如"大中华文库"工程、"中国图书对外推广计划"和"中华学术外译"项目等，但其中没有一部真正意义上的法律典籍被翻译出版，这就让研究停留在对已有译本的分析与评价上，成果也局限在狭小的受众范围内，产生的影响力较为有限。此外，参与研究的多是来自政法类和师范类高校的研究者，外语类高校参与度较低，且从高校之间的合作角度来看，尚未形成联系紧密的研究团队，这直接导致成果较为单一化、碎片化，难以形成持续、稳定的研究体系。

其次，研究的深广度有待加强。单就上述四个全译本来说，在深度方面，《大清律例》英译本是主要研究对象，但哲美森与杰弥逊发表在《中国评论》上的节译、法国人弗里克斯（Félix）基于英译本翻译的法译本等尚未引起足够重视。此外，《大明律》姜永琳译本因为出版时间较晚，受到的关注还不多，但其学术研究型的深度翻译策略使得译作成了难得的研究语料，其经典性还需进一步探索。就广度而言，关于典籍及其翻译研究已经有了多年各自为战的研究成果，但迄今为止，尚未达到一种融合、系统的状态，和研究直接相关且具有关键作用的学科如社会学、传播学、海外汉学等在一定程度上存在缺位。

最后，缺少实证研究。法律典籍多为纸质藏书，部分典籍译本由海外出版社出版，藏书于海外图书馆，这都增加了研究的难度。因此，现有研究多为文本分析和理论思辨。然而，一个完整的法律典籍翻译研究体系的建构离不开实证性研究和定性、定量相结合的混合型研究。与之相关的语料库和术语库亟待建立，这不仅可以数据化、定量化的方式呈现译者与译本风格，而且能够直观呈现古代法律术语译名的变迁，指导翻译实践。

问：由此可见，完善相关研究具有重要意义，既能丰富典籍翻译理论，提高法律典籍翻译的质量，也利于现代法律语言文化的对外译介和传播。这就赋予了后续研究者们百尺竿头更进一步的继承性使命。对于未来的法律典籍翻译研究，您可以给我们一些建议吗？

答：法律典籍翻译研究仍有较大的探索空间，可以从很多方面入手。

1. 法律典籍翻译规划研究。构建政府主导、多主体并行的法律典籍翻译规划框架极为必要。从"法律典籍"的概念出发，号召专家学者依托研究中心或研究所，组成翻译与研究团队，绘制法律典籍翻译路线图，一方面对西方人译本中的蓄意性改写进行纠正、重译，一方面明确遴选标准，将更多彰显优秀传统法律文化的典籍进行选译、编译、全译，让研究建立在一定数量和质量的语料研究基础之上，以提高法律典籍翻译能力，丰富法律典籍翻译研究成果。

2. 传统法律文化的译介与研究。法律典籍承载着中华民族祖先对社会、法律、文化、哲学的体悟和思考，对传统法律文化的考察，一方面需要在新的历史方位下，继续挖掘、传承、翻译传统法律文化；另一方面还需关注译本推介，关照言外的文化性和社会性，考查已有译介行为中的受众、渠道和影响，总结宝贵经验和有益启示，找到传统法律文化精华输出与海外接受的契合之处，将传统法律文化更有效地引入国际视野。

3. 古代法律术语英译规范化研究。古代法律术语的英译对译者来说绝非易事。西方译者不仅受到自身宗教、思想、文化背景、读者、接受环境的影响，还受到中西文化关系大环境的影响，其译本中不乏一些"隐性的书写"。如何对已有译名进行较为系统全面的审定，充分考虑源语和目的语的语言文化差异，合理取舍与调整，做好语际转换，确保概念阐释层面的准确性、语符表征层面的一致性，推动形成古代法律术语译名统一与规范化体系，同样值得深入探究。

4. 法律典籍译本的副文本研究。副文本对于译本正文本起到了丰富、阐释、细化、验证的作用。探索副文本作为独立文体形态所蕴含的丰富意蕴，有助于体悟译者英译目的，寻绎不同特色的副文本在建构译者与读者关系中的功能。

5. 法律典籍译者研究。在翻译社会学视域下，可借助多元文化理论、译者行为批评理论等译学理论，借鉴比较文学、叙事学、社会学、接受美学等相关理论，继续加强对译者文化身份和译本的研究。

6. 法律典籍翻译的跨学科研究。法律典籍翻译研究的重要推动力来源于跨学科能力。挖掘法律典籍里蕴含的思想精华，激发其生命力，赋予其时代性，需要吸收其他学科的理论来丰富研究视角。如从历史角度勾勒古代法律术语译名的生成、发展史，从传播角度考证法律典籍译本旅行史，从形象学角度探究中国法律形象的域外建构、传播与变异，从符号学角度勾勒古代法律术语的符号意义以确立双语符号系统对接原则，等等，赋予法律典籍翻译研究深入且丰富的学术内涵。

7. 法律典籍翻译的实证性研究。基于现代技术的典籍数字化是"互联网+"时代的方向，建立包括基于网络、大数据等的法律典籍语料库或电子平台必然会给研究带来便利。借助于汉英对照语料库，研究者可以迅速确定较为合理的术语译文；利用 USAS（在线语义标注系统）对比权力关系总量及多个下级语义域，再现不同译本中的权力关系；多语平行语料库也有助于从词汇、句法、语篇等层面以定量对比的方法探析译者风格。

8. 法律典籍翻译与研究队伍培养研究。国内已有不少高校拥有翻译专业的硕士点和翻译学方向的博士点，但实际从事法律典籍翻译与研究的人才非常稀缺。研究成果的可持续产出需要高校有意识地承担起培养法律典籍翻译与研究人才的责任，在课程设置、教学模式及考核方式等方面进行创新，这就需要研究者调研我国高校法律典籍翻译与研究人才培养现状，制订合理的人才培养方案。

总之，开展法律典籍的翻译和研究，研究者必须站在新时代海外中国学的视野里，提升研究的前瞻性、深广度、理论性、应用性和持续性，力争向世界更好地讲述真实、立体、全面的中国传统法律故事。

参考文献

[1] Geng, Qiang (耿强). *Chinese Literature Walking towards the Worle through Literary Translation: A Study of English Translation in Panda Books Series* (文学译介与中国文学"走向世界"——"熊猫丛书"英译中国文学研究) [D]. Shanghai International Studies University (上海外国语大学), 2010.

[2] Guo, Jie & Dong, Xiaobo (郭洁, 董晓波). "An Visual Analysis of Translation Studies of Chinese Legal Classics from 1983 to 2021" (中国法律典籍翻译研究的可视化分析(1983—2021)) [J]. *Minority Translators Journal* (民族翻译), 2022(06): 63-74.

[3] Hu, Bo (胡波). "On the Three Paradigms of Translation Studies on Chinese Traditional Legal Classics and its Research Prospects" (中国法律典籍翻译研究中的"三大范式"及其研究展望) [J/OL]. *Journal of Zhejiang Sci-Tech University (Social Science Edition)* (浙江理工大学学报(社会科学版)), 2023-04-04: 25-30.

[4] Hu, Bo & Dong, Xiaobo (胡波, 董晓波). "Is It Cultural Communication or Cultural Hegemony: An Analysis of the Cultural Misleading in the First English Translation of *Ta Tsing Leu Lee*" (是文化交流, 还是文化霸权?——从《大清律例》首个英译本中的文化误读切入) [J]. *Chinese Culture Research* (中国文化研究), 2021(2): 161-170.

[5] Xiong, Demi (熊德米). "On the Foreign Translation of Chinese Legal Classics and its Criticism" (古代法律典籍外译及其批评研究) [N]. *Chinese Social Sciences Today* (中国社会科学报), 2018-10-19:006.

作者简介

骆怡然, 博士研究生, 金陵科技学院讲师。主要研究方向: 法律语言与翻译、典籍翻译。电子邮箱: evonneluo@jit.edu.cn。

董晓波, 博士生导师, 南京师范大学外国语学院教授, 中国法治现代化研究院"一带一路"法治发展研究中心副主任、特邀研究员。主要研究方向: 法律语言与翻译、语言政策与规划。

翻译大众化与大众翻译话语

——德布雷媒介学视阈下的考察

⊙ 肖维青　王 景（上海外国语大学英语学院，上海）

[摘　要] 翻译本身即是一种跨语言、跨文化的媒介，沟通原文与译文、源语文化与译入语文化，起到传播知识、观念、思想的作用。媒介学理论属于传播学的研究范畴，由法国学者雷吉斯·德布雷提出，本文以之为理论框架，引介其"媒介域"等核心概念，以此透视媒介变革进化的逻辑进路，并结合用户生成翻译这一实例，观照翻译活动的发展趋势，即翻译的大众化现象。大众化的翻译产生了丰富的大众翻译话语资源。针对后者，文章分别从本体论、范畴论、方法论、价值论等方面对其进行了阐释，旨在关注翻译发展动态，扩展翻译话语的研究领域，对深化翻译话语的跨学科研究、充实翻译话语研究内涵有积极的推动作用。

[关键词] 翻译大众化；大众翻译话语；德布雷；媒介；媒介学

Mediological Review of How the Discourse of Mass Translation Forms and Develops

XIAO Weiqing　WANG Jing (Shanghai International Studies University, Shanghai)

Abstract: As a bridge between the source and target texts and the two cultures, translation can be regarded as the cross-linguistic and cross-cultural medium to disseminate knowledge, ideas and thoughts. In light of the theory of Mediology, which was proposed by French scholar Régis Debray as a sub-discipline to Communication studies, this paper introduces its core conceptions to examine the inner logic of media evolution, and then reviews how the mass translation becomes mainstream with the help of the example of User-generated Translation. Mass translation brings abundant discourse, which in this paper is explored from the perspectives of its ontology, categories, methodologies, values, etc., as an effort to stay in tune with the status quo of the translation and promote interdisciplinary studies.

Key words: mass translation; the discourse of mass translation; Régis Debray; media; Mediology

一、引　言

作为一项跨语言、跨文化交际的工具，翻译也是一种形式的媒介（孙迎春，2012：56）。观念、理论、知识的旅行必然要借助翻译作为媒介（耿强，2022：78），翻译的媒介作用不仅表现在沟通两种语言、两种文化上，还表现在储存文化信息、推动文化传播上。同时，翻译研究中出现的多次转向均带有跨学科的特点。

法国学者德布雷所提出的媒介学理论专门针对媒介展开研究。本文以媒介学理论为出发点，通过分析其中的核心概念，归纳预测媒介的变革进化逻辑，结合翻译活动当前及未来的发展趋势，探讨翻译的大众化以及大众翻译话语的问题。翻译的传播过程及其效果在翻译学界已经是一个备受关注的课题，目前从传播学角度思考翻译问题的研究不一而足，而研究形式上主要可以分为三种：

一是采用传播学理论结合某一具体翻译领域开展研究，该类型的研究目前已经全面铺开，呈现百花齐放的态势：文学翻译、新闻翻译、外宣翻译、网站翻译、影视字幕翻译、民族和民俗翻译、典籍翻译、旅游翻译，甚至是武术翻译、陶瓷翻译、京剧翻译、中医药翻译等切入点更为微观的研究。但值得注意的是，部分研究有嵌套理论之嫌，导致研究程式化、呆板化、缺乏新意。

二是从传播学的角度聚焦于翻译过程中的某一主体，如李庆明和赵颖（2012）研究了《老残游记》两个译本中译者的主体性问题；牟佳、周桂君（2019）关注纪实文学翻译中译者的历史认知情况；李振（2009）从受众角度出发，分析其存在的选择性心理。这类研究融合了传播学和翻译学的方法论，关注的也不再是文本，而是聚焦于诸如译者和接受者这样的翻译活动者。

三是从翻译研究和传播学两门学科的高度出发，研究两者之间的关系，如吕俊（1997）认为翻译学是传播学的一个特殊领域，姚亮生（2004）提出要建立传播学的翻译观。还有一部分学者直接提出建立一门独立的学科——翻译传播学，提出其已在事实上成为一门新的交叉学科（谢柯、廖雪汝，2016；尹飞舟、余承法，2020）。这类研究目前还较为少见，可见目前相关研究主要关注的仍是微观和中观层面，而鲜少从宏观角度进行跨学科的审视。

然而，无论形式如何，上述研究基本是着眼于论文发表时翻译活动的特点，根据其当时的翻译实践经验得出结论，而并未把握翻译活动的发展趋势；同时，结合传播学中媒介学理论研究翻译的成果近乎空白。本文旨在从翻译作为媒介这一本质特征出发，发现两者在进化逻辑上的共同点，同时提出大众翻译话语这一概念，在翻译研究中开辟出一个较新的研究领域。

二、德布雷与媒介学：理论来源和关键词

（一）理论来源

媒介学的提出者雷吉斯·德布雷（Régis Debray）是一位著述颇丰的法国学者，先后出版十余部著作及多篇论文、访谈。德布雷的思想形成有两个关键因素：自身经历和学术环境。德布雷的自身经历极富传奇色彩：早年他与著名的革命家切·格瓦拉并肩战斗，亲身经历了波澜壮阔的拉美游击战争。同时，德布雷的毕业院校巴黎高等师范学院当年也是左翼思潮和革命思想的大本营，著名的马克思主义哲学家、《保卫马克思》的作者路易·阿尔都塞（Louis Althusser）便是德布雷的老师。现实生活中的经历导致德布雷的学术理念深受马克思主义与革命思想的影响，让他关注人民大众、关注事物的进化与发展、关注社会的权力关系。

此外，德布雷的学术思想也发端于其祖国的"法国理论"（French Theory），即20世纪五六十年代法国的社会人文理论思潮，代表人物有米歇尔·福柯（Michel Foucault）、雅克·德里达（Jacques Derrida）、皮埃尔·布迪厄（Pierre Bourdieu）等。德布雷的媒介学理论中的核心概念"传承"（transmission），以及媒介域的划分、演进等等，显然是受到了福柯谱系学方法论的影响，无论是认知论还是方法论，我们完全可以用谱系学来描述媒介学（朱振明，2019：87），同时媒介学也关注权力与话语的关系，和福柯的知识考古学一样，媒介学注重技术史的梳理与发掘，致力于阐发社会与资本的关系等等。可以说，媒介学是在法国的社会人文学术环境中生发的，与其同时代的其他理论一脉相承，在方法论、研究角度等方面都具有一定的共性。

（二）理论关键词

1. 媒介学与媒介

要讨论媒介学，首先我们需要对何为"媒介"和"媒介学"给出定义。德布雷于1979年的著作《法国的知识权力》（*Le Pouvoir Intellectuel en France*）中第一次提出了媒介学（Mediology）这个概念（陈卫星，2015：1），并在此后的《普通媒介学教程》（*Cours de Médiologie Générale*）、《媒介学引论》（*Introduction á la Médiologie*）、《媒介学宣言》（*Manifestes Médiologiques*）等著作中构建、完善了媒介学的整个体系框架。德布雷认为，媒介学是"一种对文化领域和技术领域的互动研究"（Debray，2015：102），研究的是"一个观念通过哪些媒介成为一种力量？一个话语如何能造成事件？一个精神如何能获得实体？"（Debray，2014：96）而对于媒介，德布雷将其定义为介于符号生成和事件生成之间的、一套程序和中介体的动态集合（Debray，1996：17）。由此可见，媒介学是从技术的观点观照话语、思想和文化的传播，特别强调的便是技术与媒介、文化、社会、权力等因素的关系如何。

2. 媒介域

媒介域（mediaspheres）是德布雷媒介学学说中的一个核心概念，集中体现了其基本观点和内在逻辑，是我们进一步研究媒介进化逻辑的理论起点。所谓媒介域，就是信息传播的媒体化配置所形成的包括社会制度和政治权力的一个文明史分期（陈卫星，2015：9）。德布雷在《普通媒介学教程》中划分了三个媒介域：文字（逻各斯域）、印刷（书写域）和视听（图像域），在每一个媒介域中都有相对稳定的社会制度和文化随之产生，而它们赖以维系的支柱便是各自占据支配地位的技术，如口头叙述之于逻各斯域，印刷术之于书写域，电视、电影等视听技术之于图像域。德布雷认为，媒介域是随着技术进步而不断进化的，但一个新的媒介域的出现并不代表着前一个媒介域的绝对消亡，媒介域的演进并不是完全线性的，反而是相互交错，不断协调甚至是彼此激活的（Debray，2014：51）。比如视听设备的出现，一方面使传统纸媒的地位大大下降，另一方面也促成了电子纸媒的兴起。媒介域更替背后的规律，就是媒介的演化逻辑。

3. 媒介演化逻辑

近年，德布雷在与中国传媒大学陈卫星教授的学术谈话中明确地指出，我们现在已经身处一个全新的，也就是第四个媒介域——数字域中。数字域"是一个二维码的、影像的和符号的世界"，而数字域的出现是因为信息技术载体的碎片化趋向，这种碎片化"稀释了社会的内聚力，弱化了集体身份"，在这里每个人都是信息的发出者和散布者，"我们从一个以发出者为中心向大众传递某个信息的大众媒介系统开始过渡"（Debray，2015：15）。

德布雷认为，媒介的演化进入了一个新的阶段，而在这个新的媒介域中，最突出的特质就是媒介的进一步大众化，即所有人都同时成为传播的发起者和参与者。当前，新媒体、社交网络已经成为最主要的媒介形式。仅以微博为例，据统计，截至2022年第一季度末，微博月活跃用户达到5.82亿，同比净增5100万，日活跃用户达到2.52亿，同比净增2200万[①]，充分体现了大众参与、大众传播的特点。

我们在前文提到，技术的更新是媒介域演进的根本动力，数字域的出现也不例外。与德布雷写成《普通媒介学教程》之时相比，当今互联网世界已进入web 2.0时代，网络已不再是静态的文本和图形，而应被视作一种交互性的传输机制（DiNucci，1999：220），网络连接的不再是用户与内容，而是用户和用户，正是这种技术上的进步促成了数字域的到来。我们已经进入了"众媒时代"，媒介形式更加多样，信息生产主体和接受主体彻底大众化。

基于上述的媒介演化逻辑，下一个媒介域或许即将出现在离我们触手可及的未来。目前传播学界已经关注到了技术上的又一次革命性演进，即以元宇宙为代表的虚拟现实技术的勃兴，互联网的 web 3.0 时代正在来临。有识之士早已对此有所观察，并针对性地提出了一系列新的概念，观照媒介层面相应会发生的变革与进化。有观点认为，在新一轮技术的驱动下，未来媒介发展趋势将会是"万物皆媒"，泛媒化时代即将到来（彭兰，2016：5）。与当下的"数字域"时期相比，虚拟现实技术所带来的突破主要在于"万物互联，终端显化"。从 web 1.0 到 2.0，互联网的重心从信息传递逐步过渡到人际关系，而 web 3.0 将进一步突出用户终端（人）的地位，通过高互动性和高智能性形成"一个高度以'人'为中心的网络"（方凌智、沈煌南，2021：2）。人正从互联网这张大网上连接的一个个终端节点走向网格的核心位置。可以看出，无论是现在还是不远的未来，媒介都将会更深入、更彻底、更全面地实现大众化的演变，向无数个终端——个体存在的人无限靠近，这就是当下和未来的媒介进化逻辑。

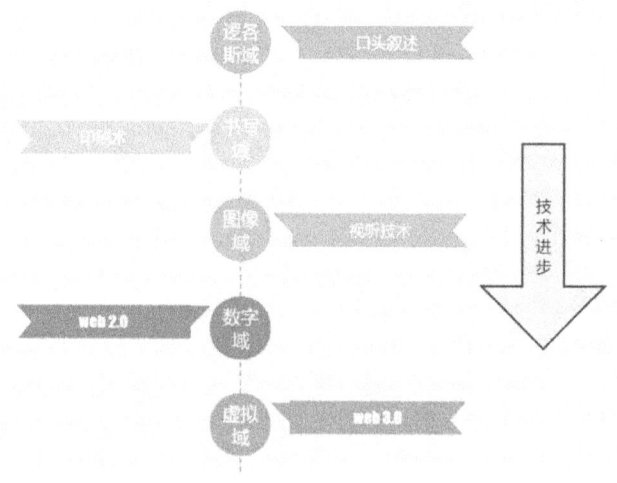

图 1 媒介域与媒介进化逻辑

三、翻译的大众化：以用户生成翻译为例

（一）翻译的大众化

媒介学的观点为我们提供了一个新的视角和理论进路，让我们可以重新审视翻译活动的发展和演变趋势。事实上，作为一种特殊的媒介，翻译完全符合上述的媒介进化逻辑，也在发生大众化的演变。然而，在历史上翻译作为一种人类活动的发展过程中，创作主体在很长一段时间内都是小众化，甚至精英化的。回顾翻译的发展史，无论是西方的《圣经》翻译还是中国的佛经翻译，翻译的开端总是与宗教联系在一起，只有一小部分掌握多门语言的宗教界人士才能进行翻译，翻译被蒙上了一层神秘色彩。何况宗教翻译对于译者的要求苛刻，不仅需要完全忠实于原文，做到极高的精准度和还原度，还要拥有广博的知识。《圣经》的翻译甚至与教权主义和反教权主义的斗争有关，罗马教廷禁止平教徒私下阅读、阐释、翻译《圣经》，翻译被视为教会和教士独有的权力。

在欧洲文艺复兴和启蒙运动之后，翻译的接受者逐渐变得大众化，越来越多的平民百姓可以通过翻译来接触《圣经》等宗教读物以及其他的文学作品。但翻译活动本身却依然与普通民众联系甚少，仅为文学界、哲学界等知识精英阶层接触。一直到翻译确立独立学科地位后，情况也没有特别明显的改变，翻译还是少数人的私家爱好。

但近年来，随着互联网技术突飞猛进的发展，全球化进程不断深入，世界已然变成了"地球村"，经济、政治、文化交流日益频繁，对于翻译的日常需求大大上升。同时，世界各国普遍加大对教育的重视程度，推行教育改革，实行教育的国际化，外语教育得到了广泛的普及。语言的工具性日益突出，翻译活动的创作主体也出现了明显的下沉倾向，翻译已经彻底不是束之高阁的秘宝，我们进入了一个几乎人人都能说几句外语，人人都会做一点翻译的时代。有学者指出，今日世界，翻译实践参与面之广前所未有，整个翻译活动链的参与人群早已突破了以往的文化精英圈，无论是语言转换、作品欣赏还是翻译批评，参与者都变得更加大众化，翻译日益成为一种平常的活动、普通大众也有话语权的文化场域（莫爱屏等，2014：52）。虽然翻译的大众化也带来了许多问题，最明显的即是由空前庞杂的译者队伍规模所带来的翻译水平的参差不齐（魏向清，2016：152），但翻译实践已经不再是知识精英阶层的专利，在普罗大众也获得了翻译王国的入场券之后，翻译参与的主体得到了很大的丰富与扩充。

尽管如此，有调查表明，翻译研究者和翻译从业者对于众包翻译（outsourcing translation）等大众化趋向的翻译行为关注兴趣不高，并且多数持负面态度（Zwischenberger，2022：11）。可见翻译研究学界仍未将翻译业外的大众群体作为翻译活动的重要参与和创作主体展开研究，对其创作特点、趋势产生的原因、对翻译活动的影响等仍然没有给予足够重视。目前，翻译研究者重点关注的还是传统翻译研究对象，如作家、学者、译者，原文、译文，以及相关历史、相关事件等等。

（二）用户生成翻译

翻译大众化的大潮中最为普遍、参与面最广，也因此最具代表性的一种翻译形式当属用户生成翻译（User-generated Translation, UGT）。这个概念实际上来自用户生成内容（User-generated Content, UGC）这一信息领域的术语，后者的定义是"web 2.0 下一种新兴的网络信息资源创作与组织模式"（赵宇翔等，2012：68），可见这种翻译形式正是技术变革下媒介域演进的产物，符合媒介演化逻辑。有了 web 2.0 技术层面的进步，个人就可以通过社会化媒体向所有人展示自己产生的内容（钱洁、潘洪涛，2012：105）。用户生成内容在 web 2.0 时代得到迅速发展，目前已经成为互联网世界主流的创作方式和内容构成。用户生成翻译对其在范畴上对用户生成内容加以进一步的限制，即仅限通过翻译活动产生的内容。

用户生成翻译的创作者"因为对某一领域或某一主题感兴趣，自愿成为无翻译版本作品的补救者，并凭借自身知识背景成为翻译的直接生成者"（O'Hagan，2009：97），因此大多是业余爱好者，虽然可能具备一些某一特定方面的相关知识，但一般并不具备专业的翻译学科背景。他们在翻译和创作过程中并不会以某种翻译标准为框架约束自己，也不会一以贯之地采用某种翻译策略，主要翻译目的为试笔和娱乐，以满足个人审美情趣，而非出于特定的政治因素，也没有实现学术价值的追求。

用户生成翻译体量非常庞大，有不计其数的来源渠道，包括网络用户创造生成的论坛、主贴、图片、博客、视频等各种内容（Chua，2014：7），也包括粉丝影视字幕组、民间动漫和游戏汉化组等翻译活动形式。但由于其非专业性、主观随意性较强、翻译质量良莠不齐等因素，在现阶段并没有得到充分和系统的研究。已有研究往往聚焦于某个具体领域（如字幕组翻译或是游戏本地化翻译等），研究中的跨学科意识也存在缺位现象。

四、大众翻译话语：意涵与维度

翻译话语这一概念目前在中国学界尚属早期形成阶段。当代杰出的翻译家、著名翻译理论学者张佩瑶教授曾在著作《中国翻译话语英译选集（上下册）》中提出"翻译话语"的概念，将其基本定义为译论和译思。在中国知网以"翻译话语"为关键词检索，发现针对这一概念的论述绝大多数仍处于自发认识阶段，而学界似未达成共识。相当一部分学者将其定义为"具体某一领域翻译的用语模式或模型"，如"儿歌翻译话语"（崔若男，2022）、"山水诗翻译话语"（陈琳、魏春莲，2021），也有研究将翻译话语定义为"翻译中的术语"（陈德用，2022）。虽然针对翻译话语的研究整体数量仍相对较少且发刊层次较低，但近几年来（自2021年开始）学界对该概念的关注度显著提高，相关研究频频刊登在《中国翻译》《外国语》《中国外语》《上海翻译》等权威刊物上。中国学者耿强在几篇论文中较为详细和系统地阐述了翻译话语的意涵与理路，将其定义为"翻译事实、有关翻译的知识与观念以及知识生产过程中知识与权力的相互作用和生产、传播、消费的各个环节"（耿强，2020：7）。该定义从适用范围、过程链条等方面较为完整全面地描述了翻译话语。因此本文借用这一概念，并在此基础上提出大众翻译话语这一新的术语。翻译的大众化必然会产生丰富的大众翻译话语资源，因为"翻译话语是翻译实践的直接产物，有什么样的翻译实践，就会产生与之相匹配的翻译话语"（耿强，2018：171）。本文分别从本体论、范畴论、方法论、价值论这四个层面对大众翻译话语这一议题展开探究，以期能够较为深入、全面地阐发大众翻译话语的意涵与维度。

（一）本体论

首先，我们要对大众翻译话语的概念做出定义，明确其属性和特质。本文认为，大众翻译话语是技术进步和文化结构互动关系下的伴随性产物，与媒介进化具有逻辑一致性。它可以被认为是在翻译大众化趋势下，围绕不具备翻译学科专业背景、未经过专业训练的普通大众的翻译行为所产生的话语和话语体系。

大众翻译话语具有以下几个特点：

第一，具有高度的共享性、交互性和社交性。大众翻译话语最主要的生成渠道是社会化的媒体平台。比如，手机上音乐软件中的非中文歌曲的歌词翻译，都是由软件用户自行翻译上传的，在其上传后，其他用户都可以在听歌时看到该翻译，也可以在评论中分享、交流自己对该翻译的看法；视频网站中有一些原本没有翻译的"生肉"视频，有通晓该语言的用户以弹幕的形式发送自己的翻译作为字幕，从而给其他不懂该语言的用户以方便，而其他用户在观看的同时，也可以通过发表自己的弹幕或者在评论区留言的方式给弹幕提供者反馈，还可以通过在软件内转发或是跨平台分享等形式去继续传播这些大众翻译话语。因此，交互和社交属性是影响大众翻译话语生成、传播、消费的重要因素。

第二，价值判断具有强烈的个性化特征。由于参与主体是广大大众群体，不同个体之间审美情趣、学识阅历、生活环境等相差甚远，再加上大部分人没有翻译专业的学科背景，大众所形成的翻译话语在对于翻译的观念看法、翻译质量的评判等方面也是千差万别，带有鲜明的个人烙印。

第三，话语涉及的内容和领域十分丰富。大众翻译话语包罗万象，无论是政治、经济、军事、音乐、体育、科技，只要涉及语言转换，就都可能存在大众翻译话语的踪迹，因为大众文化存在于社会各个领域。

第四，话语出处具有模糊性。大众翻译话语生成的技术基础是互联网技术，而互联网本身就具有匿名性强的特点。与传统翻译话语基本出自身份明确的名家学者不同，大众翻译话语的来源大都是以网络虚拟身份参与的普通大众，话语出处具有多元性和模糊性。

第五，相较于传统翻译话语，受众广、影响大，但语域较低、主观随意。虽然大众翻译话语已经跨越了翻译学科的范畴而真正成为大众文化生活的一部分，但作为创作主体的大众只是用日常用语来描述翻译，且带有很强的主观随意性，需要我们对其加以整合和提炼，找到对于翻译活动和翻译研究有价值和启示作用的部分，从整体的角度探寻规律，并用专业的语言表述出来。

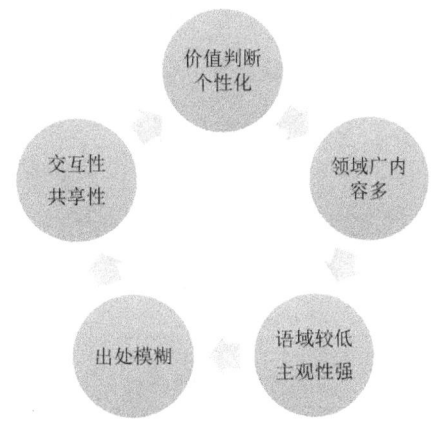

图 2 大众翻译话语的特点

（二）范畴论

范畴论主要研究大众翻译话语的存在形态。首先是由大众直接创作的翻译，翻译实践构成了最基础的话语形态；其次是围绕大众的翻译实践所产生的心得感悟、批评议论等等，还有新闻媒体对于热点大众翻译事件的报道，以及相应的规章制度、纲领文件等等。

大众翻译话语的研究对象包括其活动者，即生产者、传播者以及消费者，如活动者的动机和心理、评判标准，抑或是翻译过程、译文特点、翻译质量、翻译现象等等。

（三）方法论

方法论关注的是我们怎样着手研究大众翻译话语的问题。既然大众翻译话语是技术进步的产物，我们当然要从技术层面对其展开研究。上文提到，大众翻译话语十分庞杂，且主观性、差异性很强，因此我们需要以计算机辅助翻译为技术手段对其加以分类整理、总结提炼，如使用语料库技术对话语进行批量化的筛选，归纳翻译模型，寻找话语生成规律；通过大数据对大众翻译话语进行系统的统计和分析，对其生产者、传播者、消费者划分不同的类群，并描摹类群的整体画像，分析不同类群的行为模式及其对翻译的影响，以及深层次的文化因素、经济因素等等。

我们也可以分别从共时和历时的角度展开研究。历时研究方面，梳理大众翻译话语的发展脉络，聚焦其中的重要事件及其影响（如智能手机和个人电脑的普及、社交媒体的主流化等等）；共时研究方面，可以分析在现代语境下，大众翻译话语和传统翻译话语的关系，二者是否存在相互作用、相互影响。

（四）价值论

价值论主要研究大众翻译话语所产生的影响，包括对翻译自身以及在更宏观层面上的影响。对于翻译本身来说，研究大众翻译话语有助于我们更好地把握翻译活动发展的趋势，描绘当下翻译活动的整体面貌，广泛了解受众的审美和需求。

一方面，大众翻译话语的主流化给翻译活动带来了一些积极的改变，如提高了公众对于翻译的兴趣和参与度，使更多的群体能够参与到翻译活动和相关的讨论中来。相对完成质量较高的译作促进了翻译风格的多元化，丰富了译者队伍构成，降低了参与翻译活动的门槛，有助于翻译活动打破学科藩篱，收获更高的关注。另一方面，大众翻译话语也可能会对翻译活动、翻译研究造成负面影响。大量低质量翻译的流行、混乱的翻译质量评估标准会使大众形成对翻译的错误认知，并在社会层面引起一种错误的翻译导向和翻译风气。

"一个时代的文化心理、社会思潮、政治观念、行为模式与这个时代的信息传播结构有关系，这是相互塑造的互动过程的结果"（陈卫星，2016：118）。作为一种新的翻译话语形态，大众翻译话语的影响不仅仅局限在翻译层面，更会带来权力关系的重塑，对社会生态产生一定的影响。例如，关于翻译的学科设置、定位以及相关的教育制度可能需要更新；大众翻译话语表达了大众对于翻译的需求，可能出现为其服务的配套产业等等。

五、结 语

德布雷的媒介学关注的是技术与文化结构的互动，他提出了媒介域的概念，认为不同的技术条件会催生不同的媒介域，而媒介域是在不断发展、进化的。借助媒介域的内在逻辑，我们可以论证媒介的变革和演化进路：在互联网技术进一步发展的技术基础上，第四个甚至是第五个媒介域已然出现，为信息的生产、传播和消费带来了大众化的变化，而这也影响了翻译活动，翻译出现了大众化浪潮，翻译链全过程的参与主体得到了极大的拓展，以用户生成翻译为代表的大众翻译形式应运而生。大众化的翻译实践带来了大众翻译话语，作为一种重要的翻译话语存在形态，我们可以从本体论、范畴论、方法论、价值论等方面对其展开初步研究，厘清研究思路，为今后更为系统的研究铺路架桥。

翻译话语本身就是翻译研究中一个全新的研究领域，而大众翻译话语则是这个新领域中又一次"开疆拓土"的尝试。在翻译大众化的大潮下，翻译从业者和研究者更要注重自己的专业身份，用敏锐的眼光把握翻译发展趋势，捕捉具有研究意义的翻译现象，从学科的高度和理论的高度出发审视、阐发大众翻译话语，真正成为翻译和翻译研究的引路者、护航人。

注释

① https://baijiahao.baidu.com/s?id=1734435532847267443&wfr=spider&for=pc

参考文献

[1] Chen, Deyong (陈德用). "Technical Terms Employed in Tang China's Discourse on Translation" (从《全唐文》透视唐朝翻译话语中的术语体系) [J]. *Chinese Translators Journal* (中国翻译), 2022(2): 32-41.

[2] Chen, Lin & Wei, Chunlian (陈琳，魏春莲). "On the Ecological Implication of Hinton's Translational Discourse in Translating the Rivers-and-Mountains Poetry" (论欣顿山水诗翻译话语的生态哲学意义) [J]. *Foreign Languages in China* (中国外语), 2008(2): 89-96.

[3] Chen, Weixing (陈卫星). "Communication and Mediaspheres: Another Historical Approach of Interpretation" (传播与媒介域：

另一种历史阐释) [J]. *Global Journal of Media Studies* (全球传媒学刊), 2015(1): 1-21.

[4] Chen, Weixing (陈卫星). "The Mediological Problematic of New Media" (新媒体的媒介学问题) [J]. *Nanjing Journal of Social Sciences* (南京社会科学), 2016(2): 114-122.

[5] Chen, Weixing & Debray, Régis (陈卫星, 雷吉斯·德布雷). "Mediology: Ideas and Propositions: An Academic Dialogue on Mediology" (媒介学：观念与命题——关于媒介学的学术对谈) [J]. *Nanjing Journal of Social Sciences* (南京社会科学), 2015(4): 101-106.

[6] Chua, Tat-Seng & Li, Juanzi & Moens, Marie-Francine. *Mining User Generated Content* [M]. New York /London: Chapman and Hall, 2014.

[7] Cui, Ruonan (崔若男). "Study on the Translation Discourse of Chinese Nursery Rhymes by Westerners in Modern Time" (近代西方人中国儿歌翻译话语研究) [J]. *Folk Culture Forum* (民间文化论坛), 2022(5): 99-108.

[8] Debray, Régis. *Introduccion a la Mediologia* [M]. Barcelona: Paidos, 2000.

[9] Debray, Régis. *Media Manifestos* [M]. London: Verso Books, 1996.

[10] DiNucci, Darcy. *Design & new media: Fragmented Future-web Development Faces a Process of Mitosis, Mutation, and Natural Selection* [M]. New York: Print, 1999.

[11] Geng, Qiang (耿强). "Genealogical Review of How Travelling Theory Develops to Transknowletology" (从观念的旅行到知识翻译学：一个谱系学的考察) [J]. *Contemporary Foreign Languages Studies* (当代外语研究), 2022(3): 74-83.

[12] Geng, Qiang (耿强). "Problems and Strategies of the Double Marginalization of Chinese Discourses on Translation" (中译外翻译话语的双重边缘化：问题与对策) [J]. *Fudan Forum on Foreign Languages and Literature* (复旦外国语言文学论丛), 2018(01): 170-176.

[13] Geng, Qiang (耿强). "Remarks on Chinese Discourses on Translation" (中国翻译理论话语：内涵与意义) [J]. *Shanghai Journal of Translators* (上海翻译), 2020(03): 7-11+95.

[14] Li, Qingming & Zhao, Ying (李庆明, 赵颖). "A Study on Translator Subjectivity from Communication Theory Perspective on the Two Versions of Laocan Youji" (传播学视域下的译者主体性探究——以《老残游记》两译本为例) [J]. *Journal of Chongqing Jiaotong University (Social Sciences Edition)* (重庆交通大学学报(社会科学版)), 2012,12(05): 134-137.

[15] Li, Zhen (李振). "A Study on Recipients' Psychology of Choices of Relevance Translation from the Perspective of Communication" (传播学视角下关联翻译的受众选择性心理) [J]. *Journal of Chongqing University of Technology(Social Science)* (重庆工学院学报(社会科学版)), 2009, 23(07): 148-150.

[16] Lv, Jun (吕俊). "Translotology: A Special Sphere of Communication" (翻译学——传播学的一个特殊领域) [J]. *Journal of Foreign Languages* (外国语), 1997(02): 40-45.

[17] Mo, Aiping & Hao, Junjie & Wu, Di (莫爱屏, 郝俊杰, 吴笛). "The Transformation of Translation through Industrialization in the Context of Popular Culture" (大众文化语境下翻译转型的产业化途径) [J]. *Chinese Science & Technology Translators Journal* (中国科技翻译), 2014, 27(03): 51-54+47.

[18] Mu, Jia & Zhou, Guijun (牟佳, 周桂君). "A Study of Historical Understanding in Documentary Literature from the Perspective of Communication" (传播学视阈下纪实文学翻译中译者的历史认知研究) [J]. *Foreign Language Research* (外语学刊), 2019(06): 108-112.

[19] O'Hagan, Minako. Evolution of User-generated Translation: Fansubs, Translation Hacking and Crowdsourcing [J]. *Journal of Internationalization & Localization*. 2009, 1: 94 - 121.

[20] Peng, Lan (彭兰). "Everything is Media: The Pan-Media Trend Driven by New Technologies" (万物皆媒——新一轮技术驱动的泛媒化趋势) [J]. *Editorial Friend* (编辑之友), 2016(03): 5-10.

[21] Qian, Jie & Pan, Hongtao (钱洁, 潘洪涛). "Effect of Using and Satisfaction of User Generated Content on Brand Attitude: An

Example for Audio and Video of User Generated Content" (用户生成内容使用与满足对品牌态度的影响研究——以音视频类用户生成内容为例) [J]. *Finance and Trade Research* (财贸研究), 2012, 23(03): 105-115.

[22] Sun, Yingchun (孙迎春). "Translation as Media" (翻译作为媒介) [J]. *New Perspectives in Translation Studies* (译苑新谭), 2012(00): 54-65.

[23] Wei Xiangqing (魏向清). "On Translators' Terminological Consciousness and Competence — A Case Study of Translating the English Term "Hallucinatory Realism" into Chinese" (论大众翻译时代译者的术语意识与素养——从莫言诺贝尔文学奖评语中的术语翻译谈起) [J]. *Foreign Language Research* (外语学刊), 2016(01): 150-153.

[24] Xie, Ke & Liao, Xueru (谢柯，廖雪汝). "The Name and Nature of Transcommunication" ("翻译传播学"的名与实) [J]. *Shanghai Journal of Translators* (上海翻译), 2016(01): 14-18.

[25] Yao, Liangsheng (姚亮生). "A Two-way Dialogue: Intrapersonal and Interpersonal Communication - Transtology in the Perspective of Communication Science" (内向传播和人际传播的双向对话——论建立传播学的翻译观) [J]. *Journal of Nanjing University (Philosophy,Humanities and Social Sciences)* （南京大学学报（哲学·人文科学·社会科学版）），2004(03): 135-139.

[26] Yin, Feizhou & Yu, Chengfa (尹飞舟，余承法). "Toward Constructing Translational Communication Studies" (翻译传播学论纲) [J]. *Journal of Xiangtan University (Philosophy and Social Sciences)* (湘潭大学学报(哲学社会科学版)), 2020, 44(05): 170-176.

[27] Zhao, Yuxiang & Fan, Zhe & Zhu, Qinghua (赵宇翔，范哲，朱庆华). "Conceptualization and Research Progress on User-Generated Content" (用户生成内容(UGC)概念解析及研究进展) [J]. *Journal of Library Science in China* (中国图书馆学报), 2012, 38(05): 68-81.

[28] Zhu, Zhenming (朱振明). "Genealogical Traces in Régis Debray's Mediology: A Methodological Analysis" (媒介学中的系谱学迹线——试析德布雷的方法论) [J]. *Journalism & Communication Review* (新闻与传播评论), 2019, 72(03): 87-97.

[29] Zwischenberger, Cornelia. Online Collaborative Translation: Its Ethical, Social, and Conceptual Conditions and Consequences [J]. *Perspectives: Studies in Translation Theory and Practice*. 2022, 30: 1 - 18.

作者简介

肖维青，上海外国语大学英语学院教授、博士生导师。研究方向：翻译教学、视听翻译。电子邮箱：wqxiao@shisu.edu.cn。

王景，上海外国语大学英语学院英语语言文学专业翻译研究（笔译）方向2021级硕士研究生。

党的"十九大"以来《习近平谈治国理政》翻译研究综述

⊙ 戴若愚 王玥月（西南交通大学外国语学院，成都）

[摘　要] 文章对党的"十九大"以来《习近平谈治国理政》的翻译研究进行梳理总结后发现：现阶段研究成果主要集中在英语译本的研究，较少关注少数民族语言和小语种译本的研究；大部分研究关注文本内的对比分析，总结译者运用的翻译策略与方法，较少有研究涉及文本的外部因素。基于此，未来《习近平谈治国理政》的翻译研究应该在评价现有翻译模式的同时，运用跨学科知识，将微观的文本分析与宏观的社会、历史和文化等因素相结合，促进《习近平谈治国理政》翻译研究的持续深入发展。

[关键词] 《习近平谈治国理政》；翻译研究；研究综述

Literature Review on Translation Studies of *Xi Jinping: The Governance of China*

DAI Ruoyu WANG Yueyue (Southwest Jiaotong University, Chengdu)

Abstract: Based on the previous studies on the translations of *Xi Jinping: The Governance of China* since the 19th CPC National Congress, the article finds that most academic studies focus on the English translation of *Xi Jinping: The Governance of China* and pay little attention to the translations in other languages, most of which probe into translation strategies and methods at the linguistic levels but fail to involve external factors. Therefore, the article puts forward that the academic research on translations of *Xi Jinping: The Governance of China* should not only interpret the present translation model, but also, based on interdisciplinary studies, combine social, historical and cultural factors affecting the whole process of translation process at macro level and with text analysis at micro level, so as to further the research on the translations of *Xi Jinping: The Governance of China*.

Key words: *Xi Jinping: The Governance of China*; translation studies; literature review

一、引　言

党的"十九大"将"习近平新时代中国特色社会主义思想"确立为党必须长期坚持的重要指导思想并写入党章，之后这一思想在十三届全国人大一次会议中写入宪法，成为指导中国特色社会主义伟大实践的一面新旗帜。《习近平谈治国理政》作为以习近平同志为核心的党中央集体智慧的结晶，是习近平新时代中国特色社会主义思想的重要体现。自2014年第一卷出版以来，《习近平谈治国理政》已连续出版四卷。目前，

基金项目：2022年西南交通大学学位与研究生教育教学改革项目"国际工程合同翻译案例库"（YJG5-2022-AL06）。

该著作已出版33个语种，发行覆盖170多个国家和地区，受到了国内外读者的广泛关注。

《习近平谈治国理政》多语种的出版发行，也吸引了国内学者在翻译学领域开展研究。但是国内相关翻译综述研究仍处于起步阶段，目前仅有两篇论文对《习近平谈治国理政》的翻译研究成果进行综述。杨立学（2021）梳理了2015-2019年有关《习近平谈治国理政》英译的代表性研究成果，从翻译策略、对外传播和话语分析三个方面进行总结，认为未来使用话语分析工具进行翻译研究有待成为新的热点。栗慧敏、牛桂玲（2021）借助Citespace软件从翻译研究对象、研究视角与方法、外宣策略、传播目的与路径等五个方面，对《习近平谈治国理政》的多语种翻译与传播情况进行了梳理总结，认为运用中国本土译学理论和跨学科理论，加强话语分析，更加注重传播效果的研究会成为新的热点。以上两篇论文均能从不同角度对《习近平谈治国理政》的翻译研究成果进行梳理，并提出未来值得深入研究的方向，但杨立学（2021）只梳理了英译本的成果，没有提及少数民族语言译本和小语种译本的研究成果，而且只针对部分专著和发表在核心期刊上的文章，研究数据不够全面。栗慧敏、牛桂玲（2021）重点依靠Citespace软件的统计结果对《习近平谈治国理政》的研究成果进行分析，缺少对问题的总结和反思，而且对未来的展望局限在翻译与传播研究，未能考虑到翻译学领域内的其他研究方向。随着党的"二十大"的胜利召开以及进一步加强中国国际话语体系建设的需要，有必要对党的"十九大"以来《习近平谈治国理政》翻译研究的成果进行梳理分析，把握近五年该领域的研究动态，在总结已有经验和不足的同时，提出未来值得继续深入的研究方向。

本文运用文献计量分析法，以中国知网（CNKI）为数据源，设置"习近平谈治国理政"为主题词进行检索，筛选出"十九大"后（2017.10.31-2022.10.31）有关翻译研究的文章，在剔除无关文献后共得到有效数据374篇。其中期刊220篇，研究生学位论文154篇。借助Citespace软件对党的"十九大"以来《习近平谈治国理政》翻译研究的历年发文情况、发文作者、机构和期刊来源进行分析，同时结合文本细读的方法对翻译研究成果进行介评。在此基础上，指出现阶段研究中存在的5个问题，提出了4个在该领域值得深入研究的方向，以期为未来《习近平谈治国理政》的翻译研究提供新的思路。

二、党的"十九大"以来《习近平谈治国理政》翻译研究历年发文分析

对党的"十九大"以来《习近平谈治国理政》翻译研究领域的总发文量、期刊和研究生学位论文发文量分别统计后，绘制了如下所示的折线图（图1）。如图所示，总发文量在2017-2019年增长势头强劲，并在2019年达到顶峰。其中的原因一方面与研究内容的不断更新有关。自2014年《习近平谈治国理政》第一卷出版发行以来，到2019年已出版两卷，收录的都是习近平总书记在不同时间不同地点不同主题的讲话，研究者可以从这些不断更新的内容中持续不断地发掘新的思路和研究方向。另一方面，习近平总书记在多次讲话中反复强调"讲好中国故事，传播中国声音，增强我国国际传播能力建设"的重要任务，《习近平谈治国理政》中蕴含着丰富的中国智慧和中国态度，是习近平中国特色社会主义思想的集中体现，其翻译研究的持续发展也是国内学者不断响应这一政策号召的具体表现。除此之外，相关科研立项的增加也为《习近平谈治国理政》的翻译研究提供了广阔的平台。据统计，党的"十九大"以来《习近平谈治国理政》翻译研究领域的期刊论文中共有124篇与科研项目有关。这些项目为学者们提供资助的同时，也源源不断地吸引着更多学

者在该领域开拓创新，发展新的研究方向。期刊的发文量在 2019-2020 年有所回落后，在 2020-2021 年间又再次增长，对这两年文献的摘要和关键词进行阅读后发现，研究对象逐渐从《习近平谈治国理政》前两卷及其多语种译本向第三卷的多语种译本转变，这是因为 2020 年《习近平谈治国理政》第三卷及其多语种译本正式出版，展现出《习近平谈治国理政》翻译研究与时事紧密联系的特点。

研究生学位论文的数量同样在 2017-2019 年间迅猛增长，但与期刊不同的是，研究生学位论文在 2019-2020 年间继续增长，并在 2020 年达到顶峰。这可能和相关政策的推进有关。2019 年底，中央宣传部组织的《习近平谈治国理政》多语种版本进高校、进教材、进课堂（以下简称"三进"）试点工作，在北京外国语大学、上海外国语大学、四川外国语大学启动。随着"三进"工作的持续推进，越来越多的研究生选择《习近平谈治国理政》的多语种译本作为自己学位论文的研究方向。

从整体上看，2019 年以来《习近平谈治国理政》翻译研究领域文章数量趋于平缓，研究进入潜伏期，随着党的"二十大"的胜利召开以及《习近平谈治国理政》第四卷及其多语种译本的出版发行，未来该领域的研究热度仍将受到国内学者的持续关注。

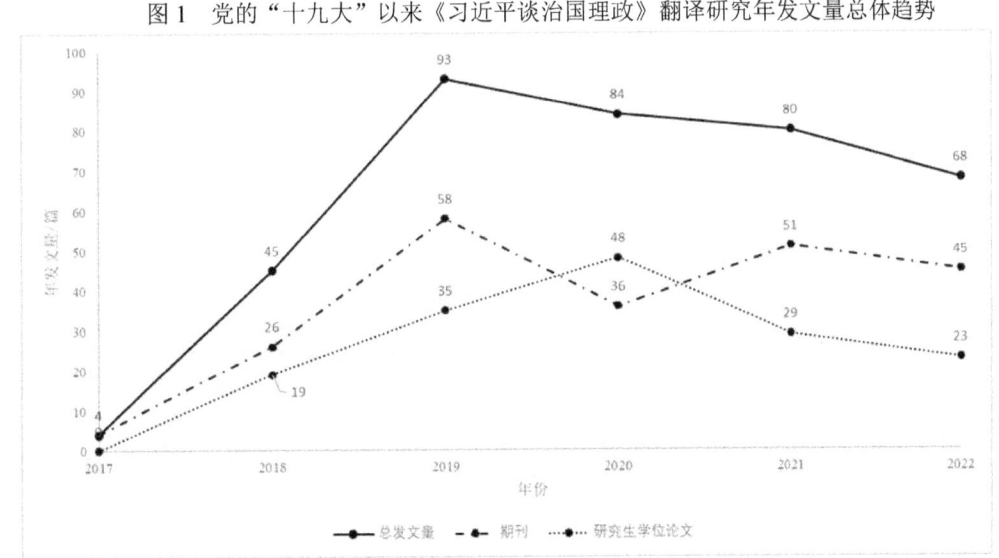

图 1　党的"十九大"以来《习近平谈治国理政》翻译研究年发文量总体趋势

三、党的"十九大"以来《习近平谈治国理政》翻译研究发文期刊作者和机构分析

通过对文献来源进行确认后发现，党的"十九大"以来《习近平谈治国理政》翻译研究领域的文章主要分为期刊和硕博士学位论文两大类，分别约占总发文量的 41% 和 59%。文章作者主要是硕博士研究生和相关领域的研究者。由于硕博士研究生学位论文的作者和机构之间不存在合作网络关系，因此本研究只分析期刊作者以及机构间的合作关系。借助 Citespace 软件对期刊发文作者和机构进行分析后发现，从总体上看，《习近平谈治国理政》翻译研究的期刊作者之间合作程度较低，少数作者之间存在合作关系（见图 2），领域内并没有形成专业的核心研究团队，这可能是因为作者本身出自较高水平的研究机构，具有一定的科研实力，相互之间的学术联系较少。从期刊发文机构看，大部分发文机构之间联系程度薄弱，研究较为孤立，只

有少数发文机构之间存在合作关系（见图3）。可以看出近年来的主要发文机构以语言类院校和研究机构为主，如天津外国语大学中央文献翻译研究基地和四川外国语大学等，这说明研究机构能利用自身的语言专业优势和学科特色，在《习近平谈治国理政》翻译研究领域开展研究。

图2 党的"十九大"以来《习近平谈治国理政》翻译研究的期刊发文作者

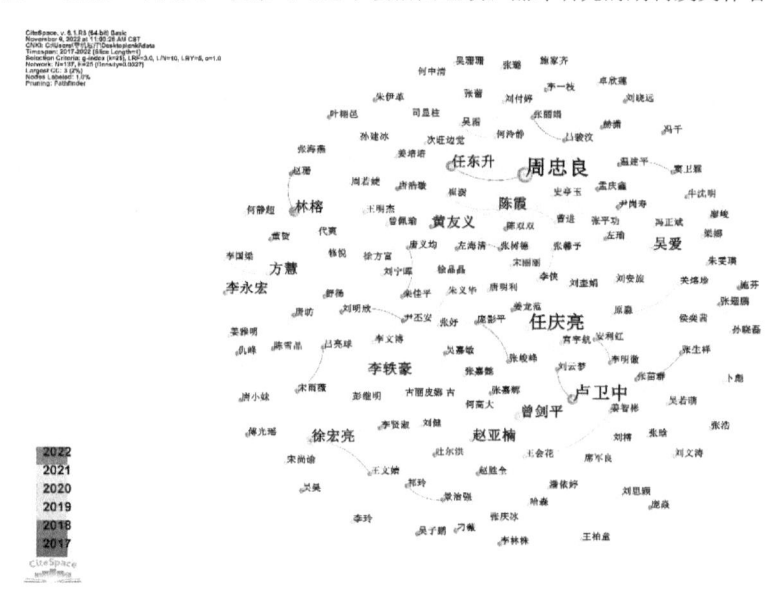

图3 党的"十九大"以来《习近平谈治国理政》翻译研究的期刊发文机构

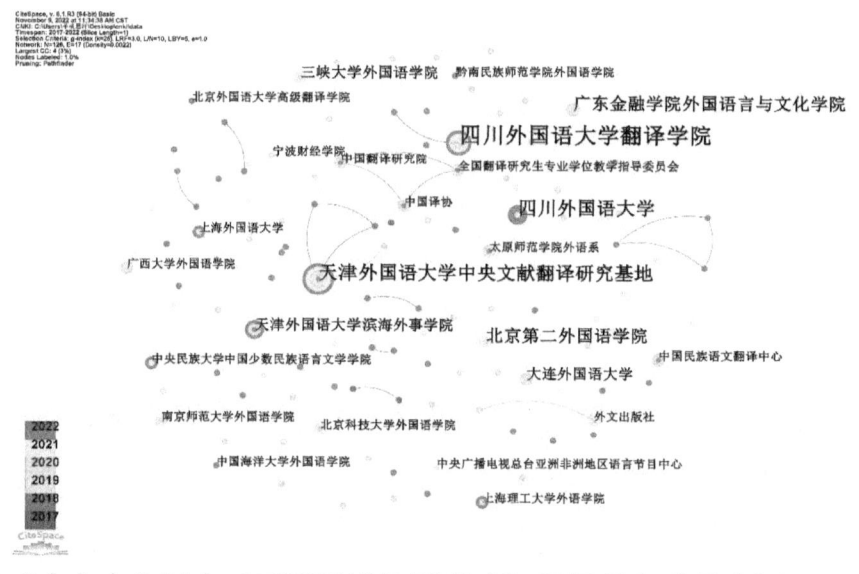

四、党的"十九大"以来《习近平谈治国理政》翻译研究成果介评

通过对374条文献进行梳理汇总后，本文根据译本语种，将党的"十九大"以来《习近平谈治国理政》的翻译研究成果分为两大方向：《习近平谈治国理政》英译本研究和《习近平谈治国理政》少数民族语言和小语种译本研究。对两大方向的成果具体分析如下：

（一）《习近平谈治国理政》英译本研究

在对 374 篇文献研究的译本语种进行分类统计后发现，《习近平谈治国理政》英译本研究文献共有 285 篇，约占整体发文量的 76%。具体研究内容主要涉及以下四类：

（1）针对英译本运用的翻译策略进行分类总结，重点关注典故、古诗词、俗语、具有中国特色文化内涵的概念隐喻和政治术语等微观语言学层面翻译。大部分文献都是运用翻译理论对翻译现象进行阐释，出现频次较高的理论有目的论、功能对等、关联理论、翻译转换、生态翻译学等。研究者大多从语言和文本分析的角度，对具有中国特色文化内涵的词汇和句子进行解读，归纳译者运用的翻译技巧和方法，研究对象集中在语言和文本分析层面，研究目的大多是为同类型的政治文献提供借鉴，研究思路趋同化。部分学者尝试借助语料库工具，采用定性研究和定量研究相结合的方法，对《习近平谈治国理政》英译本运用的翻译策略讨论反思。例如陈国兴、菅爱丽（2019）通过自建小型双语平行语料库，对《习近平治国理政》前两卷中的科技隐喻进行梳理，发现科技隐喻具有人文性特征，使整个政治语篇清新自然，而直译、意译、中英融通这三种翻译策略的结合既保留了原汁原味的中国文化特色，又符合西方读者的阅读习惯。祝朝伟（2020）通过自建语料库和文本细读相结合的方法，将《习近平谈治国理政》中的典故分为三类并总结了英译本中运用的六种翻译策略，同时指出只有对译者自身过硬的素质到严格的审校程序层层把关才能真正做到"讲好中国故事，传播好中国声音"。这些学者在创新研究方法的同时，对研究对象也进行了穷尽式的探索。仅有少数学者从宏观角度对《习近平谈治国理政》的整体翻译策略及其指导原则进行总结。例如，司显柱、曾剑平（2021）通过言内判断和言外调查的方式，总结《习近平谈治国理政》的英译本采纳了释疑解惑的语言融通策略、趋向目标语修辞策略和中国特色政治话语的翻译创新策略，提出这种翻译策略的运用正是《习近平谈治国理政》英译本能够取得成功的关键。上述将宏观策略的把握和微观案例分析相结合的方法，也进一步拓展了《习近平谈治国理政》英译本翻译策略研究的深度。

（2）将《习近平谈治国理政》英译本作为教材应用在翻译教学活动中，探究思政教育与翻译教学相结合的途径。这一研究方向下的成果主要分间接和直接呈现两种形式。间接呈现的成果就是在"三进"试点工作的推进下，有关《习近平谈治国理政》翻译研究的硕博士学位论文数量持续增长。直接成果主要以期刊论文的形式呈现，共 5 篇，其中有两篇来自核心期刊，这表明该方向的研究尚处于起步阶段。一方面可能是因为该方向的研究对学者的身份和翻译教学经验有一定要求。另一方面是因为研究周期相对较长，从课程设置到实际开展再到积累研究数据，需要一定的试错周期。但可以看出该方向已有研究成果的质量处于较高水平，一定程度上能够为未来该方向研究的深入提供借鉴经验。例如，曹进、陈霞（2019）指出了翻译硕士培养过程中思政教育与翻译专业学习脱节的问题，并以西北师范大学"国策与省情"翻译素养类课程为例，通过引入《习近平谈治国理政》前两卷的英译本，指出思政教育与专业相结合的显性和隐性塑造功能。该研究成果建立在五年教学实践的基础上，既能结合《习近平谈治国理政》及其英译本的具体内容又能结合培养单位实际情况，研究较为系统完备，是对翻译教学和思政教育相结合的一次有益尝试。唐昉（2022）在已有的译者能力研究基础上，从社会翻译学出发重构面向国际传播的译者能力培养模式，通过开展《习近平谈治国理政》（前三卷）英译赏析课程，针对学生的认知能力、翻译能力和传播能力进行训练。该研究不仅认识到将

《习近平谈治国理政》英译本引入翻译教学课堂对学生思想的指引作用，更重要的是将其作为对外传播翻译的典范，探索翻译人才培养的新模式。

（3）关注《习近平谈治国理政》英译本的海外传播模式和接受效果，探究其在建构国家形象，提升中国国际话语权等方面的影响。此类研究多站在宏观角度，结合传播学和形象学知识，总结《习近平谈治国理政》英译本成功的海外传播经验。此类研究的目的可分为两个方面，一是利用《习近平谈治国理政》英译本纠正西方媒体对中国的负面评价所造成的影响，达到提升中国国际话语权的目的。例如，朱伊革（2018）认为《习近平谈治国理政》（第一卷）英译本塑造了亲仁善邻、民主法制、和平发展的国家形象，强调了翻译文本对于中国人主动"自塑"形象，改变中国国际话语权被动局面的积极作用。张生祥、张苗群（2018）针对《习近平谈治国理政》英译本在美国的传播现状和情况，总结出座谈会、新闻媒体、期刊三种行之有效的传播渠道，借助政治精英、社会精英和学术精英三种精英力量引导舆论风向，从而达到提升中国国际话语权的目的。二是通过分析《习近平谈治国理政》海外传播的方式和效果，为同类型下的中央政治文献的出版提供借鉴经验。周忠良（2019）从《习近平谈治国理政》的翻译模式、发行策略和海外传播模式，总结其在海外广受好评的原因，并提出加强顶层设计，创新宣传方法和实施本地化策略对当前我国政治文献的出版的启示。以上两方面的研究都能从对《习近平谈治国理政》英译本研究的语言文本分析层面，转向关注译本的传播效果和传播途径，为《习近平谈治国理政》翻译研究提供了新的研究思路和方向。

（4）围绕《习近平谈治国理政》的英译本开展译文质量评估。此类研究大多从语言和文本分析层面出发，可以分为两个方面：一方面是关注《习近平谈治国理政》中的中国特色政治和文化术语，对其译文质量进行评价。例如，唐义均、栾佳平（2018）基于语料库语言学的知识，从词语搭配出发调查"深化改革"一词的英译，发现中国译者初稿更注重语义对应，英美专家审稿后更符合自然英语的典型搭配，既肯定了《习近平谈治国理政》英译本采用中外合作翻译的模式，又肯定了其在词语搭配上的译文质量。王伟（2019）、康凯（2020）、周群（2019）同样运用语料库工具，结合元功能对等理论、互文语境重构理论对《习近平谈治国理政》英译本的排比结构和典故翻译做出质量评价，这些研究能够利用语料库工具对《习近平谈治国理政》的英译本进行质量评估，在创新研究方法的同时又为该领域的研究提供了新的视角，但这些研究未能根据发现的不足提出个人的改进建议。另一方面就是利用《习近平谈治国理政》的英译本为参考译文，对机器翻译的文化翻译和隐喻翻译质量进行评价。例如，王思琳（2020）以概念隐喻为理论框架，《习近平谈治国理政》第二卷为研究语料，通过与人工隐喻翻译对比，发现 GNMT（Google Natural Machine Translation）翻译系统在涉及文化因素的隐喻翻译中表现较弱。田青炜（2021）通过提取 112 段《习近平谈治国理政》包含用典翻译的段落，选择 DeepL、谷歌和搜狗三种机器工具进行翻译，与官方译文对比后发现三种机器翻译在不同类型的翻译方面存在可靠性，但仍需要结合语境减少错译。此类研究能够将《习近平谈治国理政》英译本引入机器翻译质量评估模式，为机器翻译质量的评估提供了新的研究视角，但研究者未能说明选取《习近平谈治国理政》英译本作为研究语料和评价标准的原因，在数据获取和评级方法方面缺少一定的客观依据。

（二）《习近平谈治国理政》少数民族语言译本和小语种译本研究

据统计，研究《习近平谈治国理政》少数民族语言和小语种译本的文献数量共89篇，占总发文量的24%左右。一共涉及15种语言，其中小语种有日语、阿拉伯语、俄语、韩语、朝鲜语、葡萄牙语、德语、法语、老挝语、西班牙语、蒙古语和哈萨克语，少数民族语言有藏语、维吾尔语和壮语，展现出党的"十九大"以来《习近平谈治国理政》多语种译本研究共同发展的态势。根据对文献的筛查分析后发现，少数民族和小语种译本研究的学者大多出自语言特色鲜明、专业性较强的外国语院校，或是地处少数民族自治区，具有语言地理优势的院校。例如，来自四川外国语大学的学者在日语、韩语、俄语、西班牙语等语种译本的研究中均有涉猎。研究维语译本的学者大都出自位于新疆维吾尔自治区的院校，如喀什大学、新疆师范大学、新疆大学等。这些学者能够充分利用院校专业优势和地理位置优势，开展《习近平谈治国理政》多语种译本的翻译研究。

从研究内容看，少数民族语言和小语种译本研究内容和英译本内容趋同，以《习近平谈治国理政》多语种译本的翻译策略研究和在翻译教学中的应用研究为主。首先，从翻译策略的研究来看，大部分学者从语言学层面切入，针对《习近平谈治国理政》中的中国特色文化术语和政治术语的翻译，总结译者运用的翻译策略，并探究影响翻译策略选择的原因。例如，廖峻、汤恬（2021）以变译理论为基础，认为《习近平谈治国理政》（一、二卷）德译本主要采用编译、改译和译述三种翻译策略，使译文更加符合德语读者的阅读习惯。黄进财、罗兹深（2021）以概念隐喻理论为基础，采用定量分析和定性分析相结合的方法，对《习近平谈治国理政》中出现的隐喻进行识别、提取、分类、统计，总结出其中翻译方法，使韩译本达到了良好的翻译效果。可以看出，此类研究一定程度上能够推动小语种译本及其同类型的政治文献翻译的研究，但分析后发现依旧没有走出英译本研究思路的范式。《习近平谈治国理政》多语种版本的第二类研究同样集中在探索思政教育和翻译教学相结合的途径上。例如，胡业爽、徐曼琳（2022）以《习近平谈治国理政》俄译本为依托，开展翻译鉴赏课程，从"道"和"术"的层面提升学生的翻译能力，更重要的是从逆向探析课堂教学设计，推动"三进"课程更加科学化、丰富化和趣味化。王田、童亚星（2021）以四川外国语大学西班牙语专业的教改实践为基础，提出《习近平谈治国理政》"三进"课程和思政一体化模式，从个人、家国和国际层面进行一体化思政教育。与英译本在翻译教学应用中的研究不同的是，少数民族语言和小语种译本在翻译教学中的应用研究起步较晚，第一篇论文发表于2021年，这可能是因为国内在少数民族语言和小语种专业学习人数明显少于英语专业学习人数，人才队伍建设仍处于发展阶段，相关课程实践和研究有一定的滞后性。

五、《习近平谈治国理政》翻译研究的不足与展望

随着我国综合国力的提升，对提升我国国际话语权，塑造良好的大国国际形象的要求更为迫切。党的"十九大"以来《习近平谈治国理政》的翻译研究进入快速发展阶段，成为翻译学研究领域新的热点，越来越多的学者投入该领域的研究，但本文在对此类研究进行综述后发现存在着以下不足：（1）研究思路趋同化：无论是英译本的研究还是多语种译本的研究，大部分学者都选择从语言和文本分析层面出发，尤其关注译者处理典故、古诗词、概念隐喻和中国特色政治术语时运用的翻译策略和翻译方法，切入点多集中在微观层面，通常情况下还会选择一种翻译理论进行指导，但大部分研究中的理论与实际结合过于生硬，结论偏重

于对某种理论对《习近平谈治国理政》翻译实践的指导作用。（2）整体研究质量不高，需要进一步向深度拓展。据统计，核心期刊仅有 22 篇约占文章总数的 0.06%，比重较低。此类研究大部分停留在实践层面，深度有待加强。通过细读硕博士学位论文后发现，部分硕士研究生学位论文的研究内容相似率较高，大部分都在针对语言学层面的翻译问题，总结相应的翻译策略，对运用的翻译理论理解程度不够。（3）跨学科研究成果较少。作为一门科学的翻译研究，其跨学科性未能被充分发掘出来。大部分研究都集中对文本内部因素的讨论，鲜少涉及文化、社会、政治等文本外因素对译本的传播、出版甚至译者行为影响的研究。（4）少数民族语言和小语种译本的研究较少，不同语种的译本研究发展不平衡。少数民族语言和小语种译本研究较英译本研究具有一定的滞后性，研究内容略显单一。（5）研究语料不够全面。截至目前，《习近平谈治国理政》及其多语种译本已连续出版四卷，但大部分研究仍是选取四卷中的一卷文本进行分析，对研究对象的选择缺少充足的依据，而且较少有学者能运用语料库工具对四卷内容做穷尽性分析。

基于以上出现的不足，本文认为《习近平谈治国理政》翻译研究未来可以在以下四个方面继续开展深入研究：

（1）结合当代语言学知识，对现有译本的翻译质量进行评估。现阶段对《习近平谈治国理政》的翻译研究绝大部分关注的是译者是否实现了语义"对等"，研究者的角度也大多从传统语言学出发，尤其是将原文划分成词汇、句子和语篇等多种层次进行研究，视角略显单一。当代语言学经过发展，融合了多学科的知识，例如认知语言学、语用学、语料库语言学等。这些新知识在提供新视角的同时，又能指导研究者对《习近平谈治国理政》的译文进行批判性阅读，提出个人改进建议。

近年来，语用翻译理论得到了国内学者的关注，尤其是探讨顺应论对翻译理论和实践研究的启示。"顺应论强调：人们使用语言的过程是一个基于语言内部与外部的原因，在不同的意识程度下做出语言选择的过程"（戈玲玲，2021:9）。由此可见，语境因素、语言结构因素、语言的使用和选择等等都是译者在翻译过程中需要考虑的内容，意义的生成变成一种动态的过程，即所谓的"动态顺应"。基于此，"译文语言的选择也应该是做出顺应的动态过程，这种顺应要根据不同的语境，不同的语言结构而变化，从而最大限度地满足交际双方的需要"（同上：10）。由此可见，动态顺应对翻译提出了新的标准和要求。学者们在对《习近平谈治国理政》的多语种译本时可以重点关注译文语言是否顺应了不同的语境，比如根据习近平总书记讲话场合和背景的不同采取不同的翻译策略；译文的语言是否能够反映原文的语体和语言风格，比如说面对一些号召语、音律节奏感强的句子时译者是选择还原语义还是再现原文的语言结构。

随着计算机技术的飞速发展，语料库语言学也进入了新的发展阶段。目前，国内已经有学者运用语料库工具对《习近平谈治国理政》的排比句翻译质量进行评估，但相关内容仍然较少。"语料库途径的翻译质量评估是传统翻译质量评估的有效补充。专门领域内的专业信息可以通过相应的翻译评估语料库得以充分挖掘，个人直觉也可以通过语料库证据得到验证。传统词典工具与双语（多语）平行文本中提供的专业术语"（戴光荣、左尚君，2001：95）。语料库工具的引入让翻译质量的评估更有说服力。学者们既可以通过自建《习近平谈治国理政》四卷的双语语料库作为其他政治文献的质量评估标准，也可以通过平行语料库对《习近平谈治国理政》中的术语统一，尤其是具有中国特色的政治术语的统一，提出自己的新译文和新看法。

（2）关注译者主体性，对现有的翻译模式进行阐释。翻译不仅是停留在语言文字层面的转换，同时也是一项跨文化人际交往活动。"翻译活动不仅涉及原作者、译者与译文读者三者的关系，还牵涉到与翻译委托人、译文编辑以及原文读者等多重纷繁复杂的关系"（李民，2013:77）。这种人与人之间的多层次互动，自然存在着伦理关系。"译者角色从翻译活动伊始便与伦理有着密切联系，译者活动的实施是在伦理意识下做出的行为"（同上:77）。在翻译理论的"文化转向"后，译者的中心地位逐渐凸显，对译者的伦理研究也受到了学者们的广泛关注。李庆明、刘婷婷（2011）认为译者伦理不仅体现在译者对作品的具体理解，也体现在翻译文本的选择、翻译的文化目的及翻译策略方面。《习近平谈治国理政》作为官方主导的翻译活动，译者在翻译的过程中势必会受到官方政策的影响，由此也就产生了有关译者伦理关系的讨论。从译者伦理的角度可以开展的研究如下：1）译者伦理对翻译过程的影响：译者个人的教育背景、文化知识、审美意识、跨文化思维等等都会影响翻译过程。《习近平谈治国理政》的翻译团队由多名译者共同组成，这些多种因素的交织势必对翻译过程产生一定的影响；2）译者伦理对翻译策略和翻译方法的影响：译者在翻译的过程中很可能受到官方政策的干预，这种干预是否会影响译者最终的翻译策略，影响的程度如何，译者可否拒绝这种干预等等。

对译者伦理的关注其实也是对译者的身份从"隐形"到"显形"，从附属到主动选择地位的一种肯定。对《习近平谈治国理政》中译者伦理的关注也是对现有翻译模式合理性的一种全新阐释。

（3）关注文本外部因素，从文本内部研究向文本外部研究拓展。翻译不仅仅是语言学层面的文字转换，而是由原作者、译者和读者等多方共同参与的活动，割裂任何一方都无法完整地阐释翻译过程。已有的研究能够做到对文本内部进行分析，总结出对应的翻译策略，但有的忽略了文本外部因素，尤其是目标语读者的接受情况对翻译过程的影响。《习近平谈治国理政》被视为世界读懂中国的"思想之窗"，其译文既要保证忠实原著，又要让读者看得懂，既能感悟原文的语言风格，又能理解其中蕴含的中国思想和中国智慧。因此译文有必要考虑跨文化语境下读者的接受情况和认知心理等，从而达到最佳的传播效果。

接受美学理论起源于 20 世纪 60 年代，最初是在研究文学和文学史中提到要重视读者的接受过程。接受美学掀起一场文学理论改革的同时，也为翻译理论提供了新的视角。接受美学认为，"翻译在本质上是一种阅读，译者首先是读者，是原语文本的接受者。译者在对原语文本的阅读中，总会带着自己的'前理解'对文本中的空白和不确定因素借助想象加工，使其具体化"（孙淑芬，2007:157）。因此，"翻译不应只是原作者或原作品的独白，而是接受者带着'期待视野'在文本'召唤结构'的作用下，与隐含的作者进行对话和交流后形成的'视野融合'"（Ibid:157）。接受美学理论和翻译理论的融合大部分体现在文学翻译的研究上，《习近平谈治国理政》中也引用了大量的典故和古诗词，具有典型的文学翻译特征，但大部分学者并没有从读者接受的视角来研究这些翻译。结合接受美学理论，《习近平谈治国理政》翻译研究可以在以下两个方面展开：1）从读者的期待视野出发，探究在翻译过程中译者要采用何种方式能够让目标语读者理解和接受译文。例如，《习近平谈治国理政》多语种译本的出版术语由政府主导推进的对外传工作，翻译活动自然也是由政府负责组织开展的，其文本中又蕴含着大量政治术语，采用何种翻译策略不会在目标语读者中产生歧义，最大限度地消解意识形态的隔阂；2）从追求语义信息的传递，到追求读者的审美感受。除了文学翻译可以感受美，《习近平谈治国理政》音调的叠韵之美、用词的简洁之美、句式的和谐之美，译者如何在翻译过程中再现这些美学上的特点都是学者们在研究中可以挖掘的新方向。

（4）把握国家对外宣传方向，开展跨学科研究。随着我国综合国力和国际地位的提升，对外传播事业也进入了新的发展阶段。但意识形态上的分歧导致还有很多西方国家对中国政策进行"污名化"报道。因此，有必要通过外宣翻译树立积极的国家形象，提高中国的国际话语权。目前已经有学者运用形象学的知识对《习近平谈治国理政》的译本开展研究。"翻译研究中关于形象的问题可分为形象的建构、原因、传播和影响等，既涉及文本，也涉及文化、心理、传播、国际关系等多个层面"（闫晓珊、蓝红军，2021：115）。国内学者对《习近平谈治国理政》的翻译主要围绕国家形象的塑造和传播展开，未来相关研究还可以向国家形象塑造的过程、原因和影响等方面深入。同时，学者也可以思考译者在翻译形象塑造过程中是否进行了干预，这种干预是积极的还是消极的，目标语读者的接受情况如何，这是否会导致原文塑造的形象发生变异等等。另一方面，《习近平谈治国理政》不仅集中展现了中国智慧和中国态度，也包含了源远流长、博大精深的中华文化，学者还可以对译本中塑造的中国传统文化形象加以研究。

翻译学与传播学的结合也是当前的研究热点所在。"一般来说，翻译活动具有一定的目的性，特别是对外传播性质的翻译活动，其目的性更强。比如文学翻译的主要目的是译介优秀的外国文学作品以满足他们的什么需求；外宣翻译的主要目的是满足目标读者对特定信息的需求以及试图通过特定信息的传播来达到传播方预期的目标，常常是争取获得目标语读者的认同进而改变他们的态度或行为"（谢柯，2016:15）。吕俊（1997）指出翻译传播过程涉及七个要素：谁传播；传播什么；通过什么渠道传播；向谁传播；传播的目的是什么；传播在什么场合下进行；传播的效果如何。谢柯、廖雪汝（2016:16）根据以上七种要素将翻译传播学的研究对象分成了七个方面，结合《习近平谈治国理政》多语种译本的研究，本文认为具体的研究内容可以涉及：1）翻译的传播主体研究：翻译活动的特殊性体现在其跨文化和跨语言上，因此这一过程中的传播主题也从原来的一个，变成了原文作者与译者两个。对于《习近平谈治国理政》的翻译研究来说，可以研究现有的翻译模式是否合理，在现有的翻译模式下对译者的角色和作用进行重构，还可以探究传播过程中译者的形象是否发生了变化，是否影响到了最终的翻译效果；2）翻译的传播媒介研究：包括《习近平谈治国理政》多语种译本通过什么媒介传播、这些媒介的特点是什么、这些媒介是否适用于此类翻译文本，能否为外宣翻译总结出普适性的传播规律；3）翻译的传播受众研究：传统的翻译研究对受众的忽略使得翻译过程研究往往忽略了目标语读者，无法构成一个连续的整体。可以结合心理学、跨文化传播学、社会学等知识分析目标语读者的群体特点、心理期待和需求等；4）翻译的传播效果研究：即对《习近平谈治国理政》的翻译效果进行研究，既包括在某一个人上产生的影响，也可以包括在某一个国家或地区产生的影响，可以采用实地调研的方式来完成。除此之外，可以根据翻译传播效果，反向评估翻译传播的主客体和翻译传播过程。

（5）翻译的传播环境研究：包括对传播受众所处的社会环境、政治环境、人文环境和经济环境的考察，以及这些环境对传播过程的制约和对传播效果的影响。（6）翻译的传播过程研究：既涉及对翻译过程的研究，又涉及跨文化传播过程的研究，可以通过研究《习近平谈治国理政》的翻译过程，总结出适用于同类型文本的翻译传播特质。

《习近平谈治国理政》作为海外读者了解中国社会政治制度和历史文化的重要窗口，结合形象学和传播学的知识，对译者、译文传播的媒介、目标语受众、译文传播效果等等的研究，有助于把握《习近平谈治国理政》多语种译本整体的传播过程，树立积极的国家形象，讲好中国故事，传播中国声音。

六、结 语

本文经过研究后发现，党的"十九大"以来，《习近平谈治国理政》翻译研究主要局限在翻译策略的分析层面，缺少从语言和文本分析出发的微观层面和涉及社会、文化、历史等因素的宏观层面的系统结合，研究思路趋同化，研究内容略显单一。由国家主导的翻译活动，其内容的权威性较少受到质疑，大部分学者都将其视为业内典范，这可能是《习近平谈治国理政》翻译研究思路受限的原因之一。跳出语言对等的思维惯式后可以发现，《习近平谈治国理政》的翻译研究不仅仅可以集中在语言和文本分析层面的讨论，还可以结合当代语言学知识，对译文提出个人修改建议，探讨文本外部因素对翻译策略选择的影响，对译者主体性和现有的翻译进行阐释、或者结合翻译传播学、翻译形象学研究等跨学科知识等，这些都是值得深入挖掘的新方向。同时，鼓励来自不同学科和不同研究机构的作者加强合作，开展多学科、多视角和多维度的研究，提升《习近平谈治国理政》翻译研究的整体质量。随着党的"二十大"的召开以及《习近平谈治国理政》第四卷的出版，未来在该领域的研究有望进一步深入拓展。

参考文献

[1] Chen Guoxing & Jian Aili (陈国兴，菅爱丽). "A Corpus-Based Study on Metaphors of Science and Technology in Political Discourse and the English Translation Strategies: A Case Study of *Xi Jinping: The Governance of China*" (政治语篇中的科技隐喻及其英译策略研究——基于《习近平谈治国理政》的平行语料库) [J]. *Technology Enhanced Foreign Language Education* (外语电化教学), 2019, (05): 56-61.

[2] Cao Jin & Chen Xia (曹进，陈霞). "Ideological and Political Education in MTI Courses: A Case Study of the Course about National and Provincial Policies in Northwest Normal University" (翻译硕士培养过程中的思政教育实践研究——以西北师范大学"国策与省情"课程为例) [J]. *Chinese Translators Journal*(中国翻译), 2019, 40(03):105-113.

[3] Dai Guangrong & Zuo Shangjun (戴光荣，左尚君). " Corpus Applied in Translation Quality Assessment" (翻译质量评估中语料库的运用与研究)[J] *Foreign Language Education* (外语教学), 2001, 42(2):92-96.

[4] Ge Lingling (戈玲玲). "Adaptability Theory on Translation Studies: with Discussions on Standards of Pragmatic Translation" (顺应论对翻译研究的启示——兼论语用翻译标准) [J]. *Foreign Language Research* (外语学刊), 2002(03): 7-11.

[5] Huang Jincai & Luo Zishen (黄进财，罗兹深). "A Study of Korean Translation Methods of Metaphors in *Xi Jinping: The Governance of China* from the Perspective of Conceptual Metaphor" (概念隐喻视角下《习近平谈治国理政》中隐喻的韩译方法研究) [J]. *Foreign Languages and Literature* (外国语文), 2021, 37(05):17-26.

[6] Hu Yeshuang & Xu Manlin (胡业爽，徐曼琳). "Reverse Analysis of Teaching Design Path of Courses Based on the "Three-into" Pilot Reform: A Case Study on the Appreciation of the Russian Version of *Xi Jinping: The Governance of China*" ("三进"课程的课堂教学设计路径逆向探析——以《习近平谈治国理政》俄文版翻译鉴赏课程为例) [J]. *Foreign Languages and Literature* (外国语文)，2022, 38(03): 25-32.

[7] Li Huimin & Niu Guiling (栗慧敏，牛桂玲). "The Translating of Party Literature plus the Current State and Future Trend of Communication Studies: with *The Governance of China by Xi Jinping* as a Case for Analysis" (中央文献翻译与传播研究的现状与趋势——以《习近平谈治国理政》为例) [J]. *Minority Translators Journal*(民族翻译)，2021, (04):22-32.

[8] Liao Jun & Tang Tian (廖峻，汤恬). "Translation Variation Theory" of Chinese Colloquialism: A Study of Colloquialism Translation in German Version of *Xi Jinping: The Governance of China*" (中国俗语之"变译"——《习近平谈治国理政》德译本中的俗语翻译研究) [J]. *Foreign Languages and Literature* (外国语文)，2021, 37(05): 10-16.

[9] Li Min (李民). "The Ethical Characteristics of the Translator's Role" (论译者角色的伦理特性) [J]. *Foreign Languages and Their Teaching*(外语与外语教学)，2013,(06):77-80.

[10] Li Qingming & Liu Tingting (李庆明，刘婷婷). "An Exploration into the Translator's Subjectivity and its Influence on the Literary Translation Process from an Ethical Perspective" (译者主体性与翻译过程的伦理思考——以文学翻译为例) [J]. *Foreign Language Education* (外语教学)，2011, 32(04):101-105.

[11] Lv Jun (吕俊). " Translation Communication Studies: A Specific Field in Communication Studies" (翻译学——传播学的一个特殊领域) [J]. *Journal of Foreign Languages* (外国语)，1997, (2):39-44.

[12] Kang Kai (康凯). "The Meta-functional Equivalence in the English Translation of Chinese Allusions in *The Governance of China by Xi Jinping*" (元功能对等理论视域下《习近平谈治国理政》中用典的英译研究) [D]. Huaqiao University (华侨大学)，2020.

[13] Si Xianzhu & Zeng Jianping (司显柱，曾剑平). "Remarks on the Translation of Political Discourse: Principles, Strategies and Effect—A Case Study of English Version of *Xi Jinping: The Governance of China*" (对外政治话语翻译:原则、策略、成效——以《习近平谈治国理政》的英译为例) [J]. *Shanghai Journal of Translators* (上海翻译)，2021, (02): 18-24.

[14] Sun Shufen (孙淑芬). "Reception Aesthetics and Receptions in Literary Translation" (接受美学与文学翻译中的接受者)[J]. *Jiangxi Social Science* (江西社会科学)，2007,(12):156-158.

[15] Tang Fang (唐昉). "Developing Translator Competence for International Communication: A Case Study of English version of *Xi Jinping: The Governance of China*" (面向国际传播的译者能力培养——以《习近平谈治国理政》英译赏析课程为例) [J]. *Foreign Languages and Literature* (外国语文)，2022, 38(3): 33-41.

[16] Tian Qingwei (田青炜). "Assessing Machine Translation Quality of Chinese Allusion: A Case Study of *Xi Jinping: The Governance of China* (Volume III)" (汉语典故的机器翻译质量评估研究——以《习近平谈治国理政》（第三卷）为例) [D]. Beijing Foreign Studies University (北京外国语大学)，2021.

[17] Tang Yijun & Luan Jiaping (唐义均，栾佳平). "English Translation of Chinese Phrase *shēn huà gǎi gé*" (从"深化改革"的英译看中式词语搭配) [J]. *Chinese Science & Technology Translators Journal* (中国科技翻译)，2018, 31(3):47-50.

[18] Wang Wei (王伟). "A Corpus-based Study of the Translation of Parallel Structures in *The Governance of China* from the Perspective of Metafunctions" 基于语料库的《习近平谈治国理政》中排比结构英译的语言元功能研究[D]. China University of Petroleum (中国石油大学)，2019.

[19] Wang Silin (王思琳). "Comparing Google's Neural Machine Translation and Human Translation of Conceptual Metaphors: The Case of *Xi Jinping: The Governance of China II*" (概念隐喻视角下 GNMT 汉英隐喻翻译质量评估) [D]. Beijing Foreign Studies University (北京外国语大学)，2020.

[20] Wang Tian & Tong Yaxing (王田，童亚星). "Integration of Ideological and Political Education in the Course Based on *Xi Jinping: The Governance of China* in Universities, Textbooks and Classrooms" (《习近平谈治国理政》"三进"课程中的思政一体化研究) [J]. *Foreign Languages and Literature* (外国语文)，2021, 37(05): 27-31.

[21] Xie Ke & Liao Xueru (谢柯，廖雪汝). "Discussions on Translation Communication Studies" (翻译传播学的名与实) [J]. *Shanghai Journal of Translators* (上海翻译), 2016 (01): 14-18.

[22] Yang Lixue (杨立学). "Review of the English Translation Studies on *Xi Jinping: The Governance of China* Based on the Important Academic Literature (2015-2019)" (《习近平谈治国理政》英译研究综述——基于重要研究文献（2015-2019）的分析) [J]. *Journal of Tianjin Foreign Studies University* (天津外国语大学学报)，2021, 28(02): 45-56+159.

[23] Yan Xiaoshan & Lan Hongjun (闫晓珊，蓝红军). " The Theoretical Approaches and Methodologies of Translation Studies from the Perspective of Imagology" (翻译形象研究的途径与方法) [J]. *Shandong Foreign Language Teaching* (山东外语教学)，2021, 42(03): 108-117.

[24] Zhu Chaowei (祝朝伟). "What Can Foreign-Oriented Publicity Translators Learn From the Successful Translation of *Xi Jinping: The Governance of China*?" (《习近平谈治国理政》中典故的英译方法及对外宣翻译的启示) [J]. *Foreign Languages and Literature* (外国语文), 2020, 36(03)：83-90.

[25] Zhou Qun (周群). " A Study of the Translation of Classical Sayings in *Xi Jinping: The Governance of China (II)* from the Perspective of Intertextual Recontextualization" (互文语境重构视角下《习近平谈治国理政二》用典翻译研究) [D]. China University of Petroleum (中国石油大学)，2019：1-44.

[26] Zhu Yige (朱伊革). " The English Translation of *Xi Jinping: The Governance of China* and the transmission of China's image in the world" (《习近平谈治国理政》英译与中国形象在海外的传播) [J]. *Journal of Xi'an International Studies University*(西安外国语大学学报), 2018, 26(2):82-93.

[27] Zhang Shengxiang & Zhang Miaoqun (张生祥，张苗群). "On the Publicity of Chinese Leader's Discourse in America and the Strategies of Enhancing China's International Discourse Power: Taking the English translation of *Xi Jinping: The Governance of China* as an example" (国家领导人话语在美国的传播与中国国际话语权提升——以《习近平谈治国理政》英译本为例) [J]. *Foreign Language Education* (外语教学)，2018, 39(1):91-96.

[28] Zhou Zhongliang (周忠良). "The Overseas Publishing Influence of *Xi Jinping: The Governance of China*" (《习近平谈治国理政》海外出版影响力研究) [J]. *China Publishing Journal* (中国出版), 2019,(17):51-55.

作者简介

戴若愚，西南交通大学外国语学院副教授。研究方向：译介学、翻译理论与实践。电子邮箱：ralphdai@swjtu.edu.cn。
王玥月，硕士，西南交通大学外国语学院硕士生。研究方向：翻译理论与实践。电子邮箱:wyyassassin@163.com。

2021年中国翻译研究年度综述

⊙ 皮伟男 赖春梅 蓝红军（广东外语外贸大学高级翻译学院，广州）

[摘 要] 2021年于中国译学界而言是非常重要的一年，研究成果丰硕，值得称道。本文以中国重要外语类期刊为主要考察对象，回顾和述评2021年中国的翻译研究状况，主要包括翻译认识研究以及翻译实践研究两方面。翻译认识研究包括翻译理论研究、应用翻译学研究、翻译史研究以及翻译学科建设研究，旨在加深人们对翻译的认识，而翻译实践研究则包括翻译自身实践研究、翻译行业实践研究以及翻译批评实践研究，旨在帮助人们更好进行翻译实践。

[关键词] 翻译认识研究；翻译实践研究；年度综述

An Annual Literature Review of Translation Studies in China in 2021

Pi Weinan LAI Chunmei LAN Hongjun (Guangdong University of Foreign Studies, Guangzhou)

Abstract: 2021 is a very important year for Chinese translation studies, and the research results are fruitful and worthy of praise. This article focuses on important China's foreign language journals to review and comment on the status quo of translation research in China in 2021, mainly including translation cognition research and translation practice research. Translation cognition research includes translation theory research, applied translation studies, translation history research and translation discipline construction research, aiming to deepen people's understanding of translation, while translation practice research includes translation practice research, translation industry practice research and translation criticism practice research aimed at helping people better practice translation.

Key words: translation cognition research; translation practice research; annual review

一、引 言

2021年于中国以及与中国翻译学界而言都是意义非凡的一年。2021年是中国共产党建党100周年，党的成立为中国带来了翻天覆地的变化。100年来，中国的翻译事业与之共振，为了庆祝建党100周年，各地举办了多场主题各异的研讨会，多个期刊也组织了专栏回顾与党的成立相关的翻译活动。2021年5月22日，国家翻译能力研究中心正式成立；9月18日至19日，第二届国家翻译实践与对外话语体系建构高层论坛在青岛举行，与会专家围绕"国家翻译实践理论建构研究"等议题进行讨论；上述两个活动分别受到了央视新闻和中国社会科学网的关注，表明国家翻译学迈入了崭新的发展阶段。生态翻译学作为开创性的本土翻

本文系中国国家社科基金一般项目"中国翻译思想发生机制与发展路径研究研究（23BYY119）"和2021年广东外语外贸大学研究生科研创新项目"从拉图尔行动者网络理论看傅译《撒哈拉的故事》（21GWCXXM-107）"的阶段性成果。

译理论迎来了其建构的第 20 周年，在其原创精神的影响下，2021 年创建本土的翻译理论蔚然成风，为译学界注入了新鲜血液，贡献了中国学者的智慧，也有助于提高中国译学界的话语权。

综上，有必要对 2021 年翻译研究进行学术回顾。一门学科的研究包含实践和认识研究两部分，翻译学不外如是。实践研究旨在帮助人们获得对实践如何进行以达成目标的认识，而认识研究则旨在获得对学科实践和学术研究的认识。本文以中国重要外语期刊为考察对象，从翻译认识研究以及翻译实践研究两方面综述 2021 年中国的翻译研究，翻译认识研究包括翻译理论研究、应用翻译学研究、翻译史研究以及翻译学科建设研究，而翻译实践研究则包括翻译自身实践研究、翻译行业实践研究以及翻译批评实践研究。

二、翻译认识研究

（一）翻译理论研究

1. 思想阐释

部分学者在阐发翻译家或翻译理论家的翻译思想方面做出了学术努力。《解放军外国语学院学报》第六期组织专栏对张柏然翻译思想进行研读，其他刊物也有与之相关的文章发表，如于德英（2021）采用历史化阐释的方法重释张柏然的语言观，指出其语言观呈现出的两个辩证圆览特征，并阐发其翻译美学思想的两大特点；赵奂（2021）阐释了张柏然对翻译元理论演进过程中四种偏向的批评。李奕和刘军平（2021）考察和阐释了叶君健"翻译是精品再创造活动"的思想；此外许渊冲"三化论"的翻译美学思想也得到了阐释。

同样，译学关键词的阐释也受到了译学界的重视。有的关键词虽然常用但语义模糊，为译学研究带来了混乱，需要学者补苴罅漏，如耿强（2021）厘清了翻译诗学的概念，为后人进行翻译诗学的研究铺平了道路。近年译学新概念蔚起，也需要学者们对其厘清，谭载喜（2021）和陈大亮（2021）分别对翻译界学和翻译境界论进行了界定，为译学研究提供了学术增长点的同时也为译学研究提供了中国智慧。译学关键词的审查则是译学界进行研究的逻辑起点，译学界学者需要进一步朝着这个方向进行努力，推动翻译学这一相对年轻的学科走向成熟。

近年为了推动中国译学界与西方译学界展开平等对话，中国翻译学者致力于建构立足本土的翻译学中国学派。该倡导有两条相辅相成的实现路径：一是结合传统文化和文论资源进行创新性翻译理论阐释和建构，例如严晓江（2021）归纳出中国传统诗学的核心要素以对考察典籍翻译活动以及进行翻译批评提供诗学理据。二是重新挖掘中国的传统译论，对其理论形态等进行当代阐释，将其建设成现代译学理论体系，例如王晓农（2021）从翻译范畴和翻译理论两个角度诠释了鸠摩罗什的"圆通论"；武光军和蒋雨衡（2021）也对严复"信、达、雅"的译学意义进行了重释；此外刘润泽（2021）等学者也沿着这条路径做出了努力。虽然两条路径并不完善，但他们也做出了难能可贵的贡献，其创新性也值得嘉许。

2. 概念深化

"何为译"一直是翻译学者不断追问和探讨的话题。虽然按照形式逻辑，翻译隐喻虽然不算是严格的翻译定义，但是加深了人们对翻译本质的理解，于是受到不少学者的关注。王天翼（2021）从概念隐喻视角出发，将"翻译即交际"作为根隐喻并探讨了其余四条派生性支隐喻，帮助人们更好地理解翻译的内涵及外延。岳曼曼（2021）从认知语言学的视角出发分析了深度翻译在传播文化中的作用。佛经翻译一直是译学界研究的重点，关于"何为本"人们一直模糊不清，梁娜和陈大亮（2021）则诠释了佛经翻译"本"的概念。

此外，译学界学者还进一步加深了对翻译单位、翻译策略以及译者主体性等方面的认识。关于翻译单位，有学者关注"何为翻译单位"，如冯全功（2021）从原型理论视角出发，将翻译单位分为理论和操作两个层面，该研究侧重理论层面的探讨，而袁辉和徐剑（2021）的研究则是实证性的，利用键盘记录法探讨翻译单位和语言单位、译者能力之间的关系。方梦之（2021a）则探讨了翻译策略，将翻译策略分为元策略、总策略以及分策略。就译者主体性而言，《外语学刊》组织专栏对之进行探讨，主要研究视角包括评价理论和译者行为批评等。

3. 理论建构

近年，中国译学界一改以往担当西方翻译理论"搬运工"的态势，进行原创翻译理论建构。中国本土翻译理论中，生态翻译学的影响力最大。2021年是生态翻译学的二十周年。二十年来，其理论逻辑在译界学者的共同努力下不断完善，已经成为中国译论体系的重要部分，仍具有较强的学术生命力。《外语教学》第六期组织专栏对生态翻译学的发展进行探讨，其他期刊也有学者在完善生态翻译学方面做出学理性批评。译者行为批评也是具有重大影响力的原创理论，越来越多的学者运用该理论进行相关的研究，周领顺（2021）也对如何运用该理论进行研究做了方法论指导。此外，国家翻译学的建设也受到了重视，《当代外语研究》第五期和《中国翻译》第四期都组织专栏对其进行创新探索，蓝红军（2021）等学者都有文章产出。另外，王寅（2021）在将"认知语言学"本土化为"体认语言学"的基础之上提出了体认翻译学，为学者进行翻译研究提供了新视角。杨枫（2021）也发表了知识翻译学的宣言，革新了人们对翻译本质、功用和价值的认识。创建新理论实属不易，使之完善更是难上加难，我们期待今后学者能够有新的成果问世以提高其理论的科学性。

关于如何进行中国特色翻译学派的建设，不少学者都给出了方法论层面的指导，陈东成和李艳（2021）从《周易》的"易"出发，提出"五易"原则；朱健平等（2021）也分析了目前存在的六个问题并给出了六点建议，特别强调了马克思主义哲学的作用。对中国译学界而言可喜可贺的是近些年来涌现了一大批翻译理论建设的学者，不过韩子满和钱虹（2021）也指出虽然新世纪以降中国翻译理论如雨后春笋般发展起来，但是国际译学界对中国原创的翻译理论关注度不高。希望今后中国译学界的学者能够提高在国际译学界传播中国翻译理论的意识以提高中国原创翻译理论的影响力，增强中国译学界的话语权。

（二）翻译史研究

作为翻译研究的一项重要内容，翻译史研究极大地推动了翻译学科的建立，研究队伍也在不断地壮大。近年来，翻译史研究不断深化，不再落入史料堆砌的窠臼。2021年翻译史研究内涵也在进一步提升。作为翻译史研究的主要对象，翻译家研究成果最为丰硕，其研究主要呈现出以下几个特征：1）中国文学翻译家研究依旧是主流，例如郑克鲁、朱湘、林语堂、茅盾、鲁迅以及巴金等人。值得一提的是，王祖华（2021）对林纾的研究有了新突破，纠偏了以往人们对林纾的认识，并从方法论层面对我国翻译史研究给予了建议。2）与此同时，非英汉语对的翻译家研究数量有所增加，例如德国翻译家高立希、西班牙语翻译家陈国坚以及西班牙汉学家杜善牧。过往学者大多将目光放在英汉语对的翻译家，2021年翻译家研究有了新气象，我们期待更多其他语对翻译家研究成果的推出。3）翻译家的研究对象从个人拓宽至了译者群体，例如旧体译诗的学衡派、毛泽东诗词英译群体以及《共产党》月刊的译者群体等。4）一改以往对经世致用的翻译家语焉不详的现象，让被遮蔽的科学、教育学以及农史学等学科领域的翻译家显身。王烟朦、梁林歆（2021）从译史隐逸的钩沉着手，展现了丁汉江的科技典籍译介活动；此外李善兰的科学翻译、史学家和教育家何炳松的学术翻译以及农史学家石声汉的学术外译都有探讨。对这些对社会进步和学科发展起重要作用的译家进行考察进一步明确了翻译学在人类学术史中的地位，让翻译史研究走上了与其他学科发展史接轨的道路。5）翻译家研究更多关切到了翻译家道德精神的"厚度"。例如"石声汉的翻译动机始于学术强国的远大抱负"（周鹤、张保国，2021），周春悦（2021）也考察了青年巴金的翻译立场。

翻译活动是翻译史研究的重要组成部分。2021年是中国共产党建党的第一百周年，许多期刊组织专栏为之庆祝。翻译作为一项社会活动在建党过程中发挥了不可磨灭的作用，王宁（2021a）指出翻译促成了马克思主义中国化的结晶，即毛泽东思想；还有许多学者从不同角度论述了翻译对共产党形象的塑造。同时，在党的英明领导下，新中国的翻译活动也有其特点，黄友义、黄长奇（2021）回顾了在党的领导下外文局对外翻译出版物的内容重点及其发展变化。佛经翻译一直是翻译史研究的重点，常红星（2021）补证了道安对佛经翻译"失本"的反对态度并分析了其反对译经"失本"的原因；汪东萍和庞观（2021）考察了不同时期佛经翻译的源语是"胡"还是"梵"。翻译赞助研究也得到了一定关注，有学者考察了个人的翻译赞助行为，如苏艳（2021），也有两位学者考察了国家翻译赞助机制；冯小冰（2021）则对勒弗菲尔的赞助理论进一步完善后再对中国当代小说德译的赞助机制进行考察，深化了前人的理论，使其研究更深入。

译介史也同样受到较多关注。有学者从历时角度梳理和考察某一文本在海外的译介史，如《瀛涯胜览》；也有学者结合社会文化因素考察某一作家在他国的译介与传播，如王尔德在白银时代在俄罗斯的译介；还有学者考察某一时期的译介活动，如1575-1688年传教士翻译中国神话时的矛盾态度（王敏，2021）。就译介史研究对象的体裁而言，有学者关注文学作品，如高茜和王晓辉（2021）爬梳2000-2020年中国科技小说的英译发展；也有学者关注非文学体裁，如新中国时期中央文献译介的发展历程以及《伤寒论》和《洗冤录》的译介史。

翻译史研究方法论的研究也在进一步深入。许明武和聂炜（2021）梳理了提出"重写翻译史"的背景并就如何"重写翻译史"指明路径与方向；而高玉霞和任东升（2021）提出的将国家治理作为翻译史书写的对象以及张汨（2021）详细论述的翻译微观史书写的方法都是"重写翻译史"的具体路径。关于翻译家研究，方梦之（2021b）指出要拓宽人物涉及的宽度，同时也要关注翻译家道德精神之厚度。

就研究对象而言，2021年口译史的研究成果较少，只有李忠辉（2021）考察了清代朝鲜使臣觐见时的口译活动，数量远不能和笔译史研究相比；而相对于翻译实践史而言，翻译思想史和翻译理论史也少有学者关注。就研究视角来说，学者们开始站在国家实践的层面考察翻译活动，如韩淑芹（2021）从国家翻译实践考察洋务运动时期的官办译馆，有助于国家翻译实践与国家翻译史的书写。就研究方法而言，碎片化的微观翻译史研究依旧是主流。

（三）应用翻译理论研究

2021年11月20日至21日第九届全国应用翻译研讨会线上举行，杨平强调要加强应用翻译研究基础理论的构建、系统深化对各专业领域的应用研究、关注和拓展对翻译工作相关新领域新现象的研究、优化研究方法拓展研究路径。应用翻译研究的核心在于"应用"，即应用相关理论对实用文本、应用型问题以及应用翻译研究话语系统展开研究（傅敬民、刘金龙，2021：82）。2021年，应用翻译理论研究在话语体系建设、应用文体翻译理论探索、应用型问题的理论应用提升方面取得了丰富的研究成果。

2021年在话语体系建设方面最大的贡献在于"中国特色应用翻译研究"的提出。傅敬民和刘金龙（2021）对其"特色"的四个方面进行了阐述，认为在我国的应用翻译研究话语系统中，"中国特色应用翻译研究"应占有一席之地。此外，傅敬民和喻旭东（2021）阐述了中国特色应用翻译研究的四个维度。

在应用文体翻译理论研究方面，大多数学者聚焦于法律翻译研究，尤其是法律术语翻译的研究，如李文龙和胡晓凡（2021）分析了语言规律的约定俗成对法律术语翻译的作用与价值。李晋和董晓波（2021）从翻译规范论的视角深入地分析了"shall"在我国立法文本翻译中使用的失范情况和形成原因。此外，也有研究针对法律翻译质量评估，如杨敏（2021）等学者对法律翻译质量层级分析模式的建构为我国法律翻译职业翻译评估提供了可具操作性的理论分析框架。

应用翻译理论研究离不开对语言服务行业的考察。王传英和杨靖怡（2021）详细归纳了我国本土跨国公司海外投资语言环境与语言服务需求特征。郭小洁和司显柱（2021）通过阐述高质量发展的内涵和梳理语言服务业的发展现状，提出了语言服务业高质量发展的路径。除了宏观层面的语言服务行业研究，也有从微观层面对特定领域的探索，如张法连和李文龙（2021）从法律翻译人才培养和法律翻译职业准入制度两方面探讨了法律翻译者职业伦理的建设路径。此外，张法连和曲欣（2021）提出法律翻译技术伦理建构三原则，对法律翻译技术伦理风险管控做出了有益探索。

综上可知，2021年中国应用翻译理论研究整体上呈现出"百花齐放"的局面，应用翻译话语体系的构建既强调中国特色又呼吁国际合作，法律翻译受到较多关注，多种学科理论被运用到研究当中以解决学科和行业上面临的难题，体现出应用翻译研究的跨学科性。但当下应用翻译理论研究仍有大片空白急需填充，应用翻译理论研究需要借用更多其他的学科理论来对其领域的问题进行描写和解决，同时需要进一步完善应用翻译研究话语体系的构建，尤其是需要加强对其与文学翻译研究之间的"断裂地带"（傅敬民，2021：81）的阐释力度。

（四）翻译学科建设研究

自霍姆斯（Holmes）1972年发表"翻译学的名与实"以降，翻译学作为一门独立学科经历了近半个世纪的洗礼正茁壮成长。然而相较于其他人文学科，翻译学的内涵依旧比较单薄，研究界限模糊不清，学科方法论结构的思悟不够等问题依旧存在。2021不少学者在推动翻译学走向成熟的道路上做出了努力。

有学者从不同角度勾勒出翻译学作为一个学科的发展历程和走向，如孙艺风（2021）回顾了斯坦纳（George Steiner）和图里（Gideon Toury）的翻译理论，而方梦之（2021c）则从四个方面归纳出中国原创翻译研究的发展。就翻译的功用而言，王晓路（2021）通过分析欧洲中世纪和中国近代的文化发展论述了翻译独特的历史文化功能。

按照霍姆斯的框架，翻译研究现有各分支在进一步深入。翻译批评研究成果丰硕，张道振（2021）从历时的角度对当代描写翻译批评的客观性进行了解读，并对描写翻译批评的方法进行了策略性建构；陈小慰（2021）提出将翻译修辞批评纳为翻译批评的范式之一，拓展了翻译批评研究的疆域；刘云虹（2021）从契机、问题驱动、主体的意图和策略三个维度阐述了构建翻译批评事件的主客观要素。还有学者通过研读翻译批评类著作来探讨翻译批评理论建构问题，如胡陈尧和许钧（2021）。就理论翻译学而言，黄忠廉、方仪力和朱灵慧（2021）提出从三个层面推动理论翻译学的建构。

2021年，翻译研究进一步呈现出学科分化和跨学科交叉的趋势。随着翻译实践的不断发展，译学界学者对当前发生着的翻译现象做出理论上的回应，例如在中国文化"走出去"的大背景下，中译外占据翻译实践主流，黄忠廉和孙敏庆（2021）提出了"外译学"的概念，我们期待学者进一步对其进行探索。翻译学作为一门综合性学科，其他学科对翻译学的发展有巨大的贡献，例如语料库语言学、认知语言学等。语料库翻译学是近些年的研究热点，不过2021年其研究成果不算丰硕，研究也陷入了僵局，大多数研究成果探讨译者风格，我们期待语料库翻译学能有新突破。多模态翻译研究近年也受到了学界的认可，吴赟（2021）在回顾多模态翻译研究历史的基础上论述了其重要性和必要性并阐释了其研究方法。目前多模态翻译研究也未能有大的突破和创新,我们期待其进一步发展。此外,王立非和孙疆卫(2021)则建构出了翻译经济学的框架,还有学者指出要在中国推动翻译发生学和建构翻译思想发生学,这些学术努力都将拓宽译学研究的边界,但同时也需要确保译学研究边界的清晰,确保翻译学科的独立性,以免沦为其他学科的附庸。

关于学科建设的方法论,不少学者有成果产出。王宁(2021b)和许钧(2021)等领军学者站在回应重大社会需求的角度给出了方法论指导,分别就在国家提出新文科的大背景下如何进行翻译研究以及如何深化中国文学外译的研究给出了建议,体现了学者拥抱时代和适应时代的精神。郭天骥(2021)指出在"文化转向"的影响下,翻译学作为一门学科的边界变得模糊不清,于是提出借鉴叙事学的学科发展道路,以实现翻译学跨学科融合和研究界限清晰的平衡。

三、翻译实践研究

(一)翻译自身实践研究

翻译实践自身的研究包括笔译研究、口译研究和机器翻译研究。笔译实践的研究主要包括文化外译研究和政治文献研究。习近平主席强调中华文化的独特作用,并指出要更好推动中国文化走出去以及提升中华文化的影响力。在2021年,翻译研究学者从各向度做出努力以助力中华文化走出去,回应了重大的国家需求,彰显了翻译研究学者服务家国的情怀。中国文学外译是中华文化走出的必由之路,成果最为丰赡,《外语学刊》组织两期"全球视野下的中国文学外译"专题进行探讨。而文学外译的研究成果以诗歌翻译为最,例如毛泽东诗词、白居易的《长恨歌》、王维的诗歌以及唐诗中象征性女性形象等的翻译。就毛泽东诗词英译而言,有的学者关注微观层面具体意象的翻译,如李正栓和张丹(2021),也有学者关注宏观层面毛泽东诗词文学性的英译,如周方衡(2021)。关于如何译诗,不少学者都给提出了方法,如赵彦春和连蓉(2021)的以韵译韵。此外,2021年学者不只关注文学,研究对象更为具体和丰富,例如李庆明、张恒(2021)从读者意识出发,提出秦腔剧本的翻译策略,以推动中国戏剧走出去;王密卿、朱慧敏(2021)探析《建党伟业》英文字幕的翻译策略,以助力中国电影走出去;此外,还有学者发表文章以助力中国歌曲和白酒走出去,不一而足。在中西意识形态对立冲突的今天,这些学术努力将发挥重大作用。

政治文献翻译成果依旧丰硕。学者们紧扣热点立足新时代探讨外宣翻译的理念、原则、策略与方法,助力中国形象的建构,具体包括《习近平谈治国理政》(以下简称《习谈》)、习近平讲演辞、十九大报告、中国特色扶贫术语以及十八大以来外交部发言人话语等。《天津外国语大学学报》组织了三期"中央文献外译研究"专题探讨中央文献外译。值得一提的是非通用语种(如韩语、西班牙语和德语等)的中央文献翻译也受到了学者的关注,如黄进财、罗兹深(2021)就《习谈》中隐喻的韩译方法进行探讨,不过整体而言非通用语种翻译研究相对式微,其他语种的翻译研究学者需要做出努力。

此外,笔译实践的研究对象也呈现出多样性的特征,例如"人才"一词的翻译、校训翻译、新冠肺炎有关话语的翻译、法律文本翻译和术语翻译等。就法律翻译而言,《北京第二外国语学院学报》第一期刊发了两篇与之相关的文章探究法律文本的翻译策略。就术语翻译而言,《中国科技翻译》刊发了许多与之相关的研究成果,其他期刊也有与之相关文章见刊,具体包括中国典籍术语、物联网文本专业词汇、医学术语ECMO、矿物工程英语以及土木工程英语等的翻译;研究视角包括文本类型理论、语用交互、交际术语学等。

2021年口译研究内容聚焦于同传和交传,主题多元,主要涉及口译工作过程和口译策略研究。其中,口译过程研究所占比重最大，主要采用实证研究方法，多运用眼动追踪技术和语料库技术，多围绕口译认知负荷和信息处理展开。就口译认知负荷而言，巢玥（2021）将3D虚拟技术介入译前准备活动，研究其与交替传译认知负荷的相关性；就口译过程中的信息处理而言，卢信朝（2021）对英汉同声传译过程中信息成分损耗的原因进行了研究，原蓉洁和柴明颎（2021）认为语篇结构是交替传译过程中信息处理的关键。在技术运用方面，眼动追踪和语料库依旧是口译过程研究中常用的技术方法，如苏雯超和李德凤（2021）运用眼动技术对同传中的视觉信息加工进行分析，宋姝娴等（2021）基于语料库分析输入语速对同声传译译语流利性的影响。

占比其次的是口译策略研究，涉及词汇、术语等信息的处理，如张杲和李德超（2021）从个案出发，以"问题"为例，从词汇视角分析同声传译的词汇翻译模式；王华树和李敏铃（2021）则从应用层面对口译术语管理技术所面临的问题和解决方案展开研究。整体而言，2021年口译研究主要聚焦口译过程，以实证研究为主，多是引入眼动追踪技术和语料库技术。

2021年机器翻译研究可大致分为机器翻译技术应用研究、机器翻译质量评估研究和机器翻译策略研究。机器翻译技术应用研究成果较少，鲍同、范大祺和赵灵（2021）介绍了日本机器翻译研发现状并为中国机器翻译研发提供了相应建议。在机器翻译质量评估方面，不同机器翻译译文之间的对比研究是一大亮点，如陈胜和田传茂（2021）以石油地质文献为例，对其在7个线上翻译平台的英译文进行分析评价，认为译后编辑可以弥补机器翻译的不足。在机器翻译策略研究方面，译后编辑的研究成果丰富，如王湘玲等（2021）突破传统的研究方法，基于眼动追踪和键盘记录技术，从认知负荷和译文质量两方面对人工翻译与神经网络机器翻译译后编辑的隐喻表达进行比较。以上研究对改善机器译文质量有极大的促进作用。就当下2021年的机器翻译研究而言，研究主题仍有待拓展，比如翻译技术工具的介绍以及在翻译中的应用、机器翻译与社会的联结、机器翻译所面临的伦理问题等等。

（二）翻译行业实践研究

2021年翻译行业研究主要涉及翻译教学研究。翻译教学研究成果颇丰，涵盖翻译课程改革、翻译教学模式、翻译技术等多个话题。在翻译课程改革方面，值得一提的是，《中国翻译》在其第四期和第五期连续推出以"翻译教学·翻译专业课程思政教育校长论坛"为论题的一系列研究，其他几期的翻译教学专栏也有与课程思政相关的研究，探讨翻译课程思政建设和翻译人才培养的问题，如查明建（2021）认为现今的翻译教学应当融入思政课程以增强翻译专业教育的国家意识和提升翻译专业人才培养的时代使命感，张宝钧（2021）对课程思政与思政课程、任课教师和专业课程三者的关系进行了简要阐述，深化了学界对课程思政的理解。翻译课程研究还包括对"翻译概论"这一课程的研究，如李雯等（2021）以广外"翻译概论"课程教学为例，提出该翻译课程教学应该以职业化为导向。翻译教学模式研究主要涉及PBL翻译教学和"翻译工作坊"教学模式研究，如李德超（2021）基于对内地和香港高校翻译课程教学情况的问卷调查，总结了目前PBL翻译教学所存在的问题，并对教师实施PBL翻译教学提供了可行性的建议；施雪莹和刘云虹（2021）以南京大学"翻译理论与实践"课程为例对"翻译工作坊"教学模式进行了探索。在翻译技术教学方面，程维和魏子杭（2021）以翻译技术中的本地化教学为例肯定了翻译技术类课程对学生高阶思维能力的培养。总的来说，翻译课程研究是2021年翻译教学研究热点，不论是对翻译教学模式的探索，还是对技术在翻译教学中的应用研究，这些研究都对传统的翻译教学提出了挑战，对翻译专业人才培养提出了更高的要求，为进一步完善翻译人才培养标准和翻译教学体系做出了贡献。

（三）翻译批评实践研究

翻译批评是连接翻译理论与翻译实践的桥梁和纽带。相比以往，2021年的翻译批评研究"百花齐放"，大多研究是依据周领顺的译者行为批评理论来对一种或是多种译文进行批评分析，如周领顺和高晨（2021）从人本的角度，对葛浩文英译莫言作品乡土语言比喻修辞的翻译进行译者行为批评分析，为含有比喻修辞的汉语乡土语言的英译实践提供了方法上的指导，深化了译者行为批评研分析的"求真"与"务实"分析模式。黄勤和信萧萧（2021）运用译者行为批评理论，从译者身份的角度对比分析沙博理和王际真英译《家》的译者行为，阐明不同的译者身份对其译者行为的影响。另外，还有的学者专门研究译者行为批评中的译评者类型，如朱芬（2021）。由此可见，2021年译者行为批评研究的研究对象更加多元，不仅仅限于对译者行为批评理论相关概念的运用，而是将译者行为与其他方面相结合，如译者身份和译评者类型，这是对译者行为批评理论的深化与延展。

此外，有的学者从其他视角对多个译本进行比较批评研究，如王洪涛和王海珠（2021）基于图里的翻译规范理论，对方志彤和黄兆杰英译的《文赋》两个译本进行描写性、解释性比较研究；丁立和刘泽权（2021）从评价理论视角，对比分析了《红楼梦》王熙凤话语"笑道"的四个英译本。以上研究为多译本比较批评研究提供了多种理论视角，但其理论的普遍实用性有待商榷。也有的研究未借用理论，但侧重于对史的考察，如荣立宇和王洪涛（2021）围绕着《人间词话》"境界"理论及其相关核心概念，对该著涂经诒、李又安两个译本的相关英译做了系统、深入的对比研究。然而，作为"冰山一角"的网络翻译批评研究依旧较少，王一多（2021）从传播学的视角，对《飞鸟集》冯唐译本网络翻译批评的六度传播模式的运行过程进行分析，拓宽了网络翻译批评模式研究路径以及传播学理论在翻译批评研究中的应用。朱安博和刘畅（2021）通过豆瓣网上收藏人数最多的莎剧三个译本，对莎剧网络翻译批评的现状进行分析和思考，对网络翻译批评的规范性研究有建设性作用。

整体来看，以上研究基本上是属于文学翻译批评研究，而且大多是译者行为批评，非文学文本的翻译批评研究凤毛麟角，是未来翻译批评研究的一块新地。此外，翻译批评形式的研究也较为单一，除了传统的翻译批评形式，还可以大力扩展新的批评形式，如网络翻译批评、众包翻译等。

四、结 语

2021年是人类历史发展长河中的沧海一粟，然而对于中国译学界而言则是值得记录的一年。译学界学者进一步关注自身，建构立足本土的译学理论，为译学界贡献中国力量，我们期待学者们能完善方法推动中国翻译学派的建立。此外，就学科建设而言，我们也发现了现阶段的不足，也希望各位学者能弥补之，推动翻译学这一相对年轻的学科走向成熟，牢固其学科地位。相比以往，应用翻译理论研究获得了进一步的发展，话语体系建设有所完善。而随着译者行为批评理论相关概念的不断深化与拓展，翻译批评实践研究对象更加多元，但批评形式和批评文本依旧有待扩展。就实践而言，翻译是一门社会性活动，翻译行业是一门独特的行业，因此翻译与社会、翻译与教育、翻译与互联网等行业领域的研究需要得到重视。在中国共产党向下一个一百年奋进的征程上，翻译实践以及翻译研究将会更加繁荣，为国家与社会贡献更多力量。

参考文献

[1] Bao, Tong et al (鲍同等). "The Experience and Inspiration of Machine Translation R&D and Application in Japan" (日本机器翻译研发应用的经验及启示) [J]. *Chinese Translators Journal* (中国翻译), 2021(3):124-132.

[2] Chang, Hongxing (常红星). "Dao'an's Opposition Against Translation-caused Losses of Buddhist Scripture's 'Original Look' " (释道安译经"失本"态度问题补证) [J]. *Chinese Translators Journal* (中国翻译), 2021(1):41-47.

[3] Chao, Yue (巢玥). "A Study on the Correlation between Pre-interpretation Preparation and Cognitive Load of Consecutive Interpreting with the Intervention of 3D Virtual Reality Technology" (3D虚拟现实技术介入的译前准备与交替传译认知负荷的相关性研究) [J]. *Foreign Language Education* (外语教学), 2021(5):93-97.

[4] Chen, Daliang (陈大亮). "Toward a Theory of Translation Horizon" (何谓翻译境界论) [J]. *Chinese Translators Journal* (中国翻译), 2021(2):13-21.

[5] Chen, Dongcheng & Yan, Li (陈东成，李艳). "Discussion on the Construction Principles of Chinese School of Translation Studies" (翻译学中国学派之构建原则探讨) [J]. *Shanghai Journal of Translators* (上海翻译), 2021(6):17-22.

[6] Chen, Sheng & Chuanmo, Tian (陈胜，田传茂). "Problems of Chinese-English Translation and Post-translation Editing on Online Translation Platforms: Taking Petroleum Geology Literature as an Example" (在线翻译平台汉英翻译的问题及译后编辑——以石油地质文献为例) [J]. *Chinese Science & Technology Translators Journal* (中国科技翻译), 2021(1):31-34.

[7] Chen, Xiaowei (陈小慰). "Dimensions of Translational Rhetoric Criticism" (翻译修辞批评的几个维度) [J]. *Shanghai Journal of Translators* (上海翻译), 2021(1):1-6.

[8] Cheng, Wei & Zihang, Wei (程维，魏子杭). "High Order Thinking Skills in Translation Technology Teaching" (翻译技术教学中的高阶思维培养) [J]. *Shanghai Journal of Translators* (上海翻译), 2021(3):39-44.

[9] Ding, Li & Zequan, Liu (丁立，刘泽权). "An Examination of the Evaluative Meaning and English Translation of Reporting Verbs: Taking Wang Xifeng's 'XIAO DAO' as an Example" (报道动词的评价意义及英译考察——以王熙凤的"笑道"为例) [J]. *Shanghai Journal of Translators* (上海翻译), 2021(1):77-82.

[10] Fang, Mengzhi (方梦之). "Meta-Strategies, General Strategies and Special Strategies of Translation" (翻译的元策略、总策略和分策略) [J]. *Shanghai Journal of Translators* (上海翻译), 2021(3):1-6.

[11] Fang, Mengzhi (方梦之). "Research on Translators: Objects and Their Spiritual Ethics" (翻译家研究的"宽度"和"厚度") [J]. *English Studies* (英语研究), 2021(1):11-20.

[12] Fang, Mengzhi (方梦之). "The Way to Construct the Chinese Translation Discourse System" (我国译学话语体系的勃兴之路) [J]. *Contemporary Foreign Languages Studies* (当代外语研究), 2021(1):29-37.

[13] Feng, Quangong (冯全功). "Rethinking the Unit of Translation from the Perspective of Prototype Theory" (原型理论观照下的翻译单位辨析) [J]. *Chinese Translators Journal* (中国翻译), 2021(1):21-29.

[14] Feng, Xiaobing 冯小冰. "A Study on the Sponsorship Mechanism of German Translation of Contemporary Chinese Novels" (中国当代小说德译的赞助机制研究) [J]. *Journal of Xi'an International Studies University* (西安外国语大学学报), 2021(3):104-108.

[15] Fu, Jingmin & Jinlong, Liu (傅敬民，刘金龙). "On the Characteristics of Chinese Pragmatic Translation Studies" (中国特色应用翻译研究的特色问题) [J]. *Journal of Foreign Languages* (外国语), 2021(2):80-85.

[16] Fu, Jingmin & Xudong, Yu (傅敬民，喻旭东). "Pragmatic Translation Studies with Chinese Characteristics in an Era of Great Change: Status Quo and Trends" (大变局时代中国特色应用翻译研究：现状与趋势) [J]. *Journal of Shanghai University (Social Sciences Edition)* (上海大学学报(社会科学版)), 2021(4):128-140.

[17] Gao, Qian & Xiaohui, Wang (高茜，王晓辉). "An Overview of English Translation and Dissemination of Chinese Science Fiction: 2000-2020" (中国科幻小说英译发展述评：2000-2020 年) [J]. *Chinese Translators Journal* (中国翻译), 2021(5):57-64.

[18] Gao, Yuxia & Dongsheng, Ren (高玉霞，任东升). "Writing Translation History Based on National Governance: Justifications and Paths" (基于国家治理的翻译史书写：理据与路径) [J]. *Contemporary Foreign Languages Studies* (当代外语研究), 2021(5):30-39.

[19] Geng, Qiang (耿强). "Poetics of Translation: An Epistemological Survey of a Keyword in TS" (翻译诗学：一个学科关键词考察) [J]. *Journal of PLA University of Foreign Languages* (解放军外国语学院学报), 2021(3):129-136.

[20] Guo, Tianji (郭天骥). "Tracing, Reflecting, and Drawing on the Disciplinary Boundaries of Translation Studies: Taking the 'Post-Classical Turn' in Narratology as Reference" (溯源·反思·借鉴——论翻译研究的学科界限：以叙事学的"后经典转向"为参照) [J]. *Foreign Languages Research* (外语研究), 2021(6):72-77.

[21] Guo, Xiaojie & Xianzhu, Si (郭小洁，司显柱). "Exploring the Development Path of China's Language Service Industry from the Perspective of High-Quality Development" (高质量发展视角下中国语言服务业发展路径探索) [J]. *Chinese Translators Journal* (中国翻译), 2021(3):117-123.

[22] Han, Shuqin (韩淑芹). "The 'Rule' and 'System' of National Translation Program—The Case of Translation in Government-run Translation Centers in the Period of the Foreign Affairs Movement" (国家翻译实践之"治"与"制"——以洋务运动时期官办译馆翻译为例) [J]. *Shanghai Journal of Translators* (上海翻译), 2021(5):79-84.

[23] Han, Ziman & Hong, Qian (韩子满，钱虹). "International Dessemination of Contemporary Chinese Translation Theories: Present Status and Prospect" (当代中国翻译理论国际传播：现状与展望) [J]. *Chinese Translators Journal* (中国翻译), 2021(6):103-110.

[24] Hu, Chenyao & Jun, Xu (胡陈尧，许钧). "Historical Reflection, Practical Problems and Development Path of Translation Criticism—A Review of Criticism of Criticism: Theoretical Construction and Reflection on Translation Criticism" (翻译批评的历史反思、现实问题与发展路径——兼评《批评之批评：翻译批评理论建构与反思》) [J]. *Shanghai Journal of Translators* (上海翻译), 2021(2):8-12.

[25] Huang, Jincai & Zishen, Luo (黄进财，罗兹深). "A Study of Korean Translation Methods of Metaphors in *Xi Jinping: The Governance of China* from the Perspective of Conceptual Metaphor" (概念隐喻视角下《习近平谈治国理政》中隐喻的韩译方法研究) [J]. *Foreign Languages and Literature* (外国语文), 2021(5):17-26.

[26] Huang, Qin & Xiaoxiao, Xin (黄勤，信萧萧). "A Study on the Relationship between Translator Identity and Translator Behavior in Cultural Translation: An Example from the English Translation of *The Family* by Shapiro and Wang Jizhen" (文化外译中译者身份与译者行为之关系研究——以沙博理和王际真英译《家》为例) [J]. *Shanghai Journal of Translators* (上海翻译), 2021(1):33-38.

[27] Huang, Youyi & Changqi, Huang (黄友义，黄长奇). "Review of the Development of New China's Foreign Translation and Publishing Under the Leadership of the Communist Party of China: Taking China Foreign Language Bureau as an Example" (党领导下的新中国对外翻译出版事业发展回顾——以中国外文局为例) [J]. *Chinese Translators Journal* (中国翻译), 2021(3):28-35.

[28] Huang, Zhonglian & MinQing, Sun (黄忠廉，孙敏庆). "On the Construction of the Studies on Outward Translation" (外译学管论与外译详解) [J]. *Foreign Languages in China* (中国外语), 2021(1):91-97.

[29] Huang, Zhonglian *et al* (黄忠廉等). "Three Tendencies of Theoretical Translation Studies: Directionality, Dominance and Instrumentality" (理论翻译学研究:方向性、主导性与工具性) [J]. *Shanghai Journal of Translators* (上海翻译), 2021(5):6-10.

[30] Lan, Hongjun (蓝红军). "Theoretical Construction of National Translation Capacity: Values and Objectives" (国家翻译能力的理

论建构：价值与目标) [J]. *Chinese Translators Journal* (中国翻译), 2021(4):20-25.

[31] Li, Dechao (李德超). "Applying Problem-based Learning to Translation Classrooms: Challenges and Solutions" (PBL 在翻译教学中的应用：挑战与对策) [J]. *Shandong Foreign Language Teaching Journal* (山东外语教学), 2021(6):101-111.

[32] Li, Jin & Xiaobo, Dong (李晋，董晓波). "A Study on 'Shall' in Legislative Text Translation on China" (我国立法文本翻译中"shall"的失范分析及改进策略研究) [J]. *Foreign Language Learning Theory and Practice* (外语教学理论与实践), 2021(3):128-140.

[33] Li, Qingming & Heng, Zhang (李庆明，张恒). "The Concern of Audience Awareness in the Translation of Shaanxi Opera Scripts" (秦腔剧本翻译之读者意识关照) [J]. *Foreign Language Research* (外语学刊), 2021(4):95-100.

[34] Li, Wen *et al* (李雯等). "A Probe into the Teaching Model of Introduction to Translation Guided by Translation Professionalization" (以翻译职业化为导向的"翻译概论"课程教学模式探析) [J]. *Foreign Language Learning Theory and Practice* (外语教学理论与实践), 2021(2):136-144.

[35] Li, Wenlong & Xiaofan, Hu (李文龙，胡晓凡). "On Conventionality in the Translated of Legal Terms" (法律术语译名的约定俗成研究) [J]. *Journal of Tianjin Foreign Studies University* (天津外国语大学学报), 2021(3):53-62.

[36] Li, Yi & Junping, Liu (李奕，刘军平). "Explanation of Ye Junjian's Translation Thought of 'Re-creation of Excellence': Taking the English Translation of Mao Dun's *Rural Trilogy* as an Example" (叶君健"精品再创造"翻译思想阐释——以茅盾"农村三部曲"英译为例) [J]. *Journal of Xi'an International Studies University* (西安外国语大学学报), 2021(3):98-103.

[37] Li, Zhengshuan & Dan, Zhang (李正栓，张丹). "The Implication and Translation of the Flag in Mao Zedong's Poems" (毛泽东诗词中旗帜意象的意义及其英译) [J]. *Journal of Tianjin Foreign Studies University* (天津外国语大学学报), 2021(3):1-10.

[38] Li, Zhonghui (李忠辉). "Principles, Strategies, and Evaluation of Chinese and North Korean Interpretation during the Hajj of Qing Dynasty Korean Envoys: Based on Bourdieu's Theory of Field, Habitus, and Capital" (清代朝鲜使臣觐见时中朝口译的原则、策略与评价——基于布迪厄的场域、惯习与资本理论) [J]. *Foreign Languages Research* (外语研究), 2021(2):84-89.

[39] Liang, Na & Daliang, Chen (梁娜，陈大亮). "Concept, Historical Development and Modern Interpretation of *Ben* in Discussing Sutra Translation" (佛经译论之"本"的概念、发展脉络与现代诠释) [J]. *Foreign Languages Research* (外语研究), 2021(6):60-65.

[40] Liu, Runze (刘润泽). "Terminological Knowledge Restructuring in the Development of Traditional Discourse on Translation: Methodological Reconsideration Based on the Case of *Wen* and *Zhi*" (面向中国传统译学话语构建的术语重塑——文质论话语转型实践与反思) [J]. *Foreign Languages and Their Teaching* (外语与外语教学), 2021(5):121-128.

[41] Liu, Yunhong (刘云虹). "Criticism as Event and Construction of Translation Theory" (文学翻译批评事件与翻译理论建构) [J]. *Journal of Foreign Languages* (外国语), 2021(1):106-114.

[42] Lu, Xinchao (卢信朝). "A Study on the Causes and Mechanisms of Information Component Loss in English-Chinese Simultaneous Interpretation." (英汉同声传译信息成分损耗原因及机制研究) [J]. *Chinese Translators Journal* (中国翻译), 2021(3):157-167.

[43] Rong, Liyu & Hongtao, Wang (荣立宇，王洪涛). "A Comparative Study of English Translation of the 'Jingjie' Theory in the Two Versions of *Jen-chien Tz' u-hua* Respectively by Tu Jingyi and Adele Rickett" (《人间词话》"境界"理论的英译对比研究——以涂经诒译本与李又安译本为例) [J]. *Shandong Foreign Language Teaching Journal* (山东外语教学), 2021(5):104-114.

[44] Shi, Xueying & Yunhong, Liu (施雪莹，刘云虹). "Translation Teaching with Emphasis on Process Analysis and Ability Cultivation: Exploration and Practice of 'Translation Workshop' Teaching Mode" (重过程剖析与能力培养的翻译教学——"翻译工作坊"教学模式探索与实践) [J]. *Shanghai Journal of Translators* (上海翻译), 2021(4):53-57.

[45] Song, Shuxian *et al* (宋姝娴等). "An Empirical and Corpus-based Study on the Effects of Input Rate on Fluency in Simultaneous

Interpreting" (输入语速对同声传译译语流利性的影响:基于实证及语料库的研究) [J]. *Foreign Language Research* (外语学刊), 2021(3):103-108.

[46] Su, Wenchao & Defeng, Li (苏雯超, 李德凤). "A Study of Eye Movements in Visual Information Processing for Simultaneous Interpretation" (同声传译视觉信息加工中的眼动研究) [J]. *Chinese Science & Technology Translators Journal* (中国科技翻译), 2021(2):17-20.

[47] Su, Yan (苏艳). "Zhang Zhidong's Patronage of Translators in His Viceroy Office of Huguang" (张之洞督鄂期间翻译赞助行为研究) [J]. *Foreign Languages Research* (外语研究), 2021(5):70-76.

[48] Sun, Yifeng (孙艺风). "*After Babel* and Beyond" (《通天塔》与"Beyond") [J]. *Chinese Translators Journal* (中国翻译), 2021(1):5-20.

[49] Tan, Zaixi (谭载喜). "The Duality and Multiplicity of Translation: A Boundary Theory Based Interpretation" (翻译的界、两界与多界：一个关于翻译的界学阐释) [J]. *Foreign Language Teaching and Research* (外语教学与研究), 2021(6):937-947.

[50] Wang, Chuanying & Jingyi, Yang (王传英, 杨靖怡). "Overseas Language Environments Facing China's MNCs and the Challenges They Pose for the Country's Language Service Industry" (我国本土跨国公司海外投资语言环境与语言服务业发展) [J]. *Chinese Translators Journal* (中国翻译), 2021(4):106-114.

[51] Wang, Dongping & Guanli, Pang (汪东萍, 庞观丽). "*Hu* or Sanskrit? A Re-examination of the Source Languages of Chinese Translation of Buddhist Scriptures" (佛典汉译的源语是"胡"还是"梵") [J]. *Chinese Translators Journal* (中国翻译), 2021(4):133-140.

[52] Wang, Hongtao & Haizhu, Wang (王洪涛, 王海珠). "A Comparative Study of Two English Translation of *Wen Fu* Based on Gideon Toury's Theory of Translational Norms" (基于图里翻译规范理论的《文赋》两英译本比较研究) [J]. *Foreign Languages and Literature* (外国语文), 2021(5):110-118.

[53] Wang, Huashu & Minling, Li (王华树, 李敏铃). "Terminology Management Techniques for Interpreters: Needs, Problems and Options" (口译术语管理技术：需求、问题与方案) [J]. *Chinese Science & Technology Translators Journal* (中国科技翻译), 2021(4):24-27.

[54] Wang, Lifei & Jiangwei, Sun (王立非, 孙疆卫). "Analysis of Hot Spots of Translation Economy Research at Home and Abroad and Construction of Theoretical Models" (国内外翻译经济研究热点分析与理论模型构建) [J]. *Chinese Translators Journal* (中国翻译), 2021(2):117-124.

[55] Wang, Min (王敏). "To Translate or not to Translate: Early Translation of Chinese Myths by European Missionaries (1575-1688)" ("译"与"不译"之间：早期欧洲传教士对中国神话的翻译（1575-1688）) [J]. *Foreign Language Teaching and Research* (外语教学与研究), 2021(2):273-283.

[56] Wang, Miqing & Huimin, Zhu (王密卿, 朱慧敏). "A Study of English Subtitling Translation Strategies from the Perspective of Functional Equivalence Theory Based on the Chinese Film *Beginning of the Great Revival*" (从功能对等理论视角探析英文字幕的翻译策略——以《建党伟业》为例) [J]. *Journal of Tianjin Foreign Studies University* (天津外国语大学学报), 2021(3):21-29.

[57] Wang, Ning (王宁). "Translation and the Sinicization of Marxism: A Literary and Cultural Dimension" (翻译与马克思主义中国化:文学和文化的维度) [J]. *Shanghai Journal of Translators* (上海翻译), 2021(6):1-6.

[58] Wang, Ning (王宁). "Translation Studies from the Perspectives of New Liberal Arts" (新文科视域下的翻译研究) [J]. *Journal of Foreign Languages* (外国语), 2021(2):75-79.

[59] Wang, Tianyi (王天翼). "The Analysis of Metaphorical Expressions on Translation Based on Conceptual Metaphor Theory" (基于概念隐喻论分析翻译的隐喻表达式) [J]. *Foreign Languages in China* (中国外语), 2021(6):88-94.

[60] Wang, Xiangling *et al* (王湘玲等). "A Comparative Study of HT and NMT Post-editing: Data from Eye-tracking and Key-logging on Metaphor Translation" (人工翻译与神经网络机器翻译译后编辑比较研究——基于对隐喻翻译的眼动追踪与键盘记录数据) [J]. *Foreign Language Learning Theory and Practice* (外语教学理论与实践), 2021(4):115-126.

[61] Wang, Xiaolu (王晓路). "The Historical and Cultural Function of Translation: Cognitive Patterns and Knowledge Genealogy" (论翻译的历史文化功能：认知模式与知识谱系) [J]. *Foreign Language Teaching and Research* (外语教学与研究), 2021(2):263-272.

[62] Wang, Xiaonong (王晓农). "Kumarajiva's Discourse on Buddhist Sutra Translation: A Reexamination" (令文义圆通,使微言不坠——鸠摩罗什佛经翻译"圆通论"诠释) [J]. *Chinese Translators Journal* (中国翻译), 2021(2):29-36.

[63] Wang, Yanmeng & Linxin, Liang (王烟朦, 梁林歆). "An Overview of Ding Wenjiang's Translation Activities of Scientific and Technical Texts" (丁文江的科技典籍译介活动钩沉) [J]. *Shanghai Journal of Translators* (上海翻译), 2021(3):70-75.

[64] Wang, Yiduo (王一多). "A Study of Online Translation Criticism Models from the Perspective of Communication Studies" (传播学视角下网络翻译批评模式研究) [J]. *Shanghai Journal of Translators* (上海翻译), 2021(1):7-12.

[65] Wang, Yin (王寅). "Defining Embodied-Cognitive Translatology" (体认翻译学的理论建构与实践应用) [J]. *Chinese Translators Journal* (中国翻译), 2021(3):43-49.

[66] Wang, Zuhua (王祖华). "New Breakthroughs in Lin Shu's Studies and Their Implications" (林纾研究的新突破及其启示) [J]. *Shanghai Journal of Translators* (上海翻译), 2021(4):80-84.

[67] Wu, Guangjun & Yuheng, Jiang (武光军, 蒋雨衡). "The Origin of Yan Fu's '*Xin, Da* and *Ya*' and Their Reinterpretation in Contemporary Translation Studies" (严复"信、达、雅"来源考辨及其译学意义重释) [J]. *Chinese Translators Journal* (中国翻译), 2021(3):50-56.

[68] Wu, Yun (吴赟). "The Medial Turn and Multimodal Translation Studies" (媒介转向下的多模态翻译研究) [J]. *Journal of Foreign Languages* (外国语), 2021(1):115-123.

[69] Xu, Jun (许钧). "A Few Suggestions for Strengthening Studies on Translation of Chinese Literature into Other Languages" (关于深化中国文学外译研究的几点意见) [J]. *Foreign Languages and Their Teaching* (外语与外语教学), 2021(6):68-72.

[70] Xu, Mingwu & Wei, Nie (许明武, 聂炜). " 'Rewriting Translation History': Origin, Methods and Future Directions in Chinese Translation History Field" ("重写翻译史"：缘起、路径与面向) [J]. *Foreign Languages and Literature* (外国语文), 2021(6):105-112.

[71] Yan, Xiaojiang (严晓江). "Poetic Enlightenment of Zhang Boran's Translation Thoughts with Chinese Characteristics" (张柏然中国特色翻译思想的诗学启示) [J]. *Journal of PLA University of Foreign Languages* (解放军外国语学院学报), 2021(6):27-33.

[72] Yang, Feng (杨枫). "Declaration on Epistemic Translation Studies" (知识翻译学宣言) [J]. *Contemporary Foreign Languages Studies* (当代外语研究), 2021(5):2.

[73] Yang, Min *et al* (杨敏等). "A Hierarchical Model for Analyzing the Quality of Legal Translations" (法律翻译质量的层级分析模式) [J]. *Foreign Language Education* (外语教学), 2021(2):97-101.

[74] Yu, Deying (于德英). "Zhang Boran's Translation Aesthetics Reinterpreted from His View on Language: A Dialectic and Holistic Integration" (语言·阐释：张柏然辩证圆览的翻译美学思想探究) [J]. *Journal of PLA University of Foreign Languages* (解放军外国语学院学报), 2021(6): 34-40.

[75] Yuan, Hui & Jian, Xu (袁辉, 徐剑). "A Keylogging-based Study of Translation Units: Evidence from Its Correlations with Linguistic Units and Translation Competence" (基于键盘记录的翻译单位和语言单位与译者水平关系的研究) [J]. *Foreign Languages Research* (外语研究), 2021(2):76-83.

[76] Yuan, Rongjie & Mingjiong, Chai (原蓉洁, 柴明颎). "The Key to Information Processing in Consecutive Interpreting: An Exploration Based on Discourse Structure" (交替传译中信息处理的关键——基于语篇结构的探析) [J]. *Chinese Translators Journal* (中国翻译), 2021(2):139-145.

[77] Yue, Manman (岳曼曼). "The Cognitive Value and Conceptual Operations of Thick Translation" (深度翻译的认知价值与实现方式) [J]. *Foreign Language Teaching and Research* (外语教学与研究), 2021(4):594-605.

[78] Zha, Mingjian (查明建). "Leading the Connotation Construction and Innovative Development of Translation Profession with Curriculum Civics and Politics" (以课程思政引领翻译专业内涵建设与创新发展) [J]. *Chinese Translators Journal* (中国翻译), 2021(5):77-80.

[79] Zhang, Baojun (张宝钧). "On the Three Groups of Relationships in Curricular Civic Education" (论课程思政教育的三组关系) [J]. *Chinese Translators Journal* (中国翻译), 2021(5):70-72.

[80] Zhang, Daozhen (张道振). "From Traditional to Modern—On the Concept, Methodology and Tasks of Descriptive Translation Criticism" (从传统走向现代——论描写翻译批评的现代理念、方法和任务) [J]. *Journal of Foreign Languages* (外国语), 2021(6):94-102.

[81] Zhang, Falian & Wenlong, Li (张法连, 李文龙). "A Perspective on Professional Ethics of Legal Translators and Interpreters" (法律翻译者职业伦理构建探索) [J]. *Chinese Translators Journal* (中国翻译), 2021(1):104-112.

[82] Zhang, Falian & Xin, Qu (张法连, 曲欣). "Ethical Review of Legal Translation Technology" (法律翻译技术伦理建构探索) [J]. *Foreign Languages in China* (中国外语), 2021(6):17-22.

[83] Zhang, Gao & Dechao, Li (张昊, 李德超). "A Lexical Translation Model for Simultaneous Interpreting from a Lexical Trigger Perspective: The Example of 'Problem' " (词汇触发视角下同声传译的词汇翻译模式——以"问题"为例) [J]. *Chinese Translators Journal* (中国翻译), 2021(1):147-153.

[84] Zhang, Mi (张汨). "Writing the Microhistory of Translation: Theories and Methods" (翻译微观史书写:理论与方法) [J]. *Foreign Languages and Their Teaching* (外语与外语教学), 2021(5):129-137.

[85] Zhao, Huan (赵奂). "Translation Bias and Translation Criticism: The Metatheoretical Direction of Zhang Boran's Translation Thought" (翻译偏向与翻译批评:张柏然翻译思想的元理论向度) [J]. *Journal of PLA University of Foreign Languages* (解放军外国语学院学报), 2021(6):41-47.

[86] Zhao, Yanchun & Rong, Lian (赵彦春, 连蓉). "Translating Rhyme: The Way to Translating Poetics into Poetics" (韵不绝,诗乃存——"以诗译诗、以韵译韵"方为正道) [J]. *Foreign Language Research* (外语学刊), 2021(2):84-89.

[87] Zhou, Chunyue (周春悦). "The Establishment of Young Bakhtin Translators' Subjectivity: 'Translation Stance' and 'Translation Impulse' in the Translation of *The Night is Not Yet Done*" (青年巴金译者主体性的建立——《夜未央》译本中的"翻译立场"和"翻译冲动") [J]. *Chinese Translators Journal* (中国翻译), 2021(2):94-101.

[88] Zhou, Fangheng (周方衡). "A Study of the English Translation of Literariness of Mao Zedong's Poems" (毛泽东诗词文学性英译研究)[J]. *Journal of Tianjin Foreign Studies University* (天津外国语大学学报), 2021(3):11-20.

[89] Zhou, He & Baoguo, Zhang (周鹤, 张保国). "The Translation Way of Chinese Academics Going Global: Taking Agricultural Historian Shi Shenghan's Academic Translations as an Example" (中国学术"走出去"的翻译之道——以农史学家石声汉的学术外译为例) [J]. *Shanghai Journal of Translators* (上海翻译), 2021(1):39-43.

[90] Zhou, Lingshun & Chen, Gao (周领顺, 高晨). "Goldblatt's Translation of the Chinese Folk Languages Metaphors from the Perspective of Translator Behavior Criticism" (葛译乡土语言比喻修辞译者行为批评分析) [J]. *Journal of PLA University of Foreign Languages* (解放军外国语学院学报), 2021(5):102-110.

[91] Zhou, Lingshun (周领顺). "Translator Behavior Research Methodology" (译者行为研究方法论) [J]. *Foreign Language Education* (外语教学), 2021(1):87-93.

[92] Zhu, Anbo & Chang, Liu (朱安博，刘畅). "A Critical Study of Online Translation of Shakespeare's Plays" (莎士比亚戏剧网络翻译批评研究) [J]. *Foreign Languages Research* (外语研究), 2021(1):76-84.

[93] Zhu, Fen (朱芬). "Research on the types of translation ethics in translator's behavior criticism: with the controversy on the evaluation of the Japanese translation of MO Yan's novels as a case study" (译者行为批评中的译评者类型研究——以莫言小说日译评价争议为例) [J]. *Foreign Language Learning Theory and Practice* (外语教学理论与实践), 2021(4):153-161.

[94] Zhu, Jianping *et al* (朱健平等). "Shifting the Focus from Learning from the West to Learning on the Tradition: A Reflection on Constructing the Discourse System of Translation Studies with Chinese Characteristics" (从借鸡生蛋到借镜传统——关于中国特色翻译研究话语体系建设的一点思考) [J]. *Journal of Foreign Languages* (外国语), 2021(6):83-93.

作者简介

皮伟男，广东外语外贸大学高级翻译学院硕士研究生。主要研究方向：中国当代文学外译、翻译理论。电子邮箱：634274261@qq.com。

赖春梅，广东外语外贸大学高级翻译学院硕士研究生。主要研究方向：翻译理论与实践。电子邮箱：lai18883705915@126.com。

蓝红军，广东外语外贸大学高级翻译学院教授、博士生导师。主要研究方向：译学理论批评、翻译思想史。电子邮箱：alan.lan@163.com。

传承优秀文化 规范景区英译 讲好中国故事

——泉州著名世界遗产点九日山景区信息英译问题及解决方案

⊙ 陈 彬（泉州信息工程学院，泉州）
⊙ 李跃平（西南民族大学，成都；泉州信息工程学院，泉州）

[摘 要] 景点是一个城市的名片之一。著名景点是一个城市最靓丽的名片。景区的英语信息和英语标识具有鲜明的标识特征，不仅是沟通信息和文化的桥梁，在旅游业以及对外交流中发挥着重要的作用，而且在满足人民精神文化需求、推进文化自信自强中同样发挥着不可忽视和或缺的作用。文章以泉州著名世界遗产点之一的九日山景区信息为例，对景区部分具有中国特色的景点名称、景点信息的英语信息和英文标识存在的翻译问题，提出了针对性的解决策略，使用音译直译结合、音译意译结合以及注释法等技巧予以校正改译，希望能够对当地的旅游景区英语信息及英语标识的表述与规范使用有所促进，以达到"讲好中华优秀传统文化故事，推动中华文化更好走向世界"的目的。

[关键词] 九日山；世界遗产点；规范标识；著名景区；景点信息；英语标识；世遗泉州；中国故事

Inheriting Excellent Traditional Chinese Culture, Normalizing Scenic Area English Translation, Telling Chinese Stories Well: Problems of English Translation of Information in Jiuri Mountain Scenic Area, a Famous World Heritage Site in Quanzhou and Their Solutions

CHEN Bin (Quanzhou University of Information Engineering)

LI Yueping (Southwest Minzu University; Quanzhou University of Information Engineering)

Abstract: Scenic spot is one of a city's business cards. Famous scenic spot is the most beautiful business card. The English information and English signs of the scenic areas have distinct identification characteristics, which not only are bridges for communicating information and culture, and play an important role in tourism and foreign exchanges, but also play an important and indispensable role in meeting the spiritual and cultural needs of the people and promoting cultural self-confidence and self-improvement. Taking Jiuri Mountain Scenic Area, one of the famous world heritage sites in Quanzhou as an example, the article proposes targeted solutions to the English translation problems of some names of scenic spots with Chinese characteristics, English information of scenic spots information

---

基金项目：泉州信息工程学院教改项目"'中国文化'融入'大学英语'教学的课程思政实践研究"（项目编号：2022JXGG021）。

and English signs, using techniques such as the combination of transliteration and literal translation, the combination of transliteration and meaning translation, and the annotation method to correct and retranslate, hoping to promote the expression and standardized use of English information and English signs in local tourist attractions so as to achieve the purpose of "telling the story of excellent traditional Chinese culture and promoting Chinese culture to better go to the world".

Key words: Jiuri Mountain; world heritage site; formal expressions; famous scenic area; information of scenic spots; English signs; the world heritage of Quanzhou; Chinese stories

一、引 言

2021年7月中国的文化遗产申报项目"泉州：宋元中国的世界海洋商贸中心"成功列入《世界遗产名录》以来，泉州市文旅管理部门积极采取行动，对泉州的景区景点，尤其是对"泉州申遗项目的遗产整体由22处代表性古迹遗址及其关联环境构成"的系列文化遗产地进一步进行提升管理理念和水平，更换了部分标识标牌，增添新的景区介绍信息，重塑景区形象，以新的姿态迎接国内外游客。中共中央总书记、国家主席、中央军委主席习近平在2022年12月12日对非物质文化遗产保护工作作出重要指示强调，"要扎实做好非物质文化遗产的系统性保护，更好满足人民日益增长的精神文化需求，推进文化自信自强。要推动中华优秀传统文化创造性转化、创新性发展，不断增强中华民族凝聚力和中华文化影响力，深化文明交流互鉴，讲好中华优秀传统文化故事，推动中华文化更好走向世界。"（习近平，2022）

景区景点信息和标识的英译是景区不可或缺的重要管理任务和内容。英语信息和英语标识是"指引游客愉快安全开展旅游的保证，也是展示景区服务水平的窗口，因此对国外游客而言，准确翻译景区标识具有重要意义。"（齐卓然，2019）"旅游景点英文翻译作为国外游客了解中国文化的工具，在中国的涉外旅游中发挥着越来越重要的作用。"（朱艳宁、向丹，2018）通过景区景点使用规范英语用语，助力中国"文化走出去"，让世界上更多的人了解中国、认识中国，让来中国旅游、来泉州旅游的外国朋友感知中国文化的博大精深，让他们喜欢中国文化、爱上中国文化，让他们觉得不虚此行，来得值得，值得再来（周绪琳、李跃平，2022）。笔者采用人类学田野调查法对泉州著名世界遗产点之一的九日山景区部分具有中国特色的景点名称、景点信息的中英文信息和中英文标识进行了多次的实地考察、拍照备存，调查发现该著名景区里具有中国特色的景点名称、景点信息的中英文信息和中英文标识存在大量的翻译问题，这对"更好满足人民日益增长的精神文化需求，推进文化自信自强"都十分不利，应该引起当地政府及主管部门的重视，采取有力措施予以纠正。只有这样，才能"做优秀传统文化传承者""讲好中国故事"。

二、泉州著名世界遗产点九日山景区信息英译错漏及校译

"九日山祈风石刻"位列由22处代表性古迹遗址及其关联环境构成的系列遗产中之首位，除了"九日山祈风石刻"外，九日山风景区内还有众多的人文景观。然而，在世界遗产点著名的九日山风景区里，却出现了"景区信息少有英译不出错"的情况，一些较为严重的中文信息错误，也导致其英译信息错误。有关"九日山祈风石刻"内容的英译问题已撰专文阐述[①]，本文不再涉及此内容。

（一）"九日山片区简介"中的英译错漏

九日山景区是泉州清源山国家级风景区不可或缺的重要组成部分。但在"清源山片区简介""九日山片区简介"和"灵山圣墓片区简介"三片区简介"三合一"告示牌上的"九日山片区简介"中的英译错误不少，详见图1、图2中的标注处。

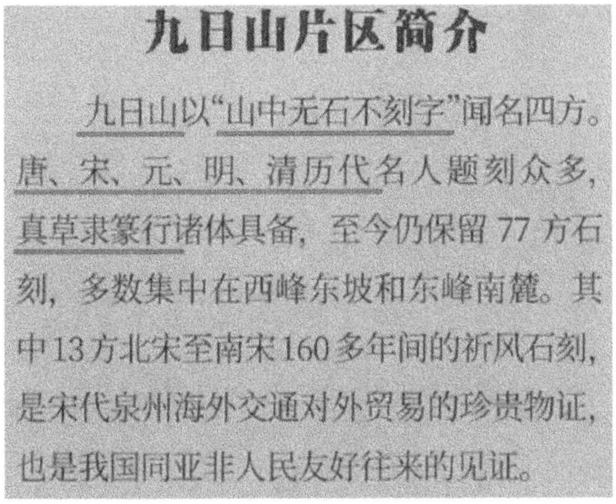

图1 "九日山片区简介"（中文） 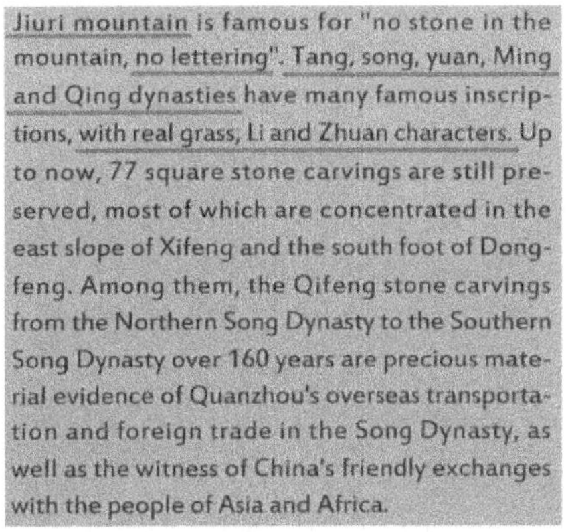　　图2 "九日山片区简介"（英文）

1. "九日山"，英译为"Jiuri mountain"有误。专有名词，首字母必须大写。建议改译为"Jiuri Mountain"，以便与九日山景区中其他处的"九日山"英译保持一致。

2. "山中无石不刻字"，英译为"no stone in the mountain, no lettering"不妥。首先，"no lettering"与"No littering"（禁止乱扔垃圾）结构相似，"鱼龙混杂"，有误译之嫌。此句的翻译直接按照汉语字面意思直译，导致英语翻译与原句语义有出入，英语译文的理解是"山中没有石头，禁止乱刻字"，不是原句含义的正确表达。其次，"字"是被"刻"，英语要用被动式，即"being engraved"。第三，汉语的字与英语字（母）并非同一个字，此"字"非彼"字"，也非同一含义，不能混用。汉语的字为"character"，而英语的字（母）为"letter"。建议改译为"no stone in the mountain without being engraved characters"。

3. "唐、宋、元、明、清历代"，英译为"Tang, song, yuan, Ming and Qing dynasties"有误。朝代名首字母必须大写，不能随意大小写，更不能"厚此薄彼"，一些大写一些小写。建议改译为"Tang, Song, Yuan, Ming and Qing Dynasties"。

4. "真草隶篆行诸体具备"，英译为"with real grass, Li and Zhuan characters"有错。首先，"真草"译为"with real grass"，此译真的有点草率，是错译。据查，按草书的四类分法，分别是章草、小草、大草和狂草。请教书法专家得知，"真草"的意思是真书和草书，真书一般指楷书，故应英译为"Kai"。其次，"行"漏译了，应为"Xing"。建议改译为"with Kai and Cao, Li, Zhuan and Xing characters"。

（二）"九日山"国保碑碑文中的英译错漏

在九日山景区里，泉州市文物管理委员会立的"九日山"国保碑十分引人注目（周绪琳、李跃平，2022）（见图3）。然而，在"九日山"国保碑的英译碑文中有不少错误，对"九日山"国保碑碑文英译中的错漏（详见图4、图5碑文英文标注下划线处），为保持已有三十余年历史的国保碑原文，本文纠错校译也力求尽量少改动。比如，此碑的"九日山"碑题英译为"HILL JIU-RI HILL NINE DAY"，而其他地方均译为"Jiuri Mountain"。

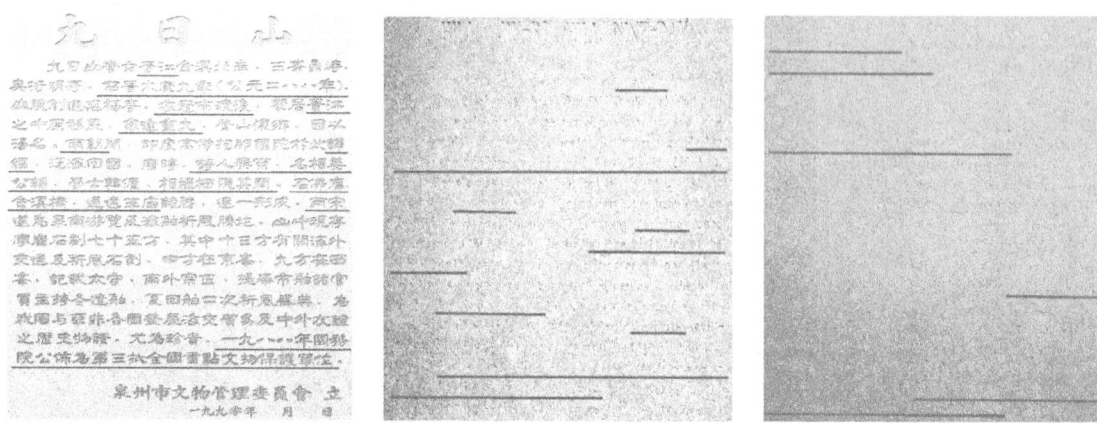

图3 "九日山"国保碑碑文（中文） 图4 "九日山"国保碑碑文（英文上半部） 图5 "九日山"国保碑碑文（英文下半部）

1. "晋江"，英译为"river Jin"是错译，应该是"Jin River"。下文的"晋江"，英译为"Jin river"有误，应该是"Jin River"。

2. "西晋太康九年（公元288年）"，英译为"In the ninth year of Tai-Kong reign of West Jin or 288 A.D."有误；依照《汉语拼音方案》的规定，"太康"应该音译为"Taikang"，而不应该译为"Tai-Kong"；"西晋"因与位置有关，应该译为"Western Jin"，而不是"West Jin"；"公元288年"不应译为"or 288 A.D."，而应译为"288 A.D."。建议改译为"In the ninth year of Taikang reign of Western Jin (288 A.D.)."。

3. "北宋"（中文碑文中没有！），英译为"North Song"不妥。因与位置有关，应译为"Northern Song"，并与其他相关表达，如南宋、南朝、北朝、西晋等的英译保持一致。中国历史上几次人口、经济、文化中心的较大的转移，一般都以"衣冠南渡"名之。"国保碑"碑文中的"衣冠南渡"指的是中国历史上的第三次因动乱而发生的大规模人口南迁现象：北宋末，宋高宗渡江，以临安（今杭州）为行都，建立南宋及相关的大批缙绅、士大夫及庶民百姓随之南下。

4. "重九"，英译为"on the ninth day of the ninth month"有误，不准确。"重九"是指农历（阴历）的"九月初九"，而不是指阳历年的9月9日。建议改译为"on the ninth day of the ninth lunar month"。

5. "南朝"，英译为"South Dynasty"不妥。按笔者在上述第3点提出的"一致性"原则，"南朝"应英译为"Southern Dynasty"。

6. "译经"，英译"translate the Buddhits scripture"中的"Buddhits"有误，应为"translate the Buddhist scripture"。

7. "诗人秦系、名相姜公辅、学士韩偓，相继栖隐其间"，英译为"poet Chin-Xi the wellknown premier Jiang-Go-ng-Fu and the scholar Han Chang …"，其中，三人的名字、"著名的"及第一个和第三个顿号的英译均有误。依照《汉语拼音方案》和《中国人名汉语拼音字母拼写法》的规定，改译为"poet Qin Xi, the well-known premier Jiang Gongfu and the scholar Han Wo had one after the other come to seclude themselves in the recess of the hill"。

8. "石佛岩、金溪桥、通远王庙"，英译为"Grotto Stone Buddha Golden Creek Bridge and the Temple of King Tong-Yua"有误。"石佛岩"与"金溪桥"的英译之间应该有一逗号，"通远王庙"的"通远"错译

为"Tong-Yua"。建议改译为"Grotto Stone Buddha, Golden Creek Bridge and the Temple of King Tong Yuan"。

9. "两宋"即"南宋和北宋",英译为"the North and South Song Dynasties"不妥。"两宋"因与方位有关,建议改译为"the Northern and Southern Song Dynasties",以与其他相关的朝代表达的英译保持一致。

10. "九日山"国保碑碑文最后一句表达有逻辑错误。从上下文来看,"山中现存摩崖石刻七十五方,其中十三方有关海外交通及祈风石刻"是主语,物为主语,不能发出带宾语的"及物"动作,自己不能"公布",只能"被公布"。"一九八八年国务院公布为第三批全国重点文物保护单位",英译为". and are under State protection as key-protected units ever since 1988."有误。英语 since 后接过去时间,意为"从过去某个时间以来",句子的谓语通常要求用现在完成时态,而不能用一般时态;State 也不用首字母大写。

从表面上看,译文"These stone-engraving and inscriptions are the most precious historic evidences … and are under State protection as Key-protected units ever since 1988."是由 and 连接的两个系动词 are 的并列系表结构,但是,因为句末有"ever since 1988",所表达的意义和时间是完全不一样的——前一句陈述的是一个事实,不受时间限制;而后一句表述的事实有一个时间限制,即"since 1988",在此时间以前不存在这个事实,所以两个句子不能并列,必须独立成句,而且逻辑关系也要按照英语的句法逻辑进行重新调整。建议改译为"It was listed as the third batch of national key cultural relics protection catalogues in 1988."或"It became state priority protected sites proclaimed by the State Council of China in 1988."

笔者认为,在如此有重要价值和意义的著名景区,实属不该出现如此低级的错、漏翻译。"九日山"国保碑的碑文刻成之后应该有专人认真检查和审核。自1990年立碑以来,三十余年过去了,错、漏至今犹在。想必立碑当初,中英文字都应该是朱红色的,十分醒目耀眼,却无一人注意到这些错、漏的存在,让人感到十分遗憾和不可理解。

(三)"九日山"石刻的英译错漏

在九日山景区里,最耀眼的石刻是"九日山"三个硕大的字刻(详见图6)。然而,这一载入史册、位列九日山景区唐、宋、元、明、清历代题刻的七十多方摩崖石刻之冠的代表之作简介的英文翻译错误不少(详见图8中的标注)。

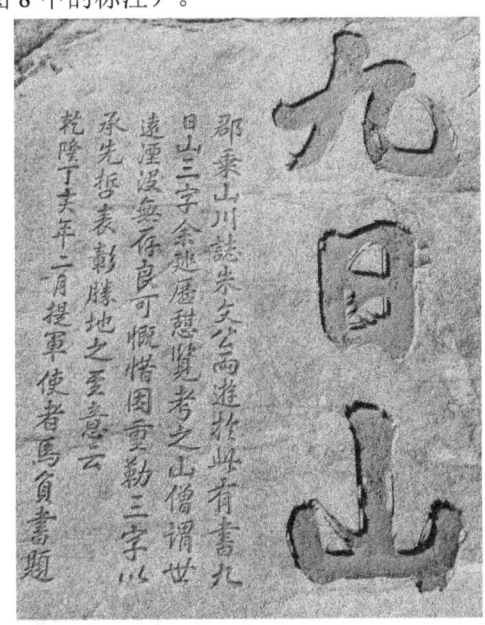

图6 "九日山"石刻　　图7 "九日山"石刻(中文)　　图8 "九日山"石刻(英文)

1. "九日山"石刻简介的中文题目属于歧义，涉嫌误导。咋一看标题："九日山石刻"，难道不会误认为是介绍九日山景区里的石刻？简介正文中的表述才是正确的："九日山"石刻！而且英译为"Jiurishan Stone Inscriptions"更是误导性的译文。首先，九日山景区里多处的"九日山"英译都是用的"Jiuri Mountain"，这里突然出现"Jiurishan"，让人"措手不及"，回不过神来。其次，"石刻"英译为"Stone Inscriptions"，复数的使用，无疑"证实了"是"九日山（景区里的）诸多石刻"之意，而不是指"九日山"这个山名的字刻！建议改译为"Stone Inscription of 'Jiuri Mountain'"或"'Jiuri Mountain' Stone Inscription"。

2. "'九日山'石刻为全山最大的字刻"，英译为"'Jlurishan (Jiuri Mountain)' is the largest stone Inscription in the mountain."有误。首先，有无必要使用"Jiurishan"值得商榷，而且还把字母"i"错写为"l"（Jlurishan）。其次，"最大的字刻"，英译为"the largest stone Inscription"不妥，没把"字刻"的韵味体现出来，而且还错用大写字母（Inscription）。建议改译为"The 'Jiuri Mountain' stone carving is the largest character carving in the whole mountain."或"The stone inscription of 'Jiuri Mountain' is the largest character inscription in the mountain."。

3. "年久风化无存"，英译为"the words have vanished for weathering"，属于严重错译。首先，朱熹1184年的题字镌刻被风化后再有马负书1736年的补题，都是过去的事情，所以，英译使用现在完成时（have vanished）是严重的错误。其次，石刻风化，不是主动风化，而是长达近600年饱受风吹日晒雨打，被冲刷、被侵蚀、被风化而"无存"的[①]，英译使用主动语态是错的，必须用被动语态。建议改译为"the words had been weathered for a long time"或"the words had been vanished for weathering"。

4. "补题刊刻'九日山'于石崖上"，英译为"wrote an inscription 'Jiuri Mountain' on the cliff"有误。首先，"补题"英译为"wrote an inscription"，缺了"补"的含义，少了"承先哲表彰胜地之至意"的韵味。其次，"补题"与"刊刻"肯定是不同的人的行为，也不可能是同时行为！难道是时任福建提督的马负书亲自"操刀"勒刻的吗？所以，也不能仅以"wrote"概括。建议改译为"supplemented to write 'Jiuri Mountain' engraved on the (stone) cliff by craftsmen"。

5. "尤擅擘窠大字"，英译为"is particularly good at ..."不妥。马负书生辰不详，卒于1767年，清乾隆年间的大才子纪晓岚称马负书"性耽翰墨"，但"擅长擘窠大字"已是250多年前的事了，同一个英语句子中的一个人的两个动作（谓语动词）分别是"was endowed with"和"is good at"，一个是过去时，一个是现在时，不妥。如果认为他"尤擅擘窠大字"是一个事实，故使用现在时态，难道他"文武双全"就不是事实？因此，两个动词的时态须要保持一致。建议改译为"was particularly good at ..."。

6. "是年补题山名后"，英译为"That year, after the inscription of the mountain"有误。"补题"的是"山名"，而不是"山"，"the inscription of the mountain（山的题字）"与"the inscription of the mountain name（山名的题字）"是有区别的。上文已述"补题"的英译，为保持上下文一致，建议改译为"That year, after supplementing the inscription of the mountain name"或"That year, after adding the inscription of the

mountain name"。

（四）九日山祈风石刻展示馆里"泉州境内奉祀通远王的主要庙宇"名称英译问题

"泉州境内奉祀通远王的主要庙宇"图（图9）中各"庙宇名称"的英译译名不统一，生硬对译，过度使用音译，译名结构"五花八门"，随心所欲，毫无"章法"。

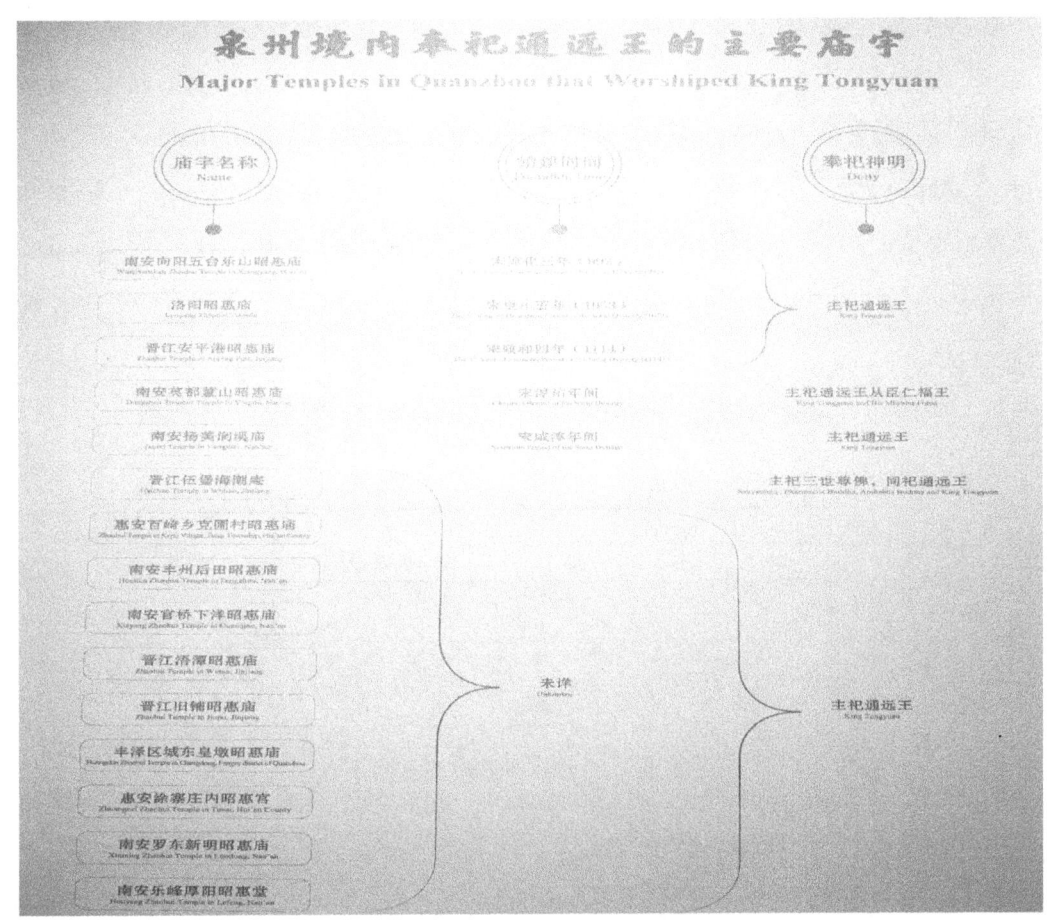

图 9　泉州境内奉祀通远王的主要庙宇

为了便于比较，我们将图中的庙宇名称按地域分布进行排序，标注出各庙宇所在的地址，并对其英译进行结构分析。详见表 1

表 1　泉州境内奉祀通远王的主要庙宇名称英译及英译结构

序号	名　　称	地　　址	英　　译	英译结构
1	丰泽区城东皇墩昭惠庙	泉州市丰泽区刘墩村	Huangdun Zhaohui Temple in Chengdong, Fengze district of Quanzhou	街区名+核心词 in 城区名, 市区县名
2	惠安百崎乡克圃昭惠庙	惠安县百崎乡下崎村克圃村	Zhaohui Temple in Kepu Village, Baiqi Township, Hui'an County	核心词 in 村名, 乡镇名, 市区县名
3	（惠安）洛阳昭惠庙	惠安县洛阳镇洛阳街	Luoyang Zhaohui Temple	乡镇名+核心词
4	惠安涂寨庄内昭惠宫	惠安县涂寨镇庄内村	Zhuangnei Zhaohui Temple in Tuzai, Hui'an County	村名+核心词 in 乡镇名, 市区县名
5	晋江安平港昭惠庙	晋江市安平鸿滨路	Zhaohui Temple in Anping Port, Jinjiang	核心词 in 区域名, 市区县名
6	晋江旧铺昭惠庙	晋江市池店镇旧铺村	Zhaohui Temple in Jiupu, Jinjiang	核心词 in 村名, 市区县名
7	晋江浯潭昭惠庙	晋江市池店镇浯潭村	Zhaohui Temple in Wutan, Jinjiang	核心词 in 村名, 市区县名
8	晋江伍堡海潮庵	晋江市深沪镇伍堡村	Haichao Temple in Wubao, Jinjiang	核心词 in 村名, 市区县名
9	南安丰州后田昭惠庙	南安市丰州镇后田村	Houtian Zhaohui Temple in Fengzhou, Nan'an	村+核心词 in 乡镇名, 市区县名
10	南安官桥下洋昭惠庙	南安市官桥镇下洋村	Xiayang Zhaohui Temple in Guanqiao, Nan'an	村名+核心词 in 乡镇名, 市区县名
11	南安乐峰厚阳昭惠堂	南安市乐峰镇厚阳村	Houyang Zhaohui Temple in Lefeng, Nan'an	村名+核心词 in 乡镇名, 市区县名
12	南安罗东新明昭惠庙	南安市罗东镇新明村	Xinming Zhaohui Temple in Luodong, Nan'an	村名+核心词 in 乡镇名, 市区县名
13	南安向阳五台乐山昭惠庙	南安市向阳乡五台山	Wutaiyaoshan Zhaohui Temple in Xiangyang, Nan'an	两个山名+核心词 in 乡镇名, 市区县名
14	南安扬美涧溪庙	南安市洪濑镇扬美村	Jianxi Temple in Yangmei, Nan'an	核心词 in 村名, 市区县名
15	南安英都董山昭惠庙	南安市英都镇董山	Dongshan Zhaohui Temple in Yingdu, Nan'an	山名+核心词 in 乡镇名, 市区县名

从"泉州境内奉祀通远王的主要庙宇"名称的英译结构来看，有"街区名+核心词（庙宇名）+城区名+市区县名"（见序号1）"核心词+村名+乡镇名+市区县名"（见序号2）"乡镇名+核心词"（见序号3）"村名+核心词+乡镇名+市区县名"（见序号4、9、10、11、12）"核心词+区域名/村名+乡镇名+市区县名"（见序号5、6、7、8、14）"山名+核心词+乡镇名+市区县名"（见序号13、15）等6种翻译结构。我们认为："核心词+村名+乡镇名+市区县名"的翻译结构更可取，一是核心词优先，主题突出，二是地理位置作为限定词"村名+乡镇名+市区县名"由小到大自然排列，而且更加符合英文的表达习惯。由此，"惠安百崎乡克圃昭惠庙"的英译"Zhaohui Temple in Kepu Village, Baiqi Township, Hui'an County"或"Zhaohui Temple in Kepu, Baiqi, Hui'an"可作为范本，即使是外国友人、外国游客前来参观，一看就明白，不会像"丰泽区城东皇墩昭惠庙（Huangdun Zhaohui Temple in Chengdong, Fengze **district** of Quanzhou）"或"南安向阳五台乐山昭惠庙（Wutaiyaoshan Zhaohui Temple in Xiangyang, Nan'an）"等庙宇的英译，看了以后"云里雾里""一头雾水"。

泉州市共辖12个县级行政区，如图10所示，英译时应该注意"一视同仁"，不能"厚此薄彼"。

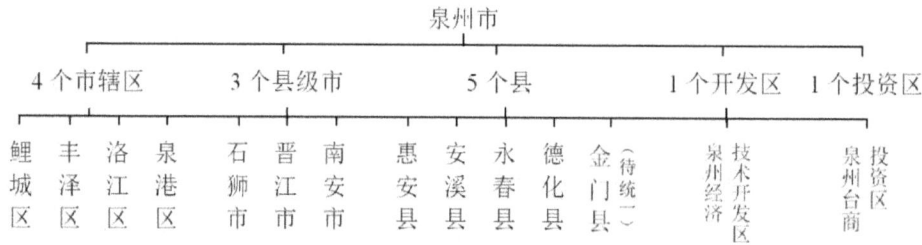

图10 泉州市下辖12个县级行政区一览

此外，这些庙宇的英译中有的用词值得商榷。

1. "丰泽区城东皇墩昭惠庙"英译为"Huangdun Zhaohui Temple in Chengdong, Fengze **district** of Quanzhou"，一是"**district**"一词如果要用其首字母必须大写，应该是"**District**"；二是"of Quanzhou"多余，丰泽区是"泉州管辖的12个县级行政区"之一，让人感觉它属于泉州，没有加"of Quanzhou"的惠安、晋江、南安，让人误解，好像不属于泉州似的。对同级别的管辖区应该"一碗水要端平"，一视同仁地对待，要加都加，要不加都不加。笔者认为，不加为妥，因为展室的图片题目已经标明"泉州境内"，各庙宇名再加上"泉州"二字，反而多此一举、画蛇添足。

2. "昭惠庙"和"海潮庵"的"寺、庙"和"庵"是有区别的，但都英译为"temple"不妥。"寺、庙"，英语为"temple"，英语释义为"a building used for the worship of a god or gods, especially in religions other than Christianity（非基督教的）庙宇，寺院，神殿，圣堂"。"庵"，英语为"nunnery"，英语释义为"a building or group of buildings in which nuns live as a religious community 尼姑庵"。故，"昭惠庙"和"海潮庵"应分别译为"Zhaohui Temple"和"Haichao Nunnery"才妥。笔者认为，同类名称的结构，用词、表达、英译应该保持一致；具有中国特色的地名、建筑物的英译，采用"修饰词汉语拼音+英语核心

词",即"音译+意译"是可取之举,相似或相近的建筑(群),但具有不同性质和差异建筑物,应该使用不同英语词汇。

3. "惠安涂寨庄内昭惠**宫**"英译为"Zhuangnei Zhaohui **Temple** in **Tuzai**, Hui'an County"不妥。一是"宫"和"庙"是有区别的,"宫"为"Palace","庙"为"Temple"。二是"涂寨"错为"Tuzai"了,应该是"Tuzhai"。三是"惠安"全称的确是"惠安县",但中文都没把"县"表达出来,其他县市的英译也没译成"Hui'an County""Jinjiang City"或"Nan'an City"。故,此处的"County"也不必译出来,以保持前后一致。

4. "南安乐峰厚阳昭惠**堂**"英译为"Houyang Zhaohui **Temple** in Lefeng, Nan'an"也不妥。"堂"与"庙"也是有区别的,"庙"在古代本是供祀祖宗的地方,故有"宗庙、私庙、家庙"之说;"堂"在佛教建筑中,是供僧众说法行道等用的地方。此处为何不叫"昭惠庙",而要叫"昭惠堂"?既然有区别,英译也应该体现区别。建议改译为"Zhaohui Hall"。

(五)"石佛亭"介绍的中文及英译错误

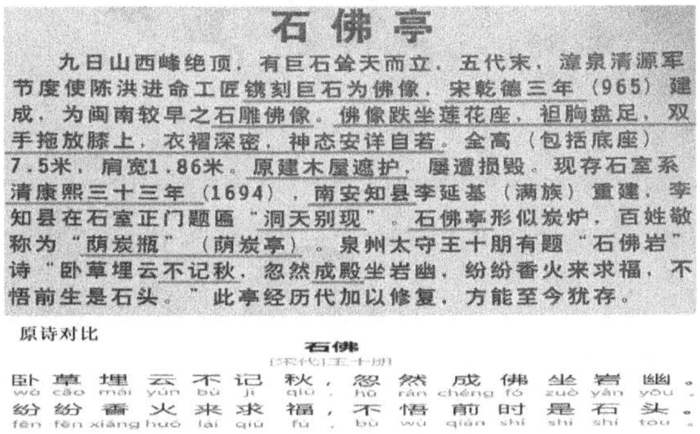

图 11 石佛亭介绍(中文)　　图 12 石佛亭介绍(英文)

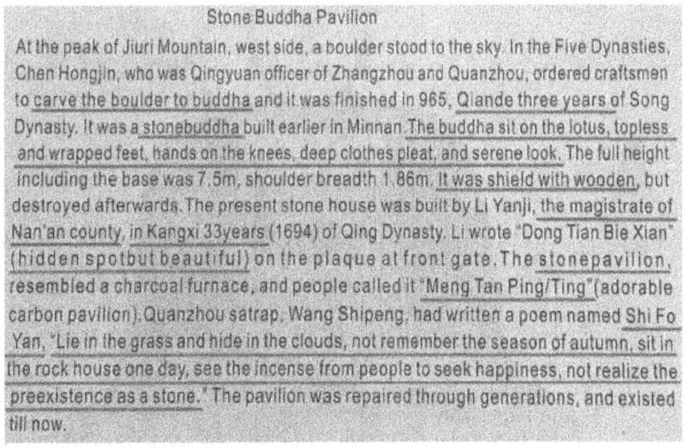

1. "镌刻巨石为佛像",英译为"carve the boulder to buddha"不妥。"把……刻成……"英译为"carve sth. into sth. else",而不是"carve sth. to sth."。"佛像"对应的英语为"Buddha (statue)",首字母必须大写,而不是"buddha"。建议改译为"carve the boulder into a Buddha statue"。

2. "宋乾德三年",英译为"Qiande three years of Song Dynasty"不妥。"宋乾德三年"意为"北宋乾德第三年"。建议改译为"the third year of the reign of Qiande in the Northern Song Dynasty"。

3. "石雕佛像",英译为"stomebuddha"有误。应为"stone Buddha (statue)"。

4. "佛像跌坐莲花座,袒胸盘足,双手施放膝上,衣褶深密,神态安详自若",英译为"The buddha sit on the lotus, topless and wrapped feet, hands on the knees, deep clothes pleat, and serene look."英译有错。动词 sit 后面的"topless and wrapped feet, hands on the knees, deep clothes pleat, and serene look"与 sit 是什么关系?起什么功能作用?均不清楚,而且整句英译用词错误不少,不能只将英语词汇堆砌起来就算"完事",也不能只做"大自然的搬运工",把中文"搬运到"英文里或"对译"成英文就"万事大吉"!如果认为是作后置修饰,补充说明"sit"的状态,但词性相同的词或者词类相同的词才能并列,否则不能并列!必须确保英语句子结构完整、语意通顺。该句英译错误,首先,"佛"的英文一定要用"Buddha",即首字母必须大写,否则何谈"**敬佛**"?其次,"坐"不能用动词原形,而要用第三人称现在时,即"sits"。再次,"袒胸"英译为"topless",错得有些离谱,《牛津英语词典》对 topless 的释义是:(of a woman) not wearing any clothes on the upper part of the body so that her breasts are not covered (女人)上身裸露的;不穿上装的。这里用于佛,是对佛的不敬,难道译者认为此佛为"雌"佛?应该用"bare"一词。第四,"盘足",英译为"wrapped feet"是错译。大智大慧的佛怎么可以译成"裹脚"者了呢?不要忘了"裹脚"或"缠脚",在中国是有特殊含义的!"盘足"实为"盘腿",应该是"cross his legs"。建议全句改译为"The Buddha statue sits on a lotus, with bare chest and cross-legged feet, both hands on his knees, his deep clothing pleat and serene and composed demeanor."。

5. "原建木屋遮护",英译为"It was shield with wooden"有错。首先,"wooden"不是"木屋",而是形容词"木头的、木制的",也不能跟在介词 with 之后作其宾语。"木屋"应该是"wooden house" "wooden hut"或"log cabin"。其次,"遮护"表达成"It was shield"不妥。"shield"用作名词是"盾(牌);防护物",用作动词是"保护,保卫;遮挡;给……加防护罩",但不能是"It was shield",应该是"It was shielded by …",可改用"shelter"一词,名词意为"居所,住处;(尤指用以躲避风雨或攻击的)遮蔽物,庇护处;遮蔽,庇护",用作动词意为"提供庇护,提供保护"。考虑到与下文"(木屋)屡遭损毁",后建"石室(遮护)"的逻辑关系,建议改译为"A wooden house was built to shelter it."。

6. "南安知县",英译为"the magistrate of Nan'an county"小有错误。应为"the magistrate of Nan'an County"。

7. "清康熙三十三年(1694)",英译为"in Kangxi 33year (1694) of Qing Dynasty"不妥。应为"in the 33rd year of the reign of Kangxi in the Qing Dynasty (1694)"或"in the thirty-third year of the reign of Kangxi in the Qing Dynasty (1694)"。

8. "洞天别现",英译为"hidden spotbut (原英文此处就是错在一起的) beautiful"不妥。并列连词"but"前后的词要属于相同词性或相同词类才能并列,"spot"是名词,而"beautiful"是形容词,不能并列连用。建议改译为"hidden spot but beauty"或"hidden spot but peculiar scenery"。

9. "石佛亭","stone pavilion"英译不妥。"stone pavilion"是"石亭",不见"佛",关键信息缺失。"石佛亭"介绍的英文题目明明白白已译为"Stone Buddha Pavilion",介绍文中为何出现"stone pavilion(石亭)"的表达?建议改译为"stone Buddha pavilion"。

10. "荫炭瓶"(荫炭亭)的"荫"是错字,应为"萌",否则英译就不该是"Meng Tan Ping / Ting"。如果"荫"字没错,则英译的"Meng"就是错的!二者必有一错。建议相关部门确认并纠正。

11. 王太守的七绝诗的中英文都出了问题。首先,泉州太守王十朋的诗,名为"石佛",而不是"石佛岩",英译为"Shi Fo Yan",属于错译。建议改译为"Stone Buddha"。其次,英译者对王太守的"石佛"诗理解有误,诗中的"不记秋"的"秋"不是指"秋天",而是指"年岁、年华流逝",所以"不记秋",不是"不记得秋天了(not remember the season of autumn)",而是"不知道年华流逝",英译"跑偏"了。第三,诗文中文的"成佛"错为"成殿"。第四,"忽然成佛坐岩幽",英译为"sit in the rock house one day",毫无"忽然成佛"的韵味和意境。第五,"不悟前生是石头",英译为"not realize the preexistence as a stone"不妥。谁"不悟"?几句英译的动词分别是"lie … and hide" "not remember" "sit" "see"和"not realize",前面四个/组动词的"动作发出者",即"(逻辑)主语"应该是"I",即"佛",而最后一个动作"not realize"的发出者不是"佛(I)"而应该是"纷纷香火来求福"的善男信女，故"not realize"的主语不能省去，即使是不把主语表达出来，至少不能让读者误解是佛"不悟"！

"卧草埋云不记秋，忽然成佛坐岩幽。纷纷香火来求福，不悟前生是石头。"用通俗的话语来说就是：（我）这块石头原来躺在草里，埋在云里，即藏在高山的野草里不知道过了多少年，忽然之间被凿成了佛像端坐在幽静的岩上石亭中。世上的善男信女纷纷前来送上香火祈求福气，却没有人领悟到我的前身也只是一块荒野的石头。对这首七言绝句诗的英译，笔者不敢妄加评判，遂与一喜爱诗词的同仁朋友交流讨教，他如此评价道：这个诗译"没有韵律，没有节奏，没有意境"。后来朋友说"胡诌了几句，想试试如何把意和型结合"，并将他译的诗文赠予笔者分享，征求意见能否引用于本文，他欣然同意[⑧]。改译诗如下：

Stone Buddha
by Wang Shipeng (Song Dynasty)

Lying alone in the endless wild, clouds adrift overhead,
I almost forgot the seasons of the mortal world.
Before I was suddenly enshrined in an abode of rock,
Peering down the bustling crowd in pretence.
While streams of pilgrims in the mist of incense,
Piously prayed to me for their fortune and luck.
Simply unaware, once a stone of obscurity,
Now a Buddha, worshiped and almighty.

改英译诗

Shi Fo Yan
Wang Shipeng

Lie in the grass and hide in the clouds,
 not remember the season of autumn,
sit in the rock house one day,
 see the incense from people to seek happiness,
not realize the preexistence as a stone.

原英译诗

此外，就这尊石佛，王十朋还题有一首七言绝句《观石佛》："土木涂金巧逼真，总随浮幻化埃尘。何人著意镌山骨，长现金刚不坏身。"如果"石佛亭"介绍中，将这首诗也加进去，必将使"石佛亭"的介绍内容信息更加丰富，一定增色不少。笔者试译了这首七言绝句，权当为"石佛亭"介绍增加一点新意，以飨读者和中外游客：

Viewing the Stone Buddha
by Wang Shipeng (Song Dynasty)

Coated with a layer of gold,
Exquisite and realistic wooden and clay Buddha statues look.
Whereas dust they always decay into,
As time passes and circumstances transform.
Who came up with the idea I know not,
To engrave Buddha statue on the mountain rock.
That's why the stone Buddha, the Vajra,
Here forever stand without rot.

由于篇幅有限，九日山景区中还有一些指路牌、告示牌、警示牌、微信公众号告示牌上等，也有不少的英译小错，不再一一赘述。

三、结 语

正如"教无定法"一样，亦或"译无定法"。"翻译没有标准答案""翻译没有唯一答案"，但也必须遵守一定的翻译规范，做到"译词达意"（周绪琳、李跃平，2022），"使语言翻译符合既定原则，且能够反应文化背后的内涵。"（吴继琴、龙婷，2018）然而，诸如以上九日山这一著名景区的信息英语翻译缺乏规范，错译颇多，这一现象应该引起当地政府有关部门，特别是文化旅游管理部门的重视。

因受条件限制和诸多因素的影响，笔者不能做到全面、详细记录、核查落实九日山景区信息的全部英译问题，难免挂一漏万，只能将随机捕捉到的部分英译错漏现象作为样本进行探讨、商榷、校译，以提醒当地政府及有关管理部门重视外宣工作，加强日常管理，更要严格按照"世界遗产保护名录"的保护要求进行管理。以负责任的态度、精神和行动，尽快复查、核实相关的信息，对确有错误的外宣信息，用积极的态度和行动予以纠正。让景区、景点"成为展示中国形象的重要窗口，同时，景区景点的翻译和宣传工作也成为景区、景点建设的重要一环。"（陈珊珊、毛雨婷等，2020）

只有这样，才能"力争达到形式、内容和意义的完美结合，推动中外融通，促进世界文化多元化，加快中国文化向世界传播。在翻译时，深入研究所翻译内容的语里意义，达到传播中华文化的目的。"（连真然、许立红，2021）

注 释

① 2021年7月25日，在福建省福州市举行的第44届联合国教科文组织世界遗产委员会会议（世界遗产大会）上，中国的文化遗产申报项目"泉州：宋元中国的世界海洋商贸中心"成功列入《世界遗产名录》。

② 关于"九日山祈风石刻"英译问题的论述，请参见周绪琳、李跃平合作撰写发表在《译苑新谭》（2022年1期）的"规范景区英译，讲好中国故事——泉州著名世界遗产点九日山景区祈风石刻英译问题及建议"一文。

③ 据查，"朱熹知漳州府时，于淳熙十一年（1184年）到永春拜访年已古稀的老朋友陈知柔，两人结伴重游九日山。在延福寺受到寺僧的热情接待，延福寺住持久闻朱熹大名，恳请他为九日山题写山名。朱熹欣然写了"九日山"三字，住持即请名匠将朱熹题字镌刻于隐君亭旁的摩崖石壁上。后来因为年代久远，朱熹的题字随着岁月的流逝，渐渐湮没无存。""乾隆三十二年（1767年），武状元、时任福建提督的马负书游历九日山，见朱熹当年的题字已风化不清，在寺僧的请求下，重书"九日山"三字，刻在原石崖上，并附一石刻小记：'郡乘山川志，朱文公两游于此，有书九日山三字，余巡历憩览，考之山僧，谓世久远湮没无存，良至可慨惜，因重勒三字，以承先哲表彰胜地之至意云。'"（资料来源：颜雅婷、陈明华．九日山：山下祈风，山中石刻——九日山保存最完整祈风石刻群[N]．东南早报，2009-06-11（B23-B24）.）

④ 按照学术引用规范，本应注明该诗的英译者，但译者坚持当"无名英雄"，再三表示"不用注明"，笔者尊重译者的意见；但需申明一下：该诗的英译者为某大学外国语学院副教授王先生。

参考文献

[1] Chen Shanshan, Mao Yuting et al.（陈珊珊、毛雨婷等）. "Research and Practice on the Translation of Tourism Resources in Suzhou Xinbianhe Scenic Spot"（宿州市新汴河风景区旅游资源翻译研究与实践）[J]. *Journal of Hebei University of Engineering(Social Science Edition)*（河北工程大学学报（社会科学版））, 2020(03): 103-105.

[2] Qi, Zhuoran（齐卓然）. "A Study on Mis-translation of Signs in Scenic Spots"（景区标识误译研究）[J]. *Tourism Overview*（旅游纵览）, 2019(22): 227-228.

[3] Lian Zenran, Xu Lihong（连真然，许立红）. " 'With the Chinese Culture as the Initiative' Innovation Translation Principle and its Significance ——And Discussion on Innovation of China's City-type Administrative Division Unit City"（"以我为主"的创新翻译原则及意义——兼谈城市型行政区划单位市的创新翻译）[J]. *New Perspectives in Translation Studies*（译苑新谭）, 2021（2）: 55-64.

[4] Wu Jqin, Long Ting（吴继琴，龙婷）. "Analysis of Sign English in Jiangxi 5A Scenic Spots from the Perspective of Ecological Translation Studies"（基于生态翻译学视角下江西5A景区牌示英语浅析）[J]. *Learning Weekly*（学周刊）, 2018(22): 182-183.

[5] Xi Jinping（习近平）. Solidly Implement Systematic Protection of Intangible Cultural Heritage and Promote the Chinese Culture to Better Go Global（扎实做好非物质文化遗产的系统性保护，推动中华文化更好走向世界）. [Online] Available: https://baijiahao.baidu.com/s?id=1752020522447368783&wfr=spider&for=pc

[6] Zhou Xulin, Li Yueping(周绪琳、李跃平). "Normalizing Scenic Area English Translation, Telling Chinese Stories Well: Problems of English Translation of Wind-praying Inscriptions in Jiuri Mountain Scenic Area, a Famous World Heritage Site in Quanzhou and Their Solutions"（规范景区英译，讲好中国故事——泉州著名世界遗产点九日山景区祈风石刻英译问题及建议）[J]. *New Perspectives in Translation Studies*（译苑新谭）, 2022（1）: 75-86.

[7] Zhu Yanning, Xiang Dan(朱艳宁、向丹). "Study on English Translation Skills of Tourist Attractions with Ethnic Characteristics under Cross-cultural Background"（跨文化背景下民族特色旅游景点的英译技巧研究）[J]. *Guizhou Ethnic Studies*（贵州民族研究）, 2018(04): 148-151.

作者简介

陈 彬，泉州信息工程学院教师，硕士，研究方向：英语翻译，英语教学。电子邮箱：1004658563@qq.com。

李跃平，西南民族大学教授，泉州信息工程学院特聘教授，研究方向：英语语言文学，民俗民风，民族史料信息，数据统计分析。电子邮箱：735941922@qq.com。

《三国演义》三个英文全译本中典故的英译策略研究

⊙ 冉明志（攀枝花学院外国语学院，攀枝花）

[摘 要] 通过对邓罗、罗慕士和虞苏美《三国演义》全译本中典故的翻译策略对比分析发现，邓罗以不打扰译文读者为出发点，采用归化为主的翻译策略；罗慕士追求译文读者与源语读者获得相同阅读体验，采用以异化为主的翻译策略；虞苏美则采用异化与归化相结合的翻译策略，以照顾译文读者并获得与源语读者相同的阅读体验。

[关键词] 《三国演义》；三个英文全译本；典故；英译策略

A Comparative Study of Strategies for Translating Allusions in the Three Complete English Versions of *San Guo Yan Yi*

RAN Mingzhi (Panzhihua University, Panzhihua)

Abstract: The paper conducts a comparative study on strategies adopted by C. H. Brewitt-Taylor, Moss Roberts and Yu Sumei for translating allusions in *San Guo Yan Yi*. As the study demonstrates, C. H. Brewitt-Taylor tends to employ domestication so as to make no interference to target readers while reading, and Moss Roberts prefers to adopt foreignization to enable both the target readers and the source language readers to acquire the same reading experience, while Yu Sumei combines the strategies of foreignization and domestication in an effort to make the translated text readable and to enable both the target readers and the source language readers to acquire the same reading experience.

Key words: *San Guo Yan Yi*; three complete English versions; allusions; English translation strategy

一、引 言

《三国演义》中丰富的典故具有鲜明浓厚的中华民族色彩，体现了中华民族深厚的文化底蕴和文化内涵。典故翻译的主要功能在于跨越文化差异有效地向译文读者传达源语典故中的文化内涵，实现文化的交流与融合。赵翠（2011）以《三国演义》中成语典故为例，从认知转喻视角对汉语成语进行阐释，探究了转喻在成语形成的认知理据及其相互关联性。刘洪辉（2012）从目的论视角比较分析了《三国演义》邓译本和罗译本中典故的英译策略，认为在翻译《三国演义》中典故时，邓罗"主要采取了归化策略"，以方便译文读者理解，而罗慕士"主要采用了异化策略"，旨在向译文读者介绍并传播中国传统文化。李翊娜（2014）从异化翻译理论角度研究了异化策略在《三国演义》罗译本中典故英译以及文化内涵传递方面的价值，发现罗慕士灵活运用了异化策略翻译典故，让译文读者能更加直接感受异质文化，有效传递典故的文化内涵。本文以自建汉英平行语料库为基础，对比分析《三国演义》三个全译本（邓罗译本、罗慕士译本以及虞苏美译本）中社会文化专有项典故的英译策略。

二、文化专有项的分类与翻译策略

（一）文化专有项的分类

"文化专有项"（culture-specific items）最初由西班牙翻译工作者哈维尔·佛朗哥·艾克西拉于1996年提出，他把文化专有项分为专有名词和常见表达两类。之后，尤金·奈达（2005）和彼得·纽马克（2000）提出了"文化词"（cultural terms）的概念。艾克西拉（2007：91）将文化专有项分为生态文化、物质文化、社会文化、宗教文化以及语言文化共五类，奈达（2000：59）进一步将文化专有项分为生态类、物质文化类、社会文化类、组织类以及手势与习惯五类。

（二）文化专有项的翻译策略

艾克西拉按照"跨文化操纵"的程度提出了关于文化专有项的处理策略：重复、转换拼写法、语言（非文化）翻译、文外解释、文内解释、使用同义词、有限泛化、绝对泛化、同化、删除、自创（1996：61-64）。张南峰认为艾克西拉的分类法"在于细致详尽，排列有序，让人看到异化和归化不是简单的二元对立，而是有不同程度的异化，不同程度的归化"（2004：22），同时"艾克西拉文化专有项翻译理论应用于英汉翻译，主要问题不在于语言特殊性而在于文化特殊性"（Ibid）。为此，张南峰建议：1."转换拼写法"改为"音译"；2.删去"使用同义词"，也许加上"重复"（以避免使用同义词）；3."自创"应定义为"引进译语文化专有项"，如需要，可考虑加上"引进原语文化专有项"；4.加上"淡化"（Ibid：22-23）。

王东风归纳出翻译界在实践中已经形成的五种"在效果及使用频率上呈等级排列"的文化缺省处理方法：文外作注、文内解释、归化、删除、硬译（1997：58-59）。总的来说，他列出的"文外作注"相当于艾克西拉的"文外解释"，"文内明示"等于"文内解释"，"同化"等于"归化"。邱懋如提出了保留源文的文化色彩、移译、音译、音译加类别词、用目的语中带有文化色彩的表达方式取代源语中带有文化色彩的表达方式、解释、译出含义等翻译方法（1998：19-22）。总的来说，他提出的"保留源文的文化色彩""移译""音译"以及"用目的语中带有文化色彩的表达方式取代源语中带有文化色彩的表达方式"分别相对于艾克西拉的"语言（非文化）翻译""重复""转换拼写法"以及"同化"。本文选择艾克西拉有关文化专有项的翻译策略进行《三国演义》全译本中典故英译的对比分析。

三、《三国演义》三个全译本中典故英译策略对比分析

《三国演义》中含有大量具有鲜明而独特中华文化内涵的文化专有项，如成语、典故、诗词、民俗、兵法谋略、军事术语等，其中的典故非常丰富，这些典故反映了中国古代的历史、文学、军事、神话传说等方面的知识，具有浓厚的民族色彩与文化内涵。按照尤金·奈达的分类法，本文研究的典故属于社会文化专有项，《三国演义》中典故可分为历史典故、文学典故、军事典故、传说典故、寓言典故等五类。

（一）历史典故的英译策略

原文：维曰："昔**韩信**不听**蒯通**之说，而有未央宫之祸；大夫**种**不从**范蠡**于五湖，卒伏剑而死。……"（第一百一十九回）

邓译文：Chiang replied, "**Han Hsin** hearkened not to **K'uai T'ung** and so blundered into trouble at the Weiyang Palace, the *T'ai-fu* **Wen Chung** would not follow **Fan Li** into retirement and fell victim to a sword on the lakes..."

罗译文: Jiang Wei replied, "When the Han Dynasty began, **Han Xin** ignored **Kuai Tong**'s counsel to establish an independent kingdom. The result was the disaster at the Weiyang Palace, where he was arrested and executed[1]. Then there was the case of **Wen Zhong**, high official to the king of Yue, Gou Jian. He ignored the advice of his colleague **Fan Li**, who urged Zhong to leave Yue with him to live as hermits in the lake district. The result was that the king of Yue forced Wen Zhong to fall on his sword[2]. ……"

[1] Kuai Tong had advised Han Xin to support neither the kingdom of Han (i.e., Liu Bang) against the kingdom of Chu (i.e., Xiang Yu) nor Chu against Han, but to exploit the Chu-Han war by creating a third kingdom of his own. Han Xin rejected Kuai Tong's advice. Remaining loyal to Liu Bang, Han Xin helped him defeat Xiang Yu and founded the Han dynasty. However, a few years after the founding of the Han, Liu Bang had Han Xin arrested and executed.

[2] After the kingdom of Yue took its revenge by conquering the kingdom of Wu, Fan Li urged Wen Zhong to retire from politics with a famous phrase: "When the sky has no more birds, the fine bows are put away; when the cunning hare has been caught, the tracker hounds are cooked."

虞译文: Jiang Wei replied, "**Han Xin** did not heed **Kuai Tong**'s advice and so lost his life at the Weiyang Palace;[1] **Wen Zhong** would not follow **Fan Li**'s advice to retire on the five lakes and ended in dying under his sword.[2] ……"

[1] Han Xin, a famous general who helped the founder of Han to win his empire, was advised by Kuai Tong to set up his own rule while he commanded the army but Han Xin failed to heed his words. Later he was deprived of his military power and he tried to rebel, but was killed at the Weiyang Palace.

[2] Wen Zhong and Fan Li were both officials of the Kingdom of Yue in ancient China. They helped their king destroy the Kingdom of Wu. Knowing that the king was not someone with whom one could share joy, Fan Li left to seek a life of leisure. Wen Zhong, however, did not follow his advice and was later forced to commit suicide.

对于上例中的历史典故的英译，邓罗采用音译和直译，未对原文中的历史典故进行任何说明，会对读者的理解造成一定的困难；罗慕士采取音译、增译与直译加注释，对其中的两个历史典故进行了文外解释，加深了译文读者对历史典故的理解，同时增译"when the Han dynasty began"，让译文读者清楚了解历史故事发生的时间；虞苏美采用音译与直译加注释，对典故文外加以注释，有助于译文读者对历史典故的理解。同时，通过比较罗译文与虞译文的注释，我们觉得罗译文中 1 的注释更好，而虞译文中 2 的注释更好。

原文：羽自幼读书，粗知礼义，观**羊角哀**、**左伯桃**之事，未尝不三叹而流涕也。（第二十六回）

邓译文：I have been a student in my youth and know somewhat of the proprieties. I sigh and weep at the memory of the fraternal affection that made **Yang Chio-ai** and **Tso Po-T'ao** die rather than separate.

罗译文：In my youth I came to know the classics and to appreciate something of our traditions and code of honor. When I reflect on the fraternal devotion and sacrifice of such ancient models as **Yangjue Ai** and **Zuo Botao**, I cannot help sighing over and over through my tears[9].

[9] This refers to an anecdote from the Warring States period. Two friends, Zuo Botao and Yangjue Ai, were bound for Chu in search of office when a snowstorm overtook them. There was not enough food and clothing to keep

them alive. So Zuo Botao sacrificed himself, giving his share to Yangjue Ai. Later Yangjue Ai became an official. He searched for and found Zuo Botao's remains, interred him, and then killed himself to demonstrate his loyalty to his friend's memory.

虞译文：I have taken up studies since my youth know something of the properties. The legendary story about the friendship between **Yang Jue-ai** and **Zuo Bo-tao**[1] has moved me to sighs and tears.

[1] Two friends during the period of Warring States (475-221 B.C.). On a journey to the Kingdom of Chu to seek office they were caught in a heavy snowstorm. Zuo Bo-tao gave all his clothes and food to his friend and died of hunger and cold himself. Later his friend who had become an important official in Chu, returned to find his corpse and buried it in great honor. Then he committed suicide.

对于上例中历史典故"羊角哀、左伯桃"的英译，邓罗采用了音译与意译，罗慕士选用了音译加注释、增译（such ancient models），而虞苏美采取了音译和注释，罗慕士和虞苏美都采用文外作注的方式对其中的历史典故进行解释，帮助读者更好理解原文。

在利用自建语料库考查31个历史典故的英译后发现，在翻译《三国演义》中历史典故时，邓罗多采用直译，有时采用增译（或文内解释），较少采用省译和意译；罗慕士主要采用直译加注释，有时采用直译、增译，鲜用意译；虞苏美大多采用直译与注释相结合的办法，有时采用意译、增译（见表1）。

表 1 《三国演义》三个英文全译本中历史典故英译策略

翻译策略	邓译本	占比	罗译本	占比	虞译本	占比
直译加注释			14	45.2%	15	48.4%
直译	15	48.4%	9	29.0%	8	25.8%
增译	8	25.8%	6	19.4%	7	22.6%
意译	3	9.7%	2	6.4%	1	3.2%
省译	5	16.1%				

（二）文学典故的英译策略

原文：玄德曰："岂不闻'运筹帷幄之中，决胜千里之外'？二弟不可违令。"（第三十九回）

邓译文：Liu Pei said, "Do you not understand that **plans elaborated in a little chamber decide success over thousands of *li*?** Do not disobey the command, my brothers."

罗译文："Brothers," Xuande said, "have you forgotten? '**Plans evolved within the tent decide victories a thousand *li* away.**' You must obey his orders."

虞译文：Liu Bei said, "Don't you understand that **the plans elaborated in a little chamber will determine victories thousands of *li* away?** Don't disobey the command, brothers."

对于上例中文学典故的英译，邓罗、罗慕士和虞苏美均采用了意译+直译并选用音译翻译其中的汉语长度计量单位"里"。

原文：操本好色之徒，久闻江东乔公有二女，长曰大乔，次曰小乔，**沉鱼落雁之容，闭月羞花之貌**。（第四十四回）

邓译文：For Ts'ao really is a sensualist. Now there are two famous beauties in Chiantung, born of the Ch'iao family. **So beautiful are they that birds alight and fishes drown, the moon hides her face and the flowers blush**

for shame at sight of them.

罗译文：Cao Cao, who is basically inclined to wantonness, has known for some time that the Southland patriarch Qiao has two daughters, **beauties whose faces would make fish forget to swim or birds to fly, abash the very blossoms and outshine the moon.**

虞译文：As you know, Cao Cao is man given to lust. Now he knows that there are two beauties in your place, born of the Qiao family. **So beautiful are these women that at sight of them, birds alight and fishes drown, the moon hides her face and flowers blush for shame.**

对于上例中的文学典故"层鱼落雁之容，闭月羞花之貌"的英译，邓罗、罗慕士和虞苏美均采用了直译，且未对其中的文化背景进行解释。

在利用自建语料库考查 22 个文学典故后发现，在翻译《三国演义》中文学典故时，邓罗多采用直译、意译、增译、直译和意译相结合，偶尔采用省译；罗慕士主要采取直译，有时采用意译，偶尔采用直译+注释、增译以及省译；虞苏美大多采用直译，有时选用意译、增译、直译加注释或直译与意译相结合等方法。可见，直译似乎成为三位译者在翻译历史典故时的主要翻译方法，同时直译加注释成为罗慕士和虞苏美共同的翻译历史典故的有效手段，而增译（或文内解释）成为邓罗翻译此类典故的常用方法（见表 2）。

表 2 《三国演义》三个英文全译本中文学典故英译策略

翻译策略	邓译本	占比	罗译本	占比	虞译本	占比
直译加注释			2	9.1%	3	13.6%
直译	6	27.3%	10	45.5%	9	40.9%
增译	5	22.7%	2	9.1%	4	18.2%
意译	6	27.3%	5	22.7%	4	18.2%
省译	1	4.5%	2	9.1%		
直译加意译	4	18.2%	1	4.5%	2	9.1%

（三）军事典故的英译策略

原文：郭图曰："不可。曹军劫粮，曹操必然亲往；操既自出，寨必空虚，可纵兵先击曹操之寨；操闻之，必速还：此孙膑"**围魏救赵**"之计也。"（第三十回）

邓译文：Kuo Tu said, "You may not go; it is certain that Ts'ao Ts'ao is there in person; wherefore his camp is undefended. Let loose our soldiers on the camp and that will bring speedily bring Ts'ao back again. This is how **Sun Pin besieged Wei and thereby rescued Han.**"

罗译文："Not a good idea," Guo Tu responded. "If they have plundered the stores, then Cao is there and Guandu is undefended. Strike Guandu first and Cao will retreat swiftly. This is exactly how **Sun Bin relieved Wei's siege of Zhao and went on to defeat Wei's army.**"[6]

[6] Sun Bin was a Warring States strategist. When the king of Qi sent Tian Ji and Sun Bin to raise Wei's siege of Handan, capital of the State of Zhao, Sun Bin stormed Wei's capital city, knowing that Wei's best troops were deployed at Handan.

虞译文：The advisor Guo Tu said, "They should not go. It is certain that Cao Cao is there in person, therefore his camp is undefended. Attack the camp and Cao Cao will speedily come back. This is what the ancient military strategist Sun Bin meant by '**Besieging Wei to Rescue Zhao**'."

对于"围魏救赵"的英译,邓罗和虞苏美采取了直译,罗慕士则采用了意译加注释,应该说罗慕士的方法更有利于读者对译文的理解。

原文:孔明曰:"此乃'**假途灭虢**'之计也。虚名收川,实取荆州。等主公出城劳军,乘势拿下,杀入城来,'**攻其无备,出其不意**'也。"(第五十六回)

邓译文: "This is the ruse known as '**borrow a road to exterminate Kuo**.' Under the pretence of taking the west they intend to capture this place, and when you go out to compliment the army you will be seized and they will dash into the city which they hope to find **the unprepared**."

罗译文: "…, using **the ancient ruse of 'passing through on the pretext of conquering Guo**.'9 Their real objective is Jingzhou, not the Riverlands. They want you to come out of the city so they can nab you, '**attacking the unprepared, doing the anticipated**.'"

9In the Spring and Autumn period the Kingdom of Jin asked the Kingdom of Yu to permit its troops to pass through in order to attack the Kingdom of Guo. On their way back, the Jin army annexed Yu. See *Zuo Zhuan*, "Xigong," year 5.

虞译文: "This ruse is known as '**Borrowing a passageway to exterminate the kingdom of Guo**.'1 Under the pretense of going to attack the west they intend to capture this place, and when you go out to greet their army you will be seized; then they will dash into the city, which they hope to find **unprepared**."

1An allusion to an incident from the days of the Spring and Autumn period. The ruler of Jin borrowed a passageway from the state of Yu to attack the state of Guo, but returning from his victory in subduing Guo he also wiped out Yu.

对于军事典故"假途灭虢"和"攻其不备,出其不意"的英译,邓罗采用了直译与省译(出其不意),罗慕士选用了直译以及直译加注释,虞苏美运用了直译、直译加注释以及省译(出其不意)。

通过语料库对比考查 35 个军事典故后发现,在翻译《三国演义》中军事典故时,邓罗多采用意译和直译,偶尔采用增译;罗慕士主要采取直译,有时采取意译和直译加注释,较少采取增译;虞苏美大多采用直译,有时采用意译与增译,较少采用直译加注释。可见,直译成为三位译者在翻译军事典故时的常用方法,直译加注释成为罗慕士和虞苏美翻译此类典故惯用的翻译策略,而邓罗更喜欢采用意译法(见表3)。

表 3 《三国演义》三个英文全译本中军事典故英译策略

翻译策略	邓译本	占比	罗译本	占比	虞译本	占比
直译加注释			5	14.3%	3	8.6%
直译	14	40.0%	18	51.4%	20	57.1%
增译	2	5.7%	3	8.6%	5	14.3%
意译	19	54.3%	9	25.7%	7	20.0%

(四)传说典故的英译策略

原文:是岁八月间,报称石邑县**凤凰**来仪,临淄城**麒麟**出现,**黄龙**现于邺郡。(第七十九回)

邓译文: In the late summer of this same year it was reported that a **phoenix** had been seen to bow at

Shihihsien, and a **Ch'i-ling** had appeared at Lintzu, while a **yellow dragon** was observed in Yeh.

罗译文：In the eighth month of the year (A.D. 220), strange manifestations were reported: in Shiyi county a **phoenix** showed itself, in Linzi a **unicorn** appeared, and in Ye itself a **yellow dragon** was seen.

虞译文：In the late summer of that year various auspicious signs were reported: a **phoenix** seen to bow at Shiyi, a *qi-lin*[1] at Linzi, and a **yellow dragon** observed in Ye.

[1] A legendary animal of good fortune, resembling a deer.

对于上例中三个传说典故"凤凰、麒麟、黄龙"的英译，邓罗采取了意译和音译，罗慕士采用了意译，而虞苏美选用了意译与音译加注释。

原文：昔**虞舜**有大功二十，而**放勋**禅以天下；**大禹**有疏导之绩，而**重华**禅以帝位。（第八十回）

邓译文：In days of old, **Yao** yielded the empire to **Shun**, and Shun in turn gave it to **Yu**.

罗译文：In ancient times after **Shun** had effected twelve accomplishments, **Yao** resigned the empire into his charge; and after **Yu the Great** distinguished himself in managing the floodwaters, **Shun** abdicated in his favor.

虞译文：In the days of old, **Shun** rendered twenty meritorious services, so **Emperor Yao** abdicated and offered him the throne. Later **Shun** also abdicated and offered the kingdom to **Yu the Great**, who performed the magnificent service of taming the flooding river.

对于上例中传说典故的英译，邓罗选用了音译与省译，使用音译对"放勋"与"重华"的别名进行翻译，省译了尧禅位于舜以及舜禅位于禹的理由；罗慕士和虞苏美均采用音译，同时采用音译对"放勋"与"重华"的别名进行翻译。

通过语料库考查 13 个传说典故后发现，在翻译《三国演义》中传说典故时，邓罗主要采取意译和直译，有时采取增译（或文内解释），偶尔采用省译；罗慕士多采用直译和意译，有时采用直译加注释以及增译；虞苏美倾向于采用直译、意译与直译加注释，偶尔采用增译。可见，直译和意译成为三位译者的主要翻译手段，罗慕士和虞苏美在翻译传说典故时还运用直译加注释的方法增加译文的可理解性，加深译文读者对中华文化内涵的理解（见表 4）。

表 4 《三国演义》三个英文全译本中传说典故英译策略

翻译策略	邓译本	占比	罗译本	占比	虞译本	占比
直译加注释			2	16.7%	3	25.0%
直译	4	33.3%	5	41.6%	4	33.3%
增译	2	16.7%	2	16.7%	1	8.4%
意译	5	41.7%	3	25.0%	4	33.3%
省译	1	8.3%				

（五）寓言典故的英译策略

原文：维笑曰："吾阵法按周天三百六十五变。汝乃**井底之蛙**，安知玄奥乎！"（第一百十三回）

邓译文："My formation admits of three hundred and sixty-five variations. You are but **a frog in a well** and know nothing of the deeper mysteries."

罗译文：Jiang Wei smiled and said, "My orders of battle have three hundred and sixty-five maneuvers following the cycle of days. You are **the proverbial frog in the well who sees but a corner of the sky**. What would you know of the arcane of formations and maneuvers?"

虞译文："My formation admits of three hundred and sixty-five variations, equal to the number of days in the year. You are but **a frog in a well** and know nothing of the deeper mysteries."

对于上例中的寓言典故"井底之蛙"的英译，邓罗和虞苏美采用了直译，罗慕士选用了直译加增译。

原文：若迷而不返，则是**韩卢、东郭**自困于前，而遗田父之获也。（第三十三回）

邓译文：If you persist in following this mistaken course, remember **the hound** and **the hare**, both so wearied that the peasant got the hare.

罗译文：Unless you relent, you and your brother will end up like **the hunting dog** and **the rabbit**. Both ran themselves to death, and a passing farmer picked them up.

虞译文：If you persist in following this mistaken course, then only your enemy will benefit. Remember the story of **the fastest hound** and **the hare**, both so wearied that the peasant caught them?

对于"韩卢"和"东郭"，邓罗、罗慕士和虞苏美均未采用音译而是选用了意译进行翻译，方便译文读者的理解。

通过语料库对比分析 10 个寓言典故后发现，在英译《三国演义》中寓言典故时，邓罗主要采取直译，有时采用意译或增译，偶尔选用省译；罗慕士多运用直译、意译和增译，偶尔采用省译；虞苏美多采用直译或直译，有时选用增译。可见，直译和意译成为三位译者主要的翻译方法（见表 5）。

表 5 《三国演义》三个英文全译本中寓言典故英译策略

翻译策略	邓译本	占比	罗译本	占比	虞译本	占比
直译	5	50.0%	3	30.0%	4	40.0%
增译	2	20.0%	3	30.0%	2	20.0%
意译	2	20.0%	3	30.0%	4	40.0%
省译	1	10.0%	1	10.0%		

四、结 语

本文通过对比分析《三国演义》三个全译本中典故的英译策略发现，为实现不同的翻译目的，三位译者采用了不同的翻译策略。具体来说，为不打扰译文读者，邓罗主要采用了归化为主的翻译策略，多采用意译和直译，有时采用增译（包括释义）、音译，偶尔采用省译，但邓罗从不采用文外作注，翻译不出来时索性采用省译，不能很好地让译文读者充分领略中华文化内涵；为让译文读者获得与源语读者相同的阅读体验，罗慕士主要采用了异化为主的翻译策略，主要选用直译、直译加注释以及意译，有时选用增译、音译，很少运用省译；为照顾译文读者，虞苏美主要采用异化与归化相结合的翻译策略，主要运用直译、直译加注释、意译，有时选用音译、省译，希望译文读者在获得与源语读者相同的阅读体验时，能更充分地了解中华文化。在翻译《三国演义》中社会文化专有项的典故时，罗慕士和虞苏美采用文外解释的方式很好地向译文读者传递了这些典故的文化内涵，有助于译文读者更好了解中华文化，这种方法对中华优秀文化外译具有较高的借鉴价值与参考价值。

参考文献

[1] Cui, Zhao (赵翠). "Research on Chinese Idioms from the Perspective of Metonymy – Taking Idiomatic Allusions in *San Guo Yan Yi* as an Example" (汉语成语的转喻阐释——以《三国演义》中的成语典故为例) [J]. *Xi'an Social Science* (西安社会科学), 2011(6): 152-154.

[2] Honghui, Liu (刘洪辉). *A Comparative Study on C-E Translation of Allusions in San Guo Yan Yi from the Perspective of Skopostheorie* (目的论视角下《三国演义》典故英译的比较研究)[D]. University of South China (南华大学), 2012.

[3] Yina, Li (李翊娜). *On Moss Roberts's Translation of Allusions in Three Kingdoms from the Perspective of Foreignization* (罗慕士英译《三国演义》典故研究——异化翻译理论的视角)[D]. Qingdao University (青岛大学), 2014.

[4] Aixelá, J. F. "Culture-specific Items in Translation", in Roman Avarez and M. Carmen-Africa Vidal (eds) - *Translation, Power, Subversion*[C]. Beijing: Foreign Language Teaching and Research Press, 2007.

[5] Nida, Eugene. *Language, Culture and Translating* [M]. Shanghai: Shanghai Foreign Language Education Press, 2005.

[6] Newmark, Peter. *A Text Book of Translation* [M]. Shanghai: Shanghai Foreign Language Education Press, 2000.

[7] Nida, Eugene. *Toward A Science of Translating* [M]. Shanghai: Shanghai Foreign Language Education Press, 2007.

[8] Nanfeng, Zhang (张南峰). "A Critical Introduction to Aixelá's Strategies for Translating Culture-specific Items"(艾克西拉的文化专有项翻译策略评介)[J]. *Journal of the Translators Association of China* (中国翻译), 2004(1): 16-23.

[9] Dongfeng, Wang (王东风). "Cultural Default and Coherent Reconstruction in Translation" (文化缺省与翻译中的连贯重构)[J]. *Journal of Foreign Languages* (外国语), 1997(6): 55-60.

[10] Maoru, Qiu (邱懋如). "Culture and Its Translation" (文化及其翻译)[J]. *Journal of Foreign Languages* (外国语), 1998 (2): 19-22.

[11] C. H. Brewitt-Taylor. *Romance of the Three Kingdoms (Volumes I & II)* [M]. Hong Kong: Tuttle Publishing, 2002.

[12] Moss, Roberts. *Three Kingdoms (Volumes I-V)*[M]. Beijing (北京)：Foreign Languages Press (外文出版社), 2003.

[13] Sumei, Yu (虞苏美). *The Three Kingdoms (Volumes I- III)*[M]. Shanghai：Shanghai Foreign Language Education Press (上海：上海外语教育出版社), 2017.

作者简介

冉明志，攀枝花学院外国语学院教授。研究方向：翻译理论与实践。电子邮箱：ranscpzh@163.com。

国家形象自塑视阈下外交话语隐喻英译策略探析

——以 2020 年外交部例行记者会发言为例

⊙ 肖志清 李静霞（武汉科技大学外国语学院，武汉）

[摘 要] 外交话语中隐喻英译策略的研究有助于有效传达外交话语内涵，提升国家形象自塑效果。本文运用语料库方法，以 2020 年外交部例行记者会发言中涉及新冠疫情的隐喻为研究对象，探究了国家形象自塑视阈下外交话语隐喻的英译策略选择。研究发现，2020 年外交部例行记者会发言通过战争隐喻、拟人隐喻、自然隐喻等多种隐喻类别，在新冠疫情背景下，塑造了中国"新冠疫情的抗击者""国际抗疫的合作者和推动者""人民利益的维护者"三大主要形象。在这三大形象自塑驱动下，国家机构译者坚持"以我为主""为我所用"的翻译原则，在翻译过程中结合中国的文化、历史背景和目的语受众的思维方式、语言习惯对原文隐喻的本体、喻体和喻义适当地进行了保留、转换或省略，实现了良好的国家形象自塑效果。

[关键词] 新冠疫情；国家形象自塑；外交话语；隐喻；翻译策略

The Translation Strategies of Metaphors in Diplomatic Discourse from the Perspective of National Image Self-shaping: A Case Study of Foreign Ministry Spokesperson's Remarks on Regular Press Conferences (2020)

XIAO Zhiqing LI Jingxia (Wuhan University of Science and Technology, Wuhan)

Abstract: Study of translation strategies of metaphors in diplomatic discourse can help to effectively convey the connotation of diplomatic discourse and enhance the effect of national image self-shaping. This paper, using a corpus-based approach, has studied the translation of metaphors related to COVID-19 pandemic in 2020 Foreign Ministry Spokesperson's Remarks on Regular Press Conferences, with an aim to explore the choice of translation strategies of metaphors in diplomatic discourse from the perspective of national image self-shaping. The study finds that the 2020 Foreign Ministry Spokesperson's Remarks on Regular Press Conferences have built China into "a fighter of COVID-19 pandemic", "a partner and promoter of the international fight against COVID-19 pandemic",

---

教育部人文社会科学研究项目"基于西方媒体涉华新闻语料库的中国政治话语翻译与传播研究"（编号：20YJC740086）、武汉科技大学 2023 年研究生质量工程教研项目"MTI 融合式翻译课程思政教学改革研究"（编号：Yjg202324）以及武汉科技大学 2022 年研究生创新创业基金项目"副文本视角下基于读者评论的中国文学外译研究——以《论语》三个英译本为例"（编号：JCX2022057）的阶段性成果。

and "a champion of people's interests" against the backdrop of COVID-19 pandemic through multiple metaphors invoving war, personification, and nature. Driven by the self-shaping of these three main images, the state institutional translators, adhering to the principle of "by China and for China", appropriately preserve, transform or omit the original object, image and sense in the translation process, during which the Chinese cultural and historical backgrounds as well as the way of thinking and language habits of the target language audience have been factored in, thus a good national image self-shaping effect is achieved.

Key words: COVID-19 pandemic; national image self-shaping; diplomatic discourse; metaphor; translation strategies

一、引 言

当前，世界面临百年未有之大变局。国家形象的构建直接影响中国在国际社会中被接受和认可的程度。2020年初新冠肺炎疫情爆发后，一些西方媒体的刻意诋毁和抹黑对中国的国家形象造成了不利影响（董雁、于洋欢，2020）。在这种情况下，中国要想谋求和平、稳定的外部发展环境，通过外交场合构建良好的国家形象就显得极为重要和迫切。政治外交话语是对外传播话语内容的核心（谢莉、王银泉，2018：7），对国家形象的构建起着关键作用。而隐喻作为习近平新时代中国特色大国外交话语体系的重要构成部分，对外交话语的内涵表达和功能实现至关重要（任东升、季秀妹，2021）。因此，恰当的隐喻翻译策略将有助于提升外交话语中国家形象的构建效果。本文从国家形象自塑视角出发，以2020年外交部例行记者会发言中涉及新冠疫情的隐喻为研究对象，探究其翻译策略选择，为外交话语隐喻翻译提供经验及借鉴，使之更好地服务于国家形象构建。

二、相关文献综述

国家形象与国家命运紧密相连，构建良好的国家形象可以帮助提升国家综合国力和国际话语权，助力国家发展。"国家形象，顾名思义就是一个国家在国际社会中的形象，或者说是一个国家在别的国家民众心目中的形象"（赵雪波，2006：1）。根据构建者的不同，国家形象的塑造方式可以分为"自塑"和"他塑"，自塑可以影响他塑。当前，在西方强势话语的控制下，中国的国家形象在很大程度上仍是"他塑"而不是"自塑"，呈现出"西强我弱"的格局（谢莉、王银泉，2018：8）。新冠疫情特殊话语之下，部分"他塑"媒体歪曲事实，损害了中国的国家形象（谭文慧等，2021：38），因此急需我们创新传播方式，不断加强"自塑"能力，从而扭转不利局势，将国际话语权牢牢地把握在自己手中，消除他国对中国形象的误解和歪曲，让世界更好地聆听"中国声音"，看到更好的"中国形象"。

良好国家形象的自塑离不开有效的话语策略。而隐喻作为一种外交话语策略，"可以影响人们的思维，重塑人们的态度，甚至有助于重组现实，形成说话者期望的概念结构，从而实现国家身份的构建，强化受众群体对话语国家的身份认同"（范武邱、邹付容，2021：61）。近年来，隐喻视角下的国家形象自塑逐渐成为研究热点。部分学者从隐喻角度出发，选取多种研究对象，对国家形象的自塑进行了多维度多层次的探讨。其中，范武邱和邹付容（2021）从批评隐喻视角出发，对中国国家领导人在2007-2018年夏季达沃斯论坛开幕式致辞中的隐喻类别、使用频次进行了量化研究，发现中国国家领导人借助隐喻构建起了中国"经济建设者""旅行者""成长者"三重国家身份。谭文慧等（2021）在概念隐喻视角下分析了中国疫情题材纪录片中的国家形象自塑，发现疫情纪录片使用多种概念隐喻成功自塑了中国政治、制度、经济、科技、外交、国民不同维度下的良好国家形象。马陈静和陈笑春（2021）基于多模态隐喻理论，从图像明喻、混合隐喻、语境隐喻角度对以脱贫攻坚为素材的纪实影像进行研究，揭示了这些纪实影像作品建构出以人民为中心、共享发展、有所作为、有所担当的大国形象的方法。由此可以看出，合理使用隐喻是帮助自塑国家形象的一种重要方式和手段，隐喻与国家形象自塑之间有着密不可分的联系。

翻译作为不同国家之间交流和沟通的纽带，在一国对外传播的过程中扮演着不可或缺的角色。隐喻可以助力国家形象的构建，隐喻的翻译也应受国家形象构建的驱动，为构建良好的国家形象服务。然而，目前中国从国家形象自塑角度出发，探讨隐喻翻译的研究还较为匮乏。鉴于此，本文拟在新冠疫情的时代背景下，从国家形象自塑角度入手，通过分析2020年外交部例行记者会发言中涉及新冠疫情的隐喻及其翻译，探讨如何选择合适的外交话语隐喻翻译策略，助力自塑良好的国家形象。

长期以来，众多学者对隐喻的翻译模式进行了有益探索，提出了许多重要的理论和方法，其中包括万·登·布若克（Van den Broeck, 1981: 77）的隐喻翻译模式三分法、纽马克（Newmark, 1981: 15）的隐喻翻译模式七分法和图里（Toury, 1995: 82）的隐喻翻译模式六分法。尽管由于语言、文化的复杂性和多样性等因素，这些隐喻翻译模式都存在一定的局限（文炳、王斌华，2021），但在当今时代，随着隐喻在各类话语中扮演的角色日趋复杂，这些学者的探索为我们更好地翻译隐喻提供了指导和借鉴。国家形象自塑驱动下的隐喻翻译当然也包括在内。总的说来，这些翻译模式的共同点在于都围绕着隐喻的本体、喻体和喻义三者展开，讨论其保留、转换或省略。这为我们探讨国家形象自塑视阈下隐喻的翻译策略提供了切入点。

三、研究设计

（一）研究问题

本研究主要聚焦以下问题：（1）2020年外交部例行记者会发言中涉及新冠疫情的隐喻有哪些类型？占比如何？（2）新冠疫情背景下，这些隐喻试图帮助中国塑造怎样的国家形象？（3）在国家形象自塑驱动下，外交话语中的隐喻英译宜采取什么策略？

（二）研究工具

外交部例行记者会是外交部发言人与中外媒体记者面对面交流互动的平台，其发言直接面向国际受众，对中国国家形象自塑具有重要意义。从外交部网站上收集整理2020年外交部例行记者会发言人的汉语原文和英语译文，经过Tmxmall平台实现对齐后，建成了一个总字数为1,567,369的小型汉英平行语料库。其中的隐喻采用Pragglejaz Group（2007）提出的隐喻识别程序（MIP）进行人工识别和标记。各隐喻关键词的词频统计借助平行语料库检索软件CUC_ParaConc完成。

（三）研究步骤

第一，根据上下文背景及关键词，人工筛选出语料库中与新冠疫情相关的问答话语。第二，在涉及新冠疫情的问答语料中利用隐喻识别程序（MIP）来识别并标记其中的隐喻。限于研究角度和研究对象，本文的隐喻统计范围仅涵盖中国发言人所做的陈述和回答，中外记者的提问内容不包括在内。第三，借助CUC_ParaConc对隐喻关键词的类别和频次进行统计整理。第四，对照各隐喻关键词英译，研究外交话语隐喻的翻译策略并结合典型案例进行分析探讨。

四、研究发现与讨论

统计发现，语料中共有隐喻3633项，可分为战争、拟人、自然、集体、器物、建筑、旅程、学习、文化、商业、棋局、戏剧、家庭、实体、医学、地理、机械、音乐、交通、宗教、游戏、饮食、时间、体育、谜语、数学和其他 27 个主要类别，其中机械、音乐、交通等 15 个类别的隐喻关键词频次低于 10，为便于分析，将这 15 个类别统一归为其他类别。整理后的隐喻类别、各隐喻类别对应的关键词举例和出现频次，以及各频次占语料中隐喻总数的比率如表 1 所示，其中战争（战斗）隐喻数量最多，占一半以上，其次为拟人隐喻（15.44%）和自然隐喻（11.64%）。

表 1　2020 年外交部例行记者会发言中新冠疫情隐喻关键词分类频次统计表

序号	隐喻类别	隐喻关键词举例	隐喻频次	占比
1	战争（战斗）	抗击、战胜、武器、敌人、阻击战、防线、战线、后盾、持久战、战场、战斗、击败、遭遇战、安全之战、福祉之战、斗争、战友、组合拳	1908	52.52%
2	拟人	援手、共同体、主心骨、心血、揪心	561	15.44%
3	自然	蔓延、风雨、阴霾、彩虹、洼地	423	11.64%
4	集体	众志成城、守望相助、同舟共济、万众一心、同心协力	270	7.43%
5	器物	甩锅、标杆、健康包、旗帜、脱钩	205	5.64%
6	建筑	框架、长城、桥梁、铜墙铁壁、防火墙	59	1.62%
7	旅程	拐点、道路、方向、出发点、前行	53	1.46%
8	学习	抄作业、数数题、闭卷考、答卷、家庭作业	30	0.83%
9	棋局	部署、大局、局面	24	0.66%
10	文化	替罪羊、莫斯科保卫战、沉默的羔羊、国王的新衣、亡羊补牢	21	0.58%
11	商业	无价、赤字、认账、成本、讨价还价	12	0.33%
12	其他	旋律、处方、黑天鹅、大戏、魔法	67	1.85%

分析发现，2020 年外交部例行记者会发言中这些隐喻的使用在新冠疫情背景下，帮助中国塑造了"新冠疫情的抗击者""国际抗疫的合作者和推动者""人民利益的维护者"三大主要形象。下文结合具体隐喻翻译案例，讨论如何选择合适的隐喻翻译策略自塑国家形象。

1. "新冠疫情的抗击者"形象

这一形象自塑所涉及的隐喻类型主要包括建筑类、战争类、集体类和旅程类。发言人通过使用"众志成城""组合拳""防线"等隐喻，展现出中国对待新冠疫情的重视程度，以及与国际社会携手抗击疫情的信心与决心。

例（1）

原文：我们将一如既往支持世卫组织继续发挥协调全球抗疫的核心作用，……共同筑起抗疫的"**铜墙铁壁**"。（2020 年 5 月 6 日外交部发言人华春莹主持例行记者会①）

译文：We will continue to support WHO in continuing to play a core role in coordinating global fight against pandemic, …to jointly build an impregnable fortress against pandemic. (Hua Chunying, May 6, 2020)

新冠肺炎的爆发给中国和国际社会都带来了巨大的负面影响。在这一特殊时期，中国积极与多个国际抗疫组织合作，共同对抗新冠病毒的"入侵"。本例中，中国与国际抗疫组织科研合作的成果为本体，"铜墙铁壁"为喻体。"铜墙铁壁"属于中国特有的四字成语，具有鲜明的文化背景。这一建筑隐喻的使用充分体现了中国从各国利益出发，积极主动与国际社会合作战胜疫情的意愿与决心。但若在翻译时，在目标语中重现相同的喻体，容易给目标语读者造成理解障碍。译文采取用目的语中合适的喻体替代源语中的喻体的方式，将仅为中文所接受的意象（"墙壁"）转化为中英文中都可理解的意象（"堡垒"），不但使原文的意思更加显性化，利于读者的认知和接受，也准确地传达了原词的意义和内涵，有助于提升国家形象自塑效果。

例（2）

原文：疫情发生后，中国政府和人民万众一心，众志成城，采取了最全面、最严格、最彻底的防控举措，打响了一场抗击疫情的**人民战争、总体战、阻击战**。（2020年5月8日外交部发言人华春莹主持例行记者会）

译文：Since the epidemic broke out, the Chinese government and people, united as one, has taken the most comprehensive, rigorous and thorough measures in this all-out, people's war against the virus. (Hua Chunying, May 8, 2020)

例（2）中，中国人民和政府防控疫情的过程为本体，"人民战争、总体战、阻击战"为喻体。战争隐喻是所选材料中出现次数最多的隐喻（见表1），对国家形象自塑的作用不言而喻。中国人喜用战争隐喻有着深厚的历史渊源。语境中，战争隐喻的使用反映了抗击疫情艰辛与不易，突显了中国人敢于斗争、善于斗争的民族品质和举国同心、舍生忘死的伟大抗疫精神。但若在翻译时，保留三个喻体，三个战争隐喻并列，容易给外国受众造成中国人好战的不好印象。译文通过只保留"人民战争"这一个喻体，译出其他两项隐喻的喻义，既完整地传达了原文语义，又避免了外国受众对中国的误解，起到了良好的国家形象自塑效果。

2. "国际抗疫的合作者和推动者"形象

这一形象主要是通过自然类、拟人类、器物类和医学类等隐喻类别构建起来的。例如，"唇齿相依""铁杆朋友""雪中送炭"等隐喻的使用突出了新冠疫情背景下，中国与国际社会真诚合作、互帮互助、共克时艰的意愿和态度。

例（3）

原文：第三，**众人拾柴火焰高**。我们希望各方都能以实际行动坚持多边主义，……共同打造人类卫生健康共同体。（2020年8月11日外交部发言人赵立坚主持例行记者会）

译文：Third, a common cause calls for extensive participation. We hope all parties will take concrete actions to support multilateralism, ... It is our common cause to build a community of health for all mankind. (Zhao Lijian, August 11, 2020)

例（3）中，"众人拾柴火焰高"，众多的人都往燃烧的火里添柴，火焰就必然很高。喻义为只要各国广泛参与、通力合作，就能在世卫组织的领导下，共同建设起人类卫生健康共同体。这一自然隐喻的使用充分体现了新冠疫情背景下，中国投身国际抗疫并推动国际抗疫的积极态度和实践原则。"众人拾柴火焰高"既是成语，又是隐喻，表达精练，含蓄有致，有利于清晰地阐述道理从而给读者留下更加深刻的印象。译文省译了原文的喻体，采用了非隐喻的表达方式，虽然做到了精练，但文化含义缺失，语言表达效果似有不足。由于目标语中不用"众人拾柴火焰高"来表达原文的含义，目标语读者较难在其与"人多力量大"之间建立相似联想，为了保留原文自然隐喻的修辞，更好地传达隐喻的文化内涵，可用目标语中存在的相关修辞性表达（如One person is not as good as two. Everyone holds the firewood in high flame.）来替代"众人拾柴火焰高"这一隐喻，或采取直译的方式，保留喻体，在隐喻后加注。这种翻译策略能更好地还原原文的国家形象自塑效果，也有利于中国文化在外国的传播。

例（4）

原文：**投我以木桃，报之以琼瑶**，这是中华民族传统美德。（2020年3月18日外交部发言人耿爽主持例行记者会）

译文："You throw a peach to me, and I give you a white jade for friendship." It is China's traditional virtue to repay goodwill with greater kindness. (Geng Shuang, March 18, 2020)

例（4）中，"投我以木桃，报之以琼瑶"出自中国古诗《诗经·卫风·木瓜》，你若赠送给我木桃，我便要用美玉来回报你。这个自然隐喻的喻义为回报别人以更大的善意。这种互相赠送答谢的形式在中国已经存在了千百年。语境中，外交部发言人的这一自然隐喻既弘扬了中国滴水之恩当涌泉相报的传统美德，也传达了新冠疫情背景下，中国与国际社会互帮互助，互惠互利，共同抗击疫情的愿望与决心。译文采取直译的翻译方法，完整地保留了原文的喻体，并在后文进一步解释了隐喻的喻义，从而有效地传递了原文的文字含义和文化内涵，利于外国读者理解，也帮助中国塑造了积极的国家形象。

3. "人民利益的维护者"形象

这一形象主要是通过战争类、拟人类、器物类、自然类等隐喻类别构建起来的。"血肉联系""健康包""风雨同舟"等隐喻词的使用彰显出了中国共产党和中国政府在抗疫过程中始终将人民的生命健康放在第一位，坚持以人为本，一心为民的责任感和使命感。

例（5）

原文：最后我要再次强调，党和政府时刻牵挂着广大海外留学人员的健康与平安，祖国永远是大家坚强的**后盾**。（2020年3月24日外交部发言人耿爽主持例行记者会）

译文：Finally, I would like to stress once again that the Party and the government are always concerned about the health and safety of overseas students. For them, the motherland is always their strong backing. (Geng Shuang, March 24, 2020)

例（5）中，"后盾"是一项战争隐喻，"指背后支持和援助的力量"（中国社会科学院语言研究所词典编辑室，2012：542）。这一隐喻的使用表达了中国对海外留学人员的关切，在新冠疫情的特殊背景下给予了他们鼓舞与力量，帮助构建起中国关心人民、爱护人民、对人民负责的大国形象。译文中用"backing"替换了这一隐喻，顺应译文语境，利于读者理解，也较为准确地传达了原文隐喻的含义。

例（6）

原文：中国共产党与中国人民**鱼水情深、血肉相连**。中国人民就是中国共产党的"铜墙铁壁"，谁都别想打破。（2020年8月27日外交部发言人赵立坚主持例行记者会）

译文：The CPC and the Chinese people are always there for each other. No one can cut off the flesh and blood ties between the CPC and the Chinese people. And no one can break the CPC without breaking the Chinese people! (Zhao Lijian, August 27, 2020)

例（6）中，"鱼水情深"为自然隐喻，"血肉相连"为拟人隐喻。这里，外交部发言人将中国共产党与中国人民之间的关系比作"鱼"与"水"、"血"与"肉"之间的关系，充分表达了中国共产党和中国人民之间不可分割的密切联系，突出了新冠疫情背景下，中国共产党坚持人民至上、生命至上。原文中的"鱼水情深、血肉相连"包含两处并列的隐喻，但因其意思相近，译文做了整合处理，省略了前一个隐喻，翻译出了后一个隐喻的喻体，在不破坏原文国家形象自塑效果的前提下，既完整地传达了原文内涵，又使得译文更显精简地道。

除上述三种形象之外，外交部发言人的隐喻话语策略还帮助中国塑造了其它良好的国家形象层面，例如，全球防疫的引领者、国际公平正义的守护者、人类前途命运的关切者等。这些国家形象层面对应下的隐喻翻译策略与上述案例有众多相似之处。总体而言，国家机构译者为有效传递原文隐喻内涵，实现最佳的国家形象自塑效果，在翻译时综合考虑了源语国家的文化与历史背景以及目的语读者的认知与接受，结合目的语语境恰当地对原文隐喻的本体、喻体和喻义进行了保留、转换或省略。

五、结 语

为充分发挥外交话语中"隐喻"的国家形象自塑作用，隐喻翻译是重中之重，只有进一步了解隐喻特性，把握合适的隐喻翻译方法，才能在未来日趋复杂的国际形势下，让隐喻"为我所用"，成为推动国家发展的利器。

通过对2020年外交部例行记者会发言中涉及新冠疫情的隐喻及其英译策略的研究，我们可以看出，国家形象自塑驱动下，隐喻翻译应对源文本和目标文本进行双向分析，在具体语境中准确把握隐喻内涵。在传达理解、避免误解（文炳、王斌华，2021：104）的基础上，尽可能地结合源语国家的文化、历史背景和目的语受众的思维方式和语言习惯选择翻译策略。同时，还要坚持"以我为主"原则（肖志清、邵斌，2019），明确并贴近源文本隐喻所对应的国家形象自塑层面，使之最好地服务于国家形象构建。

意识形态在一定程度上操控和主导着翻译，而翻译反过来又能影响意识形态。本文在语料库方法的基础之上，结合批评话语分析和翻译批评学对国家形象自塑视阈下隐喻的英译进行实证研究，采用的跨学科混合范式旨在为未来的批评性译学研究拓宽新思路。

注释

① 翻译案例中的所有原译文均下载自中华人民共和国外交部官网，网址为 https://www.fmprc.gov.cn/。

参考文献

[1] Dictionary Compilation Office of the Institute of Linguistics under the Chinese Academy of Social Sciences (中国社会科学院语言研究所词典编辑室). *Modern Chinese Dictionary (6th Edition)* (现代汉语词典（第6版）[Z]). Beijing: Commercial Press (北京：商务印书馆), 2012.

[2] Dong, Yan & Yu, Yanghuan (董雁，于洋欢). "Foreign Media's Coverage of the Fight Against COVID-19 and China's National Image Construction — A Case Study of CGTN Coverage" (外宣媒体的战"疫"报道与中国国家形象塑造——以CGTN为例) [J]. *Media* (传媒), 2020(11): 42-45.

[3] Fan, Wuqiu & Zou, Furong (范武邱，邹付容). "Diplomatic Discourse and the Construction of National Identity from the Perspective of Critical Metaphor Analysis: A Case Study of Chinese Leader's Special Addresses at the Opening Ceremonies of the Summer Davos(2007-2018)" (批评隐喻分析视阈下外交话语与国家身份构建——以中国国家领导人在2007-2018年夏季达沃斯论坛开幕式上的致辞为例) [J]. *Journal of Beijing International Studies University* (北京第二外国语学院学报), 2021(3):

60-72.

[4] Ma, Chenjing & Chen, Xiaochun (马陈静，陈笑春). "Construction of China's National Image in Poverty Alleviation from the Perspective of Multimodal Metaphor" (多模态隐喻视角下我国脱贫攻坚国家形象的建构) [J]. *Youth Journalist* (青年记者), 2021(22): 73-74.

[5] Newmark, P. *Approaches to Translation* [M]. Oxford: Pergamon Press, 1981.

[6] Pragglejaz Group. MIP: A method for identifying metaphorically used words in discourse [J]. *Metaphor and Symbol*, 2007(1): 1-39.

[7] Ren, Dongsheng & Ji, Xiumei (任东升，季秀妹). "On Strategies for Interpreting Metaphors in Diplomatic Discourse for Political Equivalence: A Case Study of Chinese Foreign Ministry's 2019 Regular Press Conferences" (基于"政治等效"的外交话语隐喻英译策略——以2019年外交部例行记者会发言为例) [J]. *Contemporary Foreign Language Studies* (当代外语研究), 2021(3): 84-95.

[8] Tan, Wenhui & Zhu, Yaoyun & Wang, Junju (谭文慧，朱耀云，王俊菊). "On the Self Shaping of China's National Image from the Perspective of Conceptual Metaphor Based on COVID-19 Documentaries" (概念隐喻视角下中国国家形象自塑研究——以疫情题材纪录片为例) [J]. *Foreign Languages Research* (外语研究), 2021(5): 38-43.

[9] Toury, G. *Descriptive Translation Studies and Byond* [M]. Amsterdam & Philadelphia: John Benjamins, 1995.

[10] Van den Broeck, R. The limits of translatability exemplified by metaphor translation [J]. *Poetics Today*, 1981(4): 73-87.

[11] Wen, Bing & Wang, Binhua (文炳，王斌华). "The Continuum Pattern in the English Translation Strategies of Chinese Literary Classics:An Analysis of Goldblatt's Translation Modes of Metaphorical Expressions in *Sandalwood Death*" (中国文学经典英译策略的"连续轴规律"考察——基于葛浩文英译《檀香刑》中比喻翻译策略的分析) [J]. *Foreign Languages in China* (中国外语), 2021(5): 98-105.

[12] Xiao, Zhiqing & Shao, Bin (肖志清，邵斌). "A Corpus-based Study of the English Translations of 'Lüshui qingshan jiushi jinshan yinshan'" (基于语料库的"绿水青山就是金山银山"的英译探析) [J]. *Contemporary Foreign Language Studies*(当代外语研究), 2019(2): 95-104.

[13] Xie, Li & Wang, Yinquan (谢莉，王银泉). "A Study of Political Discourse Translation from the Perspective of China's International Image Construction" (中国国际形象建构视域下的政治话语翻译研究) [J]. *Foreign Language Education* (外语教学), 2018(5): 7-11.

[14] Zhao, Xuebo (赵雪波). "Understanding of National Image and Other Related Concepts" (关于国家形象等概念的理解) [J]. *Modern Communication (Journal of Communication University of China)* (现代传播（中国传媒大学学报）), 2006(5): 63-65.

作者简介

肖志清，硕士，武汉科技大学外国语学院副教授、硕士生导师。研究方向：翻译技术、笔译理论与实践。电子邮箱：xiaozhiqing@wust.edu.cn。

李静霞，武汉科技大学外国语学院MTI研究生。研究方向：笔译理论与实践。

从翻译美学角度比较许渊冲和翁显良的汉诗英译策略

⊙ 张紫涵（中国民航大学外国语学院，天津）

[摘　要] 在中国，古诗英译的理论主张主要分为两类，一类是许渊冲主张的三美论，即意美、音美和形美；另一类则是翁显良教授主张的散体译诗，即以散文诗体和白描手法翻译中国古诗。从流传范围和接受程度来看，目前受众最广的理论当属许渊冲倡导的三美论，其汉诗英译作品也被誉为翻译的经典。相比之下，翁显良主张的散体译诗理论，传播范围较窄，接受程度偏低。然而，三美论可以在翻译实践中得到真正意义上的践行吗？三美论是诗歌翻译的唯一原则吗？散体译诗理论是否有值得借鉴之处呢？本文试结合翻译美学理论，从译文的形式美和意境美两个方面分析许渊冲和翁显良的汉诗英译作品，探讨两种截然相反的译论指导下，译诗在传达诗歌美之时的优势和局限性，借此分析译者在汉诗英译中应遵循怎样的标准，以及如何实现译诗对原作的审美再现。

[关键词] 三美论；韵体译诗；散体译诗；翻译美学

A Comparative Study of the C-E Poetry Translation Strategies of Xu Yuanchong and Weng Xianliang in the Light of Translation Aesthetics

ZHANG Zihan (Civil Aviation University of China, Tianjin)

Abstract: In China, there are two kinds of theories on the translation of ancient Chinese poems. The most popular one is the theory of three beauties proposed by Xu Yuanchong, which can be further elaborated as the beauty of meaning, the beauty of sound and the beauty of form. The other one is the free-style poetry translation theory advocated by Weng Xianliang, which aims to translate ancient Chinese poetry in the form of free verse. Compared with the free style translation theory, the three beauties theory is more popular and more acceptable, and Xu's translations are commonly rated as translation classics. However, is the theory of three beauties fully practicable in the translation of ancient Chinese poems? Is the theory of three beauties the only rule of poetry translation? Is there anything worth learning from the free-style translation theory? In order to answer these questions, this paper attempts to analyze Xu Yuanchong's and Weng Xianliang's Chinese-English translation works from the perspectives of beauty in form and beauty in content, so as to explore the advantages and limitations of the two different poetry translation theories, and to discuss which strategies should be followed by the translators in order to fulfill the reproduction of the original Chinese poems in the light of aesthetics.

Key words: three beauties theory; rhyming translation; prose translation; aesthetics of translation

一、引言

　　作为中国最传统的文学形式，古诗凭借其华美的文字、精妙的音律、深远的意境，流传上千年之久。古诗最大的特点在于篇幅短小而意义无穷，一般古诗多以五言和七言为主，整首诗的字数不过几十字余，但诗歌所传达的意义和意境却是无穷的。正所谓"诗无达诂"，不同读者对同一首古诗有着不同的理解，而同一位读者对同一首古诗也会由于个人经历、环境变化等原因而有不同的理解。短短的古诗能承载如此丰富的含义和情感，究其原因，全在于意境。意境是古诗的灵魂和精华，它在有限的文字中承载着诗人无限的情感，给读者以无限的想象，意境可以说是评价诗歌之美的重要标志之一。其次，古诗的另一大特点是节奏鲜明，对仗工整，韵律感强，读起来朗朗上口，无论是学步儿童还是耄耋老人，都能凭借押韵的节奏、工整的对仗将一首首古诗牢记于心，这也是上千年来古诗一直为广大读者所赏玩的重要原因之一。

　　由此可见，节奏押韵、意境深远是古诗的两大美学要素。那么，究竟如何在译诗中传达古诗的这两种美？或者说，诗歌之美可以通过翻译被原封不动地传递吗？这就涉及诗歌的可译性问题。这一个颇具争议的话题，一些学者认为诗歌无法翻译，因为真正的艺术作品都是无法翻译的，即使强行把诗歌译为另一种语言，诗歌本身所蕴含的美感也会在翻译中流失，正如闻一多读小烟薰良一首英译诗时说："这到底是怎么一回事？怎么中文的浑金璞玉移到英文里来就变成这样的浅薄这样的庸琐？我说这毛病不在译者的手腕，是在他的眼光，就象这一类浑然天成的名句，他的好处太玄妙了，太精微了，是经不起翻译的。你定要翻译它，只有把它毁了完事！……美是碰不得的，一粘手它就毁了。"（翁显良，1983：263）那么，是否可以笼统地说，诗歌不可翻译呢？其实未必。诚然，由于汉语和英语语言本质上的差别，汉诗英译中诗歌之美的流失是无法避免的，但这并不意味着汉诗之美和其所表达的情感无法通过翻译传达。因为无论是哪个国家哪个民族，大家喜怒哀乐的情绪都是一样的，思维方式、逻辑推理能力也是相通的，因此，诗歌所蕴含的美感和情感也是可以通过翻译传达的。况且语言也是不断发展变化的，一种语言可以表达的东西，即使目前在另外的语言中找不到相对等的表达，随着语言的发展，总能在日后某一天找到，因此，诗歌的翻译是完全可行的。正如周仪教授所说："不可译只是相对的，可译才是绝对的。"（周仪、罗平，1999：72）

　　事实上，自汉诗英译开始以来，参与汉诗翻译的学者便数不胜数。最早将汉诗译为英文的多为西方学者，如 Herbert Giles、Arthur Waley、Ezra Pound 等人。20 世纪 80 年代，中国众多学者开始对汉诗英译的策略进行系统性的研究，并出版了一系列质量上乘的佳作，其中最有名的便是许渊冲和翁显良。然而，两位大师的译诗风格可谓截然不同，许渊冲主张以诗译诗，注重音韵的传达，并提出汉诗英译的评价标准"三美论"；而翁显良则采取散体译诗的方式，认为译诗的主要原则是再现原诗的意境。两种译论孰优孰劣，一直未有定论。不过从读者接受程度来看，无论是专门研究诗歌翻译的学者还是不懂诗歌翻译的门外汉，几乎都知道许渊冲的译诗和三美论，而翁显良译诗的读者，则多为专门研究诗歌翻译的学者，非研究诗歌翻译的学者鲜有人知。许渊冲的译诗所呈现的节奏上的押韵和美感，是其中一个原因。然而，中国古诗之美并不仅仅局限于韵律上的押韵，古诗的意象之美更是重要因素。那么，在翻译中，诗歌的意境和音韵是否可以兼得？诗歌之美在翻译中的传递是否存在局限性？应如何平衡诗歌之美在翻译中的局限？下文将从翻译美学理论出发，分析并比较许渊冲和翁显良的汉诗英译译作和策略，探讨两种译论在传达诗歌之美中的优势和局限性，并分析译者在汉诗英译中应遵循怎样的标准，以及如何实现译诗对原作的审美再现。

二、翻译美学与诗歌翻译

所谓翻译美学，顾名思义，就是翻译和美学的结合，其所关注的重心是如何在译文中传达原文的美，使译文具有和原文接近的艺术感染力，正如意大利美学家克罗齐在《美学原理》中所说："上好的译文除与原文有几分相似外，必须有它独创的艺术价值，本身即可成为一部独立的艺术作品。"（党争胜，2010: 99）那么，是否只有西方存在翻译美学这一概念呢？其实不然，虽然中国早期并没有系统命名的翻译美学理论，但早在佛经翻译时期，译界就已经开始探讨如何在译文中传递原文之美，如东晋道安的"五失本、三不易"，玄奘的"既须求真，又须喻俗"和"五不翻"。而后期的译论标准，从马建忠的"善译"、严复的"信达雅"、矛盾的"再现意境"、傅雷的"重神似而不重形似"、钱锺书的"化境"、朱光潜的"艺术论"，再到刘重德的"信达切"等译论，无不具备相应的哲学基础和美学渊源。表面上看，这些译论并未直接提及"美学"二字，但实质上，这些译论都在探讨如何在翻译中传达原文的形式和内容，也就是美学上形式之美与内容之美的辩证问题。

中国系统的翻译美学理论则要从1991年傅仲选出版的《实用翻译美学》算起，该著作是中国首部翻译美学专著，标志着中国翻译美学研究在理论上的觉醒。2005年，毛荣贵首次以"翻译美学"作为书名，出版了《翻译美学》一书。在书中，毛荣贵探讨了中国传统译论和美学的关系，他说"中国传统的译论基础就是美学"（毛荣贵，2005: 7）。但是，"中国翻译理论中虽然具有鲜明的美学特征，但这些特征大多都是'潜在'的，尚需我们去做深入细致的探讨和考究"（Ibid: 8）。这也间接说明了从美学角度研究中国译论的必要性和重要性。在《翻译美学导论》中，刘宓庆提出了翻译美学的理论框架，将美学要素按性质分为两类，一种是美学的表象要素，即原文的语言形式，如行文的音韵、节奏、遣词造句等。而另一种则是美学的非表象要素，也就是行文的意境、神韵、风貌等。

结合中国的传统译论和系统的翻译美学理论来看，文学翻译中美学的传递无外乎是美学表象要素和美学非表象要素的传递，也就是中国传统译界一直以来的"形""神"之争，因此，下文将从翻译美学的"形""神"两方面对中国现有的诗歌翻译策略进行具体分析。

三、翻译美学视角下的汉诗英译理论

作为一项审美活动，诗歌翻译最核心的内容，便是探讨语言之美，这也是中国译界几千年来一直在研究的问题。对于许渊冲为代表的格律体译诗和以翁显良为代表的散体译诗，中国译界褒贬不一，各有支持者和反对者。钱锺书这样评价许渊冲的译诗："戴着音韵和节奏的镣铐跳舞，灵活自如，令人惊奇。"（许渊冲，2003: 367）而对于翁显良的译诗，童元方赞美道："读翁的译诗，不像读译品，却像直接读创作，使人有时惊喜到一定程度因而手之舞之，足之蹈之。"（童元方，2015：50）然而，目前在中国，许渊冲的译诗理念传播范围更广、接受程度更高。

在《毛主席诗词四十二首》的序言中，许渊冲教授首次提出了三美论，他认为一首优秀的译诗"不但要传达原诗的意美，还要尽可能地传达它的音美和形美"（许渊冲，2003：85）。"意美"即意境之美，指译诗和原诗能够保持同样的意境，能够给读者带来同样的情感体验；"音美"即音律之美，指译诗和原诗保持同样的节奏和韵律；"形美"即形态之美，指译诗与原诗保持同样的长短、字数等。三美论的原则自提出开始，便一直被译界奉为圭臬。提到诗歌翻译，无论是翻译的业内人士，还是不懂翻译的行外人士，第一反应都会提到三美论，似乎三美论是诗歌翻译的唯一法则。然而，如果对比一下汉语和英语在语言本质上的差别以及汉诗和英诗的本质差异，便会发现在译诗中传达"三美"中的任何一美已非易事，同时传达"三美"更是难上加难。

在韵律方面，由于汉语是单音节词，英语多为双音节和多音节词，因此，英语的押韵远比汉语押韵困难。其次，汉语诗歌的押韵主要通过声调的重复来实现，且多以尾韵为主，而英语诗歌则多以重音来实现押韵，且多以头韵为主，押韵格式多为两行转韵（AABB）、隔行押韵（ABCB）、隔行交互押韵（ABAB）和抱韵（ABBA）等。由此可见，汉诗和英诗的韵律在本质上差异很大，这也就决定了汉诗英译中韵律转化的困难之处。至于汉诗的意境和韵味，林语堂先生认为，神韵是原文的"字神句气与言外之意"，而季羡林则说，神韵是一种"一看就懂，一问就糊涂"的东西。由此可见，所谓诗歌的"神韵"和"意境"，本就是一种虚无缥缈、看不到摸不着的东西，要将其转化为英语实非易事。因此，仅仅传达诗歌的音韵之美或意境之美已非易事，两者是否可以兼得呢？如果不可兼得，应以传达神韵为主还是以韵律为主？

对于这一问题，许渊冲认为，如果译诗"传达了原诗的意美，而没有传达音美和形美的翻译，虽然不是译得好的诗，还不失为译得好的散文；如果译诗只有音美和形美而没有意美，那就根本算不上是好的翻译"（许渊冲，2003：85）。由此可见，在许渊冲看来，"意美"是三美中最重要的，其次是"音美"，最后是"形美"。虽然三美论理论上把"意美"的传达排在第一位，然而，在许渊冲的汉诗英译实践中，却似乎都把"音美"的传达排在了第一位。而许渊冲流传度最广的译诗，也几乎都是因为节奏上的押韵而广为人知，如毛泽东《为女民兵题照》中"不爱红装爱武装"的译文"To face the powder and not to powder the face"，杜甫的《登高》中"无边落木萧萧下，不尽长江滚滚来"的译文"The boundless forest sheds its leaves shower by shower; The endless river rolls its waves hour after hour"，李商隐的《无题》中"春蚕到死丝方尽，蜡炬成灰泪始干"的译文"Spring silkworm till its death spins silk from lovesick heart; A candle but when burned up has no tears to shed"。这些译文都传达了原诗的音韵之美，读起来朗朗上口，颇具音韵之美。

然而，如果仔细阅读许渊冲的译诗便会发现，为了满足"音美"，一些原诗中没有的押韵也被译成了押韵，从而造成了因韵害义的现象。我们来看许渊冲的译诗，并比较翁显良的英译：

登幽州台歌	**On the Tower at You Zhou**	**I See Them Not**
陈子昂	Cheng Zi'ang	Cheng Zi'ang

前不见古人， 后不见来者。 念天地之悠悠， 独怆然而涕下。	Where are the great men of the past? And where are those of future years The sky and earth forever last; Here and now I alone shed tears. （许渊冲译）	Men there have been—I see them not. Men there will be— I see them not. The world goes on, world without end. But here and now, alone I stand —in tears. （翁显良译）

《登幽州台歌》慷慨悲凉、苍劲奔放，表现了诗人怀才不遇的失意境遇和深入骨髓的孤独之感。在音韵上，该诗不同于传统的绝句诗歌，诗中并没有对仗、平仄、押韵。然而，在许渊冲的译文中，却以"past"和"last"、"years"和"tears"形成了 abab 的韵，将诗歌译成了韵律整齐的格律诗。然而，这样的押韵所传达的音韵之美还是原诗的音韵之美吗？不懂中文的读者读了这首译诗，会不会以为原诗也是这样押了 abab 韵？从意境上分析，原诗并没有具体意象，却在整体上创造了一种辽阔幽远、空旷苍茫的意境。此诗的前两句缅怀古人，期待来者，感慨自己生不逢时。第三句"悠悠"二字写出时间的漫长和空间的辽阔，第四句则描绘了诗人孤单悲苦的心绪，全诗无一"悲"字，却无处不透露着诗人的悲壮之情。许渊冲的译文，似乎过于平铺直叙，并没有给人以想象的空间，第三句的译文"The sky and earth forever last"，中文回译为"天空和大地一直存在"，失去了原诗中"悠悠"二字的韵味，而最后一句"Here and now I alone shed tears"，中文回译为"此时此刻我独自落泪"，少了那种"怆然涕下"的悲壮凄凉之感。

至于翁显良的译诗，首先从形式上看，译者采取了散文的形式，对于不懂中文的读者而言，很容易以为原诗也是以散文的形式呈现的。在韵律上，翁显良也未刻意在诗歌中保留原诗的韵律。对于题目，翁显良脱离原诗的题目，直接将题目改译为"I see them not"，直接表述了原诗的主旨，有助于意义的传达。对于前两句中的"古人"和"来者"，翁显良都未直接译出原词的意思，而是笼统地用"men"和"them"指代，赋予了诗歌无限的想象空间。而对于第三句中的"天地"，翁显良依然采取泛化的形式，将其译为"world"（世界），而第四句的译诗可谓是整首译诗的点睛之笔，"in tears"这个短语将流泪的动作转化为状态，仿佛使人看到诗人独立于苍茫大地之间怅然落泪的情景。

从《登幽州台歌》的译诗中可以看出，翁显良在译诗中一直坚持意境优于韵律的原则，正如他所说的，"汉诗英译要保持本色，首先要辨明什么是本色。这本色，一不在于辞藻，二不在于典故，三不在于形式，而是在于意象以及加强其艺术效果的节奏。只要能再现原作的意象，不一定模仿其章法句法字法"（翁显良，1978: 85）。对于原诗中无韵的地方，翁显良自然不会在译文中用韵，即便是原诗中韵律锵然的诗歌，翁显良也不会在译诗中强调音韵的传达，例如《江雪》以及翁显良和许渊冲的英译：

江雪 柳宗元	**Snow** Liu Zongyuan	**Fishing in Snow** Liu Zongyuan
千山鸟飞绝， 万径人踪灭。	No sign of birds in the mountains; nor of men along the trails; nor any craft on the	From hill to hill no bird in flight; From path to path no man in sight;

孤舟蓑笠翁， 独钓寒江雪。	river but a little boat with an old man in rustic hat and cape dangling a line in the frigid waters — a solitary figure veiled in silent snow. （翁显良译）	A lonely fisherman afloat, Is fishing snow in a lonely boat. （许渊冲译）

柳宗元笔下的《江雪》仿佛一幅泼墨山水画，寥寥数笔，便描绘出一幅冬日大雪纷飞，渔翁独坐于孤舟静自垂钓的景象。诗歌作于柳宗元谪居永州期间，诗人被贬到永州，仕途失意，难免心中苦闷，于是寄情于山水，抒发自己的压抑，并表达自己清高孤傲的情怀。翁显良教授的译文可谓一气呵成，虽然在音韵上并没有保留原诗的韵律和节奏，但在意境上却将原诗的清冷感和孤傲感表现得淋漓尽致，让人读完译诗也仿佛置身于大雪纷飞的江面之上。对于前两句诗歌，翁显良并没有将原诗中的"千"和"万"译出来，而是将"千山""鸟""万径"等意象简单地译为"mountains""birds""trails"等。前两句中的"绝"和"灭"字，可谓传神地刻画了一种肃杀、冷清之感，也间接表达了诗人被贬的那种苦闷之情，对于"绝"和"灭"字的翻译，翁显良在译文中采用了"no sign"和"nor"的表达，用这种具有绝对否定意义的表达传达了原诗中的绝望感，可谓十分传神。而对于三四两句，翁显良则将其合为一句，第四句"独钓寒江雪"被处理为介词结构"with an old man in..."，并在末尾增加了"a solitary figure veiled in silent snow"，使得老翁独自垂钓的形象跃然纸上，更突显了诗歌所表达的空灵与孤寂。虽然翁显良的译文对原诗的意境做到了较好的传达，但散文的形式难免会让不懂中文的读者以为原诗的形式也是如此，从这一角度看，散体译诗的方式并不利于中国传统诗歌美学的传播。

相比于翁显良的译诗，许渊冲的《江雪》英译，不但保留了原文诗歌的形式，而且在音韵上也做到了极大程度的保留。《江雪》原诗是标准的五言格律诗，平仄相间，押 ue 的尾韵。许渊冲在译诗中统一采用了 aabb 的押韵方式，尤其是一、二句"千山鸟飞绝""万径人踪灭"的翻译，这两句译文字数音节完全相等，读来朗朗上口，完美地传递了原诗的音韵之美。在题目上，相比于翁显良的译文，许渊冲译出了"fishing"，将原诗中的垂钓之意翻译了出来，传达了诗人寒冬冒雪江边独钓的清冷与悲凉。对于前两句诗歌，许译中也未将"千"和"万"直接翻译出来，而是用"from hill to hill"和"from path to path"的重复来呈现原诗中"千"和"万"的夸张表达。而后两句的译文虽然在音韵上保留了"afloat"和"boat"的押韵，但在诗歌的意境上却似乎少了很多。后两句中的"孤"和"独"是全诗的灵魂字眼，但在译文中却没有凸显，仅"lonely"一词，似乎不足以传达那种寂静冷清的氛围和诗人的孤寂之感。而最后一句"独钓寒江雪"中的"钓雪"被译为"fishing snow"，不但原诗中的美感全无，如果没有详细的注解，不懂中文的西方读者恐怕很难理解"钓雪"的含义。

由此可见，诗体译诗并非诗歌翻译的唯一准则，无论是散体译诗还是诗体译诗，两种译诗策略在传播中国诗词的美学中各有所失，也各有所得。诗体译诗可以较好地传达原文的形式和韵律，有助于西方读者了解中国诗歌的音韵之美。然而，在传达诗歌音韵之美时，也应注意在译诗中传达音韵的限度，不要因韵害义。英语本身就比汉语韵路窄，英语的音韵总数也大大低于汉语，因此在英语中寻求押韵要比汉语困难得多。在这种情况下，如果还非要刻意搜寻押韵的词语来传播音韵之美，最后的结果，恐怕就像吕叔湘（2002）所言："即令达意，风格已殊，稍一不慎，流弊丛生。"

散体译诗的最大好处，就是不受形式和音韵的限制，译者可以最大程度地专注于原诗意境的传达。但这种译诗策略的缺点也很明显：译诗以散文的形式呈现给不懂中文的读者，很容易让读者以为汉语诗歌就是以散体的形式呈现，毫无形式对仗或音韵整齐一说，这么一来，汉诗的美感也减少了很多。正如桐城派三祖刘大櫆所说："诗成于音，音成于声，声成于言，言成于志。"（刘大櫆，1990: 84）此外，如果在散体译诗中译者过于自由，采取完全脱离原诗的翻译策略，恐怕最后读者读到的诗歌就不是原作者的诗歌，而是译者从原诗中获得灵感后重新创作的诗歌，比如美国诗人庞德的一些古诗英译。

因此，对于汉诗英译的策略，我们并不能武断地说某种译论优于另一种，或者说诗歌翻译中音韵比意境更重要，或者意境比音韵更重要。其实，诗歌的音韵和意境同样重要，就像朱光潜所说："诗以情趣为主，情趣见于声音，寓于意象。"（朱光潜，1981: 71）诗歌翻译之中美的传达，不可能做到百分之百，也没有哪种译论，可以百分之百地让译者传达诗歌中的美学，译者只能做到在音韵和意境的限度内尽可能地传达汉诗之美。正如刘宓庆教授所说："翻译美学关注的中心是：翻译文学作品将如何保证译文具有尽可能接近原作的艺术感染力，尽可能传译原文的风格。"（刘宓庆，1986: 50）这才是中国古诗英译的要害之处。

四、结 语

将中国古典诗歌译成英文传播到世界，不仅利于中国的文化传播，也可以促进世界文学的发展。古诗英译的标准一直是中国译界所争论的问题，格律体译诗忠实于汉诗的格律形式，散体译诗忠实于汉诗的内在意境，两者在传播诗歌美学上，各有优势和局限性。另外，我们也应注意到，翻译美学理论是处于不断发展之中的理论，因此译者在翻译中国古典诗词之时，也要结合翻译美学的时代变化，合理地运用各种翻译手段和策略，以便拓宽汉诗英译之路，为中国文化走出去做出切实的贡献。

参考文献

[1] Dang, Zhengsheng(党争胜). "On the Three Principles of Aesthetic Representation in Literary Translation in Light of Translation Aesthetics" (从翻译美学看文学翻译审美再现的三个原则) [J]. *Foreign Language Education* (外语教学), 2010(3): 99.

[2] Liu, Dakui(刘大櫆). *Collected Essays of Liu Dakui: the Second Volume*(刘大櫆集：第二卷[M]). Shanghai: Shanghai Classics Publishing House(上海：上海古籍出版社), 1990.

[3] Liu, Miqing(刘宓庆). "Overview of Translation Aesthetics"(翻译美学概述) [J]. *Journal of Foreign Languages*(外国语),1986(2): 50.

[4] Lv, Shuxiang(吕叔湘). *A Comparison of the Translation of Chinese Poetry*(中诗英译比录[M]). Beijing: Zhonghua Book Company(北京：中华书局), 2002.

[5] Mao, Ronggui(毛荣贵). *Translation Aesthetics* (翻译美学[M]). Shanghai: Shanghai Jiao Tong University Press (上海：上海交通大学出版社), 2005.

[6] Tong, Yuanfang (童元方). *The Art of Translation*(译心与译艺[M]). Beijing: Foreign Language Teaching and Research Press (北京：外语教学与研究出版社), 2015.

[7] Weng, Xianliang (翁显良). *A Brief Talk on the Untranslatability of Classic Chinese Poetry* (意态由来画不成 [M]). Beijing: China Translation Corporation (北京：中国对外翻译出版公司), 1983.

[8] Weng, Xianliang (翁显良). "Selected Translation of Ancient Poems"（古诗选译）[J]. *Modern Foreign Languages*(现代外语),1978(2): 85.

[9] Weng, Xianliang (翁显良). "Selected Translation of Ancient Poems"（古诗选译）[J]. *Modern Foreign Languages*(现代外语),1979(3): 40.

[10] Xu, Yuanchong & Lu, Peixuan & Wu, Juntao(许渊冲，陆佩弦，吴钧陶). *New Translation of Three Hundred Tang Poems*(唐诗三百首新译[M]). Beijing: China Translation Corporation (北京：中国对外翻译出版公司), 1988.

[11] Xu, Yuanchong(许渊冲). *Life of Poetry* (诗书人生[M]). Tianjin: Baihua Literature and Art Press (天津：百花文艺出版社), 2003.

[12] Xu, Yuanchong(许渊冲). *Literature and Translation*(文学与翻译[M]). Beijing: Peking University Press (北京：北京大学出版社), 2003.

[13] Zhu, Guangqian(朱光潜). *Essays of Poetry Review*(艺文杂谈[M]). Hefei: Anhui People's Publishing House(合肥：安徽人民出版社), 1981.

[14] Zhou, Yi & Luo, Ping (周仪，罗平). *Translation and Criticism* (翻译与批评[M]). Wuhan: Hubei Education Press (武汉：湖北教育出版社), 1999.

作者简介

张紫涵，硕士，中国民航大学外国语学院教师。研究方向：文学翻译、翻译理论与实践。电子邮箱：zihanzzz@126.com。

"跨语际性"视阈下国产动画英译研究

——以《大理寺日志》为例

⊙ 雷 静 李明明（中央民族大学外国语学院，北京）

[摘 要] 随着中国动画产业的蓬勃发展，与动画相关的各领域研究随即展开，但针对国产动画语言变体特征的翻译研究尚不多见。本文尝试运用"跨语际性"理论对2020年大热的国产动画作品《大理寺日志》中语言变体的英译方法展开研究，从"身""神""韵"三方面梳理出动画作品中的多种语言变体与动作画面、音效制作等元素之间的互动机制，并从语言、模态和象征性资源的整体性上思考多种语言变体动画作品所具有的跨越、聚合和表述特征，从而进一步阐述具有多种语言变体特点的动画作品在英译过程中的翻译策略，为国产动画成功"出海"提供方法建议。

[关键词] 跨语际性；动画；《大理寺日志》；字幕

Translation Study of Chinese Animation from the Perspective of Translingualism:
A Case Study of *White Cat Legend*

LEI Jing LI Mingming（Minzu University of China, Beijing）

Abstract: With the vigorous development of Chinese animation, animation researches of different aspects also come into view accordingly, the research directly on the translation of language variety in Chinese animation is rare. Under translingualism theory, this paper analyzes the translation of language variants in Chinese animation and sort out the interaction mechanism among language variants, action images, sound effects and other elements of animation in terms of "body", "spirit" and "rhythm", and think further about the transcending, convergence and performative features embodied in the Chinese animation with language variants from the angle of language, modality and embodied resources, in the hoping of demonstrating the transition strategy for animation with language variants and providing methods for Chinses animation going global successfully.

Key words: translingualism; animation; *White Cat Legend*; subtitling

一、引 言

本文系教育部"春晖计划"合作科研项目（HZKY20220001）、中央民族大学"民族题材视听翻译研究"校级项目（2022QNYL14）的阶段性成果。

随着中国国产动画走向崛起，一系列制作精良的国产动画作品涌现市场。越来越多的动画作品呈现出重视对外传播的特点，发行时自带的双语字幕推动了国产动画"破圈"，在国际市场获得认可与接受。为了进一步探究我国动画作品翻译研究现状，笔者在中国期刊全文数据库（CNKI）检索后发现，相较于其他学科研究（如动画作品分析、制作技术等），中国学者对动画字幕翻译的关注度远远不够。现有研究中外国动画作品汉译研究居多，且大多从目的论、顺应论、文化翻译观、功能对等、关联理论等角度切入，对动画作品的台词、歌曲、片名、配音翻译展开论述，中国动画作品外译研究则相对较少，是亟待拓展的领域。当前国内视听翻译研究大多集中于字幕文化因素转换研究，鲜少讨论音乐符号、手势语、造型、意象和图像符号等多模态符号方面（王建华，2019：33-38）。目前，尚未出现将社会语言学的"跨语际性"理论应用到动画作品英译的相关研究文章，针对具体动画作品中多种语言变体特点的翻译分析非常缺乏。本研究将从社会语言学理论"跨语际性"出发，对 2020 年大热的国产动画作品《大理寺日志》开展英译研究，对其中多种语言变体的表现形式和英译方式进行评述，对翻译的"表述行为"（performative）和象征层面开展研究，从而为国产动画的成功"出海"提供参考。

二、《大理寺日志》简介

《大理寺日志》动画版（2020）改编自同名条漫《大理寺日志》。该漫画于 2014 年开始连载，并在 2015 年和 2016 年制作了配音版动画，受欢迎程度可见一斑。《大理寺日志》的故事背景设定在唐朝武则天统治时期，李氏家族中的一员李饼变成了一只人类体型的白猫；另一个主人公陈拾机缘巧合与李饼相遇，并进入大理寺任职。他们二人与大理寺的其他职员齐心协力，破获了不少悬案，但也被卷入复杂的宫廷斗争。动画《大理寺日志》经历了由静态漫画到配音版动画，再到动态动画作品的过程。对于单纯的"身/声"（文字语言），动画作品中又增加了"神"（静态符号）和"韵"（音乐动画）的部分。这种变化使得原本平面感的作品立体生动起来，给人更加直观且有冲击力的效果。

该动画于 2020 年 4 月在哔哩哔哩网站①首播，12 集完结之后更是收获 297.8 万人追番、1.1 亿次播放、哔哩哔哩评分 9.8 分、豆瓣评分 8.5 的好成绩②。英国动画爱好者 Cuchallain 在哔哩哔哩上发布视频表示《大理寺日志》是西方观众入坑中国动漫的最佳选择。这部动画的人物设计简单而富有表现力，色调鲜艳大胆，穿插的配乐和沙雕音效为这部动画增添光彩。制作组花了大量精力重现大唐时期的衣食住行、文化习俗，并且成功地融合了其他特色文化元素。剧中人物如天真烂漫的波斯人阿里巴巴、勤劳积极的西南部落土著朗百灵、罗马帝国的怪盗一枝花、操着一口标准河南话的陈拾，带领我们领略到开放包容的盛唐气象。可以看出，《大理寺日志》的人物设定具有明显的不同语言变体特征，本篇研究主要聚焦在动画主人公陈拾的河南话方言英译上。

三、"跨语际性"理论

对"跨语际性"进行最为系统研究的学者是社会语言学家 Canagarajah，他认为"跨语际性"包括不同语言、语言变体、语域、语义及模态之间的创造性聚合；不仅仅是单一语言之间的语码转换，其范畴包括且大于语码转换，其中语言变体（language variety）是"跨语际性"（Translingualism）理论所关注的重要内容。

英国语言学家赫德森（Hudson, R. A.）把"语言变体"定义为："社会分布相似的一套语项"，指的是语言在不同使用者的使用过程中，产生的各种变异现象（1989：27）。语言变体是指在发音、语法或词汇等层次上发生的内部差异变化，发生变异的原因可能是复杂的社会因素的作用，语言形式或者语言行为也随之发生变化。

很多翻译研究的学者对"跨语际性"与翻译之间的关系进行了详细阐述。根据"跨语际性"的定义，"跨语际性"的研究范畴包括了不同语言、语言变体和不同类型的符号体系，涉及了语际翻译、语内翻译和符际翻译的不同层面。García 和 Li Wei 对"跨语际行为"（translanguaging）进行了深入分析，阐述了"跨语际性"是发言者在整体情境下具备的沟通模态（言语、视觉、姿势和象征性）的创造性选择和合并(2014：18)。García & Li 指出，"跨语际性"理论主要是强调语言、模态以及象征性资源在整体中进行创造性的聚合；而翻译在凸显多语、多模态融合的跨语际实践中处于核心位置；翻译内嵌在跨语际空间中，并由连续的跨语瞬间构成（2014：21）。在最新的研究中，Baynham 和 Lee 提出翻译研究中的"跨语际转向"是把翻译从文本之间的关系转变成将其视为多语使用者在多语整体性中进行创造性的资源部署（2019：33）。

"跨语际性"独特的属性特征包括：语言层面上的"跨越"属性、模态层面上的"聚合"属性以及象征性资源层面上的"表述"属性。本文将"跨语际性"的这三大特征应用到动画作品中语言变体的分析上。第一，本文运用"跨语际性"在语言层面上的"跨越"特征来分析动画作品中的语言变体，即动画的"身/声"（文字语言）；"跨越"语言变体的边界，即随着说话人之间语言变体的互动，在不同社会和语义环境之下能生成新的语言形式（Baynham & Lee, 2019：8）。第二，本文运用"跨语际性"在模态层面上的聚合特征来分析动画作品中的"神"（静态符号）；对语言变体边界的跨越，其实也形成了语言变体与多种符号在不同层面上的聚合：虽在不同平面，却留下聚合的痕迹，即"由不同平面构成的，并且留下一圈圈聚合的痕迹"（Ibid：2）。通过模态的聚合使得动画作品能够达到与观众沟通的目的。第三，本文运用"跨语际性"在象征性资源层面上的"表述"特征来分析动画作品中语言变体能够呈现的"韵"（动态音效）；"跨语际性"是在特定场景偶发的，由情境和沟通模态的可视性生成并受之影响（Ibid：91）。这里强调的是动画作品在美学层面的意涵，语言变体在具体的动态情境之中所"表述"出来的情感。因此，作为跨语际行为的整体性潜能就被展现出来：通过"跨越"得以生成新的语言形式、通过"聚合"得以实现模态间的沟通、通过"表述"得以传达象征性资源。

四、"跨语际性"视角下的翻译研究

本研究主要以《大理寺日志》主人公陈拾的河南方言为研究对象，分析"跨语际性"在动画作品中的语言、模态、象征性整体资源层面上是如何进行创造性活动的。

（一）语言层面：跨越"身"

"跨语际性"在多语层面的全部资源，包括结合不同的语言、语言变体和语域等诸多方面。这些不同类型的语言资源受到自我意识驱动，能够创造语言娱乐和/或讽刺某种社会条件，最终形式体现为创造性词汇（Baynham & Lee，2019：45-46）。"跨语际性"并非局限在单一语言领域，不仅包括多种语言、语言变体，还包含语域等语内、语际方面。跨语行为能通过"仿造表达"的行为产生新的英文表达法（Li，2018：13）。从跨语行为视角来看，多种语言变体的整体呈现，能够生成新的词语结构，从而丰富动画作品的词汇特点，使得动画作品的整体效果更加鲜明。下面两个例句具体说明了"跨语际性"在语言层面主要表现为生成新的词语结构和仿造表达。

例（1）：

原文：我被……架了 日落前城外向东三里界 那啥处 快来救我（第五集）

译文：I'm …dnapped … Before sundown, 3 miles eastward, outside the city, around … post …Come and rescue me.

在此例中，陈拾收到了外籍同事阿里巴巴写的求救信，但因为识字不多，只看懂了信中的部分内容，结合剧情，"我被……架了"的完整内容是"我被绑架了"。在英文字幕中，"绑架"的英文单词"kidnap"拼写并不完整，这种特殊的处理方式有两个目的，一是通过切分单词让英文字幕与动画角色的口型、台词、字幕呈现时长尽量保持一致；二是为了更加贴合与传递出陈拾的文化程度不高这一人物信息。"I'm…dnapped…"这一译法在此可以理解为塑造和传递人物背景信息而采用的新的词语结构，这种生成新的词语结构的翻译实践方法，拓展了动画作品译文的表达方式，也使得译文更贴近原文和剧情设定，整体表达效果更鲜明。

例（2）：

原文：您过去一定是过金贵日子的人 （第二集）

译文：You strike me as the kind of person that shits gold.

例2中，"过金贵日子的人"一定程度上体现了河南方言的语言表达方式，该表达被译为"person that shits gold"。该英文表达本身并没有此用法（作者在英文俚语库 The Free Dictionary 与 Urban Dictionary 中均未检索到相关用法）。译文将角色原台词"过金贵日子"转化为中文的另一个俗语"视金钱为粪土"，"shit gold"的表达是转借了中文"视金钱如粪土"的句子结构和语素而形成，把中文惯用的表达法嵌入英文的表达法。这种"仿造"能够让对话者感受到使用语言的语气和感情色彩。跨语际实践能通过"仿造表达"的行为产生新的英文表达法，从而丰富英文词汇和英语表达方式。

（二）静态模态：聚合"神"

"跨语际性"不仅包含语言维度，还包含了生成语义的符际层面，例如：图像与文本结合等实践方式。"图像文本"（Imagetext）表达了多重含义：a）给文字信息添加语义内容；b）图像与文本作为整体被读者阅读，具有一个完整形态（gestalt），因为执行该图示动作的人的主体形态也被阅读；c）图像与图标（icon）相结合，通过并列、并置、对比资源的方式构成模态整体（Baynham & Lee，2019:100-101）。以下3个例句将具体说明图像与文本相结合的实践方式。

例（3）：

陈拾：乖乖嘞 外国人 真不愧是京城啊（第一集）

译文：Oh My!!!!!!!!! A foreigner, this IS the capital after all.

"图像文本"的第一层内涵是图像文本能够给文字信息添加语义内容。此例发生在陈拾初入大理寺之际。陈拾遇到了大理寺的录事，外国青年阿里巴巴。他对在京城能看到外国人感到非常震惊。"乖乖嘞"是河南方言的体现，目的是突出陈拾淳朴的人物角色。为了表现惊讶之感，译文运用了两个小技巧：一是感叹号的连用。译文将中文句子进行了切分，在第一个小句后连用了多个感叹号，在渲染人物震惊之余，尽量贴合人物口型；二是巧妙地把动画台词"真不愧是京城啊"的中文感叹句式表达，通过"IS"大写单词强调出来，译文显得非常灵活，视觉效果更明显，取得了和动画中异曲同工之效。从"跨语际性"的符际层面来看，此译文就通过符号的连用（感叹号的连用）与单词大写向观众突出情感内容，照应了图像文本能够为文字信息增加新的语义内容这一内涵。

例（4）：

陈拾：恁还是猫不是猫啊 恁咋能这么狠心啊 猫爷 （第十集）

译文：After all he's also a kin of yours! Have a heart, will you? Catty~~~~~~

"图像文本"的第二层内涵是图像和文本能够作为一个整体被读者阅读，具有一个完整形态，在符际翻译层面形成了语言变体与多种符号的聚合。在例（4）中，陈拾收留了一只流浪猫，少卿大人发现后命令陈拾把猫丢掉，陈拾央求少卿留下猫。"恁"是河南方言的典型标志，这句话也是在塑造陈拾淳朴，善良的人物形象。为了配合与再现陈拾的哀求语气，译文中连用了"～"这一标点符号。译文中的"～"可以指变音符号，自然流露出一点点俏皮和央告请求的意味，配合动画中陈拾的央求声，极有画面感。袁孟辉指出，标点符号是荧屏的无名英雄，标点符号也有自己的声音，巧妙地运用好标点符号这一配角，就能在视觉和深意上为文字增添魅力。译文中连用的波浪号不仅与角色配音拉长的尾音相照应，也与英文译文共同构成了"完整形态"，在传递语义的基础上，无形地传递了陈拾与少卿之间的亲密关系。

例（5）：

陈拾：恁排场呀 这地方 真嘞能要俺（第一集）

译文：Look at this place. Will they…take in my sorry ass??

图 1 陈拾面部表情　　　　　　　图 2 衰的 emoji 表情

"图像文本"的第三点内涵是图像与图标相结合，通过并列、并置、对比资源的方式构成模态整体。在例（5）中，陈拾来大理寺应征杂役，随即被大理寺的气派所震慑，产生了自我怀疑。为了突出这一点，动画对陈拾的面部表情做了细节上的刻画，如瞪大的双眼，面部两旁夸张化的汗珠，都向观众传递出了陈拾的紧张和茫然不知所措。同时，通过多模态的互动——英文文本、背景的颤抖音、人物表情细节刻画——观众能收获多模态互动带来的沉浸式观影体验。在符际翻译层面的不同模态虽然处于不同平面，却留下聚合的痕迹，即"由不同平面构成的，并且留下一圈圈聚合的痕迹"（Ibid：2）。不同模态之间的聚合，能够大大提升目的语观众对动画作品译文的接受度。

此外，陈拾这个人物设定本身就可以视为一种别具匠心的符号设计。不同于其他角色甚至是路人的精细刻画，陈拾的画风显得分外简单，只有一双豆豆眼，没有眉毛，没有鼻子（如图1）。虽然这样的设定并非首例，但观众在看到陈拾的一瞬间，极易联想到汉字的"囧"字，或者"衰"的表情符号（emoji）图像（如图2）。图像文本总是存在于语言和/或模态的边界上，使得观看者需要在之间和跨越中转换，体验跨语际性和符际性，以及跨语际空间能够带来聚合效应（Baynham & Lee，2019：152）。通过人物形象设定和观众的联想，就实现了人物图像与图标的结合，也让陈拾憨厚老实、淳朴善良的人物特征跃然纸上。通过图像与图标相结合的方式，该作品在符际翻译层面上建构了"模态整体"，这反映出"跨语际性"的聚合特征。

（三）动态音效：表述"韵"

"跨语际性"在象征性层面之所以具有"表述性"，是因为每一种物质都有其可视性（affordances）：行为和姿势不能脱离彼此，并与其他符号模态协同构成整体性空间（Baynham & Lee，2019：97）。Gottileb(1998: 245) 也指出，进行视听翻译时，需要考虑以下四个方面的传播通道:(1)言语声道，包括人物对白、背景话语等；(2)非言语声道，包括背景音乐、自然声响及特殊音响效果;(3)言语视觉通道，包括视听产品本身内嵌的字幕以及屏幕上各种文字标志；(4)非言语视觉通道，包括画面的构成及运动。前两者通过声音，即听觉传递有声元素信息，后两者通过屏幕画面，即视觉传递视觉元素信息。语言和符号有着独特的象征意义：观看者与文本之间存在一种象征性交互。这种交互，通过一种动态关系超越并改变互动空间（Ibid：161）。"跨语际性"超出了"语言-身体"的界限："跨语际性"空间改变行为的同时，行为又反过来改变"跨语际性"空间。由于身体的"表述性"，使得行为和姿势本身就具有意义，进而创造性地生成具有象征意义的实践行为和沟通效果（Ibid：49）。以下两个例句将阐述"跨语际性"在象征性资源层面上的"表述"特征。

例（6）：

陈拾：这真嘞是药 偷偷尝一小口么事儿吧 恁苦 毁……身子麻了 动不了了 俺会死吗（第二集）

译文：Is it really medicine? I suppose it won't matter if I just take a sip. Too bitter!!!! WTF!!!! My body's numb. I can't move!!! Am I going to die?

在例（6）中，字幕文本与动态音效实现了有机结合，从视觉和听觉角度传递信息。本句台词出现时伴有明显的动态音效，且所有音效都紧跟人物的台词和动作。动画很巧妙地借用X光透视方法，向观众演示陈拾喝下的药流向大脑的过程：陈拾喝药时，有喝水的音效声；药在大脑中变成变大的猫头时，可以听到水的流动声、冒泡声和众多猫头之间相互挤压的摩擦声。动态音效可以归属于动画作品中的象征性资源，具有"表述"功能。上述音效是根据人物的台词和动作创作出来的，突破了"语言-身体"的界限，字幕文本与动态音效相互呼应，通过动态音效来表述"韵"，不仅能达到渲染台词的效果，还能提升观影的趣味性，创造"跨语际性"在象征性资源层面的整体性空间。

例（7）：

陈拾：俺的娘啊 亲爱的父老乡亲大爷大娘们 这只大猫 是俺的亲娘啊 （第八集）

译文：Dear MAMA! My dear neighbors, dear fellows! This big CAT! IS MY DEAR MAMA!

"跨语际性"是在特定场景偶发的，由情境和沟通模态的可视性生成并受之影响（Ibid：91），它主要强调的是动画作品在美学层面的意涵，即在动画翻译的动态情景中所"表达"出来的情感。这也就是"跨语际性"在动画翻译的象征性层面上"表述"出的意涵。在此例中，陈拾与少卿大人为寻找失踪的孙豹来到乌云神教。为保护少卿大人身份，陈拾谎称是去世的母亲附身到这只大白猫身上。伴随着悲情的背景音乐，陈拾虽然在说谎，但是双膝跪地，甚至把地跪出了裂纹，掩面痛哭的动作极易把观影群众带入剧中围观群众的视角，不由得信服了陈拾说的话，同时也打破了陈拾憨厚老实的人物设定，形成了性格反差。背景音乐，通常是指在影视剧中用于调节气氛和衬托背景的一种音乐。它通常插入人物对话，能通过不同旋律的推动和音乐形式的传达增强情感的表现力，让观众身临其境，从而更好地理解剧情（张娟，2021）。陈拾的行为和姿势具有其自身的"表述性"，使得剧情产生了幽默的效果。译文中出现的单词大写、陈拾的行为动作、悲情音效，构成了一个整体性空间，模态之间的聚合不仅让观影者代入剧中角色视角，笑点与泪点变得更加真挚，也极大地提升了动画作品的感染力。

"跨语际性"往往是一种不断更新的、流动中的形式。从动画《大理寺日志》的英译过程发现，这些语言变体在活生生的语言使用过程中，在动画作品的动作画面和动态音效的配合下，不断获得资源产生新的表述性。而这也正是"跨语际性"在象征性层面所具有的"表述"功能，使中文的视觉性通过再符号化进入一个不同的视觉秩序。借由批判性的表述，"跨语际性"总能在语言、模态和象征性资源中来回跨越和聚合，使得活生生的翻译词汇和翻译表达法不断消亡、演变和不断重生。

五、结 语

在《大理寺日志》的英译过程中，多种语言变体特征建构出了该作品独特的"身"、多模态聚合构成作品的"神"、动画跨越"语言-身体"的"韵"味更是一种艺术风格，是贯穿整部动画的统一特质。本文研究得出，动画作品《大理寺日志》的英译过程体现出"跨语际性"特征，即多语言的跨越方式、多模态的聚合路径以及象征性资源的表述过程。在动画的空间中创造性地形成了其"身体"的表述性。本文将社会语言学的"跨语际性"理论应用到国产动画作品英译的典型案例中，能够更好地了解当下流行的动画语言的特征，从而为"跨语际性"的理论分析提供有效的数据支撑。"跨语际性"能够从整体性上了解当下国产动画英译的特征和发展趋势，进而为国产动画外译成功"出海"提供理论依据和策略建议。在未来的研究中，建议对更多的国产动画作品进行数据分析，从而更加科学地验证"跨语际性"理论在动画形式中的适用性。

注释

① https://www.bilibili.com/，哔哩哔哩被网友们亲切地称为"B 站"，是一个 ACG（动画、漫画、游戏）内容创作与分享的视频网站，也是中国年青一代高度聚集的文化社区和视频平台。

② https://www.bilibili.com/bangumi/media/md28227527/?spm_id_from=666.25.b_6d656469615f6d6f64756c65.1，数据来源自 B 站《大理寺日志》网页播放端，该动画最终放映时间为 2020 年 7 月 3 日，各项数据统计时间为 2020 年 8 月 1 日。

参考文献

[1] Cu 的动画 Review. "White Cat legend is the perfect gateway into Donghua or Chinese animation"（大理寺日志.西方观众入坑国动的最佳选择）[EB/OL]. https://b23.tv/PLmh8I，2020-7-28.

[2] Baynham, Mike and Tong King Lee. "Translation and Translanguaging" [M]. New York and London: Routledge, 2019.

[3] Canagarajah, A. Suresh(ed). "Literacy as Translingual Practice: between Communities Classrooms" [C]. New York and London: Routledge, 2013.

[4] García, Ofelia and Wei Li. "Translanguage: Language, Bilingualism and Education" [M]. Bassingstoke: Palgrave Macmillan, 2014.

[5] Gottlieb，Henrik. Subtitling. In Mona Baker (ed.). Routledge Encyclopedia of Translation Studies (1st edition) [C]. London: Routledge，1998: 244-248.

[6] Hudson, R. A.（赫德森）. "*Sociolinguistics*"（社会语言学）[M]. Lu Deping(trans.),（卢德平译）. Beijing: Huaxia Publishing House(北京：华夏出版社), 1989: 27

[7] Wang, Jianhua & Zhou Ying & Zhang Jingming（王建华，周莹，张静茗）." A Scientometric Review of China's Audiovisual Translation in the Past Three Decades"（中国影视翻译研究三十年(1989-2018)——基于 CiteSpace 的可视化分析）[J]. *Shanghai Journal of Translators*（上海翻译），2019(2): 33-38.

[8] Yuan Menghui（袁孟辉）. "A study of the use and regulation of punctuation marks in television screens"（标点符号在电视荧屏中运用与规制的研究）[J]. *Intelligence*（才智），2014(14): 279-281.

[9] Zhang Juan（张娟）. "A Study on Cultural Discounts in Audiovisual Translation"（视听翻译传播通道中的文化折扣研究）[J]. *Shanghai Journal of Translators*（上海翻译），2021(04): 41-46.

作者简介

雷 静，博士，中央民族大学副教授，硕士生导师。研究方向：翻译理论与实践。电子邮箱：graceblack@126.com。
李明明，中央民族大学硕士研究生。研究方向：翻译理论与实践。电子邮箱：hayley1102@foxmail.com。

翻译目的论视角下《列女传》日译本对比研究

⊙ 杨梅竹 敬卓越（贵州大学外国语学院，贵阳）

[摘　要] 中国女训著作《列女传》在流传至日本后也成为影响深远的女性训诫用书。在目的论的指导下，发现由于北村季吟译本旨在阐发《列女传》作为教化用书对女性学习妇道伦理的作用，而塚本哲三译本旨在严谨地传播中华文化，因而在译文构成、修辞处理和文化负载词翻译三个方面存在较大差异；北村版简化了语言表达方式、对原文有一定删减、淡化了文化元素，而后者则重视解释隐含文化信息、在译文的基础上又增添了详尽译注，准确、复杂；由此可以窥视在不同的翻译目的之下创作出来的译本具有显著的差异特色，有各自的翻译价值。

[关键词]《列女传》；日译本；翻译目的论；对比

Contrastive Study of the Japanese Versions of
***The biographies of Chinese Women* Based on Skopos Theory**

YANG Meizhu JING Zhuoyue (School of Foreign Languages of Guizhou University, Guiyang)

Abstract: The Chinese book on woman discipline, *The Biographies of Chinese women*, also became an influential book of female discipline after its transmission to Japan. Guided by the skopos theory, it is found that Kitamura Jiin's version aims to explain the role of the book as the one for the education of women in female ethics, while Tsukamoto Tetsuzan's version aims to rigorously disseminate Chinese culture. So there are significant differences in three aspects of translation composition, rhetorics, and cultural-loaded words. Kitamura's version simplified the linguistic expressions, reduced the original text to a certain extent, and diluted the cultural elements, but Tsukamoto paid attention to explaining the implied cultural information and added detailed translation notes, which are accurate and complicated. Thus, it can be seen that the versions created under different translation purposes have significant differences and their own translation values.

Key words: *The Biographies of Chinese Women*; Japanese versions; skopos theory; contrast

一、引　言

《列女传》作为一部中国古代典籍著作，共记叙了110名妇女的故事，其故事中所蕴含的训诫道理大多

基金项目：本论文为贵州大学人才引进项目课题"明治维新以来日本学界阿伊努研究资料的翻译整理与研究"的阶段性成果，项目编号为：贵大人基合字(2020) 013号。

为儒家对妇女的看法，对禁锢中国妇女的思想存在客观的影响作用。《列女传》流传到邻国日本后，在不同时代经不同人手诞生了不少译本，在日本女训文学中所受关注颇高。关于翻译研究，传统翻译标准向来将原文的忠实传达作为译文的翻译标准，而翻译目的论则脱离将"对等"作为翻译标准的局限，注重从不同的翻译目的来探讨译文的价值所在（杨柳，2009），因此现已成为翻译研究中发挥重要作用的理论之一。目前，关于《列女传》日译本的研究多集中于对某一文本译者所采取的翻译方法和策略方面，鲜有从翻译目的论视角下对在不同时代背景、经不同译者创造出来的译本进行讨论。江户时期，国学家北村季吟译作了最早的日译本《假名列女传》。通晓汉学、和学的北村关注到《列女传》文章简短，内容上却极具故事性的特点，结合时代背景下假名文学的兴盛，全篇采用大量平假名译作了通俗易懂的译文，旨在通过浅显的文本让更多妇女在该译本中学习妇道伦理。1928 年，作为史书典籍重译本，塚本哲三编译的《古列女传 女四书》被收录进有朋堂出版的《汉文丛书》中，在译文的严谨性、忠实性各方面都达到很高的标准。笔者在对两个译本进行比较之后，注意到二者在文本呈现上存在较大差异。本文拟在翻译目的论的指导下从译文构成、修辞处理及文化负载词翻译三个方面对北村季吟译本和塚本哲三译本进行对比分析，探讨不同的翻译目的下译本所呈现的不同；有助于从新视角来发现两个《列女传》日译本的文学价值，对于补充《列女传》日译本的研究和中国典籍文学研究具有重要的研究意义。

二、翻译目的论与《列女传》概述

（一）翻译目的论

翻译目的论是功能派翻译理论的重要分支，最早由德国学者汉斯弗米尔在 20 世纪 70 年代末提出。目的论认为翻译这种行动中目的性是最关键的，即译文的翻译要求是重点（杨柳，2009）。因此译文是否达到了其预期的目的就成为判定译文成功与否的标准。随着翻译目的理论的发展，翻译界也逐渐摆脱了传统的将"对等"作为翻译标准的局限性，增加了译者的主体作用以及在翻译策略上的选择，对于从多个视角进行译文批判具有重要意义。文章从目的论视角对北村季吟版及塚本哲三版《列女传》日译本进行对比分析，探讨不同翻译目的下两个译本的特别之处，有助于从新视角来阐释两个《列女传》日译本的文学价值，以期能为《列女传》译文标准提供崭新思路。

（二）《列女传》流布

今广为流传的《列女传》内容上由西汉刘向所撰的《古列女传》和明朝解缙所撰《古今列女传》，以及收录在正史《后汉书》中的一部分故事组成（张天叶，2017：1）。西汉刘向所编撰的《列女传》，一共 7 卷，《古列女传》分为母仪、贤明、仁智、贞顺、节义、孽嬖 7 个部分，列叙了尧、舜的时代至战国末为止足以成为训诫模范的妇女轶事。原有 8 篇，但在六朝时原文本丢失，现行版本是清朝王照圆的补注本，又添加了班昭撰或项原撰的汉代妇女轶事集，共 8 卷本（山崎纯一，1991）。《古列女传》记载了孟母三迁等美谈，还记载了末喜、妲己等恶女亡国的故事，在后续发展中，违背道德的故事却被删减。公元 8、9 世纪，大概为日本平安时代，《列女传》传入日本，但并未得到广泛传播（王慧荣，2011：2），因为此时日本更为注重对女子的教育及才艺技能的培养，很少强调儒家的三从四德伦理。与《列女传》所传达的维护封建礼制、宣扬男尊女卑道德观的出发点是完全背道而驰的；加上当时汉文学习属于上流人士才有机会接触的高雅文化，也难以流布至寻常百姓间。但从 1192 年镰仓幕府成立，女性社会地位逐渐下降，《列女传》作为女子教化用书而得以重视，地位逐渐提高。进入江户时代后，1654 年，由朝鲜李氏等人合刻的《新续列女传》训读本刊行；之后《列女传》内容在不断得到完整充实的同时，也诞生了多个译本，甚至在日本还出现了不少以《列女传》为蓝本而创作的日本版"《列女传》"（山崎纯一，1991）。如这一时期，黑泽弘忠创作了《本朝列女传》，北村季吟译作了《假名列女传》等。多个译本的出现以及《列女传》在日本的本土再创作都是肯定其本身价值以及在日本受众广泛的证明。由此看来，《列女传》这一记载中国典范女性行为的史书在流布日本期间影响力逐渐扩大，深刻改变日本女性的教养教化以及行为规范的评判标准。

（三）中日学者对《列女传》日译本相关研究

《列女传》作为一本经典的史书典籍，对各时期的东方女训文学的影响有起有伏，对其关注的学者也不在少数。

从中国来看，笔者在知网上搜索相关研究时发现，《列女传》作为教训史书对女性地位的影响以及其文学价值总是中国学者的关注热点。比较具有代表性的有：陈志伟（2010）指出刘向所著之《列女传》对中国后世妇德著作产生了重要影响，将妇女思想牢牢禁锢，造成毒害。王慧荣（2011）在国内一众关注《列女传》文本影响的研究中，注意到其在海外日本的翻译和传播；她不仅梳理了《列女传》在日本的流布情况，以及随着时代发展，在江户时代，日本出现了很多《列女传》的汉文和刻本及日译本及许多仿作女训；并强调日本社会借用《列女传》来传达儒家三从四德的妇道伦理并以此训导女子，对规范女性行为和日本女性的生活产生了很大影响。楚永娟（2021）注意到《列女传》在日本的本土化，即近世时期出现的许多吸收借鉴《列女传》而诞生的女训书。但是关于《列女传》日译本文本的研究还有待进一步深入。

而日本学者在关注《列女传》的文学价值、文化内涵的同时，对于译本的研究较中国也更多。学者藤井佐弓（1987）总结了《列女传》对近世女训书创造的影响以及对近世女子教育的影响作用。同年，下见隆雄（1987）针对《列女传》中孼嬖篇译本的译注与解说部分展开研究分析，指出了不同译本之间存在的一些译注差异及进行了一定的原因分析。山崎纯一（1991）深刻探讨了《列女传》原著的历史价值及译本价值所在，并再次进行了《列女传》译本创作，对于《列女传》的日译本创作和传播做出了极大贡献。如今，日本学界虽不乏有关于文本内容的展开讨论和针对个别译本的研究，但大多数学者仍将目光聚集在《列女传》对女性的思想道德影响研究上。小山真子（2019）就在其研究中指出了刘向在《列女传》中所展现出的女性观对后世女性地位的影响。

如上所述，中日学者均对《列女传》有较高的关注，中国学者更为看重著作本身的文学价值，而日本学者对《列女传》的日译本的关注相对中国学者更高，但二者均没有对译本比较展开深入研究，也没有特别关注到在时代历程中做出教化贡献的北村译本和在史书典籍译作方面有很高价值的塚本译本。

在翻译目的论看来，翻译译文只要达到译者的翻译目的，即使没有做到完全的忠实原文，也称得上是凝聚作者心血的好译本。《列女传》中，刘向将"母仪卷"放到第一卷，母仪同比其余的贤明、仁智、贞顺、节义，是对妇女要求的最高准则，从女性个人、妻子以及母亲而至儿媳等几个方面都对女性行为具有要求（邹剑萍，2017）；基于翻译目的论此种打破常规观念的翻译理论，本文将从此角度关注到北村季吟版译本《假名列女传》和塚本哲三版译本《古列女传》的"母仪卷"，通过不同角度的对比分析，试图发现《假名列女传》和《古列女传》两个译本在不同翻译目的下呈现出来的译本特点，以便更好地研究译本的价值。

三、《列女传》两个日译本的对比分析

（一）译本简介

在江户时期由北村季吟译作的《假名列女传》于明治 33 年被收录在《东亚女训丛书》中，同其余的女训书目一起在当时的市面上广受好评（北村季吟，1821）。在《假名列女传》的解说部分，北村本人曾指出其翻译《列女传》的必要性，即他的翻译目的在于通过简易的假名让女流之辈能够得其中大意，用其蕴含的妇道标准约束自身（北村季吟，1821）。北村译本分为解说、目录及正文三个部分。解说部分详尽介绍了《列女传》创作者（刘向）、创作时间以及缘由和文本内容，因涉及大量名词所以解说部分汉字占比较大。目录上直接使用原文中的篇名并进行假名注音。正文部分总体分为 8 卷，即母仪、贤明、仁智、贞顺、节义、孽嬖 7 卷加 1 续篇。全文少有汉字，多用假名书写，并且所有出现的汉字都有假名注音，不另添加注解。值得一提的是，在译本中保留了原书插图。

1928 年，有朋堂将系列具有影响力的汉文史书进行再次编译之后出版了《汉文丛书》；塚本哲三译编的《古列女传 女四书》被收录其中（塚本哲三，1928）。从经典史书再译立场来看，文本应当尽力忠实原文，传达文本中的异文化符号，译文的表达也更为严谨、精准。塚本是基于今流传于日本的《列女传》补全版来进行重译（女子之友记者，1901：5）。译本由《列女传》原文序、例言、目录、解说及译文 4 个部分组成。在原文序言部分，北村为原文本标注训读点，并未对汉字再另作假名注音；例言处简言说明该译本所选用的原文版本，目录处则对章节名称进行了简要翻译处理，但无假名注音。解说部分对该书由来、内容（如所见妇德）等（日文）进行说明；正文可分为古列女传（母仪、贤明、仁智、贞顺、节义、孽嬖 7 卷加 1 续篇）8 卷、新续列女传（上中下卷）、女诫（上下卷）、女论语、内训、女范捷录等部分。

由上可知，两个译本在翻译之初所持有的目的便是不同的。注重译者在翻译过程中的主体性发挥和策略选择，是翻译目的论有意打破传统的"对等"标准之局限的体现。本节将从译本的构成、修辞的处理和文化负载词的翻译三个方面对两个日译本进行对比，进而分析其在译者主体性得到发挥之后而呈现出的译本特点。

（二）文本的构成

西汉时期，成帝后宫淫乱，刘向忧心于此便编撰《列女传》以期能够规劝皇帝、嫔妃及外戚。全书记载了一百多个关于妇女品行的故事，后代多有增补。现存全书分 8 卷，由古汉文撰写，篇幅短小，每篇故事后附有精美插图。原文文本的构成独具特色，本节主要关注在不同的翻译目的下两个译本在文本构成上所展现的不同。

例 1：

原文：有虞二妃者，帝尧之二女也。长娥皇，次女英。

北村译：有虞の二妃は帝堯のひめみこたちなり。長ぎみを娥皇といひ、次ぎみを女英といへり。

塚本译：有虞の二妃は帝堯の二女なり。長は娥皇、次は女英。

凡原文本里登场的妇女，刘向都一一对其作了简要介绍。如在母仪卷"有虞二妃"中的一开始，便是对舜的两个妃子的介绍。对比原文本，本村译本在格式上有所变化。他将原句"長は娥皇、次は女英"，处理为"長ぎみを娥皇といひ、次ぎみを女英といへり"，句子长且假名多，更符合日语表达习惯而又简单易懂；而塚本译本则在文本格式上尽量还原原文本的对仗形式，将其处理为"長は娥皇、次は女英"，行文清晰明了。

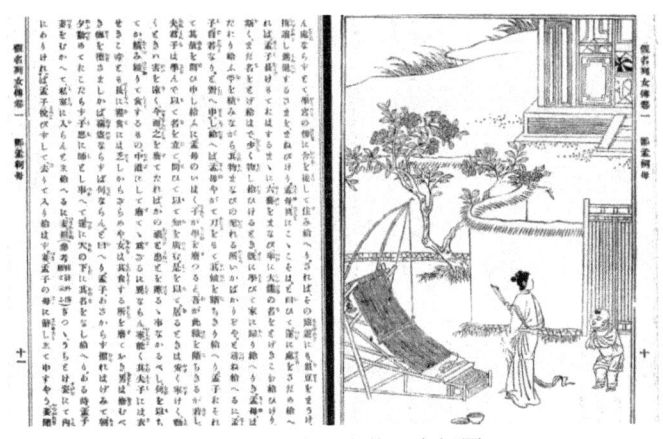

图 1. 《假名列女传》中插图

（来源：北村季吟《假名列女传》1900 年）

例 2：

原文：君子谓涂山强于教诲。诗云："厘尔士女，从以孙子。"此之谓也。颂曰：启母涂山，维配帝禹，辛壬癸甲，禹往敷土，启呱呱泣，母独论序，教训以善，卒继其父。

本村译：かの母塗山の教誨いみじく疆め給へるによりてなり。

塚本译：君子謂ふ、塗山、教誨に疆めたり。詩に云く、爾に士女を釐へて、從ふるに孫子を以てす、とは此の謂なり。頌に曰く、啓が母塗山、維れ帝禹に配す。辛壬癸甲、禹往いて土を敷つ。啓呱呱として泣く。母<u>獨り</u>序を論じて、教訓するに善を以てし、卒其の父に繼ぐ。（划线部分为另附有译注）

在《列女传》原书中，在每个故事结尾处，都伴有相应的颂词赞扬该妇女的品行。参考原书发现，北村季吟版译本将原文中表彰功绩或表达祝愿的讲话或颂词进行大量删减；如上列举的在"启母涂山"一文中"颂曰……卒继其父"部分被全部删去，使得文本篇幅上也发生一定改变。但塚本译本仍然多使用汉字，并对其进行假名注音，在此基础上又对其中个别用词另加注解；另外，译文尽量对照原文断句格式，采用古文法体表达；虽尽力还原其对仗格式，但相比原文，气势在一定程度上减弱。在文本构成上独具自我风格。

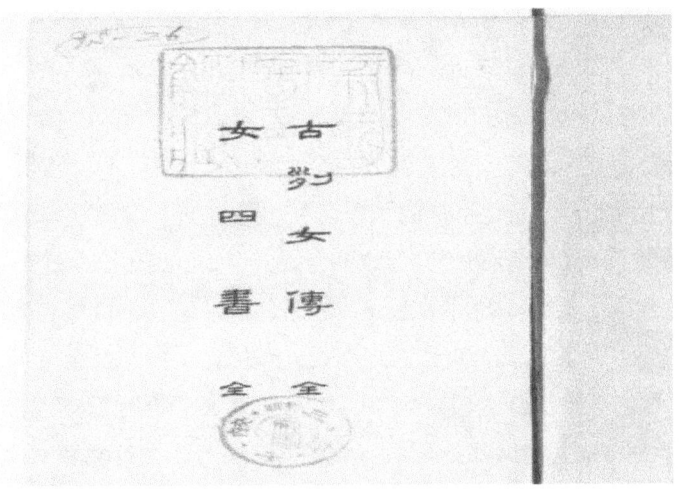

图 2. 《古列女传》封面

（来源：塚本哲三《古列女传》1928 年）

在对译本的构成上进行比较之后发现，北村不拘泥于原文本格式，主要使用假名表述，且省译大量原文本，使文本信息得到清晰、简洁的传达；同时又保留了原书插图，即趣味性，如图1。在文本构成上更加地展现出本土化特色。体现了译者的翻译意图在于方便妇女学习妇道伦理，更好发挥该著作的训诫作用，而不是为了将原文本完整呈现。

而塚本哲三注重原文内容的精彩呈现、文化内涵的精准传达，因此译文尽量还原原文格式（图2），采用古文法体表达，多汉字，汉字部分有假名注音，并附详尽注解。从正文内容翻译、编撰之详尽、严谨来看，塚本哲三收到的"翻译任务"（或翻译意图）是在于将该著作所具有的历史价值显现，而不关注其内容是否适合普罗大众阅读。因此它也更加客观地将《列女传》作为典籍藏书的历史厚重感呈现在日本人民的面前。由此看来，在翻译目的不同的情况下，译文的构成也会有所不同。

（三）修辞的处理

为了刻画恪守妇道的女性正面形象，《列女传》原著中有大量关于女性品性道德、行为举止的修辞表达。本节关注到北村季吟版译本和塚本哲三译本的"母仪卷"中关于此类品性道德的修辞形容的处理特点，并进行举例分析。

例1：

原文：女为卫庄公夫人，号曰庄姜。姜交好。始往，操行衰惰，有冶容之行，淫泆之心。傅母见其妇道不正，谕之云："子之家，世世尊荣，当为民法则。子之质，聪达于事，当为人表式。仪貌壮丽，不可不自修整。"（出自母仪篇"齐女傅母"）

北村译：傅母は齊女の傅の母なり齊女とは衛莊公の夫人莊姜をいへり。莊姜かほ容あてになまめかしく、心ばせほこりかに操行みだりに惰れるかたなんありける。衛にゆきしはじめ、傅母其婦道の正なきを見て、これを諭すに詩つくりて曰く、碩人其欣衣錦綢衣，齊侯之子衛侯之妻東宮之梅邢侯之姨、譚公維私。砥礪女之心以高節以爲人君之子弟、為國君之夫人、尤不可有邪辟之行焉。

塚本译：傅母は齊女の傅母なり。女は衛の莊公の夫人と為り、號して莊姜と曰ふ。姜狡好なり。始め往くきに、操行衰惰にして、心淫泆、冶容あり。傅母其婦道正しからざるを見て、之を論して云く、子の家は世世尊榮なり、當に民の法則と為るべし。子の質は事に聰達なり、當に人の表式と為るべし。儀貌壯麗なり、自ら修整せずんばあるべからず。錦を衣て綱裳す、飾輿に馬在り。是れ德を貴ばざるなり。（划线部分为另附有译注）

此处原文对于齐女的品行用了"交好""操行衰惰""冶容之行""淫泆之心""妇道不正"等词形容，而傅母对其教诲中有"尊荣""聪达于事""为人表式""仪貌壮丽，不可不自修整"等修辞。其修辞用词之简练生动，数语便刻画出齐女为人妻而品行不佳的形象，又将傅母的教诲得到言简意赅又发人深省的传递。北村季吟将上述修辞处理为："莊姜かほ容あてになまめかしく""心ばせほこりかに操行みだりに惰れるかたなんありける""婦道の正なき"采用了简洁的意译，通俗易懂，但又不可避免地造成在修辞上的美感缺失。而对傅母的教诲之言则直接处理为："碩人其欣衣錦綢衣，齊侯之子衛侯之妻東宮之梅邢侯之姨、譚公維私。砥礪女之心以高節以爲人君之子弟、為國君之夫人、尤不可有邪辟之行焉。"与原文相去甚远，但是基本保留了其教诲之意。塚本哲三则将上述修辞处理为："狡好なり"、"操行衰惰にして""心淫泆、冶容あり""婦道正しからざる""尊榮なり""事に聰達""人の表式と為るべし""儀貌壯麗なり、自ら修整せずんばあるべからず"基本保留原文修辞用语，附加译注。严谨、恰当的注解精确地传递出词语所承载的修辞内涵，

也便于进一步理解中华文化。但同时，译注过多也不利于通读全文和理解全文大意。

例2：

原文：尽力竭能，忠信不欺，务在效忠，必死奉命，廉洁公正，故遂而无患。（出自母仪篇"齐田稷母"）

北村译：力を盡し能を竭し、忠信にして欺かず。務めて忠をなし、必死して命を奉り、すなほに潔く、私なく、邪ならず。かるが故に遂げて患なし。

塚本译：力を盡し能を竭し、忠信にして欺かず、務は忠を效すに在りとし、必死に命を奉し、廉潔にして公正なる、故に遂げて患ふるとこなし。（划线部分为另附有译注）

例2中，对于"尽力竭能，忠信不欺，务在效忠，必死奉命"一句的翻译，两个版本采取基本相同的处理方式，无明显差异。而对于"廉洁""公正"二词，北村采取意译，译为："すなほに潔く""私なく、邪ならず"基本传达出原文意思，但稍微削弱了其所蕴含的清白高洁、公正不阿的深意；而塚本在译本中直接呈现"廉潔""公正"二词，之后将其注解为："正直にして潔白""私心なく私曲なきこと"忠实地传达出原文基本思想以及"廉洁""公正"二字的文化内涵。

以上，在修辞的处理方面，两个译本也存在差异。北村旨在将原文大意简洁明了地传达，并未将修辞的深意看作翻译重点，为了妇女的学习便利多采用简单的意译，对原文翻译进行了一定删减，并进行译文再创作。而塚本则站在尽量保留原文本所传达的意义的立场上对译本进行翻译；比起北村版理解难度虽然更大，但从史书典籍翻译这一角度考虑，其价值也更高。

（四）文化负载词的翻译

文化负载词，反映了一国文化的独特魅力，具有地域性和民族性（刘镯梦，2022：7）。本节统计了北村版译本和塚本版译本中"母仪卷"部分所有文化负载词的翻译处理，并进行对比分析（见表1）。

表1. 文化负载词翻译对比

序号	原文	北村版	塚本版
1	厥内（出自有虞二妃）	そのうち	そのうち
2	畎亩（出自有虞二妃）	秋の田の假庵	畎畝（注：圃園）
3	涂廪（出自有虞二妃）	くらを塗らせ	くらを塗らせ
4	百揆（出自有虞二妃）		百揆（注：百官を統管するの地位に置くこと）
5	卜筮禋祀（出自弃母姜嫄）	或は卜筮をなし、或は禋祀などして	占ひを立て、まつりをすること
6	稷官（出自弃母姜嫄）	しょくかん	しょくかん（注：農業を司る官）
7	玄鸟（出自弃母姜嫄）	怪しき鳥	くろきとり
8	司徒（出自弃母姜嫄）	司徒のつかさ	調教を用る官名
9	九嫔（出自汤妃有㜪）	きょうひん	女官
10	后宫（出自汤妃有㜪）	さむらひ給ひし	後宮（注：妃の住む宮殿）
11	文王治外，文母治内（出自周室三母）	陽道；陰道	陽道；陰道
12	穷闾隘巷（出自卫姑定姜）	にへをとりまかなひて、よもぎふの宿をとひ、むぐらの門にむとづれ	きゅうりょあいこう

13	黄耄倪齿（出自卫姑定姜）	かしらのゆきのふりにけるひとびと	くわうほうけいし（注：高齢の人々と云ふ、倪齒は舊齒の固か、老人の齒脱落して更に生まえたる）
14	刍豢黍梁（出自楚子发母）	さかな、物きこしめす由	芻豢黍粱
15	贾人（出自邹孟轲母）	商人	買人（注：あきんどのうりつける業）
16	俎豆（出自邹孟轲母）	そどう	俎豆（注：祭祀の禮に用ふるつくえ、もりものの器）揖譲進退（いつじょうしんたい、；行禮作法）
17	酣醲醉飽（出自鲁之母师）	たゆみつつ、うひみだれ	酣醲醉飽（注：子や嫁たちの寄集りてさかもりしたのしく十分に飲食するであらうとの意）

"卜筮禋祀"（表1序号5）为占卜祭祀之意。

北村版："或は卜筮をなし、或は禋祀などして、"

塚本版："卜筮禋祀"，附注："占ひを立て、まつりをすること。"

北村将原本的"卜筮禋祀"进行动词化处理；而塚本则又根据本土文化，将其理解为占卜和祭祀两种行为，较完整地译出其真实含义。

在"契母简狄"一篇中，"司徒"（表1序号8）一词是我国古代的一个重要官职名，文中说舜摄命契为司徒，管教化人民。

北村版："司徒のつかさ"

塚本版："調教を用る官名"

塚本版在注解中解释司徒是一个训教的官职，对其内涵稍作解释；但北村忽视了对词语的意义处理，直接使用原文。这样看，不论哪个译本都只是在对"司徒"一词进行简要处理，并未表达出这一官职的重要意义。

另在"汤妃有㜪"一篇中，刘向赞扬汤妃"统领九嫔，后宫有序"；后宫为宫廷中帝王妃嫔们所居住之地。其中对于"后宫"一词，

北村译为："あまた侍ひ給ひし中に"

塚本译为："後宮（注：妃の住む宮殿）"

北村几乎没能表达后宫一词所具备的文化深意；"妃の住む宮殿"基本译出原词含义。

由此看来，相比塚本译本，北村译本并未太过拘泥于文化负载词的精准翻译上；他或是不译，或是简言传达其基本大意，在内涵深度的传达方面虽有所欠缺，但这也很好地体现北村的翻译目的在于最大程度发挥文本的妇德教化作用。另在塚本译本中，译文常以原文原词的形式出现，尽量保持其原本简洁的风格，但对

于文化负载词基本都采取附加译注的方式处理，较为忠实地传达出原文基本思想及词语背后的文化深度，尽其翻译职守。

四、结 语

综上所述，翻译目的的不同使得北村季吟的《假名列女传》与塚本哲三的《古列女传 女四书》不论是在译文构成、修辞的处理还是文化负载词的翻译上都呈现出很大不同。译文构成上来看，北村译本几乎全部用假名书写，并且所有出现的汉字都有假名注音；相对原著存在大量的文本删减，把握住译本在易读程度上的优势。塚本也将原文信息完好传达的翻译任务完满完成，译文尽量保留了原作简洁的书写句式，译文无删减现象。修辞的处理上，为了让妇女更好地读懂译本内容，《假名列女传》尽量采取了简单明了的意译，删减了部分较难理解的内容，又或是根据自己对原文的理解进行译文再创作。而为了保留原文本的原汁原味，《古列女传 女四书》则尽量保留原文本的修辞内涵；虽比起北村版难度更大，但文化内涵更高，作为史书典籍译本的价值也更高。此外，在文化负载词的翻译上也体现出了二者翻译目的上的差异。强调文本训诫作用的《假名列女传》对于文化负载词的处理不是其关注重点；译者或是不译，或是简译，没有很好地关照到其内涵深意的传达。《古列女传 女四书》尽量保持其原本简洁的风格，对文化负载词基本采取附加译注的方式处理，使得词语所负载的文化力量得到一定传达。

北村版开创了《列女传》汉文日译的先河，促进了"三从四德"的妇道伦理在日本对其女性地位与教化方面产生进一步的影响，也推动了《列女传》在日本的传播。而塚本哲三版更为客观且严谨地将《列女传》作为典籍呈现在日本人民的面前，其在译本中的价值也是不容置疑的。一者重视女性教化和追求通俗易懂；一者重视文化传递，追求还原原本。从目的论来看，他们都达到了自己预期的翻译目的，使用不同的翻译方法从原文中提取出了不同的信息，使译者主体性得到极大发挥；并根据现实的时代背景，结合译语文化、目标读者的需求，呈现出了不同的优秀译本。

参考文献

[1] Chen, Zhiwei & Gao, Wenjun (陈志伟，高文俊). "Liu Xiang's *Biography of The Women*: the foundation work of feudal women's morality" (刘向《列女传》——封建妇德奠基之作) [J]. *Research on Library Science* (图书馆学研究), 2010(14): 93-95.

[2] Chu, Yongjuan (楚永娟). "The influence of *The Legend of Women* on moral instruction for women in early modern Japan" (《列女传》对日本近世女训的影响) [J]. *Journal of Xinyu University* (新余学院学报), 2021(01): 57-62.

[3] Fujii, Sayumi (藤井佐弓). "The Influence of *Biography of The Women* in Later Han Dynasty on Modern Women's Training Books: Taking *Biography of Lienv* in Xingrang Pavilion as a Clue" (近世女訓書における後漢書列女伝の影響：興讓館列女伝を手がかりとして) [J]. *Proceedings of the Congress of Japan Conservation Society* (日本保育学会大会研究論文集), 1987: 40.

[4] Kitamura, Jiin (北村季吟). "Kana version of *Lienv biography*" (仮名列女伝) [M]. *Tokyo: Toyo Corp* (東京: 東洋社), 1821.

[5] Koyama, Masako (小山眞子). "On Women in Liu Xiang's *Biography of Women* : Around the Role of Wife" (劉向『列女伝』における女性について：妻としての役割を中心に) [J]. *Mandarin Studies at Okayama University* (岡山大学国語研究), 2019(33): 41-55.

[6] Liu, Zhuomeng (刘镯梦). "A Study of Translation Strategies of Culture-loaded Words in Barnstone's English Translation of Mao Zedong's Poetry" (巴恩斯通英译毛泽东诗词中文化负载词的翻译策略研究) [J]. *Jingu Creative Literature* (今古文创), 2022(07): 117-119.

[7] Shitami, Takao (下見隆雄). "Annotation and Explanation of *Biography of Lienv*-3-" (「列女伝」注釈及び解説-3-) [J]. *Summary of Literature Department of Hiroshima University* (広島大学文学部紀要), 1987(01): 1-144.

[8] Tsukamoto, Tetsuzan (塚本哲三). "*Biography of Lienv & Four Books for Women*" (古列女伝 女四書) [M]. *Tokyo: Aritomo Corp* (東京: 有朋堂), 1928.

[9] The Reporter of Friends of the Women (女子之友記者). "The second part of Toyo Women Training Series: *Kana Women Biography*" (《东洋女训丛书》第二编《假名列女传·解题》) [J]. *Toyo crop* (东洋社): 1901: 5.

[10] Wang, Huirong (王慧荣). "The biography of Lienv in Japan and its influence" (《列女传》在日本的流布及其影响) [J]. *Tianjin Social Science* (天津社会科学), 2011(02): 143-144.

[11] Yang, Liu (杨柳). "The Reception History of the 20th Century Western Translation Theories in China" (20世纪西方翻译理论在中国的接受史) [M]. *Shanghai: Shanghai Foreign Language Education Press* (上海：上海外语教育出版社), 2009.

[12] Yamazaki, Junichi (山崎純一). "*Biography of Women*: Women Who Changed History" (列女伝：歴史を変えた女たち) [M]. *May study* (五月書房), 1991.

[13] Zhang, Tianye (张天叶). "The Research On Liu Xiang's *Lienvzhuan* from the Perspective of the Western Han Dynasty Culture" (西汉文化视域下的刘向《列女传》研究) [D]. *Heibei University* (河北大学), 2017(01).

[14] Zou, Jianping (邹剑萍). "To Interpret Liu Xiang's *Biography of Lienv* from the Standpiont of Feminism" (从女性主义角度看刘向《列女传》) [D]. *Fujian Normal University* (福建师范大学), 2007.

作者简介

杨梅竹，贵州大学外国语学院讲师，日本山口大学博士。研究方向：中日比较文学。电子邮箱：mzyang3@gzu.edu.cn。

敬卓越，贵州大学外国语学院21级日语语言文学硕士研究生。研究方向：日语语言文学。电子邮箱：584363277@qq.com。

基于语料库的立法文本模糊语英译策略研究

⊙ 黄宇柱（中国政法大学外国语学院，北京）

[摘　要] 法律语言的模糊性是立法文本的显著特点，致使立法文本模糊语翻译成为法律翻译译者必须面对的翻译现实。国内外有关立法语言模糊语翻译的研究比较少，也仅停留在定性分析层面，鲜有定量分析和定性分析结合的探讨。因此，本文引入语料库分析方法，基于自建立法文本汉英平行语料库，重点探讨了以下三个问题：（1）立法文本模糊语英译时主要采用哪些翻译策略？（2）对于不同类型的立法文本模糊语，是否采用不同的翻译策略？（3）该种翻译策略是否存在不足，以及改进建议？研究发现：立法文本模糊语英译策略主要有三种：直译、增译和正说反译。其中，增译策略在立法文本模糊语英译时有可行性，而直译和正说反译的翻译策略无法解决立法文本模糊语英译时存在的模糊概念和模糊蕴含的问题。因此，本研究参考法律条文中模糊语确切化的方法，将立法文本模糊语英译策略总结为模糊对模糊策略、随文注释策略、法律解释策略和语境解释策略，以期拓宽模糊语翻译研究的视野，为立法文本模糊语英译研究提供一种新的途径。

[关键词] 立法文本模糊语；模糊语翻译；语料库；翻译策略

A Corpus-based Study on Fuzzy Language Translation in Legislative Texts

HUANG Yuzhu (China University of Political Science and Law, Beijing)

Abstract: The fuzziness of legal language is a prominent feature of legislative texts, which becomes a reality that translators must face when translating legislative texts. There are relatively a few researches on the translation of fuzzy language in legislative texts at home and abroad in a qualitative methodology. However, few research on the translation of fuzzy language in legislative texts can be found in a quantitative and qualitative way. Therefore, a corpus-based method will be taken in the research. Based on self-built Chinese-English Parallel Corpus of Legislative Text, this research focuses on the following three questions: (1) What translation strategies are mainly used in translating fuzzy language in legislative texts into English? (2) Are different translation strategies adopted for different types of fuzzy language in legislative texts? (3) Are there any shortcomings in this translation strategy and suggestions for improvement? The study demonstrates that there are three main strategies: literal translation, amplification and negation. Among them, the strategy of amplification is feasible, while the translation strategies of literal translation and negation can't solve the problems of vague concepts and vague connotations in translating

---

本文系教育部产学合作协同育人项目"人机翻译交互模式下法庭口译实践课程建设"（项目编号 202002278001）和中国政法大学 MTI 翻译硕士研究生教育教学改革项目"以翻译技术为导向的法律专题口译教学方案探讨"的阶段性成果。

fuzzy language in legislative texts. Therefore, this research refers to the methods of defining fuzzy language in legal provisions, and summarizes the strategies of translating fuzzy language into English in legislative texts as fuzzy-to-fuzzy strategy, annotation strategy, legal interpretation strategy and contextual interpretation strategy in order to provide a new way for the study of the fuzzy language translation in legislative text.

Key words: fuzzy language in legislative texts; fuzzy language translation; corpus; translation strategy

一、引 言

模糊语言学起源于1965年加利福尼亚大学札德教授提出的模糊集理论。该理论的提出，逐渐推动其他学科的发展。20世纪发展为语言学的分支学科，成了语言学的一个重要术语。语言具有模糊性，作为语言的一个分支的法律语言，也存在一个认知和信息解码的问题，其模糊性同样有其存在的合理性（聂玉景、王国新，2010：6）。法律语言存在着模糊性，从立法阶段开始，法律语言的模糊性就是难以消除的现象，模糊性贯穿于法律活动的整个过程（卢秋帆，2010:20）。田力男（2016）曾对《中华人民共和国刑法》模糊语进行统计，其模糊语高频词一共出现3786次。由此可见，大量使用模糊语是立法文本的显著特点。立法文本大量使用模糊语也致使模糊语翻译成为法律翻译译者必须面对的翻译现实。然而，国内对法律模糊语翻译研究较少，也仅停留在定性分析层面，研究方法单一，鲜有通过语料库的方法来探讨立法文本模糊语英译策略研究。语料库语言学的平行语料库构建和平行语料库检索工具的开发与应用，为英汉/汉英翻译研究提供了选择，拓宽了研究路径（徐珺、自正权，2018:14）。因此，本文将语料库的研究方法引入立法文本模糊语英译策略研究，结合自建立法文本汉英平行语料库，对中文立法文本模糊语英译进行定量的统计和定性的分析，以期为立法文本模糊语翻译研究提供一个新的研究视角。

二、相关研究述评

（一）模糊语翻译

国内对模糊语翻译研究成果较少。通过知网（CNKI）以模糊语翻译为主题词进行检索，时间不限，期刊来源类别为北大核心和CSSCI，共计15篇文章。总体趋势分布图如图1所示。从时间上看，国内对模糊语翻译研究出现两个峰值，即2011年和2021年。平均发文两篇。但总体上来看，国内对模糊语翻译研究关注度不够，发文量不足，未形成研究热点。

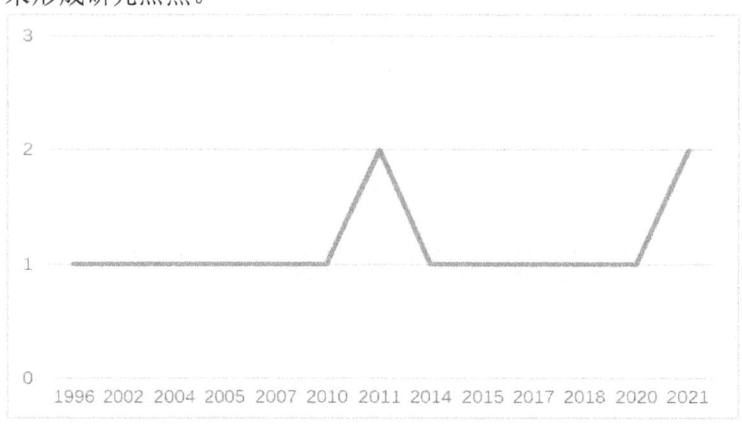

图1. 国内模糊语翻译研究总体趋势分布图

从文献统计来看，国内学者很早就关注到了语言模糊性的特点并提出了相应的翻译方法。在模糊语翻译方法方面，文旭（1996）分析了英汉语词的模糊性以及模糊语义的翻译方法，比如对等译法、变异译法和省略法等；王心洁（2005）提出模糊语的翻译需要考虑具体语境和不同民族的思维方式；在模糊语翻译研究对象方面，既有传统的文学文本模糊语翻译研究，比如唐诗、《红楼梦》（陈洁，2007；翟秋兰、阮红梅，2008），也有非文学文本中模糊语翻译研究，比如科技文本、医学文本和广告文本等（程同春，2002；张梅，2004；谭重一、姚欣，2018；关家玲、郑伟，2010）。在理论方面，学者运用功能翻译观、结构主义翻译观和翻译适应选择论研究模糊语翻译（于建平，2007；翟秋兰、阮红梅，2008；谭重一、姚欣，2018）；在模糊语翻译研究方法方面，既有定性研究方法，又有定量研究方法，尤其是2011年后，有学者通过语料库的研究方法研究模糊语翻译（赵秋荣、董元兴、刘惠华，2011；吴光亭、张涛，2020；潘峰、盛丹丹，2021）。但是，从已有文献来看，学界对立法文本模糊语翻译的研究鲜见。

（二）法律模糊语翻译

本章法律模糊语翻译是指法律语篇中的模糊语的语际翻译。本研究内容是讨论法律文本中立法文本模糊语翻译策略。从知网检索，有关法律模糊语翻译的期刊论文共计9篇，总体趋势分布图如图2所示。由图2可知，国内法律模糊语翻译研究发文数量总体起伏不大，发展缓慢。有学者是从功能对等理论、法的自创生理论以及修辞学视角下分析我国法律模糊语翻译（陈保如，2018；李晋、居方，2018；杜广才，2014）；有的学者是结合法律模糊语以及立法模糊语的一些实例分析法律模糊语的翻译方法，比如增词译法、减词译法、模糊语直译法以及模糊语精确译法等（马志民、顾维忱，2011；余菁、闫舒瑶，2008）。

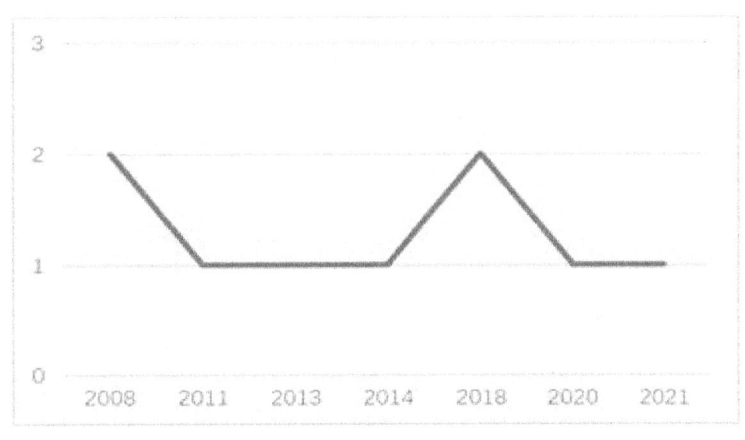

图2. 国内法律模糊语翻译研究总体趋势分布图

从以上文献综述可以看出，学界对模糊语翻译涉及科技文本、医学文本和广告文本，但研究对象较少涉及法律语篇，而且鲜有对立法文本中模糊语翻译问题进行研究，对立法文本模糊语翻译的研究成果在数量和质量上都远远不够。在研究方法上，有关法律文本模糊语翻译研究的文献只是针对一些例子进行分析，没有对某一类法律文本进行定量的梳理，缺少相应的实证研究。鉴于此，本文通过自建立法文本汉英平行语料库，运用语料库研究方法对中文立法文本中的模糊语英译进行定量统计，结合具体事例进行定性分析，以期拓宽模糊语翻译研究的研究对象，同时为立法文本模糊语的翻译研究提供一种新的途径。

三、研究设计

（一）研究目的和研究问题

鉴于立法文本模糊语的翻译研究成果较少，且研究方法单一，缺少实证研究，笔者根据自建立法文本汉英平行语料库，定量统计中文立法文本模糊语中的模糊附加词、模糊概念和模糊蕴含及其英语翻译，结合实例进行定性的分析和讨论，归纳出中文立法文本模糊语英译的主要翻译策略以及存在缺陷并提出修改建议，以期填补国内学界对立法文本模糊语翻译实证研究的不足。

本研究主要回答下列三个问题：1.译者在进行立法文本模糊语英译时主要采用哪些翻译策略？2.对于不同类型的立法文本模糊语，译者是否采用不同的翻译策略翻译？3.该种翻译策略是否存在不足，以及改进建议？

（二）语料来源和研究工具

1.语料来源：本研究语料主要选取《中华人民共和国民法典》总则编、《中华人民共和国刑法》（2020修正）、《中华人民共和国民事诉讼法》（2017修正）和《中华人民共和国刑事诉讼法》（2018修正）四种立法文本以及该四种立法文本的英译本（北大法宝版）。

2.研究工具：1.语料对齐工具"Tmxmall"；2.语料库检索工具"CUC_ParaconcV0.3"，该款软件由中国传媒大学研制。

（三）立法文本汉英平行语料库建设

本研究自建一个由中文立法文本及其对应的英文译本构成的立法文本汉英平行语料库（Chinese-English Parallel Corpus of Legislative Text，简称CEPCLT）。该语料库包含两个子语料库，即中文立法文本语料库（Chinese Corpus of Legislative Text，简称CCLT）和立法文本英译语料库（English Translated Corpus of Legislative Text，简称ETCLT）。语料库具体信息如表1所示。

表1. 立法文本汉英平行语料库（CEPCLT）

	《中华人民共和国民法典》总则编	《中华人民共和国刑法》（2020修正）	《中华人民共和国民事诉讼法》（2017修正）	《中华人民共和国刑事诉讼法》（2018修正）	总计
CCLT	15 828	77 399	2 9454	3 7601	16 0282
ETCLT	11 536	55 305	2 2489	2 7265	11 6595
文本数	2	2	2	2	8

（四）研究步骤

本研究步骤分为以下四步：

1.根据研究目的需要，自建立法文本汉英平行语料库，使用CUC_ParaconcV0.3工具对立法文本汉英平行语料库模糊语进行统计。

2.根据查奈尔模糊语言的理论，将立法文本模糊语分为三类，即模糊附加词、模糊概念和模糊蕴含（查奈尔，2000：18）。董晓波（2016：74-75）将模糊附加词、模糊概念和模糊蕴含定义如下：模糊附加词是指附加于意义明确的概念之前或之后，用来表示范畴成员的不同隶属度，相关词语有"以上""以下""以内""以外""不满""轻微""严重""特""极"等；模糊概念是法律概念的内涵不确定，分为内涵不确定，外延封闭；内涵不确定，外延开放，相关词语有"当事人""诉讼参与人"等；模糊蕴含指法律概念看似清晰，实际上蕴含某些不言自明的信息，相关词语有"从重处罚"等。本文立法文本模糊语是基于查奈尔和董晓波对立法语言的研究整理而成，如表2所示。

表2. 中文立法文本模糊语[①]

立法文本模糊语	模糊语关键词		
模糊附加词	数量范围模糊（以上、以下、以内、以外……）	程度模糊（不满、轻微、严重……）	概括模糊（其他等）
模糊概念	当事人、公序良俗、诉讼参与人……		
模糊蕴含	重大过失、从重处罚……		

3. 使用CUC_ParaconcV0.3检索软件对中文立法文本模糊语关键词进行检索和统计，如表3所示。

表3. 立法文本汉英平行语料库（CEPCLT）模糊语统计

立法文本模糊语类别	关键词	频次	总计
模糊附加词	以上、以下、以内	1103	2778
	不满、轻微、严重	510	
	其他等	796	
模糊概念	当事人、公序良俗、诉讼参与人	325	
模糊蕴含	重大过失、从重处罚	44	

4. 对检索的中文立法文本英译语句进行分析，总结出中文立法文本英译常用的翻译策略。

（五）翻译策略的界定

对翻译策略的研究，国内外均会将其与翻译方法、翻译技巧相混淆，常出现使用混乱的问题（熊兵，2014）。熊兵（2014）专门论述和区别了翻译策略、翻译方法和翻译技巧的不同。基于熊兵的论述，绘制翻译策略、翻译方法和翻译技巧关系图，如图3所示。

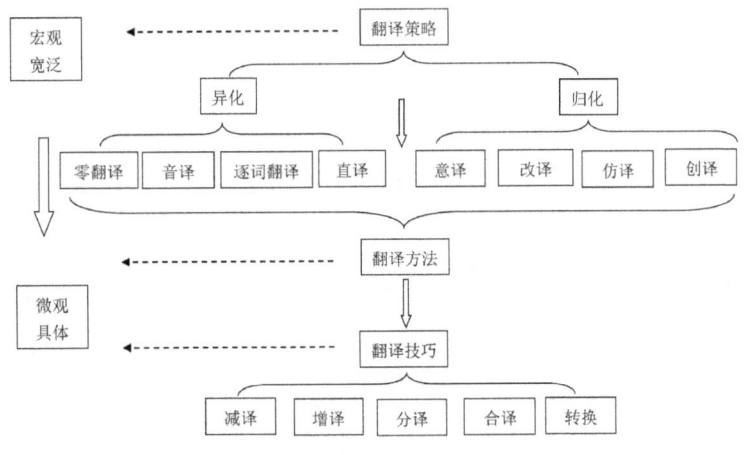

图3. 翻译策略、翻译方法和翻译技巧关系图

由图3可知，翻译策略包括异化和归化，翻译方法包括音译、直译、意译等，翻译技巧包括增译、减译、分译等。三者为从上至下的层级关系，从宏观微观，从宽泛到具体。但如果采用该分类法，翻译策略仅仅包括异化和归化两种策略，分类过于宏观。韩江洪（2015：75）通过对国内翻译策略研究，将翻译策略定义为翻译策略是从事翻译这种跨文化交际活动的具体手段和方法，约略等于翻译方法。本研究将翻译策略定义为在翻译实践中能够解决实际翻译问题的方法和技巧，但不仅仅局限于直译、意译和增译等技巧和方法。

四、研究分析

（一）主要翻译策略统计

通过对立法文本汉英平行语料库中代表性模糊语英译策略进行统计分析，统计结果如表4所示。由表4可得知，立法文本中模糊语的英译策略主要为直译、增译和正说反译策略，其中直译和正说反译占绝大多数。但直译、增译和正说反译策略是否可取以及直译、增译和正说反译策略在立法文本中模糊语英译的适用性仍然存疑，需进一步讨论。

表4. 立法文本汉英平行语料库翻译策略统计

类别	关键词	译文	直译	增译	正说反译
模糊附加词	以上	not less than（385）；attaining（4）；Number+or more（28）	864	28	929
	以下	not more than（544）			
	以内	within（48）			
	以外	except（8）			
	不满	under（17）			
	轻微	minor（7）			
	严重	serious（497）			
模糊概念	当事人	party/side（222）			
	诉讼参与人	litigation participant（8）			
	公序良俗	public order and good morals（4）			
模糊蕴含	重大过失	gross negligence（1）			
	从重处罚	be heavily punished/ give a heavier punishment/penalty（24）			

（二）立法文本模糊语英译策略可行性分析

1. 模糊附加词

（1）数量范围模糊

例1 原文：第一百七十八条 二人**以上**依法承担连带责任的，权利人有权请求部分或者全部连带责任人承担责任。

译文：Article 178 Where **two or more** persons are jointly and severally liable in accordance with the law, the obligee is entitled to request assumption of liability by part or all of the persons jointly and severally liable.

例2 原文：第一百一十条 【间谍罪】有下列间谍行为之一，危害国家安全的，处十年**以上**有期徒刑或者无期徒刑；情节较轻的，处三年以上十年以下有期徒刑：

译文：Article 110 Whoever commits any of the following acts of espionage and endangers national security is to be sentenced to **not less than** 10 years of fixed-term imprisonment or life imprisonment; when the circumstances are relatively minor, the sentence is to be not less than three years and not more than ten years of fixed-termed imprisonment:

分析：由以上两个例子可知，针对立法文本数量范围模糊语，采用增译或者正说反译的翻译策略。例1采取增译的翻译策略，将"两人以上"增译为"two or more persons"，将两人以上包括两人的模糊语具体化，因此，在立法文本模糊语英译时，可以采用增译的翻译策略。例2采取正说反译的翻译策略，将"十年以上"翻译为"not less than 10 years"。但是"十年以上"翻译为"not less than 10 years"存在一个语义模糊，"十年以上"包含两种语义。即＞10年和≥10年。法律语言准确严谨，所以必须对"10年以上"加以限定，即对"以上"进行界定，本法所称以上包括本数。因此，正说反译的翻译策略不可取。

（2）程度模糊

例3 原文：第四十八条【死刑、死缓的适用对象及核准程序】死刑只适用于罪行**极其**严重的犯罪分子。

译文：Article 48 The death penalty is only to be applied to criminal elements who commit **the most heinous** crimes.

（3）概括模糊

例4 原文：第二十五条 自然人以户籍登记或者**其他**有效身份登记记载的居所为住所；经常居所与住所不一致的，经常居所视为住所。

译文：Article 25 The domicile of a natural person shall be his or her residence recorded in the household registration or **any other** valid identity registration; but if his or her habitual residence is different from the domicile, the habitual residence shall be deemed his or her domicile.

分析：通过例3和例4的例子可以看出，立法文本程度模糊语和概括模糊语英译的翻译策略为直译。将"极其"和"其他"翻译为英文中对应的词语。虽然也存在模糊语义，但是其解决方式需要从立法技术上讨论，本文不做探讨。

2. 模糊概念

例5 原文：第五十三条 **当事人**一方人数众多的共同诉讼，可以由**当事人**推选代表人进行诉讼。

译文：Article 53 Where **the parties** on one side of a joint action is numerous, such **parties** may recommend a representative or representatives to participate in the action.

例6 原文：第十条 处理民事纠纷，应当依照法律；法律没有规定的，可以适用**习惯**，但是不得违背**公序良俗**。

译文：Article 10 Civil disputes shall be resolved in accordance with the law; or if the law is silent, **customs** may apply, but not contrary to **public order and good morals**.

分析："当事人""习惯""公序良俗"均为模糊概念。"当事人"该概念涉及广泛，指被害人、自诉人、犯罪嫌疑人等；关于民法典中"习惯"一词究竟是事实习惯还是习惯法，学界争议纷纭，另外，"习惯"在适用时的识别标准也尚未有统一意见（侯国跃，何鞠师，2021:47）。"公序良俗"是由公共秩序和善良风俗两个原则构成，公共秩序是指全体社会成员的共同利益；善良风俗是指由社会全体成员所普遍认许、遵循的道德准则（杨立新，2020：26）。仅仅将"当事人""习惯""公序良俗"直译为"party""customs""public order and good morals"并没有将其模糊概念明晰，所以，模糊概念语英译时采取直译策略不可取。

3. 模糊蕴含

例 7 原文：第一百零六条【与境外勾结的处罚规定】与境外机构、组织、个人相勾结，实施本章第一百零三条、第一百零四条、第一百零五条规定之罪的，依照各该条的规定**从重处罚**。

译文：Article 106 Whoever colludes with institutions, organizations, or individuals outside the country and commits crimes stipulated in Articles 103, 104, and 105 of this chapter are to **be heavily punished** according to the stipulations in the articles.

分析："从重处罚"该概念看似明晰，然而其处罚中"从重"的度有多大却无法得知，没有界定范围的标准。仅采用直译的策略无法将其模糊蕴含意义明晰，因此，模糊蕴含语英译时采取直译策略不可取。

综上例子分析可知，立法文本模糊语英译策略主要有三种：直译、增译和正说反译。其中，增译策略在立法文本模糊语英译时有可行性，而直译和正说反译的翻译策略无法解决立法文本模糊语英译时存在模糊概念和模糊蕴含的问题。因此，需要将其模糊语英译文本确切化。

（三）立法文本模糊语英译确切化策略

在立法过程中，模糊语是难以消除的现象，需要对法律条文中的词语作确切化的处理，以保证人们对法律理解正确。陈炯（2005:99）曾提出法律条文中模糊语确切化的方法主要有随文注释方法、语境制约方法、法律互参方法、聚合互鉴方法以及法律解释方法。本文将参考其模糊语确切化的方法，分析和总结出立法文本模糊语英译确切化策略。

1. 策略之一：模糊对模糊策略

法律语言作为自然语言的一部分，一方面客观上很难全部达到语义精确性的要求；另一方面，立法者由于无法对未来出现的法律行为与法律事实进行准确预测，故在主观上常有意在文字表述上留下空间（朱前鸿，2011：5）。由此，立法语言的模糊性及由模糊性带来的不确定性既是客观上的不可避免，也是主观上的有意为之（屈文生，2022：15）。在立法文本中，经常会使用"极其""其他"等表达程度范围模糊和概括模糊的词或短语，该类模糊语难以将其具体化，只能用同样模糊的字词或短语来翻译，将其翻译为"the most heinous"和"any other"等。因此，针对立法文本中模糊附加词类别中表达程度模糊和概括模糊的词或短语英译时，可以采用模糊对模糊的翻译策略。

2. 策略之二：随文注释策略

随文注释策略属于预先预测行为，在立法时，估计到某些词语的多义性和模糊性可能导致今后实施、执行困难，因而在制定法律同时在本文中另立法条或附则中随文加以注释（陈炯，2005:100）。随文注释策略可应用于立法文中模糊附加词类别中表达数量范围模糊的词或短语英译情况。

例 8 原文：第一百一十六条【破坏交通工具罪】破坏火车、汽车、电车、船只、航空器，足以使火车、汽车、电车、船只、航空器发生倾覆、毁坏危险，尚未造成严重后果的，处三年**以上**十年**以下**有期徒刑。

译文：Article 116 Whoever sabotages trains, motor vehicles, streetcars, ships, or airplanes in a manner sufficient to threaten the overturning or destruction of these trains, motor vehicles, streetcars, ships, or airplanes is to be sentenced to **not less than*** three years and **not more than*** ten years of fixed-term imprisonment, in cases when serious consequences have not been caused.

随文注释：* The phrases "not less than" and "not more than" include the given figure.

例 9 原文：第十八条 成年人为完全民事行为能力人，可以独立实施民事法律行为。**十六周岁以上**的未成年人，以自己的劳动收入为主要生活来源的，视为完全民事行为能力人。

译文：Article 17 A natural person attaining the age of eighteen is an adult. A minor **attaining the age of sixteen*** and primarily relying on his or her own labor income in living is deemed a person with full capacity for civil conduct.

随文注释：* The phrase "attaining the age of sixteen" includes the given number—sixteen.

分析："以上"和"以下"短语常与立法文本中表年月和数字的词或短语搭配，如"……年/月以上""……数字以下"。该类短语存在一个语义模糊，即"以上"表"≥"，"以下"表"≤"的含义。所以在英译时可以采取随文注释的策略，将其解释说明，即"not less than" and "not more than"……include the given number。

3. 策略之三：法律解释策略

法律解释就是解释法律，指司法程序中把法律文本中模糊的部分，尤其是法律条文与事实的逻辑关系，在法律规范内描绘清楚（陈金钊等，2006：2）。即法律解释是对有关法律条文含义的解释。常用的法律解释的方法包括文义解释、体系解释、目的解释、当然解释等（王利明，王叶刚，2016）。本文主要采用文义解释的方法。文义解释是对文本字面含义的解释，即按照语法结构、语言规则、通常的理解等方法的解释，常用在辨析法律概念、术语和法律条文的含义方面（魏蘅，2020；87）。立法文本中表模糊概念的术语英译时，可采用法律解释学策略。

例 10 原文：第十条 处理民事纠纷，应当依照法律；法律没有规定的，可以适用习惯，但是不得违背**公序良俗**。

译文：Article 10 Civil disputes shall be resolved in accordance with the law; or if the law is silent, customs may apply, but not contrary to **public order and good morals***.

法律解释：*The term "public order and good morals" is composed of two principles: public order and good morals. Public order refers to the common interests of all members of society. Good morals refer to the moral standards generally recognized and followed by all members of the society.

例 11 原文：第五十三条 <u>当事人</u>一方人数众多的共同诉讼，可以由当事人推选代表人进行诉讼。

译文：Article 53 Where **the parties*** on one side of a joint action is numerous, such parties may recommend a representative or representatives to participate in the action.

法律解释：* The term "party" means a victim, a private prosecutor, a criminal suspect, a defendant, or a plaintiff or defendant in an incidental civil action.

例 12 原文：第十四条 人民法院、人民检察院和公安机关应当保障犯罪嫌疑人、被告人和其他**诉讼参与人**依法享有的辩护权和其他诉讼权利。

译文：Article 14 People"s courts, people's procuratorates, and public security authorities shall protect the defense right and other procedural rights legally enjoyed by criminal suspects, defendants, and other **litigation participants***.

法律解释：*The term "litigation participants" means the parties, legal representatives, litigation representatives, defenders, witnesses, identification or evaluation experts, and interpreters.

分析：针对"公序良俗""习惯""诉讼参与人""当事人"等表模糊概念的术语英译时，可以参考现行的法律条文和司法解释，对其译文进行解释。

4. 策略之四：语境解释策略

语境解释策略是指根据法律条文上下文语境来明确其模糊语义。立法文本中表模糊蕴含的词或短语英译时，可采用语境解释策略。

例 13 原文：第一百零九条【叛逃罪】国家机关工作人员在履行公务期间，擅离岗位，叛逃境外或者在境外叛逃的，处五年以下有期徒刑、拘役、管制或者剥夺政治权利；情节严重的，处五年以上十年以下有期徒刑。

掌握国家秘密的国家工作人员叛逃境外或者在境外叛逃的，依照前款的规定<u>**从重处罚**</u>。

译文：Article 109 A state functionary who, in the course of performing his official duties, leaves his post without permission and flees this country or flees when he is already outside this country shall be sentenced to imprisonment of not more than 5 years, limited incarceration, probation or deprivation of political rights; or if the circumstances are serious, be sentenced to imprisonment of not less than 5 years but not more than 10 years.

A state functionary knowing any national secret, who flees this country or flees when he is already outside this country, shall be given **a heavier penalty*** according to the provision of the preceding paragraph.

语境解释：* A heavier penalty means a person is sentenced to imprisonment of not less than 5 years but not more than 10 years.

分析："从重处罚"该概念看似明晰，然而其处罚中"从重"的度有多大却无法得知，没有界定范围的标准。根据上下文语境，可得知，这里从重处罚指判处五年以上十年以下有期徒刑。因此，英译时，可以结合具体语境，对其进行解释。

五、结 语

　　本文以立法文本模糊语为研究对象，应用语料库的研究方法，对中文立法文本模糊附加词以及表模糊概念和模糊蕴含的词或短语及其英译策略进行定量统计分析，结果表明，中文立法文本模糊语英译时，所采用翻译策略一共有三种：直译、增译和正说反译。研究发现，直译和正说反译的翻译策略存在缺陷，无法处理立法文本中模糊语英译存在的问题。因此，本文借鉴陈炯提出的法律条文中模糊语确切化的方法，将立法文本模糊语英译策略总结如下：立法文本中表程度模糊和概括模糊的词或短语英译时可采取模糊对模糊策略；立法文本中表数量范围模糊的词或短语英译时可采取随文注释策略；立法文本中表模糊概念的词或短语英译时可采取法律解释策略；立法文本中表模糊蕴含的词或短语英译时可采取语境解释策略。

　　通过语料库的研究方法，对立法文本中的模糊语翻译进行定量统计和定性分析，这有利于法律模糊语翻译研究在实证研究方面不断深化，而且法律翻译具有较强的跨学科属性，涉及语言学、翻译学和法学等学科，借助法学方法论或法学理论也可以充实立法文本模糊语翻译研究的理论基础。

注释

① 立法文本模糊语关键词举例为代表性词汇。

参考文献

[1] Channel. *Vague Language* [M]. Shanghai: Shanghai Foreign Language Education Press，2000.

[2] Chen Jie (陈洁). "Artistic Reproduction of the Aesthetic Meaning of Ambiguity in the Translation of *Dream of the Red Chamber*" (从《红楼梦》翻译看模糊语美学意蕴的艺术再现) [J]. *Journal of Zhengzhou University(Philosophy and Social Sciences Edition)* (郑州大学学报(哲学社会科学版)),2007(03):149-152.

[3] Chen Jiong (陈炯). *Introduction to Legislative Linguistics* (立法语言学导论[M]). Guizhou: Guizhou People's Publishing House (贵州：贵州人民出版社)，2005.

[4] Chen, Baoru (陈保如). "A Study on the Translation of Legal Ambiguity in China from the Perspective of Functional Equivalence Theory" （功能对等理论视角下我国法律模糊语翻译研究）[J]. *Afterschool Education In China* （中国校外教育）,2018(18):61-62.

[5] Chen, Jinzhao et al (陈金钊等). *Legal Hermeneutics* (法律解释学[M]. Beijing: China University of Political Science and Law Press (北京: 中国政法大学出版社), 2006.

[6] Cheng, Tongchun (程同春). "The Application and Translation of Hedges in English for Science and Technology" (模糊限制语在科技英语中的运用与翻译)[J]. *Chinese Science & Technology Translators Journal* (中国科技翻译),2002(04):8-12.

[7] Dong, Xiaobo (董晓波). *Research on the Standardization of Legislative Language in China* (我国立法语言规范化研究[M]). Beijing: Beijing Jiaotong University Press (北京：北京交通大学出版社), 2016.

[8] Du, Guangcai (杜广才). "Legislative Language Ambiguity and Its Translation under the Guidance of Rhetoric" (修辞学关照下的立法语言模糊语及其翻译)[J]. *Journal of Hubei University of Science and Technology* (湖北科技学院学报),2014,34(02):98-100.

[9] Guan, Jialing & Zheng Wei (关家玲,郑伟). "Translation Methods of Fuzzy Words in English Advertising" (英语广告中模糊词汇的翻译方法"[J]. *Journalism Lover* (新闻爱好者),2010(18):92-93.

[10] Han, Jianghong (韩江洪). "A Review of Domestic Translation Strategy Research" (国内翻译策略研究述评)[J]. *Foreign Languages and Their Teaching* (外语与外语教学),2015(01):75-80.

[11] Hou, Guoyue & He, Jushi (侯国跃,何鞠师). "Identification of "Custom" in Article 10 of the Civil Code of China" (我国《民法典》第 10 条中的"习惯"之识别)[J]. *Journal of Gansu University of Political Science and Law* (甘肃政法大学学报),2021(02):46-56.

[12] Li Jin & Ju Fang (李晋,居方). "A Study on the Translation of Ambiguity in Legislative Texts from the Perspective of the Self Creation Theory of Law" (法的自创生理论视角下的立法文本模糊语翻译研究)[J]. *Language Education* (语言教育),2018,(02):79-83+97.

[13] Lu, Qiufan (卢秋帆). "Analysis of the Ambiguity of Legal Language" (法律语言的模糊性分析) [J]. *Law Review* (法学评论),2010,(02):20-26.

[14] Ma, Zhimin & Gu, Weichen (马志民,顾维忱). "Translation of Legal English from the Perspective of Linguistic Ambiguity" (从语言的模糊性看法律英语翻译)[J]. *Overseas English* (海外英语),2011(09):229-230.

[15] Nie, Yujing & Wang Guoxin (聂玉景,王国新). "Analysis of Ambiguity in Criminal Law Texts" (刑法文本中的模糊语现象分析)[J]. *Journal of Zhongzhou University* (中州大学学报),2010(04):6-8.

[16] Pan Feng & Sheng, Dandan (潘峰,盛丹丹). "Norms and Choices in Chinese English Interpretation of Press Conferences: Starting from the Translation of Hedges" (记者招待会汉英口译中的规范及选择——从模糊限制语的翻译谈起[J]. *Foreign Language Learning Theory and Practice* (外语教学理论与实践),2021(01):115-125.

[17] Qu, Wensheng (屈文生). "The System of Principles for Translating Chinese Legislative Texts into Foreign Languages: Centered on the Practice of Translating Civil Law into English" (中国立法文本对外翻译的原则体系——以民法英译实践为中心)[J]. *Foreign Languages in China* (中国外语),2022,(01):1+10-20.

[18] Tan, Zhongyi & Yao Xin (谭重一,姚欣). "On the English Translation of Ambiguous Words in the *Yellow Emperor's Inner Canon* from the Perspective of Translation Adaptation Selection Theory" (从翻译适应选择论看《黄帝内经》模糊语英译)[J]. *Journal of Basic Chinese Medicine* (中国中医基础医学杂志),2018,(09):1311-1314.

[19] Tian, Linan (田力男). *A Study on the Ambiguity of Legal Language* (法律语言的模糊性研究[M]). Heilongjiang: Heilongjiang Education Press (黑龙江：黑龙江教育出版社出版社),2016.

[20] Wang, Liming & Wang, Yegang (王利明, 王叶刚). *Legal Hermeneutics Reader* (法律解释学读本 [M]). Nanjing: Jiangsu People's Publishing House (南京：江苏人民出版社)，2016.

[21] Wang, Xinjie (王心洁). "Analysis of Fuzzy Language Translation" (模糊语翻译试析) [J]. *Foreign Languages and Their Teaching* (外语与外语教学),2005(06):55-57.

[22] Wei Heng (魏蘅). "The Legal Method of Legal Translation" (法律翻译的法学方法)[J]. *Chinese Journal of ESP* (中国ESP研究),2020(02):80-90+95.

[23] Wen Xu (文旭). "Semantic Ambiguity and Translation" (语义模糊与翻译) [J]. *Chinese Translators Journal* (中国翻译),1996(02):6-9.

[24] Wu, Guangting & Zhang Tao (吴光亭,张涛). "A Study on the Translation Strategies of Hedges into Chinese Based on the English

Chinese Bilingual Parallel Corpus" (基于英汉双语平行语料库的模糊限制语汉译策略研究)[J]. *Foreign Language Research* (外语学刊),2020(01):102-108.

[25] Xiong Bing (熊兵). "Conceptual Confusion in Translation Studies: Taking 'Translation Strategies', 'Translation Methods', and 'Translation Techniques' as Examples" (翻译研究中的概念混淆——以"翻译策略"、"翻译方法"和"翻译技巧"为例)[J]. *Chinese Translators Journal* (中国翻译),2014,(03):82-88.

[26] Xu Jun & Zi, Zheng Quan (徐珺,自正权). "A Corpus-based Study on the Translation of Metaphors in English Business Reports into Chinese" (基于语料库的英文商务报道隐喻汉译研究) [J]. *Business Languages and Communication* (商务外语研究),2018(01):13-21.

[27] Yang, Lixin (杨立新). *Interpretation and Case Commentary of the Civil Code of the People's Republic of China. General Principles Compilation* (中华人民共和国民法典释义与案例评注.总则编[M]). Beijing: China Legal Publishing House (北京:中国法制出版社), 2020.

[28] Yu Jing & Yan, Shuyao (余菁,闫舒瑶). "Legislative vague language and its translation" (立法模糊语言及其翻译)[J]. *New Science* (新学术),2008(03):264-267.

[29] Yu, Jianping (于建平). "Analysis of Several Issues in the Translation of Scientific and Technological Papers Based on a Functional Translation Perspective" (基于功能翻译观分析科技论文翻译的若干问题)[J]. *Chinese Translators Journal* (中国翻译),2007(06):61-64.

[30] Zhai, Qiulan & Ruan, Hongmei (翟秋兰,阮红梅). "From the perspective of deconstruction, the translation of vague language in Tang poetry from Chinese to English" (从解构主义看唐诗中模糊语言的汉英翻译)[J]. *Journal of Lanzhou University(Social Sciences)* (兰州大学学报(社会科学版)),2008(02):143-146.

[31] Zhang Mei (张梅). "The Function and Translation of Ambiguity in Medical English" (医学英语中模糊语的功能与翻译)[J]. *Chinese Science & Technology Translators Journal* (中国科技翻译),2004(02):5-8.

[32] Zhao, Qiulong & Dong, Yuanxing & Liu, Huihua (赵秋荣,董元兴,刘惠华). "A Comparable Corpus-based Study on Hedges" (基于类比语料库的模糊限制语研究)[J]. *Shandong Foreign Language Teaching* (山东外语教学),2011,32(04):21-26.

[33] Zhu, Qianhong (朱前鸿). *The Ambiguity of Words and Its Impact on Legal Practice* (词语的模糊性及其对法律实务的影响[M]). Beijing: China University of Political Science and Law Press (北京: 中国政法大学出版社), 2011.

作者简介

黄宇柱,中国政法大学外国语学院硕士研究生。研究方向:法律翻译。电子邮箱:huangyuzhu11@163.com。

《搜神记》日本馆藏刊本调查及译介与研究论析

⊙ 刘 毅 陈 芳（贵州大学外国语学院，贵阳）

[摘 要] 随着近年来中国大力推动中华文化走出去，以文载道、以文传声、以文化人，传统典籍外译从中扮演着向世界弘扬中国优秀传统文化，让更多人感受华夏文化独特魅力的重要角色，对外讲好中国传统故事也是更好更快构建人类命运共同体的必经步骤之一。上承《山海经》、下启《唐传奇》，《搜神记》作为中国志怪小说开山之作，其海外馆藏刊本以及译介情况值得深入研究。本文整理了日本馆藏《搜神记》刊本，用历时性手法对其在日本的译介和研究情况展开论述，同时对有关改编衍生作品进行评述，以期为中国故事走出去，让世界更好地接受中华优秀传统文化提供切实有效的参考。

[关键词]《搜神记》；日本；刊本；译介

Investigation, Translation, Introduction and Research of *Sou Shen Ji* in Japanese Library Collections

LIU Yi CHEN Fang (College of Foreign Languages, Guizhou University, Guiyang)

Abstract: As China has vigorously promoted Chinese culture to go out in recent years, the translation of traditional classics plays an important role in promoting Chinese excellent traditional culture to the world, allowing more people to experience the unique charm of Chinese culture. It is also one of the necessary steps to build a shared future for mankind better and faster. As a connecting link between *Shan Hai Jing* and *Tang Legend*, *Sou Shen Ji* is the pioneering work of Chinese mystery novels, and its overseas collections and translations are worthy of in-depth study. By sorting out the editions of *Sou Shen Ji* in Japanese collections, the translation and research in Japan are discussed in a diachronic manner, at the same time, relevant adaptations and derivative works are commented. All above is to provide practical and effective references for Chinese writings to go out and let the world better accept the excellent traditional Chinese culture.

Key words: *Sou Shen Ji*; Japan; editions; translation and introduction

一、引言

魏晋南北朝时期，社会风气逐渐开化，寻常百姓开始讨论并质疑鬼神传说以及因果报应等古来传统观念的真实性。在此背景之下，有感于父亲女婢死而复生以及兄长气绝复苏二事（《晋书》卷八十二《干宝传》），东晋史学家干宝根据前代经典史志和采集所得奇闻异事编撰成书《搜神记》，"及其著述，亦足以发明神道之不诬也"。《搜神记》又名《搜神录》，是一部搜罗、整理各种神鬼传说的著作，据《晋书》《隋书》《旧唐书》等历代书目记载，《搜神记》原本共有 30 卷，在宋代以后均已散佚而不存，如今现存于世的版本学界普遍认为是由明代学者胡应麟从《法苑珠林》、《太平广记》等类书摘录编纂而成的辑佚本。今本《搜神记》虽佚失 10 卷，全书体例也有所改变，其内容依旧十分丰富。从每卷围绕一个主题涉及的诸多故事来看，既有神仙术士的奇闻异事，也有百姓对仙凡相处的憧憬之情；既有巫觋降妖除魔的奇异事迹，也有人们祈福祓灾、重祠敬祭的风俗习惯；既有充满灵性的精怪作祟，也有人类除之而后快的"驱怪"本能；既有掌管山川河流诸神的灵异故事，也有民间对因果报应等传统观念的趋从；既有千奇百怪的瑞应恶兆，也有古人试图从世间怪力乱神实现趋利避害的愿望。如上所述，学界有一种声音认为，《搜神记》30 卷原本很有可能还包含"感应""神化""变化""妖怪"四个不同篇章或类别（李剑国，2019：287），其余均已无从考证。

目前中国学界对《搜神记》的研究车载斗量，但研究角度有一定的局限性，即从文本分析、故事形象构建和文化意蕴阐释角度出发的研究占了大多数。如，张素宁从《搜神记》中塑造的一系列女性形象出发，将其定义为"有着女人的外表，有着女人的性格，蕴含着人的味道"的"女神"群体，并肯定了"女神"的形象为后世小说女性人物的描写提供了素材（张素宁，2019：159）；樊伟峻、宋博媛列举并分析《搜神记》中的变异故事，指出特定时期人们对生命规律的认识，阐述变异说的哲学、宗教和政治意蕴（樊伟峻、宋博媛，2020：29-34）。为填补在海外视阈下《搜神记》研究之阙如，本文搜集整理了日本《搜神记》历来刊本，对日本现存馆藏刊本进行论述研究，并从历时性角度阐述评析《搜神记》在日本的译介和研究情况，以期为中华民族优秀传统文化走向世界提供切实有效的参考。

二、《搜神记》在日本的刊本调查

东晋之前亦有《楚辞》《列子》《淮南子》《神仙传》《山海经》等前代典籍，收录了大量神鬼传说，《搜神记》乃其中集大成之志怪佳作。干宝一方面继承了前人的经典史志故事，另一方面网罗身边所见所闻的奇闻异事作为故事来源，今本 20 卷《搜神记》所藏 450 余则故事之中，约 200 则为摘录前人史志内容，剩余 250 余则故事由干宝亲自采集而得。《搜神记》中保留了数量众多的关于中国古代官民日常生活的内容，是后人开展中国古代民间传说和神话研究不可或缺的珍贵藏本。日本文化深受隋唐文化影响，飞鸟时期圣德太子派遣小野妹子两度作为遣隋使出访中国，学习彼时中国先进的文化和制度，推动日本政治改革。在此之后，日本亦多次派出遣唐使，拉开了古代中日交流之盛景。众多在中国早已散佚的经典古代汉籍流传至日本，得以较为完好地保存至今，《搜神记》汉籍刊本便是其中之一。

（一）调查数据来源

调查数据来源于日本国立国会图书馆（National Diet Library, Japan）和日本国文学研究资料馆（National Institute of Japanese Literature）。日本国立国会图书馆隶属于日本国会，向公众提供国会会议记录、法令、历史文献、近现代图书等资料，是日本中国最大的公共图书馆；国文学研究资料馆创立近 50 年来馆藏了日本全国数量最多的古代典籍，囊括众多在中国早已佚失的古汉籍，其电子资料馆内新日本古典籍综合数据库（新日本古典籍総合データベース）以及日本古典籍综合目录数据库（日本古典籍総合目録データベース）为海外读者提供了便捷的远程查询服务。

本文以日本馆藏《搜神记》历代刊本为研究对象，详细检索档案标题及其所述内容包含关键字"搜神记""干宝"的电子馆藏数据，剔除重复、无效项后共得到满足条件的文献档案 17 条，详见表 1。

表 1. 日本馆藏《搜神记》刊本一览表

时间	著作名	著者/编者	出版方	馆藏所在
1592	『漢魏叢書』	程榮	出版者不明	国立国会図書館
1630	『津逮祕書』	毛晉	虞山毛氏汲古閣	東京図書館等
1647	『説郛』	陶宗儀	宛委山堂刊	国立国会図書館
1699	『二酉洞』	一色時棟	文会堂	国立国会図書館
1742	『扶桑怪談辨述鈔』	厚誉春鶯	出版者不明	京都大学附属図書館等
1767	『本朝搜神記』	厚誉春鶯	出版者不明	東洋大学附属図書館
1792	『增訂漢魏叢書』	王謨	育文書局	国立国会図書館
1794	『龍威祕書』	馬俊良	大酉山房刊	国立国会図書館
1806	『學津討原』	張海鵬	張氏照曠閣刊	国立国会図書館
1820	『搜神記20卷後記10卷』	干寶、陶潛	加賀屋善藏	不明
1846	『魏叔子文鈔6卷』	魏禧	出版者不明	名古屋大学図書館
1868	『藝苑捃華』	顧之逵	務本堂	東京大學東洋文化研究所
1875	『百子全書』	劉向等	崇文書局	国立国会図書館
明	『新刻出像增補搜神記6卷』	唐富春	大盛堂	東洋文化研究所
明末	『五朝小説』	馮夢龍	心遠堂	国立国会図書館
清初	『廣漢魏叢書』	何允中	出版者不明	国立国会図書館
出版年月不詳	『況斎叢書』	岡本況斎	出版者不明	国立国会図書館等

（二）《搜神记》主要刊本调查

1. 崇祯庚午（1630）年毛晋辑汲古阁刻本——《津逮秘书》

藏于国立国会图书馆、东京图书馆、新潟大学附属图书馆，本次调查主要涉及前两者。国立国会图书馆共藏有线装本《津逮秘书》15集共240册。版框高25.6cm，宽16.7cm。书名题"津逮秘書"，封面内页有"汲古閣藏""小寒山陳函輝先生選"字样。叙文为手写体，叙末注隶书"海鹽胡震亨題"，钤有多枚朱方印。正文四周单边有界，鱼尾上刻古籍名，下刻卷次、页次和"汲古閣"字样。每半页9行，每行18字。第3集《齐名要术》鱼尾未标注"汲古閣"字样，第10集《洛阳珈蓝记》鱼尾下刻"绿君亭"。《搜神记》前15卷内容收录于《津逮秘书》11集第149-151册，共160页；后5卷内容与《稽神录》共同收录于第152-154册，共56页。《搜神记》序文首页有"晉散騎常侍新蔡干寶令升撰"，卷头有"晉干寶撰 明胡震亨毛晉同訂"，卷末题"作是觀湖南毛晉識"。

2. 日本宽保二（1742）年厚誉春莺编河南四郎右卫门刻本——《扶桑怪谈辨述钞》

藏于京都大学附属图书馆、石川县立历史博物馆、东洋大学附属图书馆等地。全书7卷7册，石川县立历史博物馆所藏遗失第1册，且第4册有损伤。又名《净土劝化扶桑怪谈辨述钞》《本朝搜神记》，现存"宽保二年"和"明和四年"两个版本。正文四周单边无界，每半页10行，由汉字和片假名写成。卷头有"扶桑怪談辨述鈔卷之一""沙門 厚譽春鶯編"，第4卷的"编"为"撰"。封面题签左侧两边注有"淨土勸化 扶桑怪談辨述鈔 上（下）"。刊记题"寛保二壬戌歳二月十六日""京堀川通佛光寺下ル町 河南四郎右衛門"。各藏本钤朱方印"西莊文庫""長嶋町五丁目""大野屋惣八""天性寺藏書記"。全书共142页，其中，第1卷21页；第2卷17页；第3卷21页；第4卷25页；第5卷21页；第6卷19页；第7卷18页。

3. 乾隆壬子（1792）年王谟辑刻本——《增订汉魏丛书》

藏于国立国会图书馆、新潟大学附属图书馆，本次调查主要涉及前者。国立国会图书馆共藏有线装本

《增订汉魏丛书》7卷共73册。版框高25.3cm，宽15.8cm。页框高19.5cm，宽13.2cm。封面内页题记"乾隆辛亥重镌""漢魏叢書""経翼二十種""別史十六種""子餘廿二種""載籍廿八種""本衙藏版"，另钤朱印"潴湾 愛日堂發兌"。序首题记"重刻漢魏叢書"，钤有多枚朱方印。正文四周双边有界，单白鱼尾，鱼尾上刻古籍名，下刻卷次、页次。每半页9行，每行20字，注文双行。《搜神记》全8卷收录于《增订汉魏丛书》第71册，起始于56页，结束于107页，卷首有"晉 干寶撰 南昌楊先烈校"字样。卷尾提及丛书只收录8卷实为残缺，亦有提及毛氏《津逮秘书》收录的20卷版本也非原著，根据《水经注》《荆楚岁时记》所记载的内容，《搜神记》还应有"感应篇""变化篇"，而毛本均不见此体例。

三、《搜神记》在日本的译介

（一）《搜神记》最早传播追溯

据史料记载，《搜神记》作者干宝出生年月不详，西晋元康末年至太安间（299-303年）于江淮，时已成年，后卒于咸康二（336）年三月（许嵩，1986：12）。由此可推知《搜神记》成文时间应在299年至336年间。《搜神记》最早传入日本的时间尚不明确，目前所知日本关于《搜神记》最早的文字记述见于宽平三（891）年藤原佐世所撰《日本国见在书目录》（『日本国見在書目録』）（马兴国，1988：79），书中记载道："《搜神记》三十卷 干宝撰；《搜神后记》十卷 陶潜撰。"《搜神记》作为中国志怪小说开山之作著于东晋时期，此后隋唐两朝中日两国官方、民间文化交流频繁，很可能早在公元891年之前，《搜神记》业已东渡至日本。关于此观点，亦可从自古流传于日本各地的民间故事与《搜神记》所载志怪故事之间的相似性和关联性窥知一二。

日本京都府京丹后市峰山町世代流传着一个羽衣仙女传说：一男子在山上打猎时发现八个仙女在池中洗浴，男子看到池边树枝上挂着仙女的羽衣，便偷偷藏起一件羽衣，将其中一位仙女领回家中，后结为夫妻，生育三个孩子。某天，仙女从孩子口中得知羽衣所藏地，便取出羽衣飞回天宫（伴とし子，2011：156）。《搜神记》卷十四的羽衣仙女传说故事名为《羽衣女》，内容如下：

> 豫章新喻县男子，见田中有六七女，皆衣毛衣，不知是鸟。匍匐往，得其一女所解毛衣，取藏之，即往就诸鸟。诸鸟各飞去，一鸟独不得去。男子取以为妇，生三女。其母后使女问父，知衣在积稻下，得之，衣而飞去。后复以迎三女，女亦得飞去。（干宝，2019：231）

中日这两则传说，同为亚洲各国广为流传的"天鹅处女型"故事，但两者都包含三个相同的母题，即：（1）仙女脱下羽衣，被窥视，被窃走羽衣；（2）生育有三个孩子；（3）由孩子发现羽衣所在。叙事手法和故事情节如此相似，想必并非巧合。在明治维新前近千年的时间里，日本广泛地学习和吸收中国农耕、陶冶等先进科学技术以及书法绘画、乐曲诗赋等传统文化内容。从先秦时代开始，共有四次中国移民大规模迁居日本的历史记录。一是秦汉时期（公元前3世纪至公元3世纪），此时期正值日本弥生时代，徐福东渡求药寻仙为日本带去了水稻栽种和青铜器冶炼技术；二是魏晋南北朝时期（公元3世纪至6世纪），此时期正值日本古坟时代，民众为逃避西晋末年长达百年的战乱大规模迁徙日本，乃历代赴日高潮；三是隋唐时期（公元6世纪至10世纪初），此时期横跨日本飞鸟、奈良、平安三个时代，主要是学者、僧侣和手工业者东渡赴日；四是宋末元初时期（公元13世纪末），虽已无官方往来，民间仍有禅僧去日宣讲佛经。《搜神记》问世正是在上述第二个历史时期，由此可以推断，当年东渡的中原汉人将《搜神记》祖本带至日本列岛，对《搜神记》在日传播和日本本土创作"羽衣传说"一类的神话故事产生了深远的影响，也从侧面表明《搜神记》传入日本的年代已经相当久远。

（二）《搜神记》译介形式

通过在日本国立国会图书馆和国立情报学研究所数据库 CiNii 检索日本全国范围内历代出版发行的《搜神记》日译本情况，笔者整理出目前主要馆藏及在市销售的日译本如表 2 所示。

表 2.《搜神记》日译本一览表

出版时间	书名	译者/作者	出版方
1883	『通俗三世因果実験録』	義讓了淳	護法館
1922	『伝説之支那』	松井等	楠林書店
1920	『国訳漢文大成』	塩谷温	国民文庫刊行会
1935	『支那怪奇小説集』	岡本綺堂	サイレン社
1956	『馬娘婚姻譚』	今野円輔	岩崎書店
1959	『捜神記：八巻本』	荘司格一,清水栄吉,志村良治	養徳社
1964	『捜神記』	竹田晃	平凡社
1970	『岡本綺堂読物選集』	岡本綺堂	青蛙房
1992	『中国古小説選—六朝志怪・唐代伝奇』	本間洋一	和泉書院
1997	『中国怪異小説選』	八木章好	慶應義塾大学出版会
2004	『干宝 捜神記』	先坊幸子,森野繁夫	白帝社
2006	『中国古典小説選』	佐野誠子	明治書院
2016	『中国の志怪小説 捜神記 捜神後記』	久保卓哉	大学教育出版
2018	『千年狐：干宝「捜神記」より』	張六郎	KADOKAWA
2021	『中国怪談奇談集 新装増補版』	多久弘一	里文出版

《搜神记》现存日译本从文本内容上可分为二十卷本和八卷本；从译介手法上可分为节译、选译和全译本。从形式上看，多数节译本和选译本都是同其他中国史书典籍以合集的形式呈现，在介绍《搜神记》的同时亦能将其他中国古代文学作品一同向海外推广传播。明治十六（1883）年义让了淳编译《通俗三世因果实验录》作为较早版本的《搜神记》节译本颇受学界重视；大正十一（1922）年松井等人编译的《传说之中国》以及昭和十一（1935）年冈本绮堂编译的《中国怪奇小说集》则作为早期收录《搜神记》故事的选译本广为人知。1922 年楠林书店出版的《传说之中国》共收录《搜神记》7 个独立故事，分别是『盤瓠』『桑蠶』『泰山府君』『千日酒』『賣鬼』『阿紫狐』『妖蛇』，其中，『盤瓠』和『桑蠶』两则故事配有插图（松井等，1922：11-15）。文中生僻汉字有加注日文平假名，如，巴蜀（はしょく）、武陵（ぶりょう）、長沙（ちゃうさ）、廬江（ろかう）、盤瓠（はんこ）、蠶（かひこ）等。但此处"長沙（ちゃうさ）"异于现代日语"長沙（ちょうさ）"的发音，究竟是近代以来日语读音习惯发生改变，抑或是译者编写错误？都还有待考证。冈本绮堂编译的《中国怪奇小说集》作为最受日本读者欢迎的中国志怪故事合集本多次再版发行，先后由サイレン社、青蛙房、フロンティアニセン、光文社、青空文庫、サキ出版等多家出版社以精装本、文库本等多种形式数次再版，本文仅以 1935 年サイレン社发行版本为例。《中国怪奇小説集》收录『首の飛ぶ女』『攫猿』『琵琶鬼』『羽衣』『宋家の母』『盤瓠』『徐光の瓜』等 25 个《搜神记》中各具特色的神鬼故事。书中序言部分"開会の辭"提及："中国古代志怪小说从很久之前便已流入日本，并对日本文学及传说故事的创作产生了深远的影响。以《今昔物语》为始，可以说室町时代、德川时代的小说基本都受到了中国小说的影响，就算不用特别声明，但凡稍微研究过中国古代小说的人都能一眼看出那个时代的日本文学作品就是对中国文学作品在某种形式上进行的改编。甚至一直以来流传的真实历史人物轶事，亦

是从中国小说获取灵感改编而得。"冈本绮堂在《搜神记》引言部分对其历史地位进行了高度评价："谈及六朝时期最有名的文学作品非《搜神记》莫属，《搜神记》亦可称为后世小说之鼻祖。"（岡本綺堂，1935：9-12）书中收录的《搜神记》故事未进行增补或删减，在尽量保持原著内容长度的基础上为方便日本读者阅读，添加日语平假名注解，极大地降低阅读门槛、增强阅读体验，从侧面推动《搜神记》海外传播，提高其在日本的知晓度。

全译本《搜神记》分为二十卷本和八卷本，前者以昭和三十九（1964）年竹田晃编译《搜神记》（东洋文库）为代表作品；后者则是大正九（1920）年至大正十三（1924）年间盐谷温译注《国译汉文大成》以及昭和三十四（1959）年内田道夫主编，莊司格一、清水荣吉、志村良治共同翻译《搜神记：八卷本》作为主要版本广为流传。平凡社《搜神记》（东洋文库）于1964年刊印初版以来，分别又在2000年和2003年再版发行。1959年养德社出版的《搜神记：八卷本》共收录40个独立故事，其中，卷四收录『張華と狐』『酒屋の老犬』『漢の再興のきざし』『夢の真実』『易者と罪人』『陳竜文の詭弁』『東方朔と孫賓』『五人の義兄弟』8个故事，为全书收录故事数量最多的一个章节（干宝，1959：59-85）。《国译汉文大成》第十二卷《晋唐小说》用64页收录《搜神记》全8卷共40个故事，该书与其他译本最大的区别在于：（1）全文但凡出现汉字处均标注有平假名；（2）对专有名词和特殊表述在每页页脚进行译注，如提及三国时期曹魏术士管辂时，"管輅、字は公明、魏の人、周易に明かに、天文風角占相の術に精し。"又如"帰寧、帰省に同じ。"（3）每个志怪故事的标题都以通俗易懂的文字进行简要描述。以1959年养德社版《搜神记：八卷本》作为参照，该版本卷四收录的第一个故事名为『張華と狐』，而《国译汉文大成》中《国译搜神记》卷四第一个故事的标题为『狐狸張華の才を試みて却て害に遇ふ』；养德社版《搜神记：八卷本》卷四最后一个故事名为『五人の義兄弟』，《国译搜神记》则是以故事中五兄弟的孝心为关键词，将此故事取名为『孝心の感應』（国民文库刊行会，1920：1-64）。

21世纪的第二个十年，《搜神记》以青年人喜闻乐见的漫画形式全新登场。角川书店『千年狐：干宝「搜神記」より』是以原著《搜神记》中的狐妖故事为原型，凭借漫画家张六郎唯美细腻的作画手法向读者描述着一个个欢笑中夹杂着泪水，严肃却也不乏幽默的精彩故事。读者是文学译著中极为重要的一环，任何作品的优劣都能直观地反映在读者的接受程度上。全球最大网上零售商亚马逊（Amazon）的图书销售网站目前在售的共6卷『千年狐：干宝「搜神記」より』分别以1-5星让读者对其进行评分，通过分析研究不难发现，此套漫画获得读者群的压倒性好评，超过90%的读者给予4星及以上的评分，第一卷及第二卷平均分4.7，剩余4卷均为4.8。亦可从评论人数看出其受欢迎度，每卷漫画都收获超过400条评论，尤以第一卷为最，共548条；2021年12月出版发行的第六卷业已达到222条评论[①]。通过对传统志怪小说集《搜神记》的改编再创作，以全新的形式扩大原著受众面，增强海外传播影响力，在全球一体化的当下亦不失为一种打开中国古典文学作品向外走大门的新颖途径。

四、日本学者《搜神记》研究成果评述

《搜神记》作为古代志怪小说经典之作，历来受到中国学者的重视，与中国一衣带水的日本亦有大量学

者持续地致力于对《搜神记》的研究。从现行日本学界对《搜神记》的研究来看，主要是围绕文学比较与文化交流、版本起源与流传、故事形象构建与文化意蕴阐释等角度展开，其中不乏新颖的研究方向和丰硕的研究成果。

以2015年广岛大学中村有香的博士论文『六朝志怪「搜神記」の傳世過程に関する研究』（关于六朝志怪小说《搜神记》传世过程的研究）为例（中村有香，2015）。基于前人研究，目前学界对于明末编纂的二十卷本《搜神记》究竟是从类书内容摘录所得，还是整理自古流传下来的《搜神记》残卷原本所得尚无定论；此外，二十卷本《搜神记》同八卷本《搜神记》、类书之间的关联性尚有不明晰之处。中村有香先以宏观视角介绍现存各版本《搜神记》的由来与变迁，再以三种不同组别系统地探讨二十卷本、八卷本及敦煌本之间的异同和联系，探讨学界目前认为的二十卷本是以《天中记》为蓝本，用八卷本进行添补而得之假说是否合理；提出在编撰二十卷本时应该是存在自古流传下来的残卷原本，且是未被经典化的复数手抄本，才能对不同版本《搜神记》之间存在的复杂文藻差异进行解释。总的来说，中村有香对多个传本进行详尽的比较研究，异于传统的"传世说"，提出全新的"抄本分支说"理论，其研究成果为今后关于《搜神记》起源与流传的相关研究提供了可靠的参考。

通过在日本科学研究费用推动事业数据库（科学研究費助成事業データベース）KAKEN检索《搜神记》研究课题，可知已完成或在进行中的有关课题共15件，详见表3。

表3. 日本《搜神记》研究课题一览表

研究区间	课题名称	研究机构	代表学者
2020-2023	東アジア漢字文化圏における龍宮訪問譚の文化・思想交流史的研究	明治大學	金孝珍
2019-2022	日本書紀を中心とした東アジア漢字文化圏における書記用文体の成立と交流に関する研究	國學院大學	葛西太一
2014-2016	出土資料「日書」に見られる巫の研究	福岡女学院大学	高戸聰
2014-2016	中国仏教経典に占める儒教起源語彙の計量学的研究	早稲田大学	渡辺義浩
2013-2017	内容類型学からみた沖縄諸方言	大分大学	田畑千秋
2013-2016	漢魏六朝文学における「異景」描写の展開-辞賦から志怪書へ-	富山大学	大野圭介
2007-2008	二十一世紀の漢文教育テキスト作成〜長崎から世界へ	活水女子大学	荒木龍太郎
2007-2009	日中説話文学史構築のための『法苑珠林』『夷堅志』の比較説話学的研究	日本女子大学	三田明弘
2007-2010	中国語の構文及び文法範疇形成の歴史的変容と汎時的普遍性-中国語歴史文法の再構築-	東京大学	木村英樹
2006-2008	敦煌文献中にみられる説話文学資料の基礎的研究	広島大学	荒見泰史
2005-2008	英仏所蔵敦煌・吐魯番出土漢文文献の古文書学的比較研究	新潟大学	関尾史郎
2004-2006	中国魏晋南北朝志怪の成立背景-歴史意識・人間観・宗教	京都大学	佐野誠子
2003-2006	日中朝をめぐる交流と日本古代文学についての研究-渤海使と文学・『聖徳太子伝暦』-	早稲田大学	田中隆昭
2003-2004	中国古典文献における画像及びテキストデータ処理の諸問題	関西大学	二階堂善弘
1999-2001	中国古小説の類話集成に関する研究	広島大学	富永一登

从时间分布来看，较早关于《搜神记》的研究课题始于1999年，由广岛大学研究生院文学研究科富永一登教授带领团队完成了以《太平广记》《搜神记》《搜神后记》《古小说钩沈》《异苑》五部古典籍为数据库，对地名、人名、书名等专有名词以及鬼、梦、神、祠、妖怪等词汇的检索统计工作，而后在2007年

共设立新课题 3 项，为历年最多；从研究内容来看，主要分为文化圈交流、文学比较、语法构成、形象建构等主题；从机构所属地区来看，关东地区涉及 6 所大学位居第一，其后依次是九州地区、关西地区、中国地区、中部地区。

除了上述提及的博士论文与研究课题，通过对日本学术期刊登载的《搜神记》有关论文进行整理亦不难发现，其中既有围绕词汇语法进行的研究，如 2007 年刊登于『中国文化研究』上的竹田治美著『「搜神记」における程度副词について』（《搜神记》程度副词的使用）（竹田治美，2007：43-60）；也有同其他古代文学作品的比较研究，如 2002 年刊登于『二松：大学院纪要』上的河野贵美子著『「搜神记」の语る历史：史书五行志との关系』（《搜神记》述说的历史：与史书五行志的关系）（河野贵美子，2002：293-335）；还有故事形象建构与其所包含文化意蕴的解读，如 2017 年刊登于『成城国文学』上的南明希著『「搜神记」における龙：古巢老姥谭をめぐって』（《搜神记》龙的形象：以古巢老姥故事为例）（南明希，2017：92-99）。

问世于东晋时期的《搜神记》作为中国较早传入日本的文学作品，任由时光荏苒，时至今日仍在给予日本学界养分，激发学术创新活力，影响着不同时期的研究学者。中国学者亦能从海外视阈下重新审视承载于《搜神记》之中的中国古代经典文化，为今后相关研究拓展出全新的理论和方向。《搜神记》能在日本得到广泛关注并被持续深入地研究，亦是中华优秀传统文化在海外得到接受和认可的有力佐证。

五、结 语

《搜神记》作为志怪小说集大成之作，除了内容丰富、体例完备、层次清晰，其叙事手法与文藻隽永亦颇受后人称赞，是兼具直笔实录与幽悠婉转之特点的典范。就其影响而言，《搜神记》不仅是六朝志怪文学的代表作，更是唐宋传奇、宋元话本、明清小说取之不尽的素材源泉，持续受到世人的关注。《搜神记》在日本的译介呈现多样化态势，在对传统八卷本和二十卷本的译本进行补充完善的同时，亦有推出广受年轻人欢迎的漫画改编版本，一经问世便大受好评。通过搜集整理日本学界对《搜神记》有关研究不难看出，探讨《搜神记》版本起源与文化意蕴对于研究中日文学交流史，乃至比较两国民间神话故事关联性都是很有意义的。《搜神记》译介和研究过程表明，承载着经典文化的文学作品任凭时间冲刷，也必将深深地在历史长河之中刻下浓墨重彩的一笔，这是中华传统文化在海外传播取得成功的优秀范例。在推动中华文化走出去、构建人类命运共同体的时代背景下，更应该以《搜神记》为着力点开展更多中日人文对话和学术交流，在文化交流互鉴中促进民心相通，以期推动两国关系走深走实，为两国关系发展注入新动力。

注释

① 本文从日本亚马逊（https://www.amazon.co.jp/）网站采集数据的时间为 2022 年 1 月.

参考文献

[1] Ban, Toshiko (伴とし子). *The Birth of the Yamato Administration and the Kingdom of Otaba* (ヤマト政権誕生と大丹波王国) [M]. Tokyo: Shin-Jinbutsuoraisha (東京：新人物往来社), 2011.

[2] Fan, Weijun & Song, Boyuan (樊伟峻，宋博媛). "The Implications Reflected by the Mutation Story of "*Sou Shen Ji*"" (《搜神记》变异故事所反映的意蕴) [J]. *Journal of Jining Normal University* (集宁师范学院学报), 2020(04): 29-34+43.

[3] Gan, Bao (干宝). *Sou Shen Ji* (搜神记) [M]. Xian: Sanqin Press (西安：三秦出版社), 2019.

[4] Gan, Bao (干宝). "*Sou Shen Ji*" in Eight-volume Version (搜神记：八卷本)(Shouji, Kakuitsu & Shimizu, Eikichi & Shimura, Ryoji, Trans.)(荘司格一，清水栄吉，志村良治共訳) [M]. Nara: Youtokusha (奈良：養徳社), 1959.

[5] Kokumin Bunko Kanko-kai (国民文庫刊行会). *Chinese Writings Collection in Japan* (国訳漢文大成) [M]. Tokyo: Kokumin Bunko Kanko-kai (東京：国民文庫刊行会), 1920-1924.

[6] Kono, Kimiko (河野貴美子). "The Relationship between "*Sou Shen Ji*" and "*Wu-hsing Chih*"" (『搜神記』の語る歴史：史書五行志との関係) [J]. *Bulletin of Graduate Studies of Nishogakusha University* (二松：大学院紀要), 2002(03): 293-335.

[7] Li, Jianguo (李剑国). *The History of Mystery Novels before the Tang Dynasty* (唐前志怪小说史) [M]. Beijing: People's Literature Publishing House (北京：人民文学出版社), 2019.

[8] Ma, Xingguo (马兴国). "The Spread and Influence of "*Sou Shen Ji*" in Japan" (《搜神记》在日本的流传及影响) [J]. *Japan Studies* (日本研究), 1988(02): 79-84.

[9] Matsui (松井). *Legendary China* (伝説之支那) [M]. Tokyo: Kusubayashi Bookstore (東京：楠林書店), 1922.

[10] Minami, Aki (南明希). "The Image of Loong in "*Sou Shen Ji*"" (『搜神記』における龍：古巣老姥譚をめぐって) [J]. *Japanese Literature of Seijou University* (成城国文学), 2017(03): 92-99.

[11] Nakamura, Yuka (中村有香). "A Study on the Spreading Process of the Mystery Novel of Six Dynasties-"*Sou Shen Ji*"" (六朝志怪『搜神記』の傳世過程に関する研究) [D]. Hiroshima: Hiroshima University (広島：広島大学), 2015.

[12] Okamoto, Kido (岡本綺堂). *Chinese Mystery Novels Collection* (支那怪奇小説集) [M]. Tokyo: Cyren Company (東京：サイレン社), 1935.

[13] Takeda, Harumi (竹田治美). "The Adverb of Degree in "*Sou Shen Ji*"" (『搜神記』における程度副詞について) [J]. *Chinese Culture Research* (中国文化研究), 2007(03): 43-60.

[14] Xu, Song (许嵩). *Veritable Records of Jiankang* (建康实录) [M]. Shanghai: Zhonghua Book Company (上海：中华书局), 1986.

[15] Zhang, Suning (张素宁). "Analysis of the Goddess Image in "*Sou Shen Ji*"" (《搜神记》中的女神形象分析) [J]. *Tangshan Literature* (唐山文学), 2019(04): 159.

作者简介

刘毅，硕士，贵州大学外国语学院在读研究生。研究方向：日语语言文学。电子邮箱：1035996563@qq.com。

陈芳，硕士，贵州大学外国语学院教授、硕士生导师。研究方向：中日文化对比研究。电子邮箱：1271582677@qq.com。

"一带一路"推动下中国应用翻译研究的新领域
——《工程技术翻译学导论》介评

⊙ 梁富录(南开大学外国语学院,天津)

[摘 要] 在"一带一路"倡议的推动下,工程技术翻译研究逐渐从应用翻译研究中凸显出来,成为新的学术研究增长点。《工程技术翻译学导论》的出版恰逢其时。该书明确了工程技术翻译学的内涵与外延,调查了中外研究进展,论述了翻译主客体,探讨了翻译人才培养等整体性问题。该书拓宽了翻译研究领域,对翻译教育也有启发。本文首先简要介绍各章内容,然后对其特色之处进行评价。

[关键词] 一带一路;工程技术翻译;应用翻译研究;新领域

An Emerging Area of Pragmatic Translation Studies in China Driven by the Belt and Road Initiative: Comments on *An Introduction to Translatology of Industrial Engineering Interpretation & Translation*

LIANG Fulu (Nankai University, Tianjin)

Abstract: Driven by the Belt and Road Initiative, industrial engineering interpretation and translation studies gradually stands out from pragmatic translation studies as an emerging research area. In response to this trend, the book *An Introduction to Translatology of Industrial Engineering Interpretation & Translation* was published. It clarifies the connotation and denotation of industrial engineering interpretation and translation, investigates research progress worldwide, elaborates on the subject and object of translation, and discusses issues of common concern such as translation methods and translator training. This book broadens the scope of translation studies and inspires translation education. The paper first gives a brief introduction to the book, and then offers some comments on its value.

Key words: Belt and Road Initiative; industrial engineering interpretation and translation; pragmatic translation studies; emerging area

一、引言

从"师夷长技以制夷"的被迫拿来主义到"一带一路"的主动输出中国智慧,中国工程技术逐渐实现独立自主并跻身世界前列,中国也从积贫积弱的落后国家,发展成为负责任、有担当的世界大国,这其中工程技术翻译工作功不可没。工程技术翻译指引进或输出工程技术项目(工业工程项目建设、工业技术交流、工业技术和工艺引进与输出、成套工业装备及大中型单机设备引进与输出）从启动立项至结清手续全部过程中的翻译工作（刘川，2019：8）。中国工程技术翻译活动肇始于1840年鸦片战争时期，历史之悠久，规模之宏大，世界上首屈一指，是中国翻译研究的特色资源。

上世纪八九十年代，在中国经济建设和翻译学科独立意识的双重推动下，工程技术翻译曾作为科技翻译的主要类型得到一定程度的研究，但始终未成体系。至2013年，"一带一路"倡议的提出为加强工程技术翻译研究提供了新的契机和动力。首先，"一带一路"的优先领域是铁路、电力、水利等基础设施建设，需要大量工程技术翻译。其次，工程技术项目是在东道国陌生的地理、人文、法律、政治和经济环境下开展的集装备、技术和服务于一体的活动，文本外的翻译变量众多，翻译难度较大。再次，中国工程"走出去"正经历市场导向、全产业链输出、深度合作和抱团走出去四个转向（谢宜泽，2018：80），要求翻译工作与时俱进。最后，工程技术翻译同样承载着国家形象对外宣传的使命，应从战略高度认识和重视其在中国历史和当下的地位与作用。在"一带一路"倡议提出的翌年，习近平总书记出席了"国际工程科技大会"，体现了国家对工程技术"走出去"和国际合作的高度重视。中国工程技术国际贸易也随之步入了发展快车道。据刘瑾（2021）报导，2021年上半年，工程机械代表性企业三一集团和徐工集团国际销售收入同比分别大幅上涨80%和70%。

当前，工程技术翻译研究方兴未艾。2021年11月重庆交通大学外国语学院举办了"国际工程文明叙事与话语体系建设"学术论坛，就工程文明叙事与话语、技术传播人才培养、服务工程建设的语言教育、工程规范和标准的翻译及国际传播、工程典籍翻译与传播，以及工程技术话语语料库建设等议题开展了学术探讨。在此时代背景下，刘川教授以"一带一路"倡议为时代呼唤，将自身20多年工程技术翻译实践所见、所闻、所行、所思理论化，凝结成《工程技术翻译学导论》，于2019年底在上海外语教育出版社出版。方梦之和黄忠廉为该书作序，高度肯定了作者为开辟应用翻译研究新领域所做的贡献。本文首先简要介绍各章内容，然后对其特色之处进行评价。

二、内容提要

该书共16章，分为基础论、客体论、主体论和整体论四部分。

（一）基础论

基础论由第1-5章构成，从定义、历史和理论基础三方面论证了工程技术翻译学作为一门学科的可行性和必要性。第1章"工程技术翻译学的定义"指出工程技术翻译学就是研究引进或输出工程技术项目从启动立项至结清手续全过程"一条龙"翻译工作的学科。探讨了其与"科学翻译学""科技翻译研究""应用翻译学""企业翻译研究"和"商务翻译研究"的联系与区别。

第2章"中国工程技术翻译历史概述"将中国工程技术翻译史分为晚晴时期（1840-1911）、民国时期（1912-1949）、中苏友好时期（1950-1960）、自力更生时期（1961-1978）、改革开放时期（1978-2015）和援外输出工程技术项目时期（1950-2015），介绍了各个时期的翻译活动、翻译人员和翻译特点。

第3章"世界各国工程技术翻译历史概述"调查了主要国家翻译组织的性质、数量、成立时间等，重点介绍了从事工程技术翻译的组织。结合各国历史，分析翻译语言及成因。翻译人员方面，调查了翻译人员的来源、性别和素质构成等。翻译活动方面，调查了翻译内容和翻译方式。

第4章"国内外关于工程技术翻译的研究"从成果数量、发表层次、作者背景和研究内容等方面对相关研究进行了梳理和评价。总体来说，国内工程技术翻译研究规模小，发表层次走低，一线作者日渐难觅，研究内容多是对静态科普文本的语言学分析，而非对严格意义上的工程技术资料的研究。国外研究之匮乏较国内有过之而无不及。造成上述现状的原因是多方面的，既有翻译研究内部原因，也有深层社会原因。

第5章"工程技术翻译学的理论借鉴"论述了功能学派、传播学、认知科学和生态翻译学理论对工程技术翻译学的指导作用，并创造性地引入了工程哲学和ISO9000质量管理体系理论。工程哲学的借鉴作用在于工程活动基本过程、思维方式、工程理念等为构建工程技术翻译学提供了更加广阔的理论和专业知识视野。ISO9000质量管理体系则对中国制定工程技术翻译标准，提高翻译质量保证具有借鉴意义。

（二）客体论

客体论由第6-9章构成，聚焦工程技术翻译的环境和翻译内容。第6章"工程技术翻译的语境场"将语境场分为情景语境场和语篇语境场。前者是翻译内容的外部环境，包括翻译的对象、时机、时间、场所和客户等。后者是翻译语言范畴的内部结构或图式。据此构建了项目考察与预选（图式A）和项目实施（图式D）等八种翻译语篇图式。语篇图式是构建工程技术翻译学的特殊方法论，也是构建本学科其它新概念、新知识的基本依据。

第7章"工程技术翻译的话语场"借鉴语言学话语相关理论，从话语者、话语分类、话语性质、话题、话轮和话步多角度阐释了工程技术话语场的特殊之处。作者分析了工程技术翻译话语者的构成及其相互关系，从话语形态、发生地和功能三个方面对话语进行了分类。在此基础上，着重分析了工程技术翻译话语的整体同一性、长期矛盾性和可操作性特征。最后，划分出项目启动、商务经济等多个话题丛，论述了各话题丛开展的时间顺序和逻辑结构，即话题和话步。

第8章"工程技术翻译的语域"指出语域既包括方言和行话等语言形态变体，也包括公关和技术等知识范畴。据此提出工程技术翻译语域由一般语域、特殊语域、知识语域和方言语域构成，并构建了口笔译方言语域区别模式。该模式以各英语方言区距离中国的远近为距离系数，以人种、语言、文化等方面与中国的相似程度为相关系数，直观展现了各英语方言区与中国英语方言区之间的交流难度，对翻译实践、教学和研究都具有启发意义。

第9章"工程技术翻译的词汇和语句"首先论述了该领域词汇的性质，指出工程技术翻译的词汇基本语义多于附属意义、学科义位多于普通义位，词汇间存在上下义结构、总分结构、序列结构等。其次，论述了工程技术词汇民族性的产生、表现形式和意义。再次，按照客户群、项目文件和语用范围对工程技术词汇进行分类。最后，构建了面向翻译的英语和汉语语句难度计算公式。

（三）主体论

主体论由第10-12章构成，聚焦工程技术译者及其认知和思维。第10章"工程技术项目的译者"探讨了译者的分类、权力、伦理、风格和身份。本章的特色之处在于作者对工程技术翻译译者权力和伦理的分析。工程技术翻译者承袭了委托方的部分权利，其口译权力与中立性成反比，笔译权力与文件专业性成反比。译者伦理与翻译标准和译者权力形成相互作用的独立系统，并成为调整翻译标准、限制或扩大译者权力的主角，据此构建了口笔译伦理曲线。

第11章"工程技术译者的认知过程"探讨了工程技术口笔译的感知、记忆、加工、转换和产出过程。着重分析了工程技术活动的特殊环境对译员视觉、嗅觉和听觉的冲击及其对翻译感知、记忆和加工过程的作用。在此基础上，提出工程技术译者自我四重监控/修补机制，如口译的四重监控机制包括元认知监控、客户的选择性反应、现场客观语境的反馈和口译者的言语产出修补行为。

第12章"工程技术译者的思维场"明确了翻译思维场的定义、特征、发展期、类型以及工程效应。翻译思维场是译者从事翻译任务期间头脑中发生的所有思维过程和活动，具有时空性和空间性等特征，历经发展期、潜思维期和趋显思维期而逐渐成熟。它包括抽象思维场、形象思维场和灵感思维场。作者分析了每种思维场的基本形式、性质和规律。最后，借鉴工程哲学理论，阐述了翻译思维场的工程价值定向效应、逻辑-超协调逻辑效应和容错性效应。

（四）整体论

整体论由第13-16章构成，专题探讨工程技术翻译性质与特征、翻译标准体系、翻译方法论和翻译教育等关乎学科定位与发展的核心问题。第13章"工程技术翻译的性质与特征"阐释了工程技术翻译的多维性、工程性、精确性、强制性和复合性以及它们的具体表征。如工程性包括全员性、全过程性、质量监控性和客户需求至上性，其中全员性又指项目全体员工都有机会参与翻译话语的交际活动，这在其它行业翻译中是少见的。

第14章"工程技术翻译的标准体系"建立了由核心理念、共同原则和实施规范构成的宏、中、微三级标准体系。以核心理念为例。核心理念是以顾客为关注焦点的选择性忠实或精确。"以顾客为关注焦点"吸收了ISO9000质量管理体系思想，强调译者应将确保客户项目顺利建设放在首位。"选择性忠实"一是指用词应符合特定语用范围，二是指对工程技术文本及技术话语意义的全部忠实，而对其他话语的部分忠实甚至不忠实。

第15章"工程技术翻译的方法论"构建了由元方法、一级指导性方法和二级操作策略方法所构成的翻译方法体系。元方法指译者对翻译方法知识的掌握、选择及运用能力。一级方法包括基于目标、基于过程和基于手段三种方法。二级方法则是针对特定使用范围和语言特征制定的方法，比如基于过程翻译方法中的"变译（摘译）—直译"二级方法适用于某些商务资料和技术标准翻译，其译文长度明显小于原文长度。

第16章"工程技术翻译的教育论"指出工程技术翻译教育的意义及现有人才培养问题，规划了教育目标及实现路径。作者指出开展工程技术翻译教育是"一带一路"倡议和中国实现现代化、走向世界的历史趋势对外语教育事业提出的时代性要求。高校翻译教育应与时俱进，树立服务意识，建立完善的学位制度，充实课程体系，强化产学研融合，以培养"工程师+译员"等不同类型的工程技术翻译人才。

三、简 评

该书作者集工程技术翻译实践、研究和教学于一身，兼具行业认知、理论修养和教育关切，使得该书具有以下特色和价值。

（一）著述价值

该书是翻译学科对国家和社会需求的积极响应。"一带一路"倡议的提出，推动了工程翻译需求（黄友义，2017：2），使其成为部分"走出去"企业的"刚需"。根据崔启亮、刘佳鑫（2016：71）的调查，有语言服务需求的国企中工程机械企业占比最多。笔者也曾参与国内企业出口越南、印度尼西亚、印度和土耳其等国的工程技术项目翻译工作，深切感受到它们参与"一带一路"沿线国家工程技术贸易的热情。有鉴于此，加强工程技术翻译研究，是翻译学科社会价值的体现。因此，该书的出版可谓恰逢其时。

该书也是对应用翻译研究的重要拓宽。技术翻译可视为由宏观层面的科技翻译、中观层面的工程技术翻译和微观层面的冶金、铁路、石化等具体领域翻译构成的多元、多层、总分系统。以往的技术翻译著作多是宏观的"科技翻译"，知识性有余而操作性不足，且适用范围模糊，对细分领域翻译实践的指导作用有限。

当下欠缺的是一线翻译人员借鉴现有翻译理论体系，将自身翻译经验总结升华而成的中、微观翻译理论著作。这样自下而上编写的著作有望实现理论与实践的双向互动，改善科技翻译教材泛泛而谈，基本没有实际操作性的局面。该书作者一线翻译经验丰富、理论意识较强，将多个细分领域的翻译实践集结成中观翻译理论，打通理论与实践双向互动通道的同时，拓宽了应用翻译研究领域。

（二）资料价值

首先，译史资料。数十年来，中国翻译史研究重文学翻译轻科学翻译（方梦之、傅敬民，2018：67），对工程技术翻译实践史、学术史和教育史的梳理更是凤毛麟角。作者通过图书馆藏书、数据库、新闻报导等，收集并梳理了中外工程技术翻译史料，为中国科技翻译史注入了新鲜血液。其次，译例资料。该书含有大量真实译例，辅助理论阐释，可为同类著作编写提供参考。再次，文献资料。该书参考文献宏富，涉及理、工、文多学科，有助于翻译学者深入理解和借鉴相关研究成果，拓宽学术视野。

（三）理论价值

翻译大国，应有自创的译学话语体系（方梦之，2017：93）。该书立足中国大规模工程技术翻译实践，开辟了具有中国特色的应用翻译研究话语体系。该话语体系理论网络发达，涵盖了应用翻译学理论的五大来源（黄忠廉、李亚舒，2013：97）。一是从实践中提炼理论，如对工程技术翻译方法的总结（第13章）。二是借鉴基本译论，如借鉴翻译标准规范研究成果构建工程技术翻译三级标准体系（第14章）。三是工程技术翻译理论在非翻译领域的应用，如将理论化的工程技术口译方言模式用于外语专业学生语音训练（第16章）。四是挪用其他学科理论，如利用语言学中的语境理论构建工程技术翻译语境场（第6章）。五是类比适用其他学科理论，如类比适用生态翻译学理论（第5章）。这些理论丰富了翻译研究的理论路径，其改造适用过程值得借鉴。

（四）教育价值

中国外语人才数量众多，但质量不高，能胜任科技等难度较大翻译工作的人才急缺（顾俊玲，2018：36），翻译界对科技翻译教学与教材建设等译才培养关键性问题关注较少（单宇、范武邱、谢菲，2017：42）。因此，该书对工程技术翻译学科建设和人才培养的专题探讨弥足珍贵。作者调查了中国科技翻译教育现状，对办学层次、课程内容、课时数等进行了梳理和评价。制定了清晰的教育目标，包括人才定位、能力构成、授课内容、就业范围等。提出了具体的顶层办学理念和制度支持，如采取"产学研"融合的办学模式，设立研究基金等。这些建议是在现有翻译学科话语体系框架下，结合工程技术翻译教育需求提出的，具有一定的可行性。

四、结 语

中国工程技术翻译历史悠久、规模宏大、贡献卓著、特点显著，但是相关研究却较为匮乏，不成体系。"一带一路"又对工程技术翻译实践和研究提出了新的议题和需求，翻译学界应予以回应。《工程技术翻译学导论》是对工程技术翻译实践、研究和教育的系统论述，有望凝聚学术共同体，促进相关翻译研究和教学，提升翻译学科服务国家和社会发展的能力。

该书也有少数不足，如第15章"机器翻译策略"一节参考文献陈旧，对机器翻译原理和适用范围的论述没有考虑近年的神经网络技术，导致部分观点有失偏颇。尽管如此，该书仍不失为一部亮点频闪的开山之作，具有较高的学术价值和应用价值，值得深入研读。

参考文献

[1] Cui, Qiliang & Liu, Jiaxin (崔启亮, 刘佳鑫). A Survey-based Analysis of the Language Service Demand of State-owned Enterprises and its Implications (国有企业语言服务需求调查分析及启示) [J]. *Chinese Translators Journal* (中国翻译), 2016(4): 70-76.

[2] Fang, Mengzhi (方梦之). China Needs Her Own Translatological Discourse System (翻译大国需有自创的译学话语体系) [J]. *Foreign Languages in China* (中国外语), 2017(5): 93-100.

[3] Fang, Mengzhi & Fu, Jingmin (方梦之, 傅敬民). Vitalizing Research on Chinese Science Translation History — The Area of Pragmatic Translation Studies to be Explored (振兴科学翻译史的研究———应用翻译研究有待拓展的领域) [J]. *Journal of Foreign Languages* (外国语), 2018(3): 67-75.

[4] Gu, Junling (顾俊玲). Foreign Language Plus Technology: Interdisciplinary Major for Training Talents in Science and Technology Translation (外语+科技：复合专业打造科技翻译人才) [J]. *Chinese Science & Technology Translators Journal* (中国科技翻译), 2018(3): 36-38+63.

[5] Huang, Youyi (黄友义). Belt and Road Initiative and China's Translation — Reform Oriented Towards Application ("一带一路"和中国翻译——变革指向应用的方向) [J]. *Shanghai Journal of Translators* (上海翻译), 2017(3): 1-3.

[6] Huang, Zhonglian & Li, Yashu (黄忠廉, 李亚舒). The Top Five Sources of Applied Translation Studies (应用翻译学理论的五大来源) [J]. *Shandong Foreign Language Teaching Journal* (山东外语教学), 2013(2): 97-100.

[7] Liu, Chuan (刘川). *An Introduction to Translatology of Industrial Engineering Interpretation & Translation* (工程技术翻译学导论[M]). Shanghai: Shanghai Foreign Language Education Press (上海：上海外语教育出版社), 2019.

[8] Liu, Jin (刘瑾). Good News from Engineering Machinery "Going Out" (工程机械喜出"往外") [N]. *Economic Daily* (经济日报) 2021-08-17(6) [2021-08-17].

[9] Shan, Yu & Fan, Wuqiu & Xie, Fei (单宇, 范武邱, 谢菲). A Visualized Analysis of Science and Technology Translation (1985-2015) in China (国内科技翻译研究（1985—2015）可视化分析) [J]. *Shanghai Journal of Translators* (上海翻译), 2017(2): 34-42.

[10] Xie, Yize (谢宜泽). China Projects "Going Out": From Tanzam Railway to Addis Ababa-Djibouti Mode (中国工程"走出去"：从坦赞铁路到亚吉模式) [J]. *African Studies* (非洲研究), 2018(2): 80-93.

作者简介

梁富录，南开大学外国语学院博士研究生。研究方向：科技翻译、翻译技术、数字人文。电子邮箱：liang_fulu@126.com。

《人生》民俗文化形象俄译重构研究

⊙ 周一钦（黑龙江大学俄罗斯语言文学与文化研究中心，哈尔滨）

[摘　要] 民俗文化内涵丰富、地域特色显著，往往成为一个地域乃至国家的形象表征，是跨文化翻译中关注的重难点问题。路遥在《人生》中通过生态民俗文化、物质民俗文化、精神民俗文化、乡土语言民俗文化等，勾勒出陕北黄土高原一带的风土人情，塑造了80年代初城乡二元交融、鬼神信仰盛行、乡土人物形象立体的乡土中国文化形象。本文基于自建小型汉俄双语平行语料库，结合关键词表对不同类型民俗文化词汇进行定性与定量分析，考察译者在民俗文化翻译过程中的再现策略，总结《人生》对外译介中乡土中国文化形象俄译重构中的得失表征。

[关键词] 《人生》；民俗；乡土中国文化形象；俄译

Reconstruction of Folk-culture Images in the Chinese-Russian Translation of *Life*

ZHOU Yiqin (Center for Russian Language Literature and Culture Studies of HeiLongjiang University, Harbin)

Abstract: The folk-culture with affluent connotation and distinctive regional characteristics, representing the image of a region or even a country, is the keystone and difficulty in translation across cultures. The writer Lu Yao, by outlining in the novel *Life* the local customs and practices in the Loess Plateau of Northern Shaanxi through four categories, ie. ecological folk culture, material folk culture, spiritual folk culture, and local language folk culture, established the rural Chinese cultural images during the early 1980s, which contained urban-rural structure, supernature culture and farmer images. Based on the self-built small Chinese-Russian bilingual parallel corpus, this paper conducts a qualitative and quantitative analysis of different keywords of folk cultures, inspecting the translator's reproduction strategy in the process of folk culture translation, and summarizes the characterization of gains and losses in the reconstruction of rural Chinese cultural images from Chinese into Russian.

Key words: *Life*; folk culture; rural Chinese cultural images; Russian translation

一、引　言

自上自世纪80年代以来，中国当代优秀作家路遥的作品陆续以俄文、法文等语种向海外输出。其成名作《人生》于1982年发表，后荣获第二届全国优秀中篇小说奖，2018年入选"中国改革开放四十周年最有

本文为黑龙江大学2022年研究生创新科研重点项目"《人生》乡土中国文化形象俄译重构研究"（项目编号：YJSCX2022-070HLJU）的阶段性研究成果。

影响力小说"，至今已有俄法日英维蒙六个译本面世，是路遥作品中被翻译最多的一部。从历时角度看，《人生》译介起步较早，前苏联汉学家谢曼诺夫翻译的俄译本 *Судьба* 成为其流传海外的第一个译本，1988年由苏联青年近卫军出版社首次出版，2019年经由俄罗斯Шанс国际出版社再次发行，在俄罗斯读者中广受好评。

《人生》俄译本 *Судьба* 在俄罗斯的再度流行绝非偶然，路遥本人乃至20世纪中国当代文学受俄苏文学影响深远，俄苏文学中的"农村题材"小说与中国乡土文学在形成背景与精神内涵上不乏相似之处。从基层上看去，中国社会是乡土性的（费孝通，1947：10）。俄罗斯作为中国的兄弟之邦，两国文学文化深度交融，发展具有相似的历史语境。在中国文化"走出去"的战略背景下，俄译本 *Судьба* 所呈现出的乡土中国文化形象内涵值得深入研究。

二、《人生》民俗文化形象

华夏文明发轫于黄河流域一带的农耕文明，以黄土高原为己根脉，位于黄土高原核心地带的陕北是我国农耕文明的重要发祥地，是乡土中国的根基所在。在《人生》的叙事空间中，路遥"坚持文学的现实性和当代性相统一原则"，"一贯重视文学的'时代意义'和'社会意义'，重视创作题材'广阔而深刻的社会生活的内涵'"（李星，1991：88-96），通过一系列陕北民俗文化形象，即通过对陕北地域百姓衣食住行、婚丧嫁娶、祭祀祖先、日常交流等风土人情的描绘，展现出陕北乡村、乡民的世俗生活场景，初步建构出上世纪80年代乡土中国文化形象的表征情况。本文将《人生》中所呈现出的民俗文化形象分为生态民俗文化形象、物质民俗文化形象、精神民俗文化形象、乡土语言民俗文化四类（见表1）。

表1.《人生》民俗文化形象类别及部分实例

民俗文化形象类别	《人生》中的民俗文化形象部分实例
生态民俗文化	老牛山；高家村；马店村；黄土高原；大马河；南马河
物质民俗文化	的确良；蓝布衣服；蓝涤卡罩衣；蓝劳动布上衣；涤卡；尼龙袜；塑料凉鞋；浅毛蓝裤子；赤脚片；布鞋；蓝布裤；白市布瓜帽；玉米面馍；白面饼；荞面饸饹；扁食；白馍；蒸馍；八碗；合饹；油糕；寒窑；土炕；石窑洞；窗纸；风箱；五孔窑洞；架子车；"飞鸽"自行车；吉普车；拖拉机
精神民俗文化	报应；龙王爷；玉皇大帝；菩萨心肠
乡土语言民俗文化	没吃过猪肉，连猪哼哼都没听过；金花配银花，西葫芦配瓜；哪个猫都沾腥；灌清米汤；二流子；二杆子；碎脑娃娃

其中生态民俗文化形象是对某一地域自然地理、居住环境的表现，常包括山川湖泊、动植物等自然生态元素。《人生》以20世纪80年代初社会转型时期陕北农村与城镇的"交叉地带"为叙事空间，作品中生态民俗文化形象所蕴藉的"乡土味"与"市井味"浓郁，具有鲜明的地域交叉特征，如"高家村""马店村"，形象表明了乡土中国聚村而居，以地缘与血缘关系形成的差序格局。物质民俗文化形象主要包括服饰、饮食、住所、交通等，如"的确良""劳动布""馍""土炕"等再现了当时人民的物质水平与生活风貌，时代性鲜明。精神民俗文化形象反映了人民的世界观与价值观，如"因果善恶报应论"。钟敬文（1998：6）指出语言民俗包括民俗语言和民间文学，其中狭义的民俗语言指民间俗语、谚语、歇后语、街头流行语、黑话、酒令等，民间文学则指神话、民间传说、民间故事、民间歌谣、民间说唱等形式。本文所涉乡土语言民俗则包含地方方言、民歌、俚语、习语等，是特定地域人群的表达习惯与文化缩影，如"金花配银花，西葫芦配瓜"。

三、《人生》民俗文化形象欠额重构

《人生》俄译本从生态民俗、物质民俗、精神民俗与乡土语言民俗文化形象四个不同层面对乡土中国文化形象进行了详细阐释，展现出城乡二元融合、鬼神信仰盛行、乡土人物形象立体的丰富表征。但由于译者采取不同的翻译策略与方法，使这些形象的表征效果有所变化。欠额重构指译者在翻译过程中对原文文化形象进行删除或替换，使原文所呈现的文化形象轮廓或内涵消失。其中，由于文化缺省，译者常用译语文化形象替换源语文化形象。

（一）城乡欠时代性

从城乡物质基础看，译者在呈现城乡相关物质民俗文化时，部分形象进行了省译或替换，从而导致城乡二元对立现象不明显，未能完全体现出 80 年代乡土中国文化中的城乡贫富差距及城乡时代性特征，从而导致乡土中国文化形象在呈现城乡二元图式时有所缺失（见表 2）。

表 2. 物质民俗文化形象及译法频数

物质民俗文化形象	替换频数	省译频数	直译频数	增译频数
的确良	2	12	—	—
涤卡	—	2	—	—
蓝布	—	2	—	1
蓝咔叽	—	2	—	—
蓝劳动布	—	1	1	—

80 年代初正值改革开放初期，人民的物质生活并不富裕，陕北农村以及广大农村地区多采用家织棉粗布、劳动布制作服饰，故原文中常有贫苦农民身穿"蓝布""蓝咔叽""蓝劳动布"，但在译文中却多进行了省译。与之对立的"的确良"则是一种稀罕布料，是纯涤纶或与棉、毛混纺制的织物，学名为涤纶，也称涤卡，最初在粤语中音译为"的确凉"，后传至北方，改为"的确良"，相比于粗布服饰，它更为耐磨，并且易洗不褪色，材质挺括，广受大众青睐，成为上世纪风靡一时的时尚单品。尽管 1976 年至 1979 年间，"的确良"面料逐渐普及，但价格昂贵，对于农村人来说，仍旧是奢侈品。"的确良"在《人生》中一共出现了 14 次，每次都出现在一些较为重要的场合，并非人人都穿得上。例如，村中首富家的女儿巧珍在与心上人高加林见面时，才穿上"的确良"服装，但是在俄语译本中仅有两处被翻译出，有 12 处都进行了省译处理，从而弱化城乡贫富差距，未能突出时代性特征。

（二）乡土欠地域性

《人生》叙事围绕陕北黄土高原展开，地域特色显著，但在译本中极具地方色彩的民俗文化形象却进行了省译，如生态民俗文化形象"黄土高原"，物质民俗文化形象"土窑""石窑"等。窑洞，至今仍是黄土高原地区陕北广大农民的居住方式，早期雏形可追溯至西安仰韶文化半坡遗址中出现的半穴居住所，其设计理念遵循人地和谐的思想，巧妙地利用了陕北黄土及地理的特性（钱茂荣，2017：78-83），具有浓厚的历史传承底蕴与乡土文化气息。译文除进行省译外，将"窑"这一文化形象的同源词，采用"комната""дом"等词替换，归化色彩明显，使陕北居住民俗特色完全丧失。

物质民俗文化形象"玉米面馍""白蒸馍"是陕北地区的日常食物，但是上世纪 80 年代，陕北耕种环境恶劣，缺少基础水力措施等，小麦也并非高产种类，所以由小麦制成的白面十分珍贵，陕北农民们更多是以玉米、荞麦制成的面食为主。在俄译本中，"玉米面馍""白蒸馍"译作"грубые кукурузные пампушки"或"паровые пампушки"，"пампушки"由小麦粉制成，需经烤箱、烤炉烘烤，表面呈金黄色，用这一形象进行翻译，不仅扭曲了"馍"的形象轮廓，还丢失了陕北饮食民俗文化特征，未能展现出白蒸馍与玉米面馍之间的差距。

（三）农民欠粗野性

人物是读者从描写、描述或暗示主人公行为、思想、言语或感情的词语、句子、段落和篇章各要素中推断出来的（Van Peer，1989：9）。原文在进行村民动作描写时，共有六处写到"一屁股坐下"，表示动作迅速稳当，但在译文中呈现时，译者只用"сеть"翻译了"坐"这一动作，并未体现出"一屁股"的语义与形象，这种方式不仅使译文呈现更为文雅，也使农民"坐"这一行为动作不再显得粗鲁，从而淡化了农民的粗野形象。此外，还有一些方言土语形象的替换，也淡化了粗野形象，见下例：

[1] 原文：尿泡尿照照你们的影子。

译文：Вместо зеркала в собственные лужи смотрятся.

[2] 原文："高加林不光辱没了你，把咱们一家人都拿猪尿泡打了，满身的臊气！"

译文："Этот Цзялинь опозорил тебя, всю нашу семью, как боров, обмо- чил, до сих пор воняем!"

[3] 原文：只要娃娃们同意，别说娘老子，就是天王老子也管不住！

译文：Если молодые согласны пожениться, то родители в счет не идут, будь они хоть с самого неба.

将原著中对农民话语的描写与译者进行形象替换、改写后的农民话语描写进行对比，可以发现，译者对农民形象进行了重构，例[1]中，"尿泡尿"被译作"用自己的一洼水当镜子"（вместо зеркала в собственные лужи）。例[2]中方言"猪尿泡打了"，改用"猪尿湿了"（боров, обмочил）。在例[3]中，译者将"天王老子""娘老子"分别译作"самое небо""родители"，"老子"在汉语语言系统中表示"父亲"或"骄傲的人的自称，即'我'的意思"，是一种不雅的表达，译者在翻译时用"самое"强调"небо"，用"родители"将"父亲，母亲"进行了合译，表达上相比中文，更为书面文雅。

史崇文、季明举（2022）指出，俄罗斯农村小说历来的基本调性是表现俄罗斯农民生活中的苦难和农民身上的宗法观念，挖掘农民的优良道德品质，体现出浓郁的乡土情结和厚重的道德传统。当代农村小说，往往侧重体现农村的情况，集中刻画历史变迁中的农民性格，关注人与自然、人与劳动、人与土地的关系，抒发对农村的热爱和对农民的尊重，表现出俄罗斯人传统美德的颂扬。在翻译实践中，译者出于本人的文化立场、文人身份与理念，以及接受语所在地（苏联世界）农民形象的影响，对《人生》原作中农民过于粗俗的污言秽语用其他形象进行了替换改写，使原著所呈现的农民粗野形象有所淡化或丢失，以符合译语读者的审美想象。

四、《人生》民俗文化形象保额重构

在保额重构中，译者多采用直译、字面翻译或直译与意译结合的翻译方法，最大限度地保留民俗文化形象在《人生》中构建的系列表征。译者曾说："我想尽我的力量，让苏联人民通过作品了解中国人民各方面的生活实际。"当地理空间通过翻译在不同文化语境之间发生转换时，难免会有失落或形变，因此，译者应采取文化补充策略在新语境中多维度地还原和重构源文空间（王岫庐，2014：74-80）。但由于客观文化差异及译者主体性因素影响，保额重构可分为直接保额与间接保额。

直接保额偏向异化，在翻译过程中原文形象无须中间形象替换变形，原文形象外壳与内涵在译语中得以全部还原保留，具有求真性，"求真"是译者忠实于原文和语言性的本能表现，是译者行为最根本的出发点（周领顺、杜玉，2017：21-26）。因此，在直接保额中，以直译法、字面翻译为主。

（一）乡景保真

虽然《人生》中有关陕北乡土风光的景色描写仅有几处，却在行文中承担着不同的叙事功能，不仅展现了和谐清新的优美风景，同时也对情节发展、人物感情渲染具有递进作用。对于文中的生态乡景翻译，译者求真保真，遵循忠实的翻译原则，直接再现陕北乡土风光。

[4] 原文：星星如同亮闪闪的珍珠一般撒满了暗蓝色的天空。西边老牛山起伏不平的曲线，像谁用炭笔勾出来似的柔美；大马河在远处潺潺地流淌，像二胡拉出来的旋律一般好听。一阵轻风吹过来，遍地的谷叶响起了沙沙沙的响声。风停了，身边一切便又寂静下来。头顶上，婆娑的、墨绿色的叶丛中，不成熟的杜梨在朦胧的月下泛着点点青光。

译文：А в темно-голубом небе жемчужинами мерцали звезды, на западе высилась гора Старого быка, словно нарисованная углем, вдалеке звенела река Лошадиная, как будто кто-то искусно играл на китайской скрипке. Больше не слышалось ничего; ни ветерка, все вокруг замерло. В темно-зеленой листве груши над их головами колыхались блики лунного света.

译者在进行翻译时，也较为忠实地呈现出原文乡土景象，通过一系列自然景物形象"небо""звезды""гора""река""лист""груши"的组合再现，勾勒出陕北乡土恬静和谐，欣欣向荣的秀美自然风光。对于极具中国乡土特色的地理名称翻译也遵循直译原则，如将"老牛山""大马河"译作"гора Старого быка""река Лошадиная"，保留了原文语言特色与乡土中国文化形象风貌。

（二）乡语保俗

张旭（2015：87-110）指出民间话语的最大特点便落在一个"俗"字上，这个"俗"字可以同时作"通俗""低俗""粗俗"等义解。这类话语形式鲜活，语域广泛，它们往往简洁精练又通俗易懂，长期为汉民族所喜爱。《人生》中有不少形象丰富的乡土俗语，表现了陕北乡民淳朴直白的语言特点，译者在翻译这些俗语时，具有明显的保俗特点（见表3）。

表 3. 乡土俗语文化形象及其俄译

俗语	俄译
没吃过猪肉，连猪哼哼都没听过	не пробовал свинины, то хоть бы хрюканье-то слышал
刀子嘴豆腐心	язык как нож, а сердце -как соевый творог
别灌清米汤	рисового отвару не заливай
金花配银花，西葫芦配南瓜	золотые цветы липнут к серебряным, а западная тыква к южной

由表3可见，译者在处理上述俗语形象时，具有浓郁的异化色彩，译文完整保留了原文中的俗语形象，采用字面翻译，表层结构完全求真于原文，但由于文化差异的影响，译语读者可能无法完全理解表层结构下的深层含义，如"别灌清米汤"的意思是不要用甜言蜜语进行讨好、奉承，而"рисового отвару не заливай"这种字面翻译，在俄语世界中并没有相应的深层含义。

间接保额是在直接保额的基础上，部分形象发生替换变形，但译语整体表征在受众语读者中享有与原语整体表征在受众语读者中相同的效果，具有务实性。因此，在间接还原中，译者采用直译与意译相结合的翻译策略。

（三）还原因果报应论

《人生》中描写高玉德利用私权让自己的儿子顶替高加林的教师工作，高加林因为城市的诱惑而抛弃巧珍时，便多次提到老天爷的善恶报应。老天爷是中国神话中天上的主神，在中国人的思维中象征着天道与天理，其核心内涵为"积善之家，必有余庆；积不善之家，必有余殃"。在翻译过程中，译者用"небо"对"老天爷"这一形象进行进行了替换，在世界文化传统中，"天空"除了表示自然存在意义上的天，还象征着诗意性的理想世界，对阿赫马托娃等具有基督信仰的人来说，天空还是上帝的世界，但译者并未使用"бог"来阐释"老天爷"，"небо"这一翻译更为形象生动，内涵深刻，普遍接受度高，使乡土中国文化中的神灵崇拜得以充分表征，见下例：

[5] 原文：高玉德家这个坏小子，老天爷报应他呀！

译文：этот молодой подонок еще получит свое!

[6] 原文：他也认为这是老天爷终于睁了眼，给了高加林应得的报应。

译文：Все-таки есть у неба глаза, раз отплатило этому паскуднику!

[7] 原文：他做的歪事老天爷知道，将来会报应他的！

译文：небо знает, какие он дела творит, и отплатит ему!

[8] 原文：明楼！你做这事伤天理哩！老天爷总有一天要睁眼呀！

译文：Ты прогневал небо, Минлоу, оно тебя не пощадит!

译者在翻译"报应"一词时，除采用"отплатить"进行直译外，见例[6]与[7]，还融合了自己的阐释观，见例[6]中"отплатило этому паскуднику"，译者将原文中"高加林应得的报应"中隐藏的内容进行了显化，"паскудник"为俄语俚语，具有贬义，常作粗俗词汇，意为下流坏子，做卑鄙龌龊事的人，一方面体现了乡下人的随意与粗鲁，另一方面则暗示着做坏事会遭报应的因果思想。在例[5]与例[8]中，译者皆采用意译，虽然没有直接译出"报应"，但"получит свое"中也间接体现出人为自己做出的事承担后果，例[8]中，"пощадит"同样对原文语义进行显化翻译，揭示出做坏事会遭受老天惩罚的因果报应。

（四）还原神灵敬畏

在对一系列精神民俗文化形象进行翻译时，"龙王爷"，译作"царь дракона"，"玉皇大帝"译作"нефритовый владыка"，"菩萨心肠"译作"сердце бодисаты"（Буддийский святой, который отказывается от собственного спасения ради спасения других），这些形象的翻译皆体现了间接还原的特点，即借助译语文化受众读者所能理解的形象进行部分替换，使原文形象在译语文化中得到更好的诠释，比如"царь"是沙皇俄国时期君主的称呼，是最高统治者，"龙王爷"是对"龙王"的尊称，在中国古代神话中有行云布雨治水之责，故人们常常祈祷龙王，以求风调雨顺，在农耕中国里，龙王具有极高的民间信仰。译者采用"царь"一词，间接体现了龙王爷的地位。同样，"玉皇大帝"，译者采用崇高词汇"主宰"（владыка），突出"玉皇大帝"的身份与地位，较为完整地保留了原文形象。"心肠"在中国指"心地"，如果在俄语中分别译出"心"与"肠"的形象，反而令人不解，译者在进行翻译时，同时对"菩萨"这一形象进行注释，丰富了其内在含义与背景信息，帮助读者更好理解原文。以鬼神为核心构建出来的文化现象，广泛存在于中国民众的精神生活中，几千年来这一极具中国文化特色的现象，不仅影响着民众的生活、生产，而且也左右着民众的精神、心理，导致中国一般民众的思维始终处于较原始的状态，成为中国民众国民性的基本内容之一（薛文礼，2003：50-52）。

五、《人生》民俗文化形象超额重构

超额重构，指译者在保额重构的基础上，通过注释或增译等方法，对原文形象的内涵进行阐释或补充，从而达到"厚译"效果，其中"厚译"是通过给原文增补社会、历史、文化等背景信息来扩大目的语读者的视野的，从而帮助译语读者更好地理解原文（周领顺、杜玉，2017：21-26）。

（一）突出农民身份

原文中多次出现乡巴佬、老百姓、土包子老百姓、乡里人、乡下人、庄稼人、农民等词，这些身份蕴含的"土味"程度不一，体现出不同的感情色彩。俄译本中再现这些形象时，译者并非完全遵循原文语义。例如，"老百姓"在原文中共出现 8 次，学界认为"老百姓"是统治阶层以外的人群，具有特定的历史语境，在《人生》中每次都是农民身份的人物对自己或其他农民的称呼。但译者在翻译时，抛却了模糊的百姓身份，采用语义为农民的"крестьяин"及其同源词，或选用语义为农民的"деревенская девка"，补充了乡土中国基层群体是农民的想象，以及说话人的农民身份（见表 4）。

表 4. 关键词及其俄译

关键词	俄译
老百姓的儿子	крестьянский сын
土包子老百姓	простый народ；деревенская девка
土老百姓	простые крестьяне
老百姓	крестьянка；крестьяне；народ；省略

（二）增加民俗形象异质性

《人生》中具有丰富的生态、物质、精神、乡土语言等民俗文化形象，中国国家特色鲜明，异质性突出，"异"既是翻译的缘起，也是导致翻译障碍的最重要因素，无论语言之异，还是思维之异、文化之异，都会给翻译活动带来实实在在的困难（刘云虹，2021：72-80）。译者通过注释或增译方式，对这些异质文化内涵进行延伸与补充，使其文化价值有所凸显，提高译语读者的可理解度与可读性，例如：

[9] 原文：他母亲颠着小脚往炕上端饭。

Мать, ковыляя на своих бинтованных ножках, несла на кан еду.

例[9]中，小脚来自中国古代的缠足陋习，女性双脚需用布紧紧缠裹，使之畸形变小，至新中国成立后，缠足陋习才得以废除，妇女得到解放。译者增译了"缠绷带的"（бинтованных），是对"小脚"内涵的进一步补充与阐释。而"炕"的翻译，译者选择了音译与注释结合的方法，音译为"кан"，并在页面脚注位置增加了注释"Невысокая лежанка, обогреваемая изнутри и занимающая бльшую часть традиционного китайского дома"，采用异化与归化结合的翻译策略，音译保留了原文形象外壳，注释又对原文形象内涵进行了拓展与补充，彰显了东方异质文化的独特性。此外，《人生》俄译本中共有 12 处注释，其中有 9 处注释是对民俗文化形象的阐释，异质性得到更好的展现。

六、结 语

路遥着眼于"城乡交叉地带"平凡而又真实的生活，围绕陕北风土人情，再现了社会政治、经济、文化、思想、意识、道德观念等方面的矛盾，展现出我国 20 世纪 80 年代初转型时期城乡二元结构中的变动与互渗，《人生》中再现的乡土中国文化形象在俄语世界的表征有助于乡土中国文化形象的传播。由于文化缺省与文化立场影响，译者对原文民俗形象多采取欠额重构策略，对原文民俗形象进行删除省译，或借用译语文化形象进行替换，欠额重构主要对原文呈现出的城乡二元图式有所淡化；在保额重构中，译者遵循忠实的翻译原则，直译与意译结合，最大限度地保留原文民俗文化形象，使乡土中国文化形象的重要内涵得以还原；超额重构是跨文化交际中的重要桥梁，通过"厚译"向译语受众传达了异质文化的背景信息，强调了乡土中国文化形象的独特魅力。讲好中国故事，塑造中国形象，任重而道远，除西方汉学家译介之外，中国也可采取多路径多模态的方式，使中国形象在传播过程中更为生动、可理解。

参考文献

[1] Fei, Xiaotong (费孝通). *Rural China* (乡土中国[M]). Jinan: Shangdong Literature and Art Publishing House (济南：山东文艺出版社), 2019.

[2] Li, Xing (李星). "On the Way of Realism—about Lu Yao" (在现实主义的道路上——路遥论) [J]. *Journal of Literature Review*(文学评论), 1991(04): 88-96.

[3] Liu, Yunhong (刘云虹). "Further Analysis on Heterogeneitya and Translation Standpoint" (再论异质性与翻译立场) [J]. *Journal of Northwest Polytechnical University (Social Sciences Edition)* (西北工业大学学报（社会科学版）), 2021(03): 72-80.

[4] Qiang, Maorong (钱茂荣). "Cultural Context of Cave in Northern Shaanxi" (陕北窑洞的文化脉络) [J]. *Journal of Business Culture*(商业文化), 2017(35): 78-83.

[5] Shi, Congwen & Ji, Mingju (史崇文，季明举). "Native Complex of Russian Contemporary Rural Novels" (俄罗斯当代农村小说的乡土情结) [N]. *Chinese Social Sciences Weekly* (中国社会科学报), 2022-06-27.

[6] Van Peer, W (ed). *The Taming of the Text: Explorations in Language, Literature and Culture*[M]. London: Routledge, 1989.

[7] Wang, Xiulu (王岫庐). "Spatial Transformation and Reconstruction in Translation: Taking Hong Song's Adaptation *The Second Dream* for Example" (翻译中的空间转换与重构——以洪深改译剧《第二梦》为例) [J]. *Journal of Foreign Languages* (外国语(上海外国语大学学报)), 2014(06): 74-80.

[8] Xue, Wenli (薛文礼). "Custom Spirit and Cultural Transmission of Ghosts and Gods" (鬼神的礼俗精神与文化传承) [J]. *Journal of Yanbei Normal College*(雁北师范学院学报), 2003(01): 50-52.

[9] Zhong, Jingwen (钟敬文). *Introduction of Folklore* (民俗学概论[M]). Shanghai: Shanghai Literature Press (上海：上海文艺出版社), 1998.

[10] Zhou, Lingshun & Du, Yu (周领顺，杜玉). "Translator Behavior Degree of Goldblatt's Translation on Chinese 'Native Language': 'Seeking Truth and Being Pragmatic' in the Perspective of Translator Behavior Continuous Evaluation Mode" (汉语"乡土语言"葛译译者行为度——"求真-务实"译者行为连续统评价模式视阈) [J]. *Shanghai Journal of Translators* (上海翻译), 2017(06): 21-26.

[11] Zhang, Xu (张旭). "Translating Performative Texts: With Examples from Scene 2 of the English Translation of *Yuanye* by Jane Lai" (表演性文本之翻译——以黎翠珍英译《原野》第二幕为例) [J]. *Asia Pacific Interdisciplinary Translation Studies (the First Issue))*(亚太跨学科翻译研究(第一辑)). 2015(1): 87-110.

作者简介

周一钦，硕士研究生，黑龙江大学俄罗斯语言文学与文化研究中心。研究方向：文学翻译、语料库翻译。电子邮箱：y1qinzhou@163.com。

接受美学视角下《中国疫苗百年纪实》日译策略研究

⊙ 卢俊宇 王晓梅（贵州大学外国语学院，贵阳）

[摘 要] 2019年11月首次出版的纪实文学《中国疫苗百年纪实》对于当下正确把握疫情，科学应对疫情，吸取经验教训，打赢疫情防控阻击战具有重要的参考意义。从国际形势而言，该书的日译有助于抑制日本社会因疫情原因对华负面印象的攀升。本研究以文本的科普性、召唤性为出发点，从接受美学视角研究《中国疫苗百年纪实》日译策略，认为翻译一方面需照顾读者的接受视界，另一方面需保留或创造文本的召唤结构；对病名的翻译需要寻找与之对应的专业术语，若遇到民间或非官方病名的翻译，最主要是基于读者的原有图式，尽可能贴近病名的内涵意义。

[关键词] 接受美学；文本召唤；诗句日译；病名日译

A Study on the Strategy of Japanese Translation of *A Century Record of Vaccine in China* from the Perspective of Aesthetic of Reception

LU Junyu WANG Xiaomei (Guizhou University, Guiyang)

Abstract: The documentary literature *A Century Record of Vaccine in China*, first published in November 2019, is an important reference for people to correctly grasp the epidemic, scientifically respond to it, learn lessons and win the epidemic prevention and control blockade. In terms of the international situation, the Japanese translation of the book helps to curb the negative impression of Japanese society on China due to the epidemic. Based on the scientific and appealing feature of the text, this paper studes the Japanese translation of *A Century Record of Vaccine in China* from the perspective of aesthetic of reception. We hold that the translation should accommodate the receptive horizon of readers on the one hand and preserve or create the inviting structure of the text on the other hand. The translation of disease names requires the corresponding terminology. When translating the folk or unofficial disease names, the translator should base on the original schema of the readers to convey the connotative meaning of the disease names.

Key words: aesthetic of reception; textual inviting; Japanese translation of verses; Japanese translation of disease names

一、引 言

2019年11月，解放军报社原副总编江永红撰写的纪实文学作品《中国疫苗百年纪实》由人民出版社首次出版，该书以1919年北洋政府成立"中央防疫处"、现代医学进入中国防疫史为开端，通过一系列具体事件和人物，展现了中国近百年的抗疫历程，从一个特殊角度展现了中华民族坚强不屈、百折不挠的奋斗精神。2020年1月30日，突如其来的新冠疫情在中国各地蔓延之时，人民出版社及时推出该书的电子书，并在"学习强国"、中国移动、亚马逊等多家数字平台同步上线，免费供大众阅读。该书"对于当下正确把握疫情，科学应对疫情，吸取经验教训，打赢疫情防控阻击战具有重要的参考意义"（任宣，2020）。

从世界范围看，中国在新冠疫情防疫战上表现突出，获得世卫组织的高度肯定。然而，透过一些西方媒体和网友的评论可以看出，中国的抗疫效果和经验在部分国家被颠倒黑白或是嗤之以鼻。在日本，或许是受西方媒体影响，这类评论也是屡见不鲜。据日本"言論NPO"2020年9月至10月举行的"第16次日中共同舆论调查结果"显示，日本民众对中国的抗疫表现，59.1%的民众表示"对中国的印象没有改变"，23.1%的民众表示"信赖感下降"，表示"增加了对中国的信赖感"的民众只有11.4%（言論NPO，2020）。日本社会对中国抗疫成效的冷漠由此可见一斑。在此背景下，将《中国疫苗百年纪实》翻译介绍到日本，不仅可以让日本民众了解到中国近百年来不屈不挠的抗疫史，抑制因错误信息导致的对中国负面印象的产生，更可以通过纪实文学这种民众容易接受的文本形式讲述中国的抗疫故事，从而构建日本民众对中国抗疫能力的信赖感，形塑中国以人为本、以民为重的国家形象。

然而，翻译不是单纯的符号转换，更是一种以建立认同为目的的跨文化交际活动。伴随着对如何对外讲好中国故事探讨的深入，读者在对外翻译与传播中的重要性益发凸显，将读者置于中心地位的接受美学理论在翻译实践中的指导意义也得到学界的重视。朱立元将姚斯提出的"前结构"扩充至世界观和人生观、一般文化视野、艺术文化素养、文学能力这四个层次、四个要素（朱立元，2004:206）；并且从语音语调语形层、语义建构层、修辞格层、意象意境层、思想感情层的文学作品基本结构论述伊瑟尔的"本文的召唤结构"，指出以各层间的相互作用所产生的种种不确定性与空白召唤读者参与创造，以此构成文学作品的召唤结构（朱立元，2004:195）。因此，将姚斯与伊瑟尔的观点相结合共同指导翻译活动，能够避免片面地看待问题，始终保持翻译活动呈现既面向读者又尊重文本的双向开放性。有鉴于此，本研究拟以接受美学理论为指导，在文本分析、读者分析的基础上，对《中国疫苗百年纪实》的日译策略进行探讨，以期为纪实文学类文本的外译提供一定的参考。

二、《中国疫苗百年纪实》的思想精神与文本特征

《中国疫苗百年纪实》为一部纪实文学作品，"非虚构性、文化反思性和跨文体性共同构成纪实文学的基本写作伦理，这其中以充分表达作家主体诉求的、侧重于反思与批判的思想、情感或文化观念，构筑了此类文体的文化反思性"（王晖，2016），即作品表达的思想精神。"在非虚构的写作中，文学价值首先是思想价值"（冯骥才，2019），在翻译中，作品的思想精神主导着大方向，束缚着翻译不能逾越这个大框架。而文本特征主要是指文本的修辞格层，"是文学作品意义显示方式与众不同之处，是文学作品成为文学的一个关键"（朱立元，2004:160），因此，文本特征的保持与再现理应成为翻译的重点。

（一）作者背景与作品思想精神

作者江永红为一位军旅作家。1968年入伍，1977年开始发表作品，著有报告文学《蓝军司令》《看不

见的回归线》《名将解甲》等，多次获得全国好新闻奖、全国优秀报告文学奖、解放军文艺优秀作品奖。江永红认为，所谓纪实文学，"简而言之，就是写的东西要有针对性，要切中时弊，要围绕某种思想倾向或所关心的文体来写稿"（周均，2013），其荣获第二届优秀报告文学奖的作品《蓝军司令》，便揭露了军事演习中红军获胜背后的儿戏与丑陋这种表象与实质的反差，使评委组"看懂了这篇作品是刺向'左'的堡垒的匕首和投枪，是邓小平倡导的思想解放在军事领域的一声令下振聋反馈的回响"（苏梦奇，2015），而这种思想感情的表达正是纪实文学作品的主题意义之所在。

据江永红自己的介绍，他之所以关注起疫苗，也是因为"有几个有关疫苗的负面新闻在网上闹得沸沸扬扬……促使笔者思考：中国的疫苗从何而来？研制和生产疫苗的是什么人……"（江永红，2020:621），基于此类问题，作者"在一个有百余人的微信群里做了一个测试……竟然没有一人能说出 1 名疫苗专家的姓名，这似乎很不正常，但又很正常"（江永红，2020:5）。这种"似乎很不正常，但又很正常"的现象既是《蓝军司令》的成因之一，亦是《中国疫苗百年纪实》的重要成因。江永红以疫苗专家为中心写就的《中国疫苗百年纪实》这部纪实文学作品，不仅是想让民众了解中国疫苗的百年发展史，更重要的是唤起社会对疫苗专家的重视，为此才有了最后一章"对爱与责任的诠释"。

（二）文学性与科普性融合的文本特征

对于非虚构的文学性，冯骥才给出了四个要点：思想、人物、细节、语言（冯骥才，2019）。人物方面，江永红的文章常以人物报道取胜，所著《中国疫苗百年纪实》"是第一本用报告文学体裁从宏观上写中国疫苗科学家的书，所写的……是生物制品行业外所不为人知的那些人"（江永红，2020:8），其中的细节和语言便体现在人物的描写当中。如江永红所说"抓住了个性，人物就活了"，在现在的军事新闻报道中，在写作手法上要借鉴文学的写作手法来将所报道的人物个性和事件的特性表现出来（韩玄，2013）。在该文本中，人物语言的描述自不用言说，在描述人物个性和事件的特性时亦多使用四字格词语或俗语，例如"朝不保夕，日薄西山""没有金刚钻，不揽瓷器活"等，甚至掺杂"万户萧疏鬼唱歌""呼喇喇似大厦倾，昏惨惨似灯将尽"等诗词，这些修辞格使人物和事件跃然纸上，白纸黑字间被作者赋予了生动的文学潜能。"非虚构文学性主要存在于它非虚构的真实性中，这是它文学性生成的基础"（丁晓原，2019），而真实性的文章能否成为文学离不开语言的运用，"语言与文字是否精当与生动不仅关乎表现力，还直接体现一种审美"（冯骥才，2019），因此如何翻译文章中精当与生动的文字是纪实文学翻译中不可回避的难点。

朱立元认为文学语言与非文学语言的本质差异在于"前者具有被作为文学作品阅读欣赏的潜在可能性，后者则不具备这种可能性……换言之，前者具有潜在的文学性，后者则没有文学性"（朱立元，2004:137），而非文学语言缺乏文学的召唤性原因在于"科学语言尽量使相关语词的使用单一化、规范化、模式化，因而尽可能多地排除了语词意义的不确定性"（朱立元，2004:183）。非文学语言因缺乏文学的召唤性，难以激发读者的阅读兴趣，自然也不利于相关知识的科普。因此，该文本将文学的语言附着在非文学语言的前后，例如"防疫需要综合发力，最重要的是要有队伍，有'武器'——疫苗、血清等生物制品。手中没有'武器'，赤手空拳防不了疫，临时购买'武器'，人家会坐地涨价不说，而且会给中外各类骗子以可乘之机"。该句中通过"赤手空拳""武器"等手法，生动而又简洁明了地向读者科普了疫苗、血清对防疫的重要性及自主研发的重要性。读者在非文学语言与文学语言的结合中接收了科普性知识，并不会因为无机质的科学语言而导致阅读兴趣的降低，这种文学性与科普性的融合是文本生动性的原因之一。

三、日译本受众分析

从期待视野而言，日本读者对《中国疫苗百年纪实》这本纪实文学的理解程度受读者的阅读前结构所影响。其中对非文学的各种艺术的了解、爱好、兴趣为主的艺术文化素养对文学的审美阅读是很有帮助的（朱立元，2004:205）。据日本文化厅的调查，令和元年日本民众的文化艺术鉴赏活动率达到67.3%（文化厅，2020a:4），超过半数的民众具有较好的艺术文化素养。读者的文学能力主要指"姚斯所说到的文学方面的知识、阅读经验、对文学历史、文学类型、语言、主题、形式等方面的某种程度的熟悉和领悟等"（朱立元，2004:206），据调查，日本读者所阅读的主要类型前三位分别为小说、诗歌等文学作品（59.9%）；有关兴趣或体育的书籍（43.6%）；有关医疗或健康的书籍（27.5%）（文化厅国語課，2019:36）。《中国疫苗百年纪实》既属于文学作品，又跨医学领域，因此读者对该书也理应具有较高的审美期待，而对该书的内容也理应具有较高的文学能力。

另一方面，从文化圈与读者群而言，文化圈一般可分为高层次、中层次、低层次三大层次，每一层次虽可分为若干类型的圈子，但就以三大层次相对应的文学读者群而言，三个层次从高到低，人数由少到多，呈金字塔型（朱立元，2004:254）。结合原文的精神思想与科普性的翻译目标，译文的目标读者理应为人数居多的金字塔中、低两层，即以中低层次文化圈对应的读者群为主。低层次读者群的文化程度较低，知识面较窄，审美趣味较低俗，欣赏能力较薄弱，而中层次读者群在这些方面上都不高不精，平平而已（同上）。基于《中国疫苗百年纪实》是以历史为经，以人物为纬，以报告文学的方式撰写的疫苗发展史，因此低、中层次的读者群在知识储备上应具备高中水平的生物及历史知识，并且对中国的历史略知一二。从上述两方面我们能够描述出目标读者的大致轮廓：

（一）全体读者的知识素养至少具有高中水平；

（二）低层次读者具有一定的文学能力，但较为低级，审美能力较为薄弱，消遣是阅读文学的主要目的；

（三）中层次读者具有较高的文学能力，要求作品有一定的艺术性，给人以审美愉悦。

针对目标读者的一个大致轮廓，可以框定出翻译思路的大致方向。从文学语言翻译而言，因为读者都具有一定的文学能力，因此译文应该同样呈现出文学性，至于是替换为目标语社会的文学性还是依照原文的文学性表达以及何种程度的文学性适合读者等问题，还需加以具体语境和其他条件综合考虑。从非文学语言翻译而言，例如传染病名称、疫苗名称、制作工序等专有词汇若无必要不进行加注，以保证读者阅读过程的流畅性，提高文本展现文学特质的可能性。

四、接受美学视角下日译策略探析

《中国疫苗百年纪实》以人物为轴心，通过非文学语言与文学语言的相互融合推进疫苗发展史的叙述。在翻译中，文学语言的翻译毋庸置疑是翻好该文本的一大难点，也是文本的一大特征，另一方面非文学翻译中的专业术语翻译也需要慎之又慎，确保科学知识的精准传达。以下拟从文学类的诗词翻译和非文学类的病名翻译两方面加以考察。

（一）诗词的翻译策略考量

在落笔到翻译前，需考虑具体译文中微观的读者特征细节，由此才能将上文所述的宏观的读者轮廓和微观的读者特征细节与文本的召唤性结合为一体。对诗词的日译，有学者提倡"在原文加各类助译符号基础上，再附上古典日语翻译时最佳的处理方案"（李娜，2015），根据这种思路，原文中"借问瘟君欲何往？纸船明烛照天烧"可译为「借問す瘟君何れに行かんと欲するや、紙船に燭を明して天を照らして焼かん」（碇豊長，2015）这样的古典诗词，但如此一来，译文就高于目标读者的文学能力，也很难激发广大读者的审美趣味。此外日本文化厅在 2019 年度针对 28 个汉字词汇进行了社会认知调查，结果表明大部分日本民众更希望"使用汉字时标注假名"或是"改用假名书写"（文化庁，2020b:16）。

从数据而言，日本民众对汉字的掌握程度总体上越来越薄弱。此外日本学者菅原光同样认为江户时代所记学术书籍多以汉文为主，专家以外的读者通常不去翻阅，明治时期以汉文训读体所写的文章或侯文也难以阅读（菅原光，2021）。所以，将诗词译为古典诗词，译文中就不可避免出现大量汉字，而低、中层次的读者中只有少数人能够无障碍阅读汉诗中的汉字。另一方面，读者对古典日语的认知也较浅，在"视点游移"中即便能模糊地读取各个汉字的意思，在思维中仍无法将零碎、片断、单个的意象组合成意象群落，最终合成意象整体，这样读者终究无法领会到诗词的意境。因此，在诗词的翻译上，主要采取现代日语进行翻译。

采取现代日语翻译诗词是为了接近读者，那么在具体的翻译中是偏向归化还是异化呢？从读者的接受程度而言，应该采取偏于归化的策略，但这样便过于注重读者一极，而忽视且限制了文本本身的召唤结构。从文本的召唤结构而言，譬如"万户萧疏鬼唱歌"这句诗在第一层语音语调层上选用的字词"萧疏""鬼"都加强了语言消极性的情绪色彩。第二层语义建构层中读者通过"路标"，即根据词汇"万户""萧疏""鬼""唱歌"重新建构了一幅凄惨景象，营造了瘟疫的恐怖氛围，这过程便是读者在"视点游移"过程中确定意义、填补空白的过程，也是文本回应读者定向期待的过程，而"鬼唱歌"的组合采取了突兀、醒目的超常乃至反常用法，赋予了语词新的意义，这实际上是"文学语言的超常性与反常性，实质上是能指与所指、语符与意义在具体使用中的分离与偏转"（朱立元，2004:185），也是一种创新期待。第三层修辞格层是文学利用种种修辞手段造成语符与意义的分离、偏转（朱立元，2004:190），"鬼唱歌"中"唱歌"一词原有美好的意义偏转到恐怖的一极，从而造成作品意义的不确定性和增加空白意义，增加了文本的召唤性。第四层意象意境层是读者将语符转化为形象思维的过程，即读者将语符"万户""萧疏""鬼""唱歌"经过原有图式进行重组转化为意象意境，"若重组过程与原有图式一致，那么读者就同化了这个客体；若原有图式无法概括、同化客体，那么就会促进读者改变原有图式，顺应客体"（朱立元，2004:199）。因此"鬼唱歌"对某些读者可能是同化客体，也可能是顺应客体。第五层思想感情层是"隐匿在最深层的，是读者时时可以感受到而永远看不见摸不着的"（朱立元，2004:193），但对于此处的诗词而言，因为有着语境的限制，思想感情层是相对稳定、相对一致，读者无法脱离上下语境而结合个人心理图式感受到一种与文本背离的思想感情。

这五个层次是语符到形象思维的转化，其中关键的一层便是意象意境层。文学作品的意象意境层的不确定性与空白来自语义层，是作品的语言学结构预先决定了的（朱立元，2004:191），而意象意境的重组是基于个人的心理图式产生不同，它的召唤性集中体现了文学作品呼吁读者、诉诸读者的特征。因此在翻译中若是能妥善处理好意象意境层，在恰当的地方回应读者的定向期待或是激发读者的创新期待，那么译文便能在前三层的语义层和后两层的心理层中注入文学性。

（二）诗词的日译

《中国疫苗百年纪实》中仅序章中便出现了五处诗词的运用，其中三处是《聪明累》《七律二首·送瘟神》的部分运用，两处是《鼠死行》《鼠疫时的宴席》的完整引用。限于篇幅原因，以下略举两处部分引用的诗句为例。

例1：但是在宣统二年时，其政权早已是朝不保夕，日薄西山，"呼喇喇似大厦倾，昏惨惨似灯将尽"，几乎完全丧失了行政能力，已经顾不上东北这块清朝龙兴之地的子民了。（江永红，2020:3-4）

译文：宣統2年（明治43年）の時、その政権がすでに風前の灯火、西に迫る日のようなもので、まさに忽喇喇（フーラーラー）と倒れそうな高閣、昏惨惨（こんさんさん）と消えそうな灯というように政府としての機能が完全に失墜したため、清朝の発祥の地である東北地方の百姓を助ける余裕がなかったのだ。

该诗句出自《红楼梦》第五回中的《聪明累》，暗指王熙凤最终悲惨的结局。《红楼梦》在日本至今已有多个译本，那么借用母语者的译文在一般情况下是最佳的选择。著名学者曹明伦也呼吁外译需要的是"借帆出海"，而不是"闭门造车"（曹明伦，2019）。对该诗词，日本译者井波陵一将其译为「忽喇喇（フーラーラー）大厦の傾（かたむ）くが似く、昏惨惨（こんさんさん）灯（ともしび）の将（まさ）に尽きんとするが似し」（井波陵一，2015:103），可以看出此处的翻译采用了添加助译的方法将其译为文语自由诗，从读者接受角度而言无法完全照搬该译文。此外，井波陵一将此诗句作为完整的诗词进行翻译，其译文体现了原诗的风格，而此处的语境是引用该诗句来描述清政府危在旦夕的情况，强行插入风格迥异的诗句不但破坏文学的基调，而且如上文所述，带有大量汉字的译文也不适用于科普这一翻译目的。但可以借用其中一部分，例如拟声词的「忽喇喇」以及拟态词的「昏惨惨」，这两处同样也是诗句的出彩核心。因添加了音读助译，读者在阅读过程中不仅能保持连贯，而且更重要的是它打破了读者对于高楼倒塌和烛火将熄的原有图式，从另一种角度体会客体，激活读者的创新期待。创新期待会打开读者阅读的视野，缩短与克服同作品的审美距离，开拓与扩大原有的期待视界（朱立元，2004:213），随着读者不断地接受到这类文学性表达，其文学能力、审美视界等自会不断提高，译文的表达也会成为读者的原有图式，此后还需要新的文学表达去激发新的创新期待。另一方面过高的创新期待反而会打击读者的阅读兴趣，因此诗句的其余部分则按照读者的定向期待进行翻译。"似大厦倾"和"似灯将尽"都采用了比喻的手法描述事物的毁灭，日本读者对于"大厦将倾"和"烛火将熄"的心理图式和我们并无二致，因此读者是能够从「倒れそうな高閣」「消えそうな灯」的语符中轻松建构"高耸的大厦摇摇欲坠或是楼层的钢筋材料不断坠落""烛火微弱，熄灭又复燃，复燃又熄灭"等意象意境，从而与前后文的意象意境相组合进而理解该诗句对于清政府状态描述的文学性。

例2：但没有一个神灵能镇住万恶的"瘟神"，始终摆脱不了"万户萧疏鬼唱歌"的惨状。（江永红，2020:1）

译文：しかし、極悪の「疫病神」を鎮められる神がどこにもいないので、人々は長きにわたり「軒並みに荒涼として、響き渡る鬼の歌声」という惨めな苦境から脱出することができなかった。

该诗句出自毛泽东的《七律二首·送瘟神·其一》，原诗中的意思和此处所表达的意思一致，均是形容瘟疫的可怕程度。秉持着"借帆出海"的想法，笔者查阅了相关资料却未能借到"帆"，只能"造帆出海"。意象意境层是语符通过形象思维转化为意象意境，该诗句中的"万户"的所指并不是一万户人家，而是一种夸张。刘勰说夸饰是以言峻则嵩高极天，论狭则河不容舠；说多则"子孙千亿"，称少则民靡孑遗……辞虽已甚，其义无害也（刘勰，2008：271）。"萧疏"描述了气氛或环境的凄凉；"鬼唱歌"这种词义偏转使得"唱歌"的正面词义偏转到负面一极，在"萧疏"的气氛上更添一重恐怖的氛围。对于译文而言，要做的便是让目标读者能够把词汇生成的形象重组成一幅完整的意象意境，因此译的不是词汇的所指，而是寻找与所指生成的形象相同或相近的词。

例如，将"万户"的所指简单译为「多くの/数え切れない家」，那么这些表示数量多的抽象词汇较难使读者在形象思维中生成具体的画面，而「軒並み」可以使读者在思维中塑造房檐相连成片的画面，在另一角度形象地翻译出"万户"的所指。"萧疏"一词在读者思维中建构了萧条、人烟稀少的环境氛围，根据上下文的语境和"鬼唱歌"，更能让读者补充意象意境中的细节，例如家里人全都患病、街头巷尾空无一人等画面。因此译文「荒涼として」间接地将这些隐藏的或是读者需补充画面的一部分体现出来，帮助读者建构"萧疏"的意象意境。"鬼唱歌"可以说是再次加强了疫病造成的恐怖氛围，译文「響き渡る鬼の歌声」通过加译「響き渡る」向读者传达患病的人数之多和流行病的肆虐，「鬼の歌声」中的"鬼"指引发瘟疫的鬼。深受中国文化影响的日本中也存在"疫鬼"的概念（長谷川雅雄等，2018），因此无须对"鬼"的意象进行翻译。

以上对诗词的翻译中，似乎丢弃了汉诗的形和神韵，但考虑到译文的目的是让读者了解疫苗史和疫苗研究者，而并不是传递汉诗的形神韵，通俗易懂的译文能够保持读者的阅读通畅，更加贴近翻译目的，所以对汉诗独特的形神韵的翻译便降为次要地位。

（三）病名的翻译

病名的翻译属于非文学翻译，它的能指与所指在一般情况下是一一对应的，因此要求尽可能准确无误地翻译或是说在目标语中寻找到相同概念的词汇。

例 3：尽管从 1916 年北洋政府颁发的第一部《<u>传染病</u>预防条例》开始，我国一直将鼠疫列为"1 号病"，即头号烈性<u>传染病</u>……鼠疫是由鼠疫杆菌引起的恶行<u>传染病</u>……鼠疫杆菌的历史比有文字记载的<u>流行病史</u>多了约 3000 年……。（江永红，2020：2）

译文：北洋政府が 1916 年に最初の『<u>感染症</u>予防条例』を公布してから、ペストが我が国でずっと「1 号病」、つまり一類<u>感染症</u>として扱われていた……ペストとは、ペスト菌の感染によって起きる悪性<u>感染症</u>であり……ペスト菌の歴史は、文字で記録された<u>流行性疾患</u>の歴史より約 3000 年早いということだ……。

"传染病"在日语中存在「伝染病」「感染症」两种词汇，但现在的日本新闻中对新冠肺炎的称呼基本为「感染症」而并不是「伝染病」。据孙成岗、吴宏的调查，在今天无论从法律上还是日常中「伝染病」已不再用于人类间的疫病而是用于家畜，人类间的传染病译为日语时应为「感染症」（孙成岗、吴宏，2020）。那么"流行病"是否也能译为「感染症」呢？卫生部医政司对流行病的定义为："在一定时间或一定地区内，发病率明显增高、范围较广的疾病。如各种传染病、地方病等"（武广华、臧益秀、刘运祥等，2001：319）。可见流行病既包括传染病也包括流行但不具备传染的疾病，若是译为「感染症」则只包括了其中一方面，因此翻译为「流行疾患/流行性疾患」在概念上更加接近流行病。

例4：清代以后更有了鼠疫（此前称为<u>痒子症</u>、<u>核子瘟</u>等）这一病名……。（江永红，2020:5）

译文：清朝に入ってからさらにペスト（昔は<u>カユイカユイ病</u>、<u>ハレハレ病</u>など呼ばれた）という病名がつけられて……。

在"鼠疫"名称确定之前，对其病的称呼是基于人们对临床表现的认识，也表现了人们对事物认识的规律是由表及里的。当时人们对鼠疫的认识是"所感病象，无论男女壮弱，一经发热，即生痒子，或在腋下，或现两胯、两腮，或痛而不见其形，迟则三五日，速则一昼夜即毙"（陈邦贤，1937:377），因此称为"痒子症"。再看"核子瘟"，1918年《少年》杂志上刊载的《鼠疫谈》指出患此病者"初期必然头痛身热，身上会长起核子"（味鬱，1918），周镇对核子瘟也有描述，其最显著的特征是"核子遍布全身，以腋下或胯间为主"（周镇，1927）。由此可见"痒子"与"核子"都是描述腺鼠疫造成的同一症状，即受侵部位的淋巴结肿大，只不过"痒子"加入了因跳蚤蛰咬造成身体瘙痒的感觉，"核子"则更注重肿大的外观。在翻译中，这些由表象认识而来的词汇不能以现代医学的视角翻译为「リンパ節腫脹」等词汇，而应该体现当时人们是如何从表象认知鼠疫。在日本的四大公害病中就有一种叫做「イタイイタイ病」，是主要由骨质软化症引起患者全身性剧烈疼痛，不由得哭喊「痛い、痛い」而得名，也是一种对表象的认识。以「イタイイタイ病」为模板造帆，"痒子症"译为「カユイカユイ病」以体现人们对瘙痒的认识；"核子瘟"译为「ハレハレ病」以强调人们对淋巴结肿大的认识。虽然日本没有这些词汇，但读者可以在「イタイイタイ病」的原有图式上去同化或顺应新的客体。

五、结　语

本文从接受美学理论出发，基于《中国疫苗百年纪实》文本的思想精神和文本特征，对文学语言翻译和非文学语言翻译进行了简要分析。"借帆出海"对外译而言无疑是重要的，但是若所借之帆不太合适或无帆可借时，只能"造帆出海"，而所造这些帆便需要以接受美学为尺度。在文学语言翻译上，通过读者方面的审美经验期待视界和文本方面的召唤性结构两条基准的相互框定，译文一方面照顾读者的接受视界，另一方面在文本中保留召唤性。译文中偏向归化或是简单易懂的翻译迎合了读者的定向期待，使读者保持一种阅读兴趣，而为了提高文学性而形成较于难懂的翻译则是激发读者的创新期待，"它是审美经验视界得以改变和提高的动力机制和心理根源"（朱立元，2004:216），通过这一过程低、中层的读者将不断往上爬升。在非文学语言翻译上，对病名的翻译需要寻找与之对应的专业术语，若遇到"痒子症""核子瘟"等非官方病名，最主要是在读者能够理解的前提上译出病名的内涵意义。

参考文献

[1] Agency for Cultural Affairs, Japanese Language Division(文化庁国語課). *Public Opinion Survey on Japanese Language in 2018: Notation, Reading, and Language* (平成30年度国語に関する世論調査　表記・読書・言葉遣い[M]). Tokyo:gyosei(東京：ぎょうせい), 2019.

[2] Agency for Cultural Affairs, Japan(文化庁 a). *Public Opinion Survey Report on Culture*(文化に関する世論調査報告書[R]),

2020.

[3] Agency for Cultural Affairs, Japan(文化庁 b). *Summary of the Results of the 2019 Public Opinion Poll on the Japanese Language*(令和元年度「国語に関する世論調査」の結果の概要[R]). 2020.

[4] Cao, Minglun(曹明伦). "Reflections on Foreign Cultural Communication and Foreign Translation: 'Raising One's Own Voice' Requires 'Using the Sails of the Sea'"(关于对外文化传播与对外翻译的思考——兼论"自扬其声"需要"借帆出海")[J]. *Foreign Languages Research*(外语研究), 2019(5):77-84.

[5] Cao, Xueqin (writer.) Inami, Ryoichi (translator) (曹雪芹, 井波陵一訳). *New Translation of Dream of the Red Chamber* (新訳紅夢楼第一冊[M]). Tokyo:Iwanami Shoten(東京:岩波書店), 2015.

[6] Chen,Bangxian(陈邦贤). *History of Chinese Medicine*(中国医学史[M]). Shanghai:The Commercial Press(上海:商务印书馆), 1937.

[7] Ding, Xiaoyuan (丁晓原). "The Logic and Ethics of Nonfiction Literature"(非虚构文学的逻辑与伦理)[J]. *Contemporary Literary Criticism* (当代文坛),2019(5):90-96.

[8] Feng, Jicai (冯骥才). "Nonfiction Writing and Nonfiction Literature"(非虚构写作与非虚构文学)[J]. *Contemporary Literary Criticism*(当代文坛),2019(2):45-47.

[9] Han, Xuan (韩玄). Some Implications of Jiang Yonghong's Journalism for Military News Reporting(江永红新闻作品对军事新闻报道的几点启示)[J]. *News World*(新闻世界),2013(9):275-276.

[10] Hasegawa, Masao(etc.)(長谷川雅雄等). Diseases caused by "鬼" (Chin. 'guǐ', Jap. 'ki' / 'oni')(「鬼」のもたらす病－中国及び日本の古医学における病因観とその意義－（上）)[J]. *Academia. Humanities and natural sciences*(南山大学アカデミア人文・自然科学編),2018(16):1－28.

[11] Ikari, Toyonaga (碇豊長). *Mao Zedong's Seven-character Octave:Sends Off the God of Pestilence:World of Poetry:Poetry by Ikari Toyonaga* (毛沢東七律送瘟神詩詞世界碇豊長の詩詞)[OL]. http://www5a.biglobe.ne.jp/~shici/shi4_08/maoshi49.htm(accessed 2/1/2021).

[12] Jiang, Yonghong (江永红). *A Century Record of Vaccine in China*(中国疫苗百年纪实：上下卷 [M]). Beijing: People's Publishing House (北京：人民出版社), 2020.

[13] Li, Na (李娜). "The Translation of Chinese Classical Poetry into Japanese: Taking *Spring View* by Du Fu as an Example"(论汉诗日译的方法——以杜甫的《春望》为例) [J]. *Journal of Qiqihar University(Phi&Soc Sci)* (齐齐哈尔大学学报(哲学社会科学版)), 2015(2):131-133.

[14] Li, Xie (刘勰). *The Literary Mind and the Carving of Dragons*(文心雕龙[M]). Kaifeng:Henan University Press(开封:河南大学出版社),2008.

[15] Ren, Xuan (任宣). *Enhance the Determination and Confidence in the Fight Against the COVID-19 Epidemic, the People's Publishing House Published the E-book A Century Record of Vaccine in China in Advance. Free for the Public to Read!* (增强抗疫决心信心,人民出版社提前出版《中国疫苗百年纪实》电子书,免费供公众阅读!)[N]. *Wenhui Daily* (文汇报), 2020-02-02.

[16] Su, Mengqi (苏梦奇). " 'Commander of the Blue Army': Wang Jusheng's Report"("蓝军司令"王聚生报道始末)[J]. *Military*

Correspondent(军事记者),2015(4):61-62.

[17] Sun, Chenggang & Wu, Hong (孙成岗,吴宏). "Suggestions for the Construction of a Chinese-Japanese Emergency Terminology Corpus: A Case Study of Chinese-Japanese Translation in the Context of the COVID-19 Epidemic"(中日应急对译词汇库的构建设想——以新冠疫情语境下的中日词汇对译为例)[J]. *Journal of Japanese Language Study and Research*(日语学习与研究),2020(5):1-12.

[18] Sugawara, Hikaru (菅原光). "The Merits and Demerits of Modern Japanese Translation: *Selected writings of Nishi Amane* Translated by Sugawara Hikaru, Aihara Kosaku,and Shimada Hideaki: In lieu of an Introduction to My Own Book"(現代語訳の功罪：菅原光・相原耕作・島田英明訳『西周 現代語訳セレクション』：自著紹介に代えて)[J]. *The Newsletter of the CLPS, Senshu University* (専修大学法学研究所所報), 2021(62):53‐64.

[19] The Genron NPO（言論 NPO）. *The 16th Japan-China Joint Opinion Survey*(第 16 回日中共同世論調査結果)[OL]. https://www.genron-npo.net/world/archives/9354-2.html(accessed 20/12/2020).

[20] Wang, Hui (王晖). "The Non-fiction Narrative of Documentary Literature and Its Subjective Claims:The Forbidden City Trilogy as an Example"(纪实文学的非虚构叙事及其主体诉求——以"故宫三部曲"为例)[J]. *Jiangsu Social Sciences*(江苏社会科学),2016(5):203-208.

[21] Wu, Guanghua & Zang, Yixiu & Liu, Yunxiang (etc.)(武广华,臧益秀,刘运祥,等). *Chinese Health Management Dictionary* (中国卫生管理辞典[Z]). Beijing: Science and Technology of China Press (北京：中国科学技术出版社),2001.

[22] Wei, Gang (味戆). "Bubonic Plague Talk"(鼠疫谈) [J]. *Youth*(少年),1918,8(3):2.

[23] Zhu, Liyuan (朱立元). *Introduction to Reception Aesthetics*(接受美学导论[M]). Hefei: Anhui Educational Publishing House (合肥：安徽教育出版社),2004.

[24] Zhou, Jun (周均). "A Test of Winning Personality Reporting"(试论人物报道的取胜之道)[J]. *News World*(新闻世界),2013(9):14-16.

[25] Zhou, Zhen (周镇). "Plague Remedy" (鼠疫治方)[J]. *Journal of Traditional Chinese Medicine*(中医杂志(上海)), 1927(23):5.

作者简介

卢俊宇，贵州大学外国语学院硕士研究生。研究方向：中日翻译研究。电子邮箱：229477878@qq.com。

王晓梅，教授，贵州大学外国语学院副院长，硕士生导师。主要研究方向：翻译理论与实践、中日文化比较研究。电子邮箱：1344759330@qq.com。

www.ingramcontent.com/pod-product-compliance
Lightning Source LLC
LaVergne TN
LVHW081456060526
838201LV00057BA/3054